The Zondervan
1984
PASTOR'S
ANNUAL

A Planned Preaching Program for the Year

T. T. Crabtree

ZONDERVAN
PUBLISHING HOUSE OF THE ZONDERVAN CORPORATION
GRAND RAPIDS, MICHIGAN 49506

Scripture quotations are from the *King James Version* unless otherwise designated.

Additional translations used are:

American Standard Version © 1929 by International Council of Religious Education, Thomas Nelson & Sons (ASV)

Living Bible © 1971 by Tyndale House Publishers (LB)

New English Bible © 1970 by Oxford University Press (NEB)

New International Version © 1978 by New York International Bible Society (NIV)

New Testament, a New Translation by James Moffatt © 1950 by James A. R. Moffatt, Harper & Brothers

New Testament in Modern English, Revised Edition, by J. B. Phillips © 1972 by J. B. Phillips

Revised Standard Version © 1952 by Division of Christian Education of the National Council of the Churches of Christ in the United States of America, Thomas Nelson & Sons (RSV)

Today's English Version, Good News Bible © 1976 by American Bible Society (TEV)

THE ZONDERVAN PASTOR'S ANNUAL FOR 1984
Copyright © 1983 by The Zondervan Corporation
Grand Rapids, Michigan

This printing October 1983

Library of Congress Catalog Card Number 71-9126

ISBN 0-310-22671-6

Printed in the United States of America

CONTENTS

ACKNOWLEDGMENTS TO CONTRIBUTING AUTHORS

PREFACE

With gratitude in my heart to our Lord and to the fine people of Zondervan Publishing House, we send forth this nineteenth volume of the *Zondervan Pastor's Annual* with a prayer that it can be used to assist pastors as they seek to minister to their congregations. Letters from around the world encourage me to believe that this publication is proving to be helpful to those who use it as an aid rather than as a crutch in their preaching ministry.

Professors of preaching have been insisting through the years that pastors should have a planned preaching program rather than an unplanned preaching program. Dr. Vernon L. Stanfield, an outstanding professor of preaching, has stated in the revised edition of *On the Preparation and Delivery of Sermons* by Dr. John A. Broadus (New York: Harper & Row, 1979): "Planning will give purpose and direction to preaching . . . planning also helps the preacher with sermon preparation . . . planning removes much of the stress and strain of lack of preparation . . . for the pastor to plan his preaching will also help him to plan worship" (pp. 257–60). We hope that those who use the *Annual* will see it as a suggestion of how the preaching task can be done rather than a series of manuscripts that are to be used as they are printed. Hopefully if any of these are used, the Holy Spirit will enable each pastor to improve upon what has been offered.

The production of a volume like this would be impossible without the valuable assistance of the pastors, missionaries, evangelists, and professors who have supplied series of messages for use in this suggested preaching program. To them I owe a great debt of gratitude.

Without reservation I dedicate this book to my beloved wife, Bennie Elizabeth, who is the helpmate God has provided for me.

I am deeply indebted to a superb secretary, Mrs. Dale Wiser, who has worked diligently in assisting me with this task.

I am indeed grateful for the ministerial staff and to the warm and caring congregation of the First Baptist Church of Springfield, Missouri. They love their Lord, their pastor, and the world which needs the gospel of Jesus Christ. They encourage me in the task of interpreting and preaching the Word of our Lord.

Hopefully we are not being presumptuous by sending forth a publication of this kind. Our sincere desire is to provide assistance to those who serve our Lord and His people as pastors in their effort to be good undershepherds of the Great Shepherd who spoke to Peter and said, "Feed my sheep."

—T. T. Crabtree, Pastor
First Baptist Church
Springfield, Missouri 65806

A PLANNED PREACHING PROGRAM

Sunday Morning Themes

Responding to the Parables of Our Lord—*January*
"O Come, Let Us Worship and Bow Down"—*February*
Responding to God's Sorrow and Increasing God's Joy—*March*
The Purpose of the Ministry for John the Baptist—*April*
Good Housekeeping—*May, June*
Updating the Garden of Eden to the Contemporary World—*July*
Waging Successful Spiritual Warfare With the Help That Comes Through
    Prayer—*August*
Growing Quality Christians—*September*
The Urgency of Deciding for Christ Now—*October*
Understanding and Developing the Grace of Giving—*November*
Listening to the Angels' Proclamation—*December*

Sunday Evening Themes

The Lives and Lessons From Great Men—*January, February, March*
The Prophet's Message for Stressful Times—*April, May, June*
The High Cost of Disobedience to the Clear Will of God and the Chas-
    tisement Which Always Follows—*July*
The Apostle Paul Speaks to Modern Churches Also—*August*
How God Works With His People—*September*
Christ Can Bring About Great Change for Good in Your Life If You Will
    Let Him—*October*
Sharing the Good News of Salvation—*November*
Christ and Our Deepest Needs—*December*

Wednesday Evening Themes

Participating in the Privilege of Prayer—*January*
Make Good Habits, and Your Good Habits Will Make You Good—
    February, March
Let the Apostle Paul Speak to Your Needs in the Present—*April, May,
    June*
With the Lord as My Shepherd, I Shall Not Suffer the Lack of Anything I
    Need—*July, August, September*
Foregleams of Christ in the Old Testament—*October, November, De-
    cember*

SUGGESTED PREACHING PROGRAM
FOR THE MONTH OF JANUARY

Sunday Mornings

The passing of an old year and the coming of a new year provides a perspective from which we can look to the past and also view the future. As the followers of Christ, His people need to look to Him and to listen to Him. Jesus spoke powerfully to His contemporaries and to us through His parables. "Responding to the Parables of Our Lord" is the suggested theme for the Sunday morning messages.

Sunday Evenings

"The Lives and Lessons from Great Men" is the suggested theme for a series of biographical messages based on famous Old Testament characters for the evening messages.

Wednesday Evenings

"Participating In the Privilege of Prayer" is the suggested theme for the Wednesday evenings of this month. Neglect of prayer produces spiritual poverty. Participating meaningfully in a personal prayer life lets God accomplish great things through us.

* * *

SUNDAY MORNING, JANUARY 1

TITLE: **Go Out Quickly**

TEXT: **"Go out quickly to the streets and lanes of the city, and bring in the poor and maimed and blind and lame" (Luke 14:21).**

SCRIPTURE READING: **Luke 14:15–23**

HYMNS: **"We Have Heard the Joyful Sound," Kirkpatrick**
"He Included Me," Sewell
"Softly and Tenderly," Thompson

OFFERTORY PRAYER:

Holy Father, we thank You for the beginning of another year in which to worship You and witness for You. We come bringing tithes and offerings that they might be used in ministries of mercy in this community and to the ends of the earth. Bless us as we seek to give with generous hearts, and remind us always that You are the source of every good and perfect gift. In Jesus' name. Amen.

Introduction. The Bible opens with a picture of God as the life-giving Spirit whose breath causes a pile of dust to become a living human being.

In the Psalms God is pictured as a good and great shepherd who ministers to His sheep.

In the New Testament we find God described as the loving Father who loves and wants to relate to His children as a loving father.

In Jesus' parable of the marriage feast, He describes the Father God in terms of His being a generous and gracious host who has prepared a great banquet feast for those who will respond to His invitation.

Let us lift a phrase from the instructions of the householder to his servants and use it as an appropriate text and title for this first Lord's day in the year of 1984. The host said to his servants, "Go out quickly. . . ." The previous year is now history. A new year stretches out before us. The years are slipping away, and time is running out for many of us and also for many around us. What we would do for our God and what we would do for our neighbors and friends needs to be done quickly.

I. We need to go out quickly . . . because God's banquet is ready.

Did you ever arrive home to hear your mother or your wife speak and say, "Dinner will be ready in thirty minutes" or "Dinner will be ready when the rolls are done"?

The banquet that God has prepared is always ready for those who are willing to respond to Him by faith and faithfulness.

A. *God is ready to do business with you today.*

B. *The Savior lives as the conquerer of death in order that He might become your Savior and friend and teacher today.*

C. *The Holy Spirit is present to do God's work in your heart and life today.*

D. *The angels in heaven are ready to rejoice over decisions that are made by those who need to become believers in and disciples of the Lord Jesus Christ.*

II. We need to go out quickly . . . because of the swift passing of opportunity.

Time does not stand still. Yesterday is gone. Tomorrow has not arrived. Today is all we have. We must seize our opportunities quickly.

A. *Opportunity does not wait for us to extend this invitation on behalf of God.*
   1. The night will come when no one can work (John 9:4).
   2. The night will come when no one can respond.

B. *There is no invitation extended for a response to be made on tomorrow.*
   1. The prophet said, "Come now" (Isa. 1:18).
   2. The apostle said, "Behold now" (2 Cor. 6:2).

The psalmist prayed and encourages us to pray that we might number our days that we might give our hearts unto the ways of wisdom.

III. We need to go out quickly . . . because of the helplessness of the outsiders.

Almost without exception the average church member does not recognize the spiritual helplessness and hopelessness of those who do not know God.

A. *They exist in the grip of spiritual death* (Rom. 6:23; Eph. 2:1).

B. *They are in the grip of the enemy of God and the enemy of their own souls* (2 Cor. 4:3–4). The God of this world, that old serpent, the devil, has placed blindfolds on their minds lest the light of the glorious gospel of Christ should shine in so that they could be saved.

C. *They live in a state of nonbelief and noncommitment.*

D. *They will remain in this sad condition if they are never invited and persuaded to respond to God's gracious invitation to the banquet that has been prepared.*

We live in a world of unsaved people who are helpless and hopeless apart from the witness and the testimony and the help of those who already know God through faith in Jesus Christ. This means that it is urgent that we be about our Father's business.

IV. We need to go out quickly . . . because of the command of Christ.

A. *Christ gave many helpful suggestions concerning how we should face life.*

B. *Christ gave many gracious invitations to which we should respond.*

C. *Christ gave one supreme command with reference to the needs of the world.* It is contained in what we call The Great Commission (Matt. 28:19–20).

Our Lord would have each of His disciples to go out quickly into their individual and personal worlds and share the Good News of the blessings they have experienced through faith. He would encourage us to invite those who are hungry for the bread of life and the water of life to come to the feast that has been prepared.

V. We need to go out quickly . . . because of the compassion in the heart of the Father God.

Our great God is not a cold-hearted creator who is unmoved by the needs of this world.

A. *God so loved us that He gave His Son Jesus Christ. We need to recognize what all that involves.*

B. *God so loved us that He saved us in order that He might use us to save others.*

We are not free to loaf or shirk or procrastinate. We must recognize that there is some urgency involved in our being what our Lord would have us to be.

We need to go out quickly and do what God wants us to do. We need to go out quickly because of the needs of those about us.

Conclusion. Today let us go out quickly and say to those about us that a feast has been prepared.

God offers the blessing of acceptance.
God offers the blessing of forgiveness that is full and free.
God offers the blessing of spiritual renewal and restoration.
God offers peace and joy and hope and help and heaven.
Everyone is invited to come to the banquet. —*TTC*

* * *

SUNDAY EVENING, JANUARY 1

TITLE: Abraham: Man of Faith

Text: **"By faith, Abraham, when he was called to go out into a place which he should receive for an inheritance, obeyed" (Heb. 11:8a kjv).**

Scripture Reading: **Genesis 12:1–9; Hebrews 11:1–10**

Introduction. One way to know the Bible is to become familiar with those who walk up and down in its pages. As we think about Abraham the one word that is suggested by his name is the word faith. In the pages of Scripture Abraham moves before us as the man through whom faith, the living principle of true religion, becomes a force in human life. The faith of Abraham transcended mere belief; it went beyond belief to action.

Abraham was a man of faith, and we can learn three lessons from him.

I. Abraham illustrates that the man of faith interprets his life in terms of mission.

When Abraham was called (Gen. 12:1–3; Acts 7:1–4) he indulged in no bargaining with God. He allowed himself no backward glance. The Genesis account summarizes Abraham's act of faith in words of deceptive simplicity, "So Abram went, as the Lord had told him" (12:4 RSV). Faith opened up the long view and revealed the far horizon, because it lifted one isolated human being out of his hopelessness and meaninglessness and made him a part of the ongoing purpose of God.

Abraham viewed his life in terms of mission. He regarded himself as a person sent by God. This same sense of mission is found in that select company of the faithful through the centuries. The supreme example of this is Jesus who was conscious of a unique relationship with the Father at the age of twelve (Luke 2:49) and who, when He was grown up, said again and again, "He sent me" (John 7:29b).

Here is a frame in which every Christian can put his or her own picture. Such a sense of mission is not reserved for a few like Abraham and Moses and Jesus and Paul. Our faith has failed unless it has helped us interpret our lives in terms of the will of God and to know that, like Abraham, we have been called for a specific purpose. There must be something inside us that responds to something outside; and which gives us the feeling of being on the beam of reality. Such a sense of mission does two things for us.

A. *This undergirds a life with purpose that gives meaning to the day's work.* A cook in a certain household spoke the truth when she said, "Life around here is so daily." That goes for many people. Multitudes are dragging along in a kind of treadmill existence, bored to death with the whole thing. The answer to this problem lies in going back to Abraham and learning from him this sense of mission. This door stands open to every Christian.

B. *This sense of mission offers not only purpose but power.* Faith in God is not simply an exalted philosophy of life, a Savior from the darkness of unbelief, and a sustaining motive for patient service; it is also a source of power for positive achievement. When a person is doing what he is convinced is the will of God he can count on the power of God. He will have the feeling of being in harmony with "the music of the spheres"; and if in truth he is in the will of God, then indeed he is!

II. Abraham demonstrates that the man of faith is not always a man of perfect character.

God tells Abraham, "I am God Almighty; walk before me, and be thou perfect" (Gen. 17:1b). God is urging His servant to live in close touch with Him and thus live a life of moral perfection. But Abraham did not always do this. There were several letdowns from his usual high standard.

A. *Note the lapses of faith for Abraham.* In both Egypt (Gen. 12:10–20) and later in Gerar (Gen. 20), Abraham, to save his own life, palmed off his wife, Sarah, as his sister. The fact that she was his half-sister (Gen. 20:12) did not excuse this weak and sinful act. Sarah was taken into the harems of Pharaoh and Abimelech respectively. In both instances, disaster was averted by God's intervention. What a sad scene to see this man of God being rebuked by pagan rulers.

Another lapse of faith occurred when, upon Sarah's suggestion, Abraham took her Egyptian slave woman, Hagar, as a secondary wife hoping that she might bear the promised heir. According to the accepted custom of the time the children born in this relationship were considered the children of the real wife. Not only did this violate God's ideal of monogamy in marriage, but it was also a failure of faith on the part of both Sarah and Abraham when they attempted to take matters into their own hands instead of waiting on God's promise.

B. *Note the lesson for us from Abraham's failures.* Some years ago a book was published with the title, *For Sinners Only*. That would be a good motto for a church, for a Christian is not a person without sin; rather, he is a sinner saved by grace.

David, described as a man after God's own heart (1 Sam. 13:14b), was not without his failures. He was so described, and yet we can't help but think of his dark sins. In the New Testament the people who are called "saints" were not perfect. The thing that marked them as God's people is this: when they fell down they got up and tried again. The cross we are to carry is the daily battle with sin (Luke 9:23b).

Upon being asked which of his paintings he considered the best a great artist immediately replied, "The next one." This is the mark of a Christian. Granted, he has his failures, but he always wants to do better, means to do better, and tries to do better.

III. Abraham teaches that the man of faith is given courage to face the dark facts of his experience.

Abraham shows us that we are to. follow God through thick and thin, through dark days and sunshine, and through times when we do not understand, as well as those times when the way is clear.

God's command to sacrifice Isaac was the supreme test of Abraham's life. But there was neither argument nor delay. The wood was cut. The servants enlisted. The three-day trip to the mount was made. To the lad's question, "But where is the lamb for the burnt offering?" we find the answer of utter faith, "God will provide himself the lamb for the burnt offering, my son" (Gen. 22:7, 8). Then the altar was built and the wood laid in order. Isaac was bound and placed on the altar. The knife was raised, but before it fell God intervened to stay his hand and a ram was substituted for the boy.

Centuries later in the temple, which tradition says was built on this very site, Jesus said to those who had made themselves his enemies, "Abraham rejoiced to see my days; and he saw it and was glad" (John 8:56). When did Abraham see Christ's day? When he would not have withheld his "beloved son" from God. His faith went all the way.

When we find ourselves utterly tested as was Abraham, where does faith fit into the picture? In one of two ways. It may be that God will not require the sacrifice He seems to ask. When Abraham met the test his son was spared. Sometimes it works out that way.

But on the other hand, no one can talk about this test God made of Abraham, and be honest, and not admit that sometimes Isaac is not spared. When God's own Son was on the cross the voice was not heard, the hand was not stayed, and God gave His Son to die for us.

Sometimes we pray and the blow falls anyway. Does this mean that faith has failed? No! There are two ways in which God saves: He saves us from the thing we fear, or He saves us in it by giving us the grace to come through.

Conclusion. Great faith does involve great peace, assurance, and certitude; but more than that, it involves great doubt, disillusionment, and despair. It involves victories, yes; but also defeats. These darker experiences are not wholly negative or lost. They serve, as it were, as God's tools for enlarging our minds and our souls.

Our great need is faith. God give us faith!   *—WTH*

* * *

WEDNESDAY EVENING, JANUARY 4

TITLE: The Principles of Prayer

TEXT: **"And in that day ye shall ask me nothing. Verily, verily, I say unto you, Whatever ye shall ask the Father in my name, he will give it you. Hitherto have ye asked nothing in my name; ask, and ye shall receive, that your joy may be full" (John 16:23, 24).**

SCRIPTURE READING: **John 16:23, 24**

Introduction. The Bible urges us to pray. Yet many complain that their prayers are unanswered. They have not obtained the results for which they were looking. Has God failed them in His promises? Are Jesus' words empty and meaningless?

If there is no answer to our prayers, the fault lies with us. We need to search the Bible diligently and, like the disciples, ask the Lord to teach us how to pray. God has laid down certain principles of prayer which, if followed, assure us God's answer to every petition that we make.

What are some of these principles?

I. Pray according to the will of God.

We are to pray according to the will of God. "And this is the confidence that we have in him, that, if we ask any thing according to his will, he heareth us; And if we know that he hears us, whatever we ask, we know that we have the petitions that we desired of him" (1 John 5:14, 15).

We must not forget the fact that we must recognize that God is Lord of all things. We dare not dictate to the almighty, all-wise God, telling Him what He must do and how He must do it. God knows better than we know. He knows what the future has in store for us. We often think we cannot live unless we have our way. As we go to God in prayer asking Him to heal us, to give us daily bread, to give us the many things we think we need for life, let us always pray that the will of God be done.

II. Pray in the name of Jesus.

When we go to the Lord in prayer there are sins between us and Him. These sins need to be removed. But we cannot remove them. We cannot go back to our yesterdays and live our life over. We cannot by our tears wash our sins away. Jesus must remove our sins, and this He has done by the blood of the cross. Therefore, in the name of Jesus we can approach the prayer-answering God. If we come to God through Christ, we shall find a loving father who can lift our burdens or give us strength to bear them. "And whatever ye shall ask in my name, that will I do, that the Father may be glorified in the Son. If ye shall ask anything in my name, I will do it" (John 14:13–14).

His name stands for all that Jesus Christ is in the eyes of the Father. Let us ask for nothing that is not in accord with the mind of Christ.

III. Pray conscious of the ministry of the Holy Spirit.

When we do not know how to pray as we ought, the Holy Spirit will make intercession for us. "Likewise, the Spirit also helpeth our infirmity; for we know not what we should pray for as we ought; but the Spirit himself maketh intercession for us with groanings which cannot be uttered" (Rom. 8:26).

When we cannot frame our words, to express the deep yearnings of the soul, the Holy Spirit, who is a discerner of the thoughts and intents of heart, helps our infirmities by making intercession for us.

IV. Pray believing.

Praying should not be done mechanically or automatically. We do not drop a prayer into a machine, and out comes an answer. A prayer must come from the heart. We must believe God will answer. "But without faith it is impossible to please him; for he that cometh to God must believe that he is, and that he is a rewarder of them that diligently seek him" (Heb. 11:6). "But let him ask in faith, nothing wavering. For he that wavereth is like a wave of the sea driven with the wind and tossed. For let not that man think that he shall receive anything of the Lord" (James 1:6, 7).

V. Pray without being selfish.

"You ask, and receive not, because you ask amiss, that you may consume it upon your lusts" (James 4:3).

We ask amiss when we ask anything for the honor and exaltation of self. God will not give His glory to another.

VI. Pray with a forgiving spirit.

"And when ye stand praying, forgive, if ye have anything against any, that your Father also, who is in heaven, may forgive you your trespasses. But if ye do not forgive, neither will your Father, who is in heaven, forgive your trespasses" (Mark 11:25, 26).

There is no use to pray if you harbor a grudge against anyone. We must forgive one another as Christ has forgiven us. "Forbearing one another, and forgiving one another, if any man have a quarrel against any; even as Christ forgave you, so also do ye" (Col. 3:13).

VII. Pray asking the Lord to forgive your sins.

All of us are sinners. Let us see to it that we confess our sins and are cleansed by God. "If I regard iniquity in my heart, the Lord will not hear me" (Ps. 66:18).

CEMETARY - ANCIENT - CALLED
(GOD'S ACRE) -

VIII. Pray without becoming impatient.

"But without faith it is impossible to please him; for he that cometh to God must believe that he is, and that he is a rewarder of them that diligently seek him" (Heb. 11:6).

The reward may be lost for lack of perseverance. Abraham prevailed because he did not stagger at the promise of God. "He staggered not at the promise of God through unbelief, but was strong in faith, giving glory to God" (Rom. 4:20).

Conclusion. Jacob prevailed because he would not let go. Elijah prevailed on Mount Carmel because he continued in prayer when there was no sign of rain. The widow prevailed with the unjust judge because of her importunity, and Jesus added: "Shall not God avenge his own elect who cry day and night unto him though he bear long with them?" (Luke 18:7). "I tell you that he will avenge them speedily" (Luke 18:8).   *—HSK*

* * *

SUNDAY MORNING, JANUARY 8

TITLE: How Can We Compel People to Come to the Banquet?

TEXT: **"And the master said to the servant, 'Go out to the highways and hedges, and compel people to come in, that my house may be filled'"** (Luke 14:23).

SCRIPTURE READING: Luke 14:15–24

HYMNS: **"A Mighty Fortress Is Our God,"** Luther
             "Footsteps of Jesus," Everett
             "People to People," Reynolds

OFFERTORY PRAYER:

Holy Father, You are the giver of every good and perfect gift. Today we come desiring to bring ourselves to You. Accept our gifts as tokens of this desire to be useful to You and helpful to others. We pray in Jesus' name. Amen.

Introduction. Our text provides an appropriate theme for the church as the body of Christ and as the servant of Christ in the world.

Our text provides an appropriate theme for the Sunday school organization of the church. The Sunday school is charged with the responsibility of reaching out and enrolling people in Bible study so they can learn about God as He is revealed through Jesus Christ. Until people come to know something about God, there is little likelihood that they will trust Jesus Christ as Savior.

Our text serves as an appropriate theme for you individually as a follower of Christ. To you is given the privilege of inviting people to participate in God's wonderful banquet.

I. If we would be instrumental in helping people come to God's banquet, we need to recognize the nature of God's invitation.

    A. *God's invitation is the most extensive invitation that has ever been extended.*

We are to go out not only into the highways and hedges, but we are to go to the uttermost parts of the earth with the good news of God's love.

B. *God's invitation is the most inclusive invitation that has ever been extended.*

Everyone is included. Everyone can respond.

C. *God's invitation is the most intensive invitation ever extended.*

Throughout the Bible we are invited to come to God that we might enjoy all of the blessings that the Creator God prepared for us. God in all of His fullness, the angelic hosts, and the whole Christian world would like to see each individual respond to this gracious invitation.

D. *God's invitation is the most expensive invitation that has ever been extended.*

When an invitation is extended, there is always expense involved. You may invite someone to have a soft drink with you. Some expense is involved. When God extends His invitation, we need to remember that the banquet has been prepared at the cost of the sacrifice of Jesus Christ on the cross. It is to the great redemptive banquet of God that we are to invite people.

II. If we would compel people to come to Christ, we must recognize and accept our helplessness.

A. *We cannot coerce a person to come to God.*

B. *We cannot trick others into coming to God.*

C. *We must not overpersuade others to make an insincere commitment to God.*

While we are to seek to persuade people (2 Cor. 5:11), we must never violate their individual freedom. Jesus never coerced people to come to God in the sense of violating their autonomy and their freedom.

III. If we would compel people to come to Christ, we need to recognize and respond to our potential.

A. *Ours is the privilege of being spokespeople for God. We are to be witnesses for Jesus Christ.*

B. *Ours is the responsibility of inviting others to come to Jesus Christ.* This is not optional for one who is a true follower of Christ.

C. *Ours can be the joy of conveying God's invitation to needy people.*

D. *It is the birthright of one Christian to be able to help another person become a Christian.*

IV. We can be used of God to help other people be saved.

Many people do not recognize that theirs can be the joy and the privilege of helping someone experience the miracle of the new birth and come to know God in the forgiveness of their sin. If you would be useful, there are several things that can be helpful to you.

A. *Let Jesus Christ really live out His life in you.* Seek to be genuinely Christian, not only in conduct, but also in spirit and attitude.

B. *Decide that you will really live to help people come to know Jesus Christ and the best things in life.*

C. *Cultivate and develop some meaningful friendships with those who do not belong to the church.* Guard against the peril of becoming "isolated" from the unsaved world by knowing and associating only with those of your congregation.

D. *Report, as you have opportunity, what God has done and is doing in your personal life to those about you.* In a natural conversational way, do not hesitate to give testimony concerning the joy you have experienced in your faith.

E. *Recognize the deep needs of those who do not know Jesus as Savior.* Without our being aware of it, they have some great needs and some great fears. We can be helpful to them at this point. Only the Holy Spirit of God can really compel them to come to God (John 16:8). We need to recognize that those who do not know Jesus Christ have some deep needs and some great fears that can be taken care of only through faith in Jesus Christ. Only the Holy Spirit of God can convince them and call them to a saving experience of faith in Jesus Christ (John 16:8).

1. Your unsaved friend is afraid to die and yet he knows that he must.

2. Your unsaved friend feels insufficient and in many instances feels that he is the victim of luck or chance. He is not in total control over his life.

3. Your unsaved friend may be crowding his life with possessions, but he is constantly reminded that they decay and that they have not brought him any permanent happiness.

4. Your unsaved friend is afraid of being homeless, not only now but hereafter. An atomic blast could wipe out everything. An attic fire could destroy his home. War could come. An economic recession could produce a serious depression. A fatal illness could come without warning. The outsider who does not know Jesus Christ does not know how to deal with these serious problems.

Conclusion. If you would invite people to come to Jesus Christ, you can do so by a life that serves as a sample of what Christ can do when a person trusts Him sincerely and obeys Him joyfully.

You can invite your personal friends to come to know Jesus Christ with the tears of your genuine concern (Ps. 126:6). Until there is real concern in our hearts, we are not going to be very effective in extending the invitation.

Invite others to come to Jesus by reporting how God helps you with your day-to-day problems.

Invite them by pointing them to Jesus Christ. Invite them to your Sunday school class. Invite them to your church. Tell them how you came to know Jesus Christ as Savior. Trust the Holy Spirit to compel them with the gentle love of God to come to the banquet.   —*TTC*

SUNDAY EVENING, JANUARY 8

TITLE: Lot: The Road That Leads Away from God

TEXT: **"And Lot lifted up his eyes, and beheld all the Plain of the Jordan, that it was well watered everywhere before Jehovah destroyed Sodom and Gomorrah, like the garden of Jehovah, like the land of Egypt, as thou goest unto Zoar. So Lot chose him all the Plain of the Jordan; and Lot journeyed east: and they separated themselves the one from the other. Abram dwelt in** the land of Canaan, and Lot dwelt in the cities of the Plain, and moved his tent as far as Sodom. Now the men of Sodom were wicked and sinners against Jehovah exceedingly" (Gen. 13:10–13 ASV).

SCRIPTURE READING: **Genesis 13:1–13**

Introduction. A great tragedy for any minister to observe is to see some person, or some family, once interested in the things of God and active in His cause, now indifferent and worldly. Every pastor has seen that; and how depressing, how heartbreaking it is.

Such a person was Lot, nephew of Abraham. Lot did know God in his heart, or so the Scripture seems to suggest. In his second epistle Peter speaks of "righteous Lot" (2:7) and refers to his "righteous soul" (2:8). But sad indeed is the latter end of this man; and his family literally went all to pieces. The whole point of this message is this: There is a road that leads away from God and into worldliness and sin; and in Lot's experience, the signposts on that road were clearly marked.

I. The first signpost is marked contemplation.
    "And Lot lifted up his eyes, and beheld . . . " A man has taken his first step away from God when he even contemplates a choice that would lead him away from God and not toward Him. "Is not the whole land before thee?" Abraham asked Lot, when strife developed between their herdsmen. "Separate thyself, . . . from me: if thou wilt take the left hand, then I will go to the right; or if thou take the right hand, then I will go to the left" (v. 9). How generous of Abraham. He could have dismissed Lot and sent him on his way. But no, this great man, secure in his faith and in his sense of call, gave Lot first choice.
    Lot, no doubt, did not intend at first to go all the way into Sodom nor to lose all contact with his godly and gracious uncle with his smoking altars, but as he contemplated this thing the well-watered fertility and beauty of that valley was all he could think about.

II. The second signpost is marked consummation.
    When a man not only contemplates a worldly choice, but actually goes ahead and makes it, it's tragic. Listen: "So Lot chose him all the Plain of the Jordan" (v. 11a). We say, "Listen, Lot, what about your altars to God? What about the spiritual nurture and leadership you received from your uncle?"
    But Lot didn't choose on that basis. His choice, as many choose today, was calculated purely on material and business considerations. We can do some powerful rationalizing when we want to try to justify ourselves in making choices that we have already decided to make anyway. How tragic it is when we make a choice that puts the world first and leaves God out altogether.

III. The third signpost is marked separation.
    This is not separation from the world and its stain, for that would have been the right direction; but separation from his uncle Abraham, his altars, his influence. Abraham was only seeking to put distance between them to give their vast herds room to graze. As with so many today, however, prosperity turned out to be the means that saw them separated from one another.
    We have this tragic word, "And Lot journeyed east: and they separated themselves the one from the other" (v. 11b). Lot went farther away from Abra-

ham and his godly influence, and kept on pitching his tents nearer and nearer that wicked city of Sodom.

Some families do that today. They were once faithful members of a church. Then they pulled up stakes and moved. They promised themselves and God that they were going to join a church in the new town and continue to be active in the church. But they put it off and worldly interests entered in. They made friends and developed interests outside Christian circles. Their hearts grew cold. They drifted farther and farther away from God; their families, like Lot's, grew up to accept pagan moral and ethical standards.

IV. The fourth signpost is marked confirmation.

What a story in these thirteen verses of Genesis 13. Lot did not go from the blessings of Bethel to the sins of Sodom in one step, nor in one day. Step by step Lot moved away from God and godly influences and God's altars and toward sin and worldliness and heathenism. He looked, he chose, he journeyed east; and then we are told, "And Lot dwelt in the cities of the Plain, and moved his tent as far as Sodom" (v. 12b).

By way of contrast the apostle Paul entered the most godless and sinful cities of the Roman empire, not on a commercial venture, not for economic reasons, but in the power of God as an ambassador of Jesus Christ. He established churches in many of them. But Lot didn't move to Sodom to organize a church. Like many today, he moved to the new town to make money. That was his only concern.

Paul would have saved Sodom for he would surely have won nine others to faith in God (Gen. 18:32). John Wesley would have saved Sodom, as would Charles Haddon Spurgeon, or any number of soul winners through the centuries. But so confirmed was Lot in his love of the world that the angel of God almost had to pick him up by the nape of the neck and throw him out of Sodom to save his life.

V. The fifth signpost is marked dissolution.

Lot escaped from Sodom, but not with his great riches. He escaped with only "the shirt on his back." His wife, her heart more in love with Sodom than with the will of God, looked back and became a pillar of salt in the holocaust. His daughters, it turns out, had adopted the moral standards of Sodom; in shameless trickery they became the mothers of two wicked nations by their own father under the influence of strong drink.

May God have mercy! What an end for one who continues to follow on that road.

Conclusion. If a man has started down that road that leads away from God, what can he do? The prodigal son in Jesus' parable had gone far down that road. He considered his situation, turned completely around, and went back home. Any person can do that!

Years ago, Charles Clayton Morrison, then Editor of the *Christian Century,* attended an Interdenominational Committee Meeting at the Northshore Baptist Church in Chicago. It was Monday night. The pastor's Sunday morning sermon topic, "When Progress Is Backwards," was still on the illuminated bulletin board in front of the church. It fascinated Dr. Morrison.

When the meeting was over Dr. Morrison met a lay brother at the refreshment table. "Are you a member of this church?" the good Doctor asked. When

III. Jesus speaks of a limitation to the divine patience.

"Lo, these three years I have come seeking fruit on this fig tree, and I find none. Cut it down; why should it use up the ground?" (Luke 13:7).

A. *God is not in the business of encouraging parasites who use up space that could be occupied by productive plants.*

B. *God wants to replace deliberate parasites with those who will be properly productive.*

There is a national application in this parable. The patience of God with a nation can be exhausted.

There is a personal application in this parable. The patience of God with an individual who has been blessed with His favor can reach the point of exhaustion.

God makes no pets out of parasites.

IV. Jesus speaks of the gospel of a second chance.

"Let it alone sir, this year also, till I dig about it and put on manure. And if it bears fruit next year, well and good; but if not you can cut it down" (Luke 13:8–9 RSV).

Everyone who looks back and evaluates his or her performance conscientiously must admit that there have been great periods of time when we were not very productive as fig trees in the vineyard of God. We have not brought forth the fruit that would be pleasing to God or that we could be properly proud of.

While some opportunities may have flown into the past and are impossible to recall, we can rejoice in the fact that we do have the present and some portion of the future.

Let each of us decide that we will respond to the working of God's Spirit within our hearts and cooperate with the Father God that we might be a productive plant rather than a barren plant.

A. *Let us decide to make much of God's Word and not only read it, but heed it.*

B. *Let us see prayer as something more than a fire escape or a parachute project.* Let us determine to listen in order that we might receive instructions and corrections as well as commissions to do what God wants us to do.

C. *Let each of us recognize that the church is more than a place; let us see it as the body of Christ in the world today through which He would carry on His work in the world.* Let each of us rejoice over the fact that in and through the church, we can serve our Lord.

D. *Instead of neglecting and ignoring the Holy Spirit, let us recognize Him and respond to Him positively as He creates within us a hunger for fellowship with God and as He lays on us the blessing of a burden of compassionate concern for those who are about us.*

E. *Let us seize every opportunity for self-improvement through study and training.* In doing this we might become more competent in the church as members of the choir, as teachers in the Sunday school, and as participants in the outreach ministry of carrying the Good News of God's love to people in the community.

Conclusion. Where do you stand with reference to this parable of the barren fig tree? Does this parable make you ̶ ̶ ̶ ̶ ̶ ̶ ̶ If ̶ ̶ ̶u have not been converted, then it is self-evident that you have not brought forth any fruit to the glory of God. You breathe God's air which is free. You are alive because of a pump in your chest that God constructed. You are blessed with a fabulous computer between your ears that God engineered and with which you think. You live off the food produced in God's garden. It is high time that you recognize Him as creator, owner and sustainer and respond to His love by receiving Jesus Christ as Lord and Savior.

If you have received Jesus Christ as Lord and Savior and for some reason or another you have been asleep and inactive, it is high time to awake from your stupor and decide that you will become productive for God.   —*TTC*

* * *

SUNDAY EVENING, JANUARY 15

TITLE: Eliezer: The Marks of a Steward

TEXT: **"He said, 'O Lord God of my master Abraham, give me good fortune this day; and keep faith with my master Abraham'"** (Gen. 24:12 RSV).

SCRIPTURE READING: **Genesis 24:1–67**

Introduction. We have difficulty with this story because its setting is in the Near East where the manner of life is different from our own. For a man to arrange a marriage for his son, even through a third party, was the rule not the exception.

Eliezer (see Gen. 15:2, 3) was in charge of Abraham's affairs and answerable only to him. He was Abraham's steward. Though strange to us, arranging for someone else's marriage was familiar in Bible times. In Egypt Joseph became Potiphar's steward, and Jesus told a story about "a certain rich man who had a steward," who was accused of "wasting his goods" (Luke 16:1b).

The word "steward" is used to describe a Christian's relationship to Christ. As our Master He has entrusted to us, as His stewards, a portion of His goods to manage for His best interests. We are stewards, not owners. Our first concern is to be the success of our Master's affairs.

In this beautiful story about Abraham's commission to his steward and Eliezer's faithful service we see illustrated what are to be the marks of a steward. There are six of these.

I. A steward is a person who has been taken into his master's confidence and entrusted with his affairs.

Now that Abraham is old (v. 1) he is more and more dependent on this steward, "Eliezer of Damascus" (Gen. 15:2b). Having exacted of Eliezer an oath that he would not take a wife for Isaac of the Canaanites Abraham directs him to go to Mesopotamia, where some of the descendants of his brother, Nahor, still lived and seek a wife for Isaac from among his kinsmen. Eliezer makes his preparations immediately and starts on his journey.

Abraham was old and dependent on this trusted servant, but remember, God is not old, nor is He dependent on us; yet He trusts us and takes us into His confidence. He has placed a portion of His goods in our hands. He has done this because He has faith in us. We have faith in God, or say we do, but here is a sobering thought: God has faith in us. How tragic if we do not prove true to trust. What of God's has He placed in our hands? Everything we are and have (1 Cor. 4:7b).

II. A steward is a person who shares his master's faith and methods of operation.

This incident teaches us much about God's guidance of His servants. Eliezer was one whom God could guide. Why so? Because obviously he had absorbed something of his master's faith; he had imitated his master's method. He operated in the same spirit and manner as Abraham.

This we are to do. Christ is our Master. As He had faith in His Father, we are to have faith in Christ. We are not to operate in the spirit nor use the methods of the world.

Several years ago a church in a good Tennessee town got permission to put up papier-mache toll gates on the main highway and to make the last five miles into town a toll road. This was the estimated length of 50,000 one dollar bills pinned end to end. This was their goal for the amount they were seeking to raise for a proposed building. Every dollar given brought those papier-mache toll gates that much nearer town. No doubt some of those "hit for a dollar" wondered if they were being stopped by Jesse James and his gang rather than by the representatives of a church. This is not faith in God. This is not Christ's spirit nor is it His method. This smacks of the world with a commercial smell about it.

III. A steward is a person who combines faith and common sense in serving his master.

Each step Abraham's steward took was taken in fellowship with God. When the servant hesitated saying, "Peradventure the woman will not be willing to follow me unto this land" (v. 5b) Abraham assured him (v. 7). But this did not prevent the steward from weighing carefully the steps he should take. He combined faith and common sense.

Realizing that he had reached the village in Haran where Abraham's relatives lived he made the ten camels kneel and seated himself at the village well, knowing that the young ladies of the village would soon appear to draw water. How would he know who was the right girl? He wanted a chance to study the disposition and the character of the girl chosen to return with him to be his master's son's wife. His faith in the providence of a trifle is interesting. He prayed earnestly (vv. 12–14). He had ten camels. The camel is called "the ship of the desert"; and when camels come into the terminal from a long desert run they can drink a lot of water.

Rebecca was the first to appear; and she was something! She had the desired pedigree; she was physically beautiful (v. 16); and she passed the test Eliezer had set. Whatever may be the final word about Rebecca and her brother, Laban, Eliezer combines faith and common sense in the right proportions.

Why shouldn't we be as careful to combine faith and common sense? They do not conflict. They go together. They complement one another. They are allies.

IV. A steward is a person who is born zealous and urgent about his master's business.

When this man, Eliezer, had been taken into his master's confidence he entered into this highly sensitive and delicate matter with as much zeal and enthusiasm as if it had been his own private concern. He did not delay to begin, but organized his caravan and started. When he arrived in the city of Nahor he did not spend ten days to spy out the land. He began his search at once. After he had been received into Rebecca's home he would not eat anything until he had stated his errand (v. 33). When Rebecca's mother and brother tried to delay her departure ten days, after it was agreed that she should go, he replied, "Hinder me not, . . . ; send me away that I may go to my master" (v. 56b). When it was left up to Rebecca, she agreed to go immediately.

Oh, that we would be equally as intent on our Master's business! Oh, that we would be as urgent about our Master's work!

V. A steward is a person who manages to speak of his master, not of himself, whenever he has the opportunity.

Count the number of times this worthy man brings in the two words, "my master." He makes it clear from first to last that his mission is not his own; it is his master's.

Some of Jesus' disciples called Him, "Rabboni," the affectionate term for, "My Master." If only we would make it clear whose we are and whom we serve. We are His. The work of Christianity is His. He is our Master. As a boy of only twelve Jesus was conscious of His stewardship to the Father. "Knew ye not that I must be about my Father's business?" (Luke 2:49b MR) He asked his amazed parents. So must we all.

VI. A steward is a person who pleads for success in his master's name, not his own.

When Eliezer prayed that God would give him good speed in his mission he alleged, as his plea, that this would be showing kindness to his master Abraham (v. 12 ASV). As Abraham's steward this man was one with his master. Abraham's interests and concerns were his interests and concerns.

This should be our approach to stewardship. Our Master's interests and concerns should be our interests and concern. We should not hesitate to ask great things of God if we plead the name of Jesus. If we do we can be sure He will show kindness to us for Jesus' sake.

There are two approaches to time and talent, possessions and money: the owner approach and the stewardship approach. By the owner approach man is estranged, he is alienated from God and man. By the stewardship approach he is united to God and man.

Conclusion. This old world story is a beautiful lesson for all who call Jesus master and Lord. If He is your Lord, you are His steward. "It is required in stewards, that a man be found faithful" (1 Cor. 4:2b). God help us to be!

—WTH

* * *

WEDNESDAY EVENING, JANUARY 18

TITLE: The Practice of Prayer

TEXT: **"Therefore said he unto them, The harvest truly is great, but the laborers are few; pray ye, therefore the Lord of the harvest, that he would send forth laborers into his harvest" (Luke 10:2).**

SCRIPTURE READING: **Luke 10:2; 11:9; Jeremiah 33:3; Colossians 4:12**

Introduction. No sinner is saved without prayer, and no saint is sanctified without prayer. The prayer of Solomon is one of the longest in the Bible, thirty verses (1 Kings 8:23–53). Simon Peter's prayer is one of the shortest in the Bible, 1 verse, 3 words (Matt. 14:30). Whether prayer is long or short, it must be exercised, it must be practiced.

I. The person to whom we pray.
To whom should we pray? To the Father? Son? Holy Spirit? The basic New Testament rule is this: Prayer should be made to the Father, through the Holy Spirit, in the name of Jesus (Rom. 8:15, 16, 26, 27).

A. *God is eternal.* "And Moses said unto God, Behold, when I come unto the children of Israel, and shall say unto them, The God of your fathers hath sent me unto you; and they shall say to me, What is his name? what shall I say unto them? And God said unto Moses, I am that I am: and he said, Thus shalt thou say unto the children of Israel, I am hath sent me unto you" (Exod. 3:13–14).

B. *God is absolute.*

C. *God is free.*

D. *God is intelligent.*

E. *God is holy.*

F. *God is wise.*

G. *God is loving, merciful, good.*

H. *God is just.*

I. *God is omnipotent.*

J. *God is omniscient.*

K. *God is omnipresent.*

L. *God is sovereign.*

II. The positions of prayer.
The position in prayer is not as important as the heart or the soul in praying. Some biblical positions of prayer are:

A. *Standing in prayer.* "And when ye stand praying, forgive, if ye have anything against any, that your Father also, who is in heaven, may forgive you your trespasses" (Mark 11:25).

B. *Sitting in prayer* (1 Chron. 17:16–27).

C. *Bowing in prayer.* "And Moses made haste, and bowed his head toward the earth, and worshiped" (Exod. 34:8).

D. *Prostrate in prayer.* "I am weary with my groaning; all the night make I my bed to swim; I water my couch with my tears" (Ps. 6:6).

E. *On one's face in prayer.* "And he went a little further, and fell on his face, and prayed, saying, O my Father, if it be possible let this cup pass from me; nevertheless, not as I will, but as thou wilt" (Matt. 26:39).

F. *On one's knees in prayer* (1 Kings 8:54; Dan. 6:10; Luke 22:41; Acts 20:36).

G. *With the face between the knees in prayer.* "So Ahab went up to eat and to drink. And Elijah went up to the top of Carmel; and he cast himself down upon the earth, and put his face between his knees" (1 Kings 18:42).

III. The places of prayer.

A. *Privately.*

B. *Publicly.*

C. *With prayermates.*

D. *At the appointed place—God's house.*

E. *In homes*

IV. The petitions of prayer.

A. *For forgiveness.*

"And the tax collector, standing afar off, would not lift up so much as his eyes unto heaven, but smote upon his breast, saying, God be merciful to me a sinner" (Luke 18:13).

B. *For Christian graces.*

Dr. R. G. Lee tells of a dear woman who was touched by the sight of a little boy's face as he pressed it against a grocery store window, and looked wistfully at the candy and fruit display. She went inside and bought some for him. When she handed it to him, and he recognized what it was, he said, "Lady, are you God's wife?" It is not an unworthy prayer, to pray to be like God. It is a wholesome sign when the world sees in a Christian those graces that would indicate association with the Father.

C. *For the salvation of the lost* (Luke 18:13).

D. *For the harvest to be preserved for God's glory.*

E. *For accomplishing the impossible* (Mark 9:29; Acts 12:5–16; James 5:16–17).

F. *For the sick.* "Is any sick among you? Let him call for the elders of the church; and let them pray over him, anointing him with oil in the name of the Lord. And the prayer of faith shall save the sick, and the Lord shall raise him up; and if he have committed sins, they shall be forgiven him" (James 5:14, 15).

G. *For those in leadership positions.*

    1. Pastors. "And for me, that utterance may be given unto me, that I may open my mouth boldly to make known the mystery of the gospel" (Eph. 6:19).

    2. Church staff members.

    3. Government leaders.

H. *For enemies.* "But I say unto you, Love your enemies, bless them that curse you, do good to them that hate you, and pray for them who despitefully use you, and persecute you" (Matt. 5:44). "Bless them that curse you, and pray for them who despitefully use you" (Luke 6:28).

I. *For one another.* "Confess your faults one to another, and pray one for another, that ye may be healed" (James 5:16). "For God is my witness, whom I serve with my spirit in the gospel of his Son, that without ceasing I make mention of you always in my prayers" (Rom. 1:9).

Conclusion. Some pointers for prayer are suggested:

Take time to pray early in the morning. "And in the morning, rising up a great while before day, he went out, and departed into a solitary place, and there prayed" (Mark 1:35).

Take time to pray at noon. "Evening and morning, and at noon, will I pray, and cry aloud, and he shall hear my voice" (Ps. 55:17).

Take time to pray late in the afternoon. "Now Peter and John went up together into the temple at the hour of prayer, being the ninth hour" (Acts 3:1).

Take time to pray in the evening. "Let my prayer be set forth before thee as incense; and the lifting up of my hands, as the evening sacrifice" (Ps. 141:2).

Take time to pray at midnight. "And at midnight Paul and Silas prayed and sang praises unto God; and the prisoners heard them (Acts 16:25).   —*HSK*

* * *

SUNDAY MORNING, JANUARY 22

TITLE: **The Peril of Having an Empty Soul**

TEXT: **"Then he goes and brings with him seven other spirits more evil than himself, and they enter and dwell there; and the last state of that man becomes worse than the first" (Matt. 12:45 RSV).**

SCRIPTURE READING: **Matthew 12:43–45**

HYMNS: **"God, Our Father, We Adore Thee," Frazer**
       "One Day," Chapman
       "Let Jesus Come into Your Heart," Morris

OFFERTORY PRAYER:

Father God, we come into Your presence at this point in our worship service to bring our tithes and offerings. Thank You for giving to us the ability to work and the opportunity to earn. Thank You, Father, for Your thoughtfulness and Your generosity toward us at all times. We come bringing tangible evidence of our gratitude and of our desire to participate in Your effort to win the world to faith in Your Son Jesus Christ. Bless these gifts to the relief of suffering and to the spreading of the gospel. In Jesus' name we pray. Amen.

Introduction. A new sheriff was elected at a time when the community was being plagued by a lot of burglaries. He encouraged what he called "a neighborhood watch program" and encouraged the people of each community to be on the watch for the presence of suspicious looking strangers in the community. He encouraged neighbors to inform those near to them when they would be absent so that they could be on the alert for any suspicious activity next door during their absence. At the end of one year, there was a significant decrease in the number of burglaries in that county.

An empty house is in greater danger than a house that is fully occupied. Unoccupied rental property is always in danger because it presents an invitation to burglaries and vandalism.

Jesus used these known facts about empty houses to illustrate a greater truth: He pointed out the danger of having an empty soul. Jesus was speaking to His nation and to its religious leaders. The evil spirit of idolatry had been cast out of the lives of the people of Israel as a result of the pain of the exile. Never again was the nation of Israel tempted to the worship of idols. At the same time, the people of Israel had neglected to let the true God of love, grace, forgiveness, and helpfulness enter into their hearts and lives. Consequently, they possessed an empty soul. The nation and the people were experiencing the results of being empty of God and His good will for their lives. Theirs was a religion of emptiness because it was a religion of negatives and noninvolvement in ministries of reaching out to others.

Augustine is quoted as having said, "Thou hast made us for thyself and our souls are restless until they find their rest in thee." One can participate in religious activities and yet have an empty soul as far as being filled with God and His goodness is concerned.

This parable of the empty house should cause us to tremble. It is possible that some of us have not let God come in to fill our lives in such a manner as to keep the evil spirits away. This can happen without people being aware of it.

I. A religion of negatives.

The Jewish religious leaders of the day in which Jesus lived were great on emphasizing the great negatives. Their favorite verses began with, "Thou shalt not." They have many followers today who take great satisfaction in their negative goodness. They are loud and clear at the point of what they have not done. It is possible to become very pious and self-righteous on the basis of a form of negative goodness. Jesus would assert that negative goodness is not sufficient.

II. The shallow ineffectiveness of reformation.

Some people have thought that they were very religious because they turned over a new leaf and forsook a bad lifestyle.

The parable of the empty house, which has been called the haunted house, speaks to us concerning the fact that reformation is not deep enough and will prove to be ineffective.

A. *The alcoholic needs to do something besides forsaking the use of alcohol as a form of coping with the pressures of life.* Those who use alcoholic beverages are using man's most ancient tranquilizer, which dulls the pain that comes as a result of the cruelties of life. The use of this drug in the form of social beverages is very destructive and will eventually destroy many who use it. It should be recognized that "alcoholic spirits" are in reality a substitute for that which only the Spirit of God can do in the life of the individual.

B. *The lover of pleasure needs to do something more than forsake a habit that is indulgent toward his appetites and his love of ease.*

C. *The greedy person must do something more than just quit grasping for more of the possessions of the world.* He needs to become like God at the point of being a generous giver rather than a greedy grasper.

III. The aggressiveness of evil.

Jesus was not focusing on the depravity of the human heart when He gave voice to this parable of the empty house. He was recognizing the malignant aggressiveness of evil and the tendency of evil to return again and again from places from which it has been vanished.

A. *We need, with the help of God, to drive out every demon that would possess us.*

B. *We need to recognize that the demons that are driven out may come back in another form unless the place from which they were driven is filled with the presence of God.*

Only God in His fullness can prevent the return of evil into a person's life.

IV. Let God fill your life with good things.

It is not enough to merely be empty of evil. We must let God fill our hearts and lives with His goodness.

A. *The mere absence of evil in your life will not bring you fullness of joy or cause you to be well pleasing in the eyes of the Father God.*

B. *A heart that is empty of evil and cleansed from sin must be filled if it would remain clean and experience fullness of joy.*

The way to keep the weeds down in a garden is to fill that garden with seeds and plants so the weeds and the grass can be easily controlled and crowded out.

We need to do more than let Jesus come into our hearts to drive out the evil spirits that disturb and disappoint and destroy.

C. *We must let God's Spirit fill our lives.* We must fill our lives with the things of God or the evil spirits will return to plague us, and this means that the last state of that man could be worse than the first.

An empty mind and an empty heart invite disappointment and tragedy.

There are many professing Christians who are characterized by a negative form of religion who have let evil spirits come and fill their minds and fill their lives.

What about the evil spirit of self-righteousness that makes us so unattractive in the eyes of the unsaved people about us?

What about the evil spirit of self-satisfaction that causes us to live dormant and stagnant lives that are not characterized by growth?

What about the evil spirit of selfishness that causes us to assume a position of noninvolvement in reaching out to win others?

What about the evil spirit of apathy that leads to boredom and dissatisfaction with life?

What about the evil spirit of being a grouchy critic of those who try to do the will of God?

What about the evil spirit of depression that comes to disturb and to disappoint?

The evil spirits take many forms and occupy hearts that should be filled with the Spirit of God and with the goodness of God.

Conclusion. God wants to occupy and to fill the house of your soul.

God wants to help you cultivate the fruit of the Spirit (Gal. 5:22–23).

God wants to help you to love Him supremely and to love yourself properly and to love others in a helping and joyful way.

When God is permitted to fill the heart and life of a person, He gives to that individual a great inward security that replaces the fear and anxiety that dwelt there before.

When God is permitted to fill the heart and life, He enriches the person so that that person can become a giver instead of a getter.

When God is permitted to fill the heart and life of an individual, He enables that person to experience a joy that overflows and brings joy to others.

God wants to help you to be what He meant for you to be before the evil one came in and disturbed and destroyed the beauty and the peace of Eden's garden.

God wants to restore paradise in your heart, and He can do that only through Jesus Christ (John 14:6).

Let Jesus come into your heart.

There is no substitute for Jesus. —*TTC*

* * *

SUNDAY EVENING, JANUARY 22

TITLE: Moses: A Very Great Man

TEXT: **"Moreover the man Moses was very great in the land of Egypt, in the sight of Pharaoh's servants, and in the sight of the people" (Exod. 11:3b ASV).**

SCRIPTURE READING: **Exodus 11:1–8; Acts 7:20–41**

Introduction. In any list of the world's ten greatest men Moses would have to be included. Like some Colossus that will never fade from view Moses is enshrined in the memory of the Jewish people.

Several years ago a seminary professor from America was a guest for the Passover meal in the home of a Jewish family in Israel. At a certain point in the meal a knock was heard (actually the father knocking on the under side of the table). "Son," said the father to the family's youngest member, "go and see if Moses is knocking at our door." As the little fellow went the father whispered to the professor, "He has been looking forward to this moment for three years." The little boy returned to his place, disappointment written all over his face, to say, "No, father, Moses is not there." "Very well," the father replied, "maybe next year in Jerusalem." They have done this no one knows how long.

The entire Book of Exodus is in reality our text, for Moses looms like a giant out of its pages. From Exodus, and other Bible references, we learn that the life of Moses was made up of three chapters of approximately forty years each. Let us note these.

I. We see Moses as a prince in Pharaoh's household.

This is found in Exodus 2:1–15. Moses' lineage is carefully given. Of the tribe of Levi, his father's name was Amram and his mother's Jochebed. He had an older sister named Miriam and an older brother named Aaron—nothing remarkable.

But the times were remarkable. Things were dark for God's people in Egypt. Their servitude was crushing, their burdens unbearable, their slavery bitter. But worst of all a decree had gone out from Pharaoh that all boy babies were to be drowned in the river. Though the people didn't know it, the birth of a son to Amram and Jochebed was their hope.

Surely no ruler in history ever had a bigger joke played on him than Pharaoh when his own daughter rescued a castaway Hebrew baby and adopted him as her son. The future deliverer of Israel was reared in Pharaoh's household and trained and educated at state expense.

Except for a chance reference here and there, what happened during these forty years is left to the imagination. That Moses knew the secret of his Hebrew birth, his parents' religion, his people's afflictions, and their hopes for deliverance from bondage, there can be no doubt. That his own people knew his personal history and resented this Hebrew who was passing himself off as an Egyptian prince can be reasonably inferred. Referring to Moses' efforts to mediate between two fighting Hebrews Stephen tells us, "He supposed that his brethren understood that God by his hand was giving them deliverance; but they understood not" (Acts 7:25). Of course they didn't understand! They envied and resented this pampered, adopted son of Pharaoh's daughter. They would receive no help from one they considered a traitor.

But with his rash act of slaying one of Pharaoh's taskmasters the die was cast, and he fled to the land of Midian for his life. Stephen tells us that "he was well-nigh forty years old" (Acts 7:23) when this took place, marking the end of the first chapter of his life.

II. We see Moses as a shepherd in the land of Midian.

This is found in Exodus 2:16–4:26. Imagine! An Egyptian prince a sheepherder in what to the Hebrews was a despised land, Midian. But two things are significant during this period.

A. *A place of refuge for Moses.* Moses' innate sense of justice and his flair for getting involved cost him his place in Pharaoh's court, but it helped him find a job, a wife, and a home in Midian. He took the part of Jethro's daughters who were being victimized by Midianite shepherds. He was invited into their home to "eat bread" (2:20) and became Jethro's shepherd and son-in-law. No doubt this handsome young Hebrew in his royal robes, and with the gracious manner of the Egyptian court, was quite attractive to Jethro's seven daughters, especially to Zipporah whom he married.

Someone might ask: "Was God's hand in this? Was this not a terrible waste, a man 'instructed in all the wisdom of the Egyptians; and mighty in his words and works' (Acts 7:22), a shepherd?" Not so! This was God's way of preparing Moses.

B. *A time of preparation for Moses.*

1. Moses needed about forty years for his hot head to cool off. He was not "meek, above all the men that were upon the face of the earth" (Num. 12:3b) when he killed the Egyptian (Exod. 2:11–15). He learned meekness in the wilderness.

2. Moses needed to meditate on the God of his fathers and on the religion of the Hebrews he had learned at his mother's knee. That took time. A shepherd has time. Moses had forty years.

3. Moses needed to be familiar with this territory. Here he would later lead upwards of 2,000,000 people. At the end of forty years he knew every spring and every level place and hill and valley in the whole area.

After twenty-four years at Northampton, a prestigious pulpit, Jonathan Edwards, whose preaching helped to spark the "Great Awakening" in America, was dismissed by his congregation. He was in the prime of life with a large family to support. But, being a humble man, he accepted the only position open to him, as pastor-missionary on the frontier, a small place called Stockbridge. One might think, "What a waste!" Edwards' greatest works in theology and philosophy were written and published during this exile. This led to his election to what later became Princeton University.

Moses' time in Midian ended as abruptly as it began. There was the spectacle of the bush that burned and was not consumed, his reluctance to accept God's urgent call, God's equipping him with signs and wonders, and his farewell to his father-in-law. This brings us to the last chapter in his life.

III. We see Moses as God's leader in Egypt and in the wilderness.

This is given in Exodus 4:27–40:38. Moses was eighty years old when he stood before Pharaoh (Exod. 7:7) and he was 120 when he died (Deut. 34:7). Look at the main features of this period.

A. *The contest with Pharaoh.*

The ten plagues, which followed Pharaoh's initial response by increasing their burdens, were not only to break down Pharaoh's resistance, but were, as well, humiliating blows to Egypt's gods. They served also to bolster the faith of the Hebrews and of Moses.

B. *The plague of death, the institution of the Passover, and the beginning of the Exodus.*

When the angel of death struck the first-born of the Egyptians Moses had his people ready: the request for gifts from the Egyptians, the blood of the Passover lamb sprinkled on the side posts of the doors, the Passover meal eaten in haste, and their departure in the night.

When Pharaoh followed after, there were the crossing of the Red Sea on dry ground, the drowning of the Egyptians, and the song of Moses and Miriam on the other side.

C. *The trials of the march.*

The pattern seemed to be this: when there was a problem the people would complain and blame Moses; Moses would take the problem to God and God would provide deliverance. There were the bitter waters, hunger on the march, terrible thirst at Rephidim, and the God-given victory over the Amalekites.

D. *The giving of the law at Sinai.*

After centuries of slavery in an idolatrous nation the people were poorly prepared for this, but with them, as with us, God must make a start. The covenant, including the Ten Commandments, was solemnly ratified.

E. *The golden calf.*

During Moses' absence for forty days in the mount the people demanded of weak Aaron, "Up, make us gods, which shall go before us" (Exod. 32:1a ASV). Out of the gold they provided Aaron fashioned a molten calf; and proclaimed a "feast to Jehovah" on the morrow. Moses returned in the midst of the orgy that followed; burned the idol and strewed the ashes in their drinking water; and purged the camp of the offenders.

F. *Moses' return to the mount and the building of the tabernacle.*

His purpose was to intercede for the people. God heard his prayer and provided him with new tablets of the law, for he had broken those first given. The people gave willingly of their treasure for the building of the tabernacle as God instructed Moses.

G. *The failure at Kadesh-Barnea.*

The people shouted down the urging of Caleb and Joshua, the two faithful spies, in response to the evil report of the land by the ten. They were condemned to wander in this wilderness until that generation had passed on.

H. *The sin of Moses and Aaron.*

When the new generation was ready to enter the land the question was, "Would they be any better than their fathers?" They were not. They murmured because of thirst. Following a proud speech in which he failed to give God credit for the miracle Moses struck the rock and the water gushed out. For this he was denied the privilege of leading the people into the promised land.

Conclusion. Several lessons come out of Moses' life.

A. *God uses as His leaders not perfect people, but the best available to Him. He can make ordinary men great.*

B. *God can overrule an act of folly, and in the long run make it turn out for good.*

C. *God's plan for His people will not ultimately be defeated.*

D. *No matter how exalted his position before God every man is accountable for his sin.*   —*WTH*

* * *

WEDNESDAY EVENING, JANUARY 25

TITLE: Persistence in Prayer

TEXT: **"And I say unto you, Ask, and it shall be given you; seek, and ye shall find; knock, and it shall be opened unto you" (Luke 11:9).**

SCRIPTURE READING: Luke 11:5–13; 18:1–8

Introduction. The Gospel of Luke gives prominence to prayer in the life of Jesus. Luke tells us that Jesus prayed at His baptism (Luke 3:21), after cleansing the Leper (Luke 5:16), before calling the Twelve (Luke 6:12), at the Great Confession (Luke 9:18), on the Mount of Transfiguration (Luke 9:28), on the cross (Luke 23:34), and at His death (Luke 23:46). The prayer life of Jesus is precious to Luke and to every child of God.

The Parable of the Three Friends (Luke 11:5–13) and the Parable of the Widow and the Judge (Luke 18:1–8) are parables that have to do with prayer. Both parables are found only in Luke's Gospel. The main point, the salient point of the twin parables, is persistence in prayer. They teach us much about persistence in prayer, and their lessons are of utmost importance to the one who desires a life of persistent prayer.

I. Persistence in prayer assures us of an answer to our prayers (Luke 11:5–8).

The Parable of the Three Friends tells of a man who had an unexpected guest arrive at midnight. He came at the least favorable hour of the day and caught his friend without any food to set before him. The man went to another friend to secure three loaves of bread. He knocked on the door and cried to his friend inside, explaining the arrival of his guest. The friend inside said: "Stop troubling me, the door is locked, I am in bed, and I am not willing to disturb my household to give you the bread." However, the friend on the outside persisted in his request. Finally the friend on the inside arose and gave him not only three loaves but as many as he needed.

We must persist in our praying if we expect an answer.

II. Persistence in prayer unlocks God's storehouse of blessings (Luke 11:9-10).

The three present imperatives "ask," "seek," and "knock" mean we should ever be asking, seeking, and knocking. If we continue asking, seeking, and knocking, then God unlocks His storehouse to pour out His marvelous blessings on us. God is ready to give to man, but man needs to ask. He needs to ask often. He needs to ask repeatedly.

III. Persistence in prayer brings us what we need (Luke 11:11-13).

God is not going to give us the wrong gift. When we persist in prayer God will give us the right gift, His best gift. An earthly father will not give his son a stone when he asks for bread, a serpent when he asks for a fish, or a scorpion when he asks for an egg. An earthly father simply would not take advantage of his little one's ignorance and give him the wrong gift. Since earthly fathers know how to give good gifts, then how much more does God know how to give the best gifts. The argument is from the less to the greater. God's greatest gift is the Holy Spirit. It is the summum bonum that God bestows.

Persistence in prayer is the assurance that God will give His children what is required in life, even His best gift.

IV. Persistence in prayer will make us strong (Luke 18:1).

Jesus said men ought always to pray. Paul said it too (Eph. 6:18; 1 Thess. 5:17)! Persistence in prayer is a spiritual obligation. Persistence in prayer will keep us from fainting, from giving in to the pressure of evil, from turning into a coward, from losing heart, from behaving badly and denying the faith. If a man will persist in prayer he will be made strong.

V. Persistence in prayer enables us to overcome our adversaries (Luke 18:2-7).

The Parable of the Widow and the Judge gives assurance that God will deal justly in judging the wicked and avenging the righteous. If a heartless and godless judge will avenge a helpless widow because of her "continual coming," may not God do more than a judge who feared not God nor regarded man. God can be trusted to care for those who trust Him.

VI. Persistence in prayer insures faith at the coming again of our blessed Lord (Luke 18:8).

This verse is difficult to interpret. The question indicates that few will have faith at the coming again of our Lord. What kind of faith is Jesus talking about? It is faith in Jesus who will vindicate the righteous. It is the faith manifested by the widow who typifies faith in persistent prayer. Those who pray persistently stand fast; those who do not pray persistently will not stand fast.

Conclusion. How much of our weaknesses and failures is due to our failure to persist in prayer? We need to give ourselves to prayer, persistent prayer! —*HSK*

* * *

SUNDAY MORNING, JANUARY 29

TITLE: Well Done, Good and Faithful Servant

Text: "Well done, good and faithful servant; you have been faithful over a little, I will set you over much; enter into the joy of your master" (Matt. 25:23 rsv).

Scripture Reading: Matthew 25:14–30

Hymns: "Guide Me, O Thou Great Jehovah," Hastings
"Love Divine, All Loves Excelling," Zundel
"Love Is the Theme," Fisher

Offertory Prayer:

Precious Father, for Your gift of life and love, we thank You. For this day that You have made, we thank You. For the privilege of working and earning and saving and giving, we thank You. As we come today bringing our tithes and sharing an offering, accept these gifts and bless them to Your glory and to the good of a needy race. In Jesus' name. Amen.

Introduction. Jesus used parables, brief short stories, to present to us powerful pictures about God, about man, and about life. By means of these earthly stories, He communicated powerful human truths to His disciples and to those of us who are willing to listen and to learn today.

The Parable of the Talents, or the Parable of the Three Servants, is a parable that emphasizes the importance of faithfulness.

By means of this parable our Lord lets us know that in the final analysis our lives will be judged, not on the basis of our fame, but on the basis of our fidelity. We shall be rewarded, not on the basis of our genius, but on the basis of our goodness.

This parable should confront each of us in a very personal way. It can disturb us to the depths of our being. It can encourage each of us to do our best. It can challenge each of us to become a better person.

We are the children of God by grace through faith. At the same time, we are the servants of God with the privilege of helping God and others.

This pointed parable calls our attention to the possibility that we can blow our opportunity for God. We can blow our opportunity for ourselves. And we can waste our opportunity for ministering significantly to others.

This parable points out our need to have a great faith in the good character of our God. At the same time it tells us that we can enter into the joy of our God. At the same time, it should impart to each of us a healthy fear of the real peril of our experiencing a colossal failure.

The talents were measures of money and were comparable to a large sum of money. *Today's English Version* translates it in terms of $5,000, $2,000, and $1,000. These talents represent the powers and means that God has entrusted to His people for carrying on His kingdom work in the world today. They are the gifts that Paul enumerates as being distributed by the Holy Spirit in Romans 12, 1 Corinthians 12–14, and Ephesians 4. It could be said that these talents are the gospel itself, the truths that Christ preached, the training received, the energy that is available, the education that we have, the skill that has been acquired, along with Christian experience, health, wealth, time, opportunities, and effectiveness in preaching and teaching. God has entrusted to us all of the gifts and endowments of the Holy Spirit. From the Day of Pentecost, the Holy Spirit has been bestowing on the servants of God the talents and gifts that are needed for doing God's work in the world today.

I. Notice that the talents were entrusted "to each according to his ability" (v. 15).

This parable does not emphasize equality. It emphasizes the importance of faithfulness.

A. *We are unequal in our native gifts.*

B. *We are unequal in the opportunities that are open to us as individuals.*

C. *We are unequal in the matter of the advantages that we might have over others.*

D. *We are unequal in human endowments, but each of us has an equal opportunity and chance to become a good and faithful servant to God.*

This parable points out that we will be judged and rewarded on the basis of our faithfulness in using what we have that has been entrusted to us.

II. Let each of us beware of the possibility of becoming a twin brother or sister of the one-talent servant.

A. *This man failed to trust in the good character of his Lord.*

From the dawn of human history, it has been the strategy of Satan to question the goodness of God. In the Garden of Eden, he dropped the hint that God was not really good, and that He was restricting Adam and Eve from entering into what they had the right to experience.

1. The sin of no faith has been the undoing sin of God's people throughout the ages.

2. The sin of little faith causes us to refrain from attempting to do the big things that God wants us to do.

B. *This man was not a bad man.* He is not described as cruel and merciless. He is not described as a wasteful and dissipated person. He is not described as a slave of his passions.

C. *This man counted his one talent as being of no real importance.* Evidently he assumed that his one talent was not needed. It should be recognized that every talent is needed in the divine economy. He failed to appreciate the fact that every talent is precious in the eyes of God.

D. *This man lacked the faith and courage to take a risk.* He decided to be cautious and to play it safe. He is like those who never "go for broke" in order that they might succeed in a business enterprise.

1. We must take the risk of failure in the matter of trusting God to come through on His promises if we would do something significant.

2. We must expose ourselves to the peril of embarrassment and loss if we would ever do anything worthwhile.

What if Abraham had played it safe and had refused to take the risk of leaving his home and going to a far country for God?

Moses wanted to play it safe and tried every excuse possible to avoid responding to God's call. Finally he took the risk and became the great deliverer.

We can be grateful that Jesus did not play it safe. If Paul and the other apostles had played it safe and had never taken the risk of failure, we probably would have never known about the gospel of Jesus Christ.

Many people are tempted to think that their talent is so small that it does not matter, and therefore, they neglect to respond to their opportunities. When we do this we become a twin brother of the one-talent man.

III. The good news in this powerful parable.

A. *To each of us has been given talents by our King.* It is the ministry of the Holy Spirit to distribute spiritual gifts to each individual believer according to the needs of the church for the ministry that is bestowed graciously. There is no one left empty-handed. To each one there has been given a gift.

B. *You can double your capital (talents) by faithfulness.* You can have twice as much of the same things as were first entrusted to you if you will be reliable and trustworthy in using what God has placed in your hands.

You can improve your own usefulness and fruitfulness. Someone has said, "One note is a sound. Add other notes and you have a song." One color, no matter how beautiful, is monotonous; add other colors, and you have a cathedral window. Such is the reward to the person who adds to the gifts that God has given to him through faithfulness.

C. *You can receive your Lord's approval and praise.*

We receive the *acceptance* of God when we receive Jesus Christ as Savior and Lord. He receives us and forgives us and accepts us.

We can have His *approval* and His praise if we are faithful in the use of the gifts that He bestows upon us. Everyone would like to hear him say, "Well done."

D. *You can enter into the joy of your Lord.*

All of us want to enter into the joy of our Lord in the hereafter. This parable would teach us that it is possible for us to enter into the joy of our Lord in the here and now. Ours can be the joy of doing good. Ours can be the joy of being God's love to others. Ours can be the joy of seeing people come to know Jesus Christ as Savior. Ours can be the joy of becoming what God wants us to be.

Conclusion. Let us beware of thinking of ourselves as one-talent people. We need to recognize that the little person with a great gospel is mightier than a great person with no gospel.

If we neglect to use our opportunities and gifts, we will lose them.

If we bury our gifts and neglect to use them, we reveal that we do not have the character that would make it possible for us to be compatible or comfortable with God.

Let us use what God has given to us that we might bring glory to Him and that He might be glorified in us.   *—TTC*

* * *

SUNDAY EVENING, JANUARY 29

TITLE: David: Preparing for Great Encounters

TEXT: "Thy servant smote both the lion and the bear: and this uncircumcised Philistine shall be as one of them, seeing he hath defied the armies of the living God" (1 Sam. 17:36 ASV).

SCRIPTURE READING: 1 Samuel 17:17–54

Introduction. Two young men were having their mid-morning refreshment break at a soda fountain. One paid for the drinks with a dollar bill and received twenty cents change, which he immediately dropped into his pocket. A few minutes later the clerk put two dimes on the counter saying, "I believe I forgot your change." The young man who had been treated started to speak, but his friend stopped him with a knowing wink, and put the two dimes into his pocket. His partner, however, could not forget the incident. "Twenty cents isn't much money," he reasoned, "but it's the principle of the thing."

Years passed and these two, now mature men, found themselves working for the same company in a great city. The one who had been treated was the Executive Vice President in charge of personnel and the one who had received his change twice was a lesser official. The time came when the company was to open a factory and branch office in another city, and the choice for a general manager lay between the man who had filched the two dimes years before and another company official. It was the responsibility of the Executive Vice President to make the choice. His mind went back to the soda-fountain incident and he reasoned like this, "If, for no reason, my friend would steal twenty cents from a drugstore, what would he do if he should be placed in a place of trust with thousands of dollars of the company's money in his hands?" The other man got the job. Having lost the minor skirmish in the battle with dishonesty he didn't even get a chance to fight the major battle. The point is that our little battles prepare us for the great encounters which will certainly come.

When we read of David's slaughter of Goliath we are apt to forget that he had won some lesser battles before he fought the giant. He had trusted God for help and strength in the smaller battles and when he came to the supreme test he already knew how to trust God. Let us look at some of the battles David had won before he removed Goliath's head, for we fight these battles every day.

I. David had won the battle with temper.

No one can get under little brother's hide like big brother, and Eliab, David's oldest brother, sensing what David was anxious to do, was jealous. He worked little brother over good (v. 28).

This is not just another exciting, romantic tale, though it has all the elements of one. The valiant youth, as a reward for his exploit of slaying the giant, wins the hand of the king's daughter. In the format of such a story what would be Eliab's part? It is that of the ugly, elder step-sister in Cinderella. Eliab was embarrassed, jealous, and resentful; if his tongue had been a javelin and directed at Goliath, instead of his brother, he could have killed him himself at one hundred yards.

But David controlled his temper and did not reply in kind. He had bigger fish to fry than to waste time and energy fighting with big brother. Most of us do.

Nothing will disturb the accuracy of the eye or the steadiness of the hand like the passion of an uncontrolled temper. David won this lesser battle with temper before he took on the giant. So must we all.

II. David had won the battle with fear.

When David expressed his hot indignation at Goliath's insulting challenge (v. 26) he meant it. He was indignant because he felt that God's honor was being dragged in the dust. His word repeated to several, that he was not afraid to fight this giant, came to the ears of King Saul who sent for him. Saul was amazed when he saw the one who had been talking so much—he was just a big over-grown boy, a youth. But it was David who took the initiative in this interview, "Let no man's heart fail because of him," he said, "thy servant will go and fight this Philistine" (v. 32). Something had to be done, as David saw it, to remove this reproach, this insult, to God's forces. He didn't see any volunteers lining up so he said, "I'll go. I'll fight him."

There was no panic on David's part, no wasteful excitement, no shouting to keep his spirits up. He was not afraid. He was going as God's representative, to defend God's honor. He was not afraid.

How wasteful, how harmful is the emotion of fear. Few foes we have are so ruinous and destructive. It disarms us and makes us an easy prey before our enemies. Fear paralyzes and keeps us from doing what we know we ought to do. If we can conquer fear in the lesser combats we can fight the giants unafraid.

III. David had won the battle with unbelief.

Amazed at David's courage, his total lack of fear, Saul was not willing for such an uneven contest to take place (v. 33). But David enumerated some of his experiences in the rich history of God's providential dealings with him (vv. 34–37). He had known God's power when he faced the lion and the bear and now his faith that God would give the victory is unclouded and serene. "God helped me against these murderous wild beasts," David reasoned, "and He will help me against this enemy of His people."

Faith does not spring up full grown in the night like some toadstool. It grows by exercise and practice. It must be cultivated. Though David was but a youth his faith was full grown.

To David this was not primarily a contest between himself and Goliath, but between God and Goliath (v. 36)—"Seeing he has defied the armies of the living God." For David this contest had definite religious significance; and going as God's servant it never occurred to him that he could lose. His speech to Goliath was really something (vv. 45–47). But this was more than big talk. This was preaching the power of faith in God to all who would hear. This was the actual basis of the contest and, no doubt, the reason why it is preserved in such detail in the sacred record.

We need faith! We need faith, not in programs, not in slogans, not in material things, but in God. Until we can win the battle with unbelief we are not ready to fight any giants.

IV. David had won the battle with pride.

Saul agreed for David to go, but he couldn't believe that David and God could kill a giant with such crude weapons (vv. 38–39). But Saul's equipment was not the answer. It takes only a thimbleful of imagination to see how amusing and absurd this picture was. Imagine the coat of mail bumping David's knees and the brass helmet down over his eyes. But there is something deadly and danger-ous in it also, the temptation to pride—the king's armor! "Hey, big brother, Eliab, look at your kid brother now—the king's armor! Now, what do you think?"

But not David! This didn't tempt him at all. "I cannot go in these. I am not worthy and I don't know how to use them." He put them off.

God does not wage warfare as men do. He has His own methods, His own weapons, His own way and His own time. We must humble ourselves to fight His way with His weapons. Pride is deadly and self-destructive. It is deceptive. It can and it will defeat us. Pride is trust in self, which is the exact opposite of trust in God. Until we can win the battle with pride we are not ready to fight any giants.

Conclusion. Is this record relevant to our lives? Are temper and fear and unbelief and pride unknown to us? You know the answer to that. God help us in the struggle with these enemies that we may be prepared for the great encounters to come.   —*WTH*

SUGGESTED PREACHING PROGRAM
FOR THE MONTH OF FEBRUARY

Sunday Mornings

The chief end of man is to worship God and to enjoy Him forever. Genuine worship is a dynamic experience that brings about dramatic changes in the life of the worshiper. We need to improve the quality of both our public worship and our private worship activities. The suggested theme for these messages comes from the psalmist, "O come, let us worship and bow down: let us kneel before the Lord our maker" (95:6).

Sunday Evenings

Continue with the series of biographical sermons using the theme "The Lives and Lessons From Great Men."

Wednesday Evenings

The suggested theme is "Make Good Habits, and Your Good Habits Will Make You Good." We use Jesus as the Model who is worthy of our imitation. Jesus did many things by habit as well as by disposition. We need to form the good habits which our Lord had.

* * *

WEDNESDAY EVENING, FEBRUARY 1

TITLE: The Habit of Regular Church Attendance

TEXT: "And he came to Nazareth, where he had been brought up; and he went to the synagogue, as his custom was, on the sabbath day" (Luke 4:16 RSV).

SCRIPTURE READING: Luke 4:16–20

Introduction. One significant fact about this passage of Scripture in which our Lord gives the platform for His messianic ministry is Luke's calling attention to one of the habits of Jesus. Luke declares that when Jesus came to Nazareth where He had been brought up, He went to the synagogue, "as his custom was." It should not surprise us that Jesus had the regular habit of being in attendance at the place of Bible study and worship. This is one of the great habits of Jesus that should characterize the lives of those who identify themselves as His followers.

It is disturbing to see what percentage of those in each church who claim to be believers in and followers of Jesus Christ are neglectful of being regular in attendance at the house of prayer and worship. (It might be a sobering experience to compare the percentage of those who are regular in attendance for Bible study, worship, and the prayer service in your specific congregation.) In one of the great passages of exhortation in the Book of Hebrews, the readers are encouraged, ". . . not neglecting to meet together, as is the habit of some, but encouraging one another, and all the more as you see the Day drawing near" (10:25 RSV).

During the days of our Lord, He did some things which His critics considered to be as violations of the Sabbath day (cf. Matt. 12:1–8; Mark 3:1–6). Our Lord declared, "The sabbath was made for man, not man for the sabbath." He came to be Lord over the Sabbath (Mark 2:27–28).

The Jewish people had placed many restrictions upon what could be done on the Sabbath day because of their desire to avoid desecrating the Sabbath. It had become in many respects a burden rather than a blessing. Our Lord did not hesitate to minister to the suffering and to the needy and the distressed on the day which was considered a sacred day. This is not to imply that He would encourage anything that would point toward the secularization of the day of worship.

The follower of Christ who had not developed and maintained regular attendance at the house of God with the people of God is depriving himself and robbing others of the blessings that could be his and theirs through this good spiritual discipline.

I. The synagogue was a Jewish place of worship.

It is important that each believer have a place for private worship in his home or office. There must be someplace where each can go for a private talk with the Father.

It is of tremendous importance that each follower of Christ also have a group with whom he is associated in prayer, praise, witness, and sacrificial giving. Many of the blessings of God come to us through fellowship with the family of God.

To neglect to develop the habit of regular public worship is to rob ourselves.

II. The synagogue was a Jewish place for scriptural instruction.

It was to the synagogue that the Jewish people went for instruction in the Scriptures. The children were taught the Scriptures there. Adults went to hear the Scriptures read and interpreted.

Every church should be aggressive in its program of providing biblical instruction, both for its members and for nonmembers. Studies reveal that if a nonbeliever can be enrolled in Bible study, the chances of his or her becoming a convert are greatly increased.

Every new convert needs to be enrolled in regular Bible study in the church. Even the most mature followers of Christ need to be regular in their habit of studying the Word of God with others.

III. The synagogue was a Jewish place for prayer.

Our Lord had the habit of coming together with others that He might pray with them. While there is great value that comes to us through individual and private prayer, there are blessings indescribable that come to us as we pray together.

The early church was famous for its great prayer services.

Conclusion. If we would be true followers of Jesus, we need to identify with His habits. One of His habits was the habit of being regular in the synagogue worship service.

We first make our habits and then our habits make us.   —*TTC*

* * *

SUNDAY MORNING, FEBRUARY 5

TITLE: The Spiritual Prayer Retreats of Jesus

TEXT: "And in the morning, a great while before day, he rose and went out to a lonely place, and there he prayed" (Mark 1:35 RSV).

SCRIPTURE READING: Mark 1:35–39

HYMNS: "O Worship the King," Grant
      "Sweet Hour of Prayer," Walford
      "Teach Me to Pray," Reitz

OFFERTORY PRAYER:

"Father God, You you have given us this day in which to live and worship and serve. We come bringing tithes and offerings to express our love for You and our desire that the world might come to know the good news about Jesus. Bless these gifts to that end we pray. Amen.

Introduction. Our Lord not only had the habit of being regular in attendance for public worship (Luke 4:16), but He went apart repeatedly to talk with and receive help from the Father. It is interesting to note the circumstances which provided the occasion for our Lord's going apart for what we today might call a private personal worship experience.

I. Jesus was strongly led by the Spirit to go away into a desert place at the beginning of His earthly ministry (Mark 1:12–13).

Sometimes we fail to recognize that the Holy Spirit of God strongly led our Lord into a desolate place as He sought to choose the directions and the methods for His redemptive ministry. The forty days in the wilderness were a period of intense communion with God. Our Lord talked with the Father, and we can be sure that the Father talked to His Son. Even "the angels ministered to him" during this time.

II. Jesus retreated to the place of prayer when the duties and responsibilities of life weighed heavily upon Him (1:35).

Jesus found it necessary to go apart to be with God that He might receive strength and guidance and help as He faced both His opportunities and the duties that befell Him.

If Jesus needed a prayer retreat in the face of His responsibilities, it follows that we also need to go apart for communion with God.

III. When great choices needed to be made, our Lord made them after serious reflection and communion with the Father God (3:13–14).

Our lives would be more harmonious with the will of God, and we would experience far greater joy in living, if we made the decisions of life matters of earnest prayer rather than just making snap decisions along the way.

IV. Our Lord experienced a retreat when He was weary and needed rest (6:30–31).

A pastor was seeking to encourage his people to be zealous in their efforts to work for God. As he did so, he reminded them of the fact that the devil never takes a vacation. Someone responded, "That may be why he is such a devil." Jesus and the apostles found it necessary at times to go apart into a private place that they might rest and that the vital energies of life might be restored. If they needed this, surely we need it also from time to time.

V. Our Lord went apart to a private place for prayer when He experienced misunderstanding (6:45–46).

There were times when even the apostles greatly misunderstood the motive and the methods of the One whom they considered to be their Messiah. Evidently following our Lord's multiplication of the loaves and fishes, these apostles were encouraging the crowd to marshall a movement to crown Jesus as their king. Our Lord broke up this demonstration and compelled them to get into the boat in order that He might send them away. After they were gone, He needed an experience with God and went apart for prayer.

Misunderstanding is the lot of every person. There are times when this can be very painful. It is interesting to note that Jesus resorted to prayer when He was misunderstood.

VI. Jesus and the apostles needed time to be alone with each other (7:24).

Our Lord was an activist and almost a compulsive minister to the needs of the people. Though He came to minister and His heart was moved by the needs of the people, there were times when He needed to be alone with His helpers. If Jesus needed this, it follows that we are bound to need it too.

VII. Jesus retreated to a private place when He needed encouragement (9:2).

This experience in the life of our Lord took place about six months before His crucifixion. The major portion of His life and ministry was in the past. He took with Him three of the apostles that they might go with Him to the top of the mountain for a time of prayer. On the mountaintop, Jesus experienced the presence of Moses and Elijah. They discussed with Him that which was to take place by means of His death on the cross and His resurrection from the tomb (cf. Matt. 17:1–8; Luke 9:28–36). In addition to these Old Testament characters, our Lord heard the voice of the Father expressing His divine approval.

If Jesus needed to be encouraged, I am sure that all of us need to be encouraged. We can find that encouragement if we will take time out to go apart and be alone with God.

VIII. Jesus went apart into a private place for prayer when He desperately needed strength for the impossible task that He faced (Mark 14:32–42).

It is interesting to note that our Lord went apart into a private place for prayer as He faced the ordeal of His crucifixion. Repeatedly He prayed. At that time He needed also the encouragement and the strength of the prayers of His three chosen apostles who were there but who fell asleep.

Conclusion. If we are too busy to draw apart into a private place to commune with God and to let Him speak to our minds and hearts, we are entirely too busy.

All of us need to change our schedules and let God have the place that belongs to Him in our lives. Each day we should spend some time in solitude with God. We need to spend some time with His Word.

The listening side of prayer experience can be much more beneficial than the speaking portion of it.

All of us can find both time and space for private worship if we will set our hearts on it. Not to do so is to impoverish ourselves. Not to do so is to miss the blessings of God the Father.

Jesus "went out to a lonely place, and there he prayed."   —*TTC*

* * *

SUNDAY EVENING, FEBRUARY 5

TITLE: Elijah—The Education of a Prophet

TEXT: "`. . .` **And after the fire a still small voice. And it was so, when Elijah heard it, that he wrapped his face in his mantle, and went out, and stood in the entrance of the cave. And, behold, there came a voice unto him, and said, What doest thou here, Elijah?" (1 Kings 19:12b–13 ASV).**

SCRIPTURE READING: 1 Kings 19:1–18

Introduction. Like a meteor, which lights up the whole horizon for a moment then sinks beyond the rim of the sky and is gone, Elijah the Tishbite flashed across the darkest pages of Hebrew history. Elijah entered Israel's history like a tempest and went out in a whirlwind. So great was his fame, so dramatic his person during his own lifetime, that the notion persisted that Elijah was caught up into the air by the Spirit of God and carried hither and yon at will (1 Kings 18:9–15).

Elijah served God well. He was God's surgical knife, lancing the festering sore of Israel's idolatry. Elijah was the rod in God's hand chastening Israel for her disobedience. Elijah was God's mouthpiece, pronouncing the judgment of drought upon the land. Elijah was God's priest, offering a sacrifice for the sins of the people that brought down fire from heaven. At the mere mention of his name we think of earthquake, storm, and fire, the scourge of evil kings, and the prophet of doom.

But there was another side, a constructive side to Elijah's character and career. God used Elijah to anoint prophets and kings, among them the great prophet Elisha, who was to take up his mantle. God used Elijah to organize schools of prophets who lived on after him. God used Elijah to call princes and kings back to God. He was the most colorful, the most amazing, the most important man alive in his generation.

How did he come by all this? Only through a long and severe period of schooling in what we might call "God's school of faith." By means of one experience after another God taught His prophet. In the small fragments of Elijah's career given in the Scriptures we find the outline for the education of this prophet. Let us note this closely, for every prophet and child of God needs these lessons.

I. Elijah learned the lesson of provision.

Faithful as God's spokesman, Elijah had pronounced God's judgment of drought (1 Kings 17:1b), but how was he supposed to eat? In essence God said, "I'll feed you. Drink of the water of the brook, 'and I have commanded the ravens to feed thee'" (v. 4b). But the brook was drying up. Elijah had to depend upon God to provide. He *had* to do it! Elijah's part was to be faithful. God had said He would provide.

Even though Elijah saw the brook failing every day, he remained until God would send him on, even if it meant he would starve to death. And God provided for his prophet. When Elijah moved on to Zarephath, he had no fears for the failure of the meal in the widow's jar nor for the oil in the cruse. He knew they would not fail. He had already learned his lesson that God will provide; and he taught this lesson, in turn, to the widow of Zarephath.

Oh, that we could learn this lesson! Abraham learned it (Gen. 22:8). Paul learned it (Phil. 4:19). Our forefathers in a hostile wilderness learned it. But some never learn this lesson. Why? They lack Elijah's faith.

II. Elijah learned the lesson of patience.

In the widow's home Elijah was secure but secluded, away from what to him was the scene of action, Israel. His appearance in Ahab's court was a dangerous mission. He had said, "Listen, Ahab, God will judge His people. So Baal is the god of fertility and good crops, is he? I am a prophet of Jehovah. He challenges Baal to war. 'There shall not be dew nor rain these years, but according to my word'" (v. 1b). That was dangerous, dramatic, blood-tingling business; Elijah loved every minute of it.

But now he was cut out of the action, cooling his heels, day after day, week after week, month after month for three whole years, while he longed to be in Israel "preaching every Sunday." Imagine! This restless, energetic thunderbolt of a man cooling his heels in idleness for three years. But God had to teach Elijah patience and this was the only way He could do it.

Some people receive praise when they should be blamed and credit when no credit is due on this matter of patience. They have no energy for God's work, no concern about it, no zeal for Jehovah. When things at church don't go right, they take it in stride—not because they have learned God's lesson of patience, but because they don't care whether God's work goes on or not.

But God has this lesson for us, patience, the grace to wait until God is ready. God is saying to us, as He said to Elijah, "You obey Me! Do what I ask you to do! Then wait for My time!" During those three years when Elijah was idle, God was busy as with one hand He held back the rain while with the other He hurled His sunshine on the land until the nation was broken and contrite.

III. Elijah learned the lesson of power.

On Mount Carmel Elijah learned the lesson of the power of God in answer to prayer. The test by fire was for Elijah a venture of faith. He was willing to risk everything upon God's willingness to answer; and God did answer. Elijah prayed. The fire fell (18:36–38). He prayed again. The rain came in torrents (vv. 41–45). Elijah had faith to believe that the fire would fall and that the rain would descend, and his faith was vindicated by the power of God.

That power is still available. God will still answer by fire, the consuming fire of His Holy Spirit, when His people have the faith to stake everything on the answer. Elijah was not a celestial being, nor was he a creature from another world. James tells us, "Elijah was a man of like passions with us" (5:17 ASV). The only question is: Are we men of like faith with Elijah? Are we willing to pray for God's power to fall, believing so strongly that it will that we will stake our very lives on the result? I fear not. We have not learned what God's power can do because we do not have such faith, and therefore, we have not prayed in faith.

IV. Elijah learned the lesson of preservation.

There was one in Israel who was not impressed by either Elijah's prayers or God's answers of fire and rain. That person was Jezebel. Her threat could hardly be misunderstood (19:2). Had Elijah stayed close to God, he might have accepted the challenge and dared this lioness in her den, but he didn't. Instead he got up and ran for his life.

But God was patient with him, knowing that Elijah was just a man and that temptations often follow triumphs. He provided food and drink for the journey of forty days and tenderly assured him that he would be preserved, that his life was not in danger.

What Christian worker is there who has not learned that bad days follow good, and that the greatest times of weakness often follow the greatest thrills of power? How could we go on if God did not preserve us in times of weakness and defeat?

V. Elijah learned the lesson of God's presence.

Elijah had run away from Jezebel but not from God. A voice asked, "What doest thou here, Elijah?" (19:9b). Elijah laid all the cards on the table (v. 10), for there was no point in trying to hide his feelings from God. When he was told to "Go forth, and stand upon the mount before Jehovah" (v. 11a), he was shown an exhibition of awesome power (vv. 11–12), but God's essential presence was not in them. Elijah was familiar with earthquake, storm, and fire, but this "sound of gentle stillness" was a new experience, the real presence of God.

There are times when God does feed us by the ravens and answer by fire, but at other times He must lock us in a cave for a time in order for us to hear "the still small voice," and learn the wonder of His presence.

Conclusion. Do you want to go to God's school? These lessons are also for us as His servants, His children. Enroll today! —*WTH*

* * *

WEDNESDAY EVENING, FEBRUARY 8

TITLE: The Habit of Prayer

TEXT: "He was praying in a certain place, and when he ceased, one of his disciples said to him, 'Lord, teach us to pray, as John taught his disciples'" (Luke 11:1 RSV).

SCRIPTURE READING: Luke 11:1–13

Introduction. The prayer life of Jesus is most revealing. He lived in an atmosphere of daily prayer. His prayer life was never at the mercy of moods. He never permitted prayer to be crowded out of His schedule. Jesus was very persistent in His prayer life: "And in the morning, a great while before day, he arose and went out to a lonely place, and there he prayed" (Mark 1:35). "In these days he went out to the mountain to pray; and all night he continued in prayer to God" (Luke 6:12 RSV).

Jesus was found praying at all of the great crises of His life. He prayed at the time of His baptism. He prayed during the time of His temptation experience. He prayed before the selection of His apostles. He prayed on the Mount of Transfiguration. He prayed in Gethsemane. He prayed while on the cross.

When we look at the content of the prayers of Jesus, we find that He experienced communion with the Father. He offered thanksgiving to God. He presented petitions to the Father. He engaged in intercessory prayer.

The disciples noticed the difference between Jesus' prayers and their own. His were so sure and strong and real while theirs were weak and unsatisfying. They felt a great need to pray as He prayed, and consequently they requested that He teach them to pray.

I. There is an art to effective praying, and we should let Jesus be our Teacher in this matter of being effective prayers (Luke 11:2-4).

II. Jesus taught that we should have the habit of prayer and not to break it (18:1-8).

We must not "cave in" at the point of ceasing to pray. If we have the habit of not only talking to God but listening to God, this will prevent us from "caving in" when the crises of life come to us.

III. Jesus encourages us to keep on keeping on in the matter of prayer (Matt. 7:7-11).

Conclusion. How long has it been since you examined your prayer life? Is this a habit you have neglected to develop? Is it a habit which you have let drop by the wayside? Satan, your enemy, who walks about as a roaring lion seeking whom he may devour, will do everything possible to keep you out of the closet of prayer. By so doing, he will impoverish you. He will cheat God, and he will rob others.

Make good habits, and your good habits will make you good.

—TTC

* * *

SUNDAY MORNING, FEBRUARY 12

TITLE: The Nature of True Worship

TEXT: **"God is a Spirit: and they that worship him must worship him in spirit and in truth"** (John 4:24).

SCRIPTURE READING: John 4:21-24

HYMNS: **"Come, Thou Fount of Every Blessing,"** Wyeth
"Praise to the Lord, the Almighty," Gesangbuch
"Great Redeemer, We Adore Thee," Conte

OFFERTORY PRAYER:

Our Father, in giving to mankind the greatest Gift of all, Your own dear Son, You have demonstrated to us the true spirit of giving. We recognize our inherent selfishness, Father, and we ask Your forgiveness. Purify our gifts this morning, and may they bring honor and glory to Your name and promote the progress and growth of Your kingdom's work on this earth. In Jesus' name we pray. Amen.

Introduction. The conversation between Jesus and the Samaritan woman at Jacob's well is one of the high points of John's Gospel. Included in this conversation is a revelation concerning true worship which is priceless. And note that it was not made in a hushed, sacred setting, but in Samaria of all places, and to a woman whose life was jaded with moral sin! But then, this is the glory and beauty of God's truth: it knows no limit of time or place or person. It is revealed to those who are ready to receive it, whoever they are and wherever they are. So it was with the woman of Samaria. Quite without her knowing it, God had begun, by His Spirit, to control circumstances and timing in this woman's life. Actually, she tried to change the subject as Jesus began to probe deeply into her life. The popular evasive question in her day seemed to have been, "Where is the proper place to worship—in Jerusalem or on this sacred mountain in Samaria?" Jesus did not ignore the question. He used it as a springboard from which to reveal to her the classic Christian definition of worship, which is the bedrock pattern for all true worship.

I. First of all, Jesus talks about man-made worship.

A. *There are three basic weaknesses of man-made worship which are revealed in Jesus' words to the woman.* First, it is *contrived.* It is the result of man's adding a little here and taking away a little there until he has turned the Scriptures into a monstrosity. This is what the Samaritans had done in their insistence that true worship must be conducted on Mount Gerizim. They had adjusted history to suit themselves in insisting that it was on this mountain that Abraham had been willing to sacrifice Isaac, and that it was there Abraham had paid tithes to Melchizedek. Furthermore, they tampered with the Scriptures themselves when they taught that it was on this mountain that Moses first erected an altar and sacrificed to God in preparation for the entry of the people into the Promised Land. The Scriptures state clearly in Deuteronomy 27:4 that it was Mount Ebal, and not Gerizim. Every cult has done this same thing in twisting and distorting the Scriptures. A contrived gospel is a false gospel and will lead man to destruction.

B. *Not only is man-made worship contrived, it is also ignorant of the truth.* Jesus said to this woman, "Ye [meaning not only this woman, but all of the Samaritans] worship we know not what [or, what you do not know] . . ." (v. 22). The Samaritans accepted only the Pentateuch. They rejected all of the great messages of the prophets and all of the beauty and inspiration of the Psalms. They had a partial revelation of the truth. There was a fuller revelation available to them, but they would not accept it. They chose to remain in spiritual darkness. There is no excuse today for a believer in the Lord Jesus Christ to be ignorant of what he believes or of the basic teachings of the Word of God. There *was* a time when man was ignorant of spiritual things because he did not have the full revelation of God. But that time is no more; Jesus has come and has revealed God's true nature to us. We have the completed Word of God, with the ministry of the Holy Spirit available to interpret it to us.

C. *Man-made worship is also superstitious.* The Samaritans had adulterated the pure worship of Jehovah by recognizing the pagan gods of the foreigners who had come to dwell among them. They had mixed in with their worship of Jehovah all of the superstitions of the pagans. It is true today that many Christians have allowed superstition to become a basic part of their worship. There are many who will attend church *not* out of a genuine sense of need, nor out of any real desire to meet God in a worship experience. Rather they attend because they are afraid *not* to! They feel that if they do not "go through the motions" of worship, something "bad" will happen to them. They may even contribute to the church, pay the tithe, because they are afraid some calamity will befall them if they do not. This is worship out of fear (not reverential fear), and such an attitude is synonymous with superstition. A true worship experience is motivated by one's love for God and by one's gratitude for what God has done in his life and in his family.

II. Then Jesus told the woman about a God-centered worship.

In telling the Samaritan woman about a God-centered worship, Jesus gave her the eternal formula for true worship: "But the hour cometh, and now is, when the true worshippers shall worship the Father in spirit and in truth: for the Father seeketh such to worship him. God is a Spirit: and they that worship him must worship him in spirit and in truth" (vv. 23–24).

A. *The first thing Jesus said about worship is that it is God-initiated.* God makes the first move toward man in establishing a true worship experience. Man does not have to seek after God, or beg and plead with Him to meet Him in worship. This is what the prophets of Baal did on Mount Carmel in that famous contest with Elijah. They begged and cried and worked themselves up into a hysterical state—finally cutting themselves and shedding their own blood in their fanatical frenzy—trying to attract and coerce Baal to hear them and answer their call. But what did Jesus say? "The Father seeketh such [those who worship Him in spirit and in truth] to worship him." Man does not seek God; God seeks man. In other words, when we come apart privately or when we come together in our worship assemblies, God is waiting, eager to meet us! He is seeking us in order to enter into the worship experience with us.

B. *But not only is God-centered worship initiated by God, it is a spiritual experience.* "God is a Spirit," said Jesus, "and they that worship him must worship him in spirit and in truth" (v. 24). What do we mean when we say that "God is a Spirit"? Is He a vague, impersonal, ethereal Being, indescribable to man? Not at all! Rather, because He is Spirit, He is free; He is not confined to any one place or time. For thirty-three years, in a mystical union man cannot understand with his human mind, God entered human flesh in the person of His sinless Son, the Lord Jesus Christ. Then, in an even greater miracle, God *died* in the person of His Son and rose again the third day. But even during that amazing time of identification with man, God was still omnipotent, omniscient, and omnipresent.

Thus, because God is Spirit, His omnipresence makes it possible for me to worship Him anytime, anywhere. In the privacy of my room, I can worship God; in the midst of the mundane affairs of the everyday world, I can worship God. I can anticipate the blessed privilege of assembling together with my brothers and sisters in Christ at the appointed times, as we are exhorted to do in the Scriptures, and enter into an experience of corporate worship. In the midst of the rarest fellowship in the world—the *koinonia* of the people of God—I can blend my voice both audibly and silently in the midst of the congregation! Yes, God-centered worship is a spiritual experience, which is expressed both privately *and* within the blessed togetherness of God's people.

C. *Not only are we to worship in spirit, but also in truth.* In His great High Priestly Prayer, Jesus invoked the Father on our behalf, and He prayed:

"Sanctify them through thy truth: thy word is truth" (17:17). I cannot read God's Word properly without having a worship experience every time I do. For as I tune my heart to read His Holy Book, the Holy Spirit begins to open my understanding. God's Word, which is the truth of God, is the compass of the church. It keeps both the individual Christian and the church as a whole in the pathway of righteousness, ever attuned to the leadership of her Head, the Lord Jesus Christ. And not only this, but when I neglect God's Word, I find that I grope through my days, stumbling here and faltering there, unsure at this point, blundering at that decision. Only as I make my way back to the Book and to the altar of prayer *in sincere worship* do I find my life once more on an even keel.

Conclusion. What is the worship of the church? If it is a man-made worship, then it is bathed in ignorance of the true message of God's Word, and it is permeated with all kinds of false ideas, concepts, and superstitions. But if it is God-centered worship, then it is always initiated by God. He is ever seeking His children to enter into a worship experience with them. It is a spiritual experience which transcends the earthly, the mundane, the worldly; and it is Bible-centered, because God's Word is truth. It is genuine worship when God's people find a friendship and an intimacy with God, who ever seeks us and longs to have fellowship with His redeemed people. —*DLG*

* * *

SUNDAY EVENING, FEBRUARY 12

TITLE: Jeroboam—Easy Religion

TEXT: "Whereupon the king took counsel, and made two calves of gold; and he said unto them, It is too much for you to go up to Jerusalem: behold thy gods, O Israel, which brought thee up out of the land of Egypt" (1 Kings 12:28 ASV).

SCRIPTURE READING: 1 Kings 12:21–33

Introduction. When, in response to the demands of the northern ten tribes for relief from the burdens imposed by his father, Solomon, Rehoboam threatened to be a tougher kind than his father, the kingdom of Israel split into two kingdoms. Jeroboam, a former officer of Solomon's who had been in exile in Egypt, became king of the northern ten tribes.

But Jeroboam had a problem: How could he wean the people away from loyalty to the house of David so long as the most devout went up to Jerusalem to the great feasts in the temple? This he considered to be a dangerous situation and a personal threat (v. 27). But Jeroboam also had a solution. Concealing his real motives beneath a cloak of concern for the welfare of his people, he said, "It is too much for you to go up to Jerusalem" (v. 28). In other words, "This is too hard on you. You have carried this burden long enough." To cut them off completely from their ancestral roots he devised the clever strategy of making religion easy. He betrayed Jehovah for the sake of a secure throne and undisputed control, spiritual as well as secular, over his people.

This strategy is popular today. A large portion of the American people are professedly religious, but their religion is neither deep, vital, nor real. Selfishly motivated, unwisely conceived, dangerous in the extreme, Jeroboam's substitute easy religion had tragic consequences (v. 30). This is still true today. There are four things to note about this theme.

I. The characteristics of easy religion.

A. *Easy religion is not of the Lord.* After Jeroboam had sized up the facts in the religious situation we are told, "Whereupon the king took counsel" (v. 28a). He took counsel, but not with the Lord. This was in flat violation of the second commandment enjoining the worship of God without the use of images (Exod. 20:4).

B. *Easy religion is hypocritical.* "Behold thy gods, O Israel, which brought thee up out of the land of Egypt" (1 Kings 12:28b). Jeroboam was voicing the right shibboleth, but he was praising the wrong gods. Throughout all their history Israel's prophets and psalmists reminded them of God's redemption of His people from Egyptian bondage. For his own advantage Jeroboam was deliberately hypocritical.

C. *Easy religion can and does make do with substandard preachers.* The hard fact is that much easy religion comes from substandard preachers. "And he . . . made priests from among all the people, that were not of the sons of Levi" (v. 31 asv). Until this time "the sons of Levi" had dwelled in all the land; but after this move the Levites, the God-designated spiritual leaders, left northern Israel in a mass exodus—a great loss.

D. *Easy religion often makes religion a side issue.* Jeroboam's phony feast (v. 32) did nothing for the lives of the people. It was an imitation. The give-away phrase is this: "like unto the feast that is in Judah." His feast was irrelevant. One layman asked another how the members liked the new pastor. He replied, "Our new pastor can answer more questions nobody is asking than any minister we ever had."

II. The causes of easy religion.

A. *Easy religion is self-motivated, not God-motivated.* Jeroboam's real concern was for the perpetuity of his throne and the safety of his own life (vv. 26–27). Not a thought did he have in his mind nor a feeling in his heart for the real spiritual welfare of his people. To secure his own position, to save his own hide was his sole motive.

To demand a religion we can command, rather than the other way around, is to be self-deceived, for when we get it we have nothing. The British historian tells of an English nobleman of a hundred years ago who was incensed by the preaching he had been hearing. "Things have come to a pretty pass," he said, "when religion is allowed to interfere with a man's private life."

B. *Easy religion appeals to the carnal man.* It praises people; it does not judge them. Isaiah's contemporaries demanded, "Prophesy not unto us right things, speak unto us smooth things, prophesy deceits" (30:10b asv). They were saying, "Give us a comfortable religion with more emphasis on the joy of living and less on the judgment of the Lord." William James once said, "Religion is either an acute fever or a dull formalism. There is no in between."

C. *Easy religion, by its very nature, is undemanding.* To some, religious affiliation is the American sign of belonging. Popular religion has become a secularized substitute for sacrificial commitment to historic Christian faith. It is not costly. It gives way to the "cult of convenience." It fears to pay the price of ridicule. Many have an unconscious fear that to go too far in religion makes a man strange, a fool, a freak. Easy religion is the path of least resistance.

III. The cost of easy religion.

A. *Easy religion stifles growth and leads to degeneration.* If we have only a flabby, passive religion that demands nothing of us, our soul's growth will be stifled. When we do only the things we find convenient, when we never put ourselves out to do anything above and beyond the call of duty, we find ourselves shrinking and shriveling into nothing. If our religion is real, it grows. Religion is not looking at a map; it is living in the land.

B. *Easy religion is self-deceptive.* Every year at church budget-planning time someone will rise to say, "We can do whatever we want to do in this church," I agree! And the way to do it is with more tithers, more people giving liberally. But this is not what they mean. Their solution is to cut the percentage to missions in order to do some other things at home. This is the wrong solution. This is self-deceptive. This is easy religion.

C. *Easy religion is dangerous.* Of the golden calves at Bethel and Dan the writer of 1 Kings said, "And this thing became a sin: for the people went to worship each of them, even unto Dan" (12:30). Why? It led to idolatry. It always does. Easy religion progressively builds a wall between our souls and God.

D. *Easy religion can cost a nation its very life.* "And this thing became a sin" (v. 30a). Indeed it did! It was a sin from which Israel never recovered. There is a sad benediction over most of the kings in the dismal list of Israel's wicked kings. Even of Pekahiah, the seventeenth in the list, we read, "And he did that which was evil in the sight of Jehovah: he departed not from the sins of Jeroboam the son of Nebat, wherewith he made Israel to sin" (2 Kings 15:24). In round numbers that had been two hundred years. There was a general process of degeneration; and the first link in the chain was Jeroboam. No nation has ever survived the loss of its religious faith. Israel was no exception.

IV. The cure for easy religion.

A. *Easy religion can be cured by conversion.* Unless a man has been born again, he may go through all manner of religious forms but the real thing is not there. More than anything we need the example of truly transformed lives. Religion, like great music, is not in need of defense but rendition. The Wesleyan revivals saved England in the latter part of the eighteenth century. How? Thousands were converted.

B. *Easy religion is further cured by cultivation.* A man was asked what church he attended. He replied that he did not go to any church regularly, but he named one church he stayed away from the most. Unfortunately that denomination does not have a monopoly on these "stay-awayers." All of us need cultivation.

C. *Easy religion can be cured by commitment.* The test of true religion is the depth of our commitment to Christ. David and Peter were not perfect men. They blundered and fell; and Satan clapped his hands in glee over them more than once. Yet they were deeply committed men. This is the test.

"It was like a ten-mile walk in a five-and-ten-cent store," a reviewer said of a book he had read, meaning that it was a journey among cheap things, made to sell but not to use. It is amazing how a man's faith can wrap itself around things trivial and cheap. What a man seeks first and foremost in life is his religion (Matt. 6:33).

Conclusion. Years ago a Methodist bishop got off a train in a small town in the deep south. Seeing a friendly looking man on the deserted station platform he asked, "Does anyone around here enjoy religion?" The old man replied, "Yes, sir, them that has it does." Are you enjoying your religion?   *—WTH*

* * *

WEDNESDAY EVENING, FEBRUARY 15

TITLE: The Habit of Being Filled With the Holy Spirit

TEXT: **"And Jesus returned in the power of the Spirit into Galilee, and a report concerning him went out through all the surrounding country"** (Luke 4:14 RSV).

SCRIPTURE READING: **Luke 4:14–21**

Introduction. We may not customarily think of Jesus having the habit of being filled with the Holy Spirit. We may consider this to be a gift of God or an expression of the presence of God rather than a habit. However, the apostle Paul used an imperative when he said, "And do not get drunk with wine, for that is debauchery, but be filled with the Spirit" (Eph. 5:18 RSV).

I. The Holy Spirit in the life of our Lord.

   A. *The Holy Spirit effected the miraculous conception of our Lord* (Matt. 1:18, 20).

   B. *The Holy Spirit made possible the recognition of the Messiah as an infant by Simeon* (Luke 2:25–27).

   C. *The Holy Spirit descended as a dove at His baptism, giving to Him divine identification and authentication* (3:21–22).

   D. *Following His victory over the temptations of Satan, Christ returned in the power of the Holy Spirit to minister* (4:14).

   E. *The Holy Spirit equipped our Lord for His great ministry* (4:18–21).

   F. *Christ performed His great miracles in the power of the Holy Spirit* (Matt. 12:28).

II. Christ promised the gift of the Holy Spirit to His disciples as a present possession and as a continuing presence (John 14:16–18; Acts 1:8).

III. Christ bestowed the gift of the Spirit to the church on the Day of Pentecost (Acts 2:32–33).
   Pentecost was the fulfillment of a prophecy of John the Baptist that the church would be baptized with the Holy Spirit and with fire (Matt. 3:11). God gives to each of His children the gift of His Spirit at the moment of their birth into His family (Gal. 4:6–7).

Conclusion. The overwhelming majority of followers of Christ find themselves in a condition similar to that of the church at Corinth when they failed to recognize that they had received the gift of God's Holy Spirit and that He had taken up His residence within them (1 Cor. 3:16).

We need to form the daily habit of deliberately recognizing the presence of the Holy Spirit of God who has come to dwell within us. We need to recognize the workings of God's Spirit within us as He makes us spiritually allergic to sin and as He creates within us a hunger for the things of God.

We need to cooperate with the Holy Spirit as He works within us that we might experience God's full and great salvation within (Phil. 2:12–13).

We need to release ourslevs to the work of the Holy Spirit as He seeks to lead us in ministries of mercy and in announcing the Good News of God's love through Jesus Christ to all of those about us (Acts 1:8). The Holy Spirit came to equip us and to use us as witnesses for Jesus Christ to those around us who are unsaved.

We must not wait for an emotional high before we begin to do what God wants us to do. In the power of the Holy Spirit we can face each day with confidence, joy, and assurance of victory.   *—TTC*

* * *

SUNDAY MORNING, FEBRUARY 19

TITLE: **Worshiping God With Our Gifts**

TEXT: **"For all they did cast in of their abundance; but she of her want did cast in all that she had, even all her living" (Mark 12:44).**

SCRIPTURE READING: **Mark 12:41–44; 1 Chronicles 16:28–34**

HYMNS: **"A Child of the King," Buell**
"I Gave My Life for Thee," Havergal
"Our Best," Kirk

OFFERTORY PRAYER:

Father God, we thank You for another week, and we thank You for this Lord's day. We thank You for the church family with which we worship today. We thank You for the presence of the Christ, who promised to be with those who come together in His name. Accept our tithes and offerings as expressions of our love for You. Bless them to the end that others shall know of Your love. In Jesus' name. Amen.

Introduction. In the Old Testament we are encouraged to honor God by bringing the first fruits of our labors to Him as an act of worship (Prov. 3:9). In the New Testament we find Jesus honoring a person who worshiped God by bringing her generous gift to the temple. He did not honor the quantity of her gift but the quality. Jesus sat across from the place where people were making their gifts, and He watched the people as they made their contributions. The only person Jesus honored on this occasion was a poor widow who demonstrated a good spirit with her giving.

Jesus continues to honor those who give. The basis of His honors is not with the size of the gift but with the spirit of the gift. Jesus wants to honor our giving. How can He do so? Let us notice some ways that Jesus honors giving.

I. Jesus honors an interest in the treasury.

A. *Interest in the treasury represents an interest in the Lord Himself.* The widow did not go to the temple to pay a bill but to honor her God.

All through biblical history people have expressed an interest in the Lord through their giving. Cain and Abel made offerings to God. In the tabernacle, temple, and the synagogues God was worshiped by means of the treasury.

B. *Interest in the treasury represents a concern for the Lord's work.* The widow evidently went periodically to the temple, and she gave. When she gave, she knew that it was for the Lord's personnel, for temple upkeep, and for provision for the sacrifices.

One prominent reason for an interest in the treasury is for the advancement and continuation of the Lord's work. Churches are involved in the Lord's work, and people give to advance the Lord's work.

The Lord honors an interest in the treasury. We should periodically ask ourselves, "How interested am I in the treasury?" Our record of giving discloses our interest.

II. Jesus honors a proper motive toward the treasury.

A. *Jesus examines the motives of those who give.* The Lord had a good place for observing the givers. He saw those who wanted to be seen for their giving. These people probably hit the "trumpets" so that others would know that a large contribution had been made. Jesus saw those who gave; but more than merely observing who gave, He saw *why* they gave.

A poor widow made an acceptable gift. Its acceptance was not on the basis of size but its spirit. She gave because she wanted to honor the Lord, not to be seen or heard by others.

Jesus continues to examine motives for giving. He sees those who give out of guilt, self-righteousness, or ostentation. He is not pleased. The proper motive is to give out of love for the Lord Jesus Christ.

B. *Giving from the proper motive satisfies the giver.* People who give for any reason other than selflessness can never be satisfied. Those who think they can buy God never feel they have paid their bills. Those who parade their giving must work harder to have a bigger show next time.

Jesus honors unselfish giving. The rich as well as the poor can give honorably. Remember that it is not the size but the spirit of the gift.

III. Jesus honors a sacrifice for the treasury.

A. *Sacrificial giving originates with a great desire to give.* No one prompted the woman to put in the mite. The thought of giving began in her heart. She had a giving spirit before she ever gave a gift.

If you study sacrifice, you will see that one who sacrifices has a genuine desire to help others. Look at the Lord. He sacrificed His glory in heaven. Why? He had a deep desire to help others.

B. *Sacrificial giving results in personal relinquishment.* The woman gave to the treasury. Her giving was costly. "She of her want did cast in all that she had, even all her living" (Mark 12:44).

Sacrificial giving results in relinquishment. It means a costly sacrifice. If you are not a tither, and you can observe luxuries around you, then you can be assured that you are not an honorable giver.

Conclusion. This message has not been preached to gain a collection or to raise a budget. It has been prepared and delivered to develop honorable givers. God will bless those who give honorably.

Resolve this day that you are going to follow the example of the poor widow. Take an interest in the treasury. Develop the right spirit in giving to the treasury. Make the spirit of sacrifice to the treasury. God desires honorable givers.

—*HTB*

* * *

SUNDAY EVENING, FEBRUARY 19

TITLE: **Ahab—Five Chapters in a Story**

Text: **"And Naboth said to Ahab, Jehovah forbid it me, that I should give the inheritance of my fathers unto thee" (1 Kings 21:3 ASV).**

Scripture Reading: **1 Kings 21:1–26**

Introduction. This is the story of Ahab, king of Israel, and of Naboth, owner of a vineyard next to the king's summer palace in Jezreel. This is one of the strangest, most powerful, most terrible stories in the Bible. It is a story of contrasts. On one side we see innocence, courage, integrity, and the fear of God; and on the other covetousness, avarice, cruelty, perjury, death, and terrible retribution.

Ahab is one of the best-known characters in the Old Testament, where more pages are devoted to him than to any other worker of iniquity. His contrast with his adversary, the great prophet Elijah, makes him stand out the more clearly. Ahab seems to have had some residium of character and the fear of God in him, but he was under the influence of that Phoenician tigress, his pagan wife, Jezebel, the murderer of prophets.

Samaria was the capital of Israel, but Jezreel was the king's summer palace, a hide-a-way resort. Surrounded by all the pleasures and luxuries of royalty it seemed that Ahab should want for nothing. But not so! He wanted one more thing. This introduces the plot of the story.

I. The first chapter we may call coveteousness.

Next to Ahab's palace was a small but well-kept vineyard. Ahab looked over that vineyard carefully. The more he looked the more he coveted that vineyard that he might convert it into a garden of herbs.

As king, Ahab was the lord and master and, in a sense, the owner of a whole kingdom. He had palaces, servants, soldiers, silver and gold, horses, chariots, and storehouses. Yet he coveted that one small vineyard. An old myth tells of Briareus, a fifty-headed giant who had a hundred hands. If the covetous man had one hundred eyes with which to see and one hundred hands with which to take, that would not be enough. The more he has, the more he wants; the more he gets, the less satisfied he is.

Ahab proceeded at once to try to buy the vineyard outright, or to trade a larger and better vineyard for it. So fiercely did he covet that vineyard he would have given a fabulous price. But the vineyard was not for sale, and to have his covetous desire thwarted made Ahab sick. He pouted in bed. He wouldn't eat. This story resulted in intrigue, slander, perjury, and the murder of an innocent and godly man.

II. The second chapter we may call integrity.

When Ahab made his offer to trade for his vineyard or to buy it outright, Naboth replied, "Jehovah forbid it me, that I should give the inheritance of my fathers unto thee" (1 Kings 21:3b). For a man to sell his patrimony (land inherited from his father) was, in the estimation of the devout Hebrew, as serious a sin as if a man denied his own parentage.

Not all the Jews were as scrupulous in this matter as Naboth. He was a God-fearing man of integrity. He felt it would be an irreligious act, a sin against God for him to sell his inheritance to the king. The character of Naboth stands out in magnificent proportions and in unforgettable colors. Here was a man across whose brow was written, "Not for sale." Naboth was not flattered by the interview with the king, nor by the invitation to the royal palace. Principle meant more to him than worldly honor. Nor was he influenced by money. He could have asked any price for his vineyard and the covetous Ahab would have paid it.

Here was a man who was not intimidated by the king. A royal request amounted to a royal command. Naboth knew that to refuse was dangerous. Yet he stood his ground and died a martyr to conscience. Here was a man who preferred death to compromising his conscience.

III. The third chapter we may call intrigue.

Since Ahab could not have the vineyard by fair means, his wife, Jezebel, decided to secure it by foul means (vv. 7–10). Does any literature contain such a record of the court intrigue, a plot to murder an innocent man more terrible than this? The weak-kneed elders and nobles of the city carried out her orders to the letter.

By himself Ahab probably would not have thought of stealing or confiscating the vineyard, still less of murdering Naboth in order to get possession of it. The resolution of the wicked queen stirred up her husband to complicity in a crime he would have been afraid to commit had he not had Jezebel. But he had her! She was there and she went into action. She planned the whole diabolical scheme and saw that it was carried out.

IV. The fourth chapter we may call murder.

What the weak Ahab could neither devise nor do, his fierce consort carefully planned and craftily executed. The charge of the false witnesses was that Naboth had been heard to "curse God and the king" (1 Kings 21:13b). This was cruelty and hypocrisy unsurpassed. This Phoenician idolatress, Jezebel, had no regard for God or for the religion of Israel, yet she committed this crime under the guise of religion. These town elders knew that this was a crime and a sin against God, an outrage in Israel; yet for fear of Jezebel they went along.

According to custom the witnesses cast the first stones. Then all the mob joined them. Soon all that was left of Naboth was a bloody pulp. The perjured witnesses, the cowardly elders and nobles, and the fickle crowd dispersed and went back to their homes. As the darkness came on, Naboth's corpse was left alone in the vineyard. But not altogether alone, for the scavenger dogs came into the vineyard and licked up the blood of Naboth.

What a story or horror and foul play and false witnesses this is, of covetousness and murder. But the story doesn't end here.

V. The fifth chapter we may call retribution.

The story of Ahab and Naboth is not only a story of loyalty to conscience and faith in God, of intrigue and murder, but also of swift and terrible retribution.

At the queen's urging Ahab went at once to possess the vineyard. But once there he is confronted by God's prophet Elijah. Conscience was still alive in Ahab and he cried out, "Hast thou found me, O mine enemy?" Elijah replied, "I have found thee, because thou hast sold thyself to do that which is evil in the sight of Jehovah" (v. 20). Then Elijah details the terrible judgment that will fall upon Ahab and Jezebel and all their descendants (vv. 21–24). This shook up Ahab, and he rent his clothes and went in sackcloth; then he "went softly" and humbled himself before God. But his humility and apparent repentance proved to be short-lived. Let us notice how the pronounced judgment was carried out.

A. *What about Ahab?* Three years later, in spite of the warning given by the prophet, Micaiah (22:19–23, 28), Ahab went to battle against the Syrians at Ramoth-gilead. He was mortally wounded and died that evening. As they washed the blood from the chariot, the dogs came and licked his blood as the prophet had said.

B. *What about Jezebel?* She continued for a time as the queen-mother while her son Jehoram reigned over Israel. Jehu, former bodyguard of Ahab, was now one of Northern Israel's top generals. One of Elisha's assistants anointed Jehu king. All of his fellow generals pledged their loyalty, and he set out immediately for Jezreel to carry out his commission to wipe out the house of Ahab. On the way to Jezreel he slew Jehoram, king of Israel, and his nephew, Ahaziah, grandson of Ahab and king of Judah. Thundering into Jezreel, he called upon the terrified servants to throw Jezebel out of the top-story window. They did so, and Jehu ran over her body with his horses and chariot. When he sent servants later on to bury her, all they could find was her skull, her feet, and the palms of her hands. As Elijah had said, "The dogs shall eat Jezebel by the rampart of Jezreel" (21:23b).

Then follows the systematic elimination of all of Ahab's descendants and the murder of all the followers of Baal.

Conclusion. This story comes to a tremendous climax. This was mysterious, terrible, divine retribution. It teaches us in unmistakable terms that the way of the transgressor is hard and that "the Judge of all the earth" will do right (Gen. 18:25b).   *—WTH*

* * *

WEDNESDAY EVENING, FEBRUARY 22

TITLE: The Habit of Loving

TEXT: **"And Jesus looking upon him loved him, and said to him, 'You lack one thing; go, sell what you have, and give to the poor, and you will have treasure in heaven; and come, follow me'" (Mark 10:21 RSV).**

SCRIPTURE READING: **Mark 10:17–22**

Introduction. While there are many thoughts and lessons that can be drawn from this experience of Jesus with the rich young ruler, let us focus our attention specifically on the fact that "Jesus looking upon him loved him." This was one of the great habits that Jesus had as He came face to face with human beings. He saw them as the objects of God's great love. He related to them in terms of their being of infinite worth in the sight of God. He related to them in terms of love with no desire to exploit or to profit from His relationship with them.

John said concerning Jesus, "And the Word became flesh and dwelt among us, full of grace and truth; we beheld his glory, glory as of the only Son from the Father" (John 1:14). This was John's way of describing the total impact of the ministry of Jesus Christ on persons. He genuinely loved people. He related to them as the grace and the truth of God. He related to all human beings in terms of concern for their highest possible good. His habit of relating to people with love is a habit that His followers need to develop. Most of us have thought of love in terms of its being an emotional response to someone who is beautiful and admirable.

Jesus had the habit of always relating to others on the basis of divine love for them.

I. Jesus loved the Father God supremely (John 14:31).

Jesus stated that we must love the Father God supremely (Matt. 22:37).

II. Jesus declared that we must love our neighbor as ourselves (Matt. 22:39).

The average person has difficulty loving his neighbor as himself because he does not properly love himself. Many people experience the pain of self-hatred and a feeling of worthlessness. A truly genuine love for others is premised upon a proper love for oneself. Jesus is saying you need to love yourself properly and appropriately, and then you will be capable of loving your neighbor as yourself. You cannot really love your neighbor without also loving yourself. To genuinely love means that you esteem highly and affirm the other as being of unique value to God and to the world.

Genuine love has been defined as "a basic attitude of concern for the satisfaction, security, and development of the one loved."

Jesus related to both His friends and His enemies with a basic attitude of goodwill.

III. Converts to Christ are now capable of relating to others in terms of love.

People can be very difficult to love. They can be ugly and repulsive. And yet Jesus commands us to relate to them with love. Definitely He is not talking about an emotional response based upon the attractiveness of those about us.

Paul declared, "God's love has been poured into our hearts through the Holy Spirit which has been given to us" (Rom. 5:5 RSV).

Because God first loved us it is possible for us to love others (1 John 4:19).

A. *We are commanded to love our enemies* (Matt. 5:43–45).

B. *We are commanded to love our neighbors* (22:39).

C. *We are to love one another as Jesus loved us* (John 13:34). By demonstrating this kind of genuine love within the family of God, we give proof of the genuineness of our relationship with Jesus Christ (John 13:35).

    1. The love of Christ was an unmerited love.

    2. The love of Christ was a sacrificial love.

    3. The love of Christ was an appropriate love.

    4. The love of Christ was a forgiving love.

    5. The love of Christ was an affirming love.

Jesus commanded His disciples to love one another with a love greater than their love for themselves (John 15:12–13).

Conclusion. Because of God's great love for us personally, and because of God's great love for others, it is within the realm of possibility for us to develop Jesus' habit of always relating to even the most unlovely in terms of an attitude of persistent goodwill. This is the kind of love that will bless the world. This is the kind of love that will identify us as the true followers of Christ. This kind of love will authenticate us as true witnesses for Jesus Christ. *—TTC*

* * *

SUNDAY MORNING, FEBRUARY 26

TITLE: **The Hiding Place**

TEXT: **"Thou art my hiding place; thou shalt preserve me from trouble; thou shalt compass me about with songs of deliverance"** (Ps. 32:7).

SCRIPTURE READING: **Psalms 46:1; 61:1–5; 91:4; Proverbs 18:10; Isaiah 32:1–2**

HYMNS: **"Dear Lord and Father of Mankind,"** Whittier
"Take Time to Be Holy," Longstaff
"Brethren, We Have Met to Worship," Atkins

OFFERTORY PRAYER:
Father God, You are so generous to us. You have given to us Your Son as our Savior. You have given to us Your Spirit to dwell within us. You have given us the church as a caring family with which we can worship and praise You. Accept our gifts this day, and bless them to the end that suffering will be relieved and the Good News will be preached to the ends of the earth. In Christ's name. Amen.

Introduction. One of the stimulating stories to come from World War II was Corrie ten Boom's book entitled *The Hiding Place*. In this book she related her experiences of torture by the Germans when they came to Holland. The ten Boom family hid many Jewish people in a secret place they had built in their house. The Germans discovered the hiding place, and Corrie ten Boom spent many years in concentration camps. During her persecutions, dangers, and troubles she found a great solace in the presence and power of God. The Lord became a hiding place for her.

Many of the writers of the Psalms referred to God as a shelter or a hiding place. Oftentimes David testified, "Thou art my hiding place." Various situations in David's life prompted this affirmation. He was taught by his parents that God is a hiding place. He found strength in God when he fought Goliath, the Philistine giant. When he had to flee from the jealous rage of Saul, he found refuge in God. When David led the armies of Israel into battle, he knew the Lord to be a hiding place. Throughout David's life, he ran to God seeking refuge.

I. All of us need a hiding place.

A. *David's life demonstrated a definite need for a hiding place.* Many good things could be said about David—he was rich, strong, famous, a man after God's own heart. His life could be charted with ups and downs. It was a mixture of sunlight and shadows. There were the times of laughing and crying. David needed a hiding place for his diversified experiences of life.

B. *All of us need a hiding place at various times and in diversified situations.* Life brings with it sunshine and shadows, triumphs and troubles. The pressure of daily living drives us to a hiding place. Our lives are filled with so much varied activity that we live according to a watched clock and a consulted calendar.

Sin and temptation force us to a hiding place. When David was confronted with the reality of his sin, he ran to a hiding place with God. He said, "Thou art my hiding place" (Ps. 32:7). We are constantly assaulted by the satanic solicitor. Temptation is a terror to us. During times of temptation we need a hiding place. Our Lord was tempted, and He resisted. When He resisted, the angels came and ministered to Him. He, too, had a hiding place.

Dangers face us, and we are fearful. Our world lives in constant reminder that nuclear weapons could be used for a global war. People have built "fall-out shelters" to protect themselves from nuclear fall-out. God can be our refuge during the threatening dangers of life.

Sorrows and sadness teach us the need of a hiding place. During times of great grief, we need a hiding place. David lost his son Absalom, whom he loved, in death. During the time of his stress he went to God, for he needed a hiding place.

II. All of us can have a hiding place.

A. *David identified his hiding place.* His hiding place was not in his royal standing, his knowledge, his possessions, or his friends. He identified God as his hiding place. "For thou hast been a shelter for me, and a strong tower from the enemy" (Ps. 61:3).

B. *God is an amazing hiding place.* Only God is adequate for whatever life may bring. God is a proven hiding place. Through the years people have found God to be a trustworthy hiding place. David hid himself with the Lord centuries ago. Corrie ten Boom found God in this century as a hiding place.

God is a strong hiding place. People will always find that God is greater and stronger than the dangers of life. "God is our refuge and strength, a very present help in trouble" (46:1).

Places of refuge are sufficient only if they are stronger than the storms. You would not want to hide in a place which could be destroyed by a storm. God is sufficient. No trials nor troubles are stronger than God. "The name of the LORD is a strong tower: the righteous runneth into it, and is safe" (Prov. 18:10).

III. All of us can benefit from a hiding place.

A. *David testified that the secret of his life was his relationship with the Lord.* A close examination of the writings of David will disclose references to numerous testimonies about God as the Strength of his life, the Guide of his life, and his close Companion.

B. *Going to God for a hiding place will bring many benefits to our lives.*
1. First we shall enjoy the blessed presence of God. Someone greater than ourselves walks with us throughout the pilgrimage of life. The words *with us* are a great comfort as we face many situations in life.

2. A second benefit of going to God for a refuge is that we enjoy His protection. "God is our refuge and strength, a very present help in trouble" (Ps. 46:1). Of course God does not insulate His people against trouble, but He protects them *during* the trouble.

3. A third great benefit of going to God for a hiding place is that we gain God's perspective. Times of private and corporate worship give a new outlook on life.

Conclusion. Have you prepared for the storms of life? Or are the storms battering your life now? You can have a refuge in God. No one has ever been turned away who repented of his sins and opened his life to the Lord. When you make this decision, you can say, "I have found a hiding place in Jesus my Lord."

—HTB

* * *

SUNDAY EVENING, FEBRUARY 26

TITLE: Gehazi—the Unmasking of a Wicked Heart

TEXT: **"But he went in, and stood before his master. And Elisha said unto him, Whence comest thou, Gehazi? And he said, Thy servant went no whither. And he said unto him, Went not my heart with thee, when the man turned from his chariot to meet thee?" (2 Kings 5:25–26a ASV)**

SCRIPTURE READING: **2 Kings 5:1–27**

Introduction. The salient points of the story of Naaman, captain of the host of Syria, are clear. Upon the witness of a little Jewish slave girl he had come all the way to Israel seeking a cure for his leprosy. He went first to the king of Israel, and then, by invitation, to the prophet Elisha. Elisha's simple directions were, "Go and wash in the Jordan seven times, and thy flesh shall come again to thee, and thou shalt be clean" (v. 10). At first infuriated, Naaman, at the urging of his subordinates, complied and was healed. He returned in deep gratitude to the prophet and urged him to receive a gift. Elisha refused and sent him away in peace.

Up to this point the story is letter perfect. But this is inspired writing, not fiction, and it comes to a tragic end. The story turns on two words: "But Gehazi" (v. 20a). What about him? He was the servant of Elisha. He had been a witness to both appearances of the Syrian general before his master's house and of his master's dealings with him. His view of things did not agree with his master's. His avaricious soul recoiled at his master's refusal of any compensation for the miracle. So he went out on his own and came to tragedy.

Four things are to be noted in the development of the theme.

I. The growth of wickedness in Gehazi's heart.

Gehazi's character did not suddenly collapse. The process of dissolution had been going on for some time; this act of betrayal was simply the last straw.

When the Shunammite woman came to Elisha in great distress when her little son died, Gehazi was sent on ahead to greet her with the query, "Is it well with thee? is it well with thy husband? is it well with the child?" Her answer was, "It is well" (4:26). The purity of her own heart recognized the treachery of Gehazi's, and she would not unburden her grief to him. Gehazi was sent to lay

Elisha's staff upon the body of the dead child, but he had to report, "The child is not awaked" (v. 31b). Unless first there is repentance, God does not respond to a wicked heart.

The skill with which Gehazi planned and carried out his fleecing of the grateful-hearted Naaman showed that he was practiced in treachery and skilled in falsehood. This act of wickedness, like Judas' betrayal of his Master, was just the last straw before the wickedness of his heart was unmasked.

II. The proof of the wickedness of Gehazi's heart.

Gehazi's life was a living contradiction. The exterior of his life gave the lie to what he really was inside. Outward appearances and inward reality did not agree. Outwardly he was the servant of Elisha, the prophet; inwardly he was the servant of the devil. Outwardly he was one with his master, his helper and constant companion; inwardly he was far from his master in spirit, ideals, aims, and character. Outwardly he appeared to be concerned with spiritual things, the helper of a prophet; inwardly he was covetous, greedy, worldly, without any interest in spiritual things at all.

A. *Gehazi's wickedness is demonstrated by his attitudes.*

1. His attitude toward one of another race. His words, "Behold, my master hath spared this Naaman the Syrian" (5:20b), reveal his double standard on this basis, one for his own countrymen and another for Naaman because he was a Syrian. He felt there was no harm in fleecing a Syrian. This is wickedness at its worst.

2. His attitude toward his master's honor. He did not hesitate to drag his master's name in the dust and put him on the same basis as the false prophets in Israel if, by so doing, he could attain his own ends. His master's honor meant nothing to him.

3. His attitude toward simple honesty, the truth. He lied to himself: "As Jehovah liveth" (v. 20b). He lied to Naaman: "My master hath sent me" (v. 22). He lied to Elisha: "Thy servant went no whither" (v. 25b).

B. *Gehazi's wickedness is demonstrated by his motives.*

The prophet sternly asked, "Is it a time to receive money, and to receive garments, and oliveyards and vineyards, and sheep and oxen, and men-servants and maid-servants?" (v. 26) This is what Gehazi intended to do with his ill-gotten wealth.

Here is a stern lesson for us. There are many Gehazis walking about masking a wicked heart beneath a respectable exterior. We may never judge by outward appearances only.

III. The unmasking of the wickedness of Gehazi's heart.

The respectable exterior was ripped off, and the doom of leprosy on the outside would henceforth proclaim the wickedness on the inside. Gehazi had provoked God too far, and his wicked, sinful heart was laid bare. Treachery had outdone itself. Covetousness had defeated its own selfish ends. In a figure Gehazi had committed spiritual suicide (see James 1:15). Why was Gehazi's wicked heart laid bare?

A. *The honor and peace of a nation was at stake.* Recall Elisha's words to the fearful king when Naaman made his appearance at court, "Wherefore hast thou rent thy clothes? let him come now to me, and he shall know that there is a prophet in Israel" (v. 8). There had been an intermittent but deadly war with

Syria for some time, and by his act of mercy and generosity Elisha had hoped to strike a blow for peace. Gehazi had betrayed all that.

B. *The honor of the prophetic office was at stake.* There were false prophets both in Israel and in Syria. They performed for a price. Elisha was in no way like them. Gehazi's great sin was that he did this in his master's name and held him up to an open shame before a man he would have taught to honor a true prophet of God.

C. *The honor of God was at stake.* Elisha had required an act of faith so that the grace of God could be released upon Naaman. Naaman recognized that his healing had been an act of the God of Israel. Elisha had refused any gift in the name of God (v. 16). Yet Gehazi's act jeopardized all this. Naaman could have returned to Syria with the impression that the gift of God could indeed be purchased with money (see Acts 8:20).

The moral is clear. We can provoke God too far. We can hold His honor and that of His true servants up to an open shame, and He will strike us down openly. The wicked may get by with it for a time, but sooner or later the wicked heart will be unmasked.

IV. The judgment upon the wickedness of Gehazi's heart.

God's judgment followed close upon the unmasking of his heart. What terrible words are these: "The leprosy therefore of Naaman shall cleave unto thee, and unto thy seed for ever. And he went out from his presence a leper as white as snow" (v. 27 ASV). The prophet was saying, "You want Naaman's riches regardless of the cost in sin and betrayal and lies? Then take his leprosy also. Let this disease without reveal the rottenness within."

When it catches up with us, God's judgment sometimes takes an ironic turn. In the end Joseph's brothers did bow down before him. Haman was hanged on his own gallows. Gehazi reaped a living death as the leprosy of the man he had despised and cheated clung to him, an open badge advertising his sin. The worst thing that could happen to some would be this: to be forced to wear their hearts on their sleeves.

Who can miss the moral here? Our sins will catch up with us. They will track us down and find us out. The secrets of our hearts will one day be laid bare.

Conclusion. Who will be able to stand? Only those whose hearts are cleansed by the blood of the Lamb. Jeremiah said, "The heart is deceitful above all things, and it is exceedingly corrupt" (17:9a). In his first epistle John assures us, "The blood of Jesus his Son cleanseth us from all sin" (1:7b). —*WTH*

* * *

WEDNESDAY EVENING, FEBRUARY 29

TITLE: The Habit of Serving

TEXT: **"For the Son of man also came not to be served but to serve, and to give his life as a ransom for many" (Mark 10:45 RSV).**

SCRIPTURE READING: **Mark 10:35–45**

Introduction. G. D. Boardman has said, "Sow an act, and you reap a habit; sow a habit, and you reap a character; sow a character, and you reap a destiny."

Jesus had many gracious and great habits that characterized His life, which has been admired through the centuries.

In the new-birth experience we receive the nature of God which imparts to us the capability of sincerely imitating the traits, characteristics, and habits of Jesus Christ. If we would truly be recognized as the followers of Christ and be effective as His servants, we must be characterized by the habits which He exhibited perfectly.

While Jesus was a Teacher come from God, He was also a servant of God and a servant to those about Him. If we would truly be His followers, we must identify with Him in the role of a servant.

Christ repudiated the pagan pattern for greatness in His temptation experience (Matt. 4:3-10). He affirmed that the purpose for life is something other than the satisfaction of human appetites, the craving of human applause, and the accumulation of property.

Man is on a perpetual search for happiness which he believes can be found through either position, power, prominence, pleasure, success, or security.

To secure significance, man seeks it by education, diligence, shrewdness, by appropriate connections and appointments, or by means of election, hard work, or investments. Some seek happiness through deceit and theft. Jesus defined life totally in terms of an opportunity and responsibility to serve.

I. Christ came into the world to serve God.

In His healing of the paralytic who was brought to Him, our Lord responded to human need in such a way that the people were filled with amazement, and they glorified God and were filled with awe (Luke 5:26). In all that Jesus did for people, He brought glory to God. As the servant of God, He was ministering to the needs of those about Him.

II. Jesus ministered to the needs of people.

In Peter's statement to the household of Cornelius, he said regarding Jesus, "He went about doing good" (Acts 10:38). The life of Jesus was a life of continual gracious and unselfish service to people.

A. *He ministered to their physical needs.*

B. *He ministered to their spiritual needs.*

C. *He ministered to their emotional needs.*

III. Jesus encourages us to have the habit of serving (John 12:26).

A. *By His example He would encourage us to be servants.*

B. *By His teachings He would encourage us to be servants.*

C. *His call to discipleship is an invitation to assume the role of a servant.*

D. *By the blessings He bestows upon us, He calls us to assume the role of servant.*

Conclusion. In His description of the final judgment, Jesus reveals that service rendered to the needy is in reality a service rendered to Him (Matt. 25:31-40).

We need to follow the example of others who have had the habit of always trying to be a servant of God and of others.

The key to true greatness is to be found through having the habit of Jesus to be a servant. The last sentence on the tomb of General Chinese Gordon in St. Paul's Cathedral in London is comprised of these words concerning him, "Who at all times and everywhere gave his strength to the weak, his substance to the poor, his sympathy to the suffering, and his heart to God." May our Lord help us to be imitators of the Christ and General Chinese Gordon. —*TTC*

* * *

SUGGESTED PREACHING PROGRAM
FOR THE MONTH OF MARCH

Sunday Mornings

Most great passages of Scripture are gold mines of spiritual truth to be discovered and mined. Luke 15 is one of those great chapters. The suggested theme for this month's morning messages is "Responding to God's Sorrow and Increasing God's Joy." Effort should be put forth to communicate the contemporary applications of this well-known parable, which portrays God's sorrow, God's activity, and God's joy.

Sunday Evenings

Continue the series of biographical messages using the theme "The Lives and Lessons From Great Men."

Wednesday Evenings

Continue the series using the theme "Make Good Habits, and Your Good Habits Will Make You Good," with Christ as the model for our imitation.

*   *   *

SUNDAY MORNING, MARCH 4

TITLE: **The Savior's Concern and Our Concern**

TEXT: **"And the Pharisees and the scribes murmured, saying, 'This man receives sinners and eats with them'"** (Luke 15:2 RSV).

SCRIPTURE READING: Luke 15:1-7

HYMNS: **"There Is a Green Hill Far Away," Alexander**
        "Alas, and Did My Saviour Bleed," Watts
        "The Ninety and Nine," Clephane

OFFERTORY PRAYER:

Father God, thank You for giving Your Son to live and love and to die on a cross for our sins. Thank You for giving to us the gift of Your divine Spirit. Thank You for giving to us the fellowship of the church. Thank You for giving to us Your precious book, the Bible. We come bringing tithes and offerings today to the end that others will come to experience these gifts. Through Jesus Christ our Lord. Amen.

Introduction. Our Lord came into a world that believed that God cared only for the good and obedient. The people of His day thought that God was impassive and unconcerned and unmoved about those who were nonreligious. They thought that God could not be interested in anyone except the very best of people. Consequently, the conduct of Jesus was greatly misunderstood by them.

They severely criticized Jesus because He associated with nonreligious people. He responded to this charge with the great parables found in Luke 15, which are really one parable made up of three short stories which deal with a great truth about God.

Let us try to put ourselves into the middle of this parable, and listen to what Jesus was trying to communicate to His contemporaries.

Jesus was severely criticized by the religious people of His day because He was concerned for the welfare of and fellowship with the nonreligious people around Him. He responded with the stories of the lost sheep, the lost coin, and the lost son to reveal the heart concern of God for man.

I. The ninety and nine who were safe.

When we followers of Christ in the present day read this parable, we immediately identify with the ninety-nine sheep that were safe in the fold. We rejoice over being one of the ninety-nine. We are content to be included in the fortunate majority of this parable. We are grateful for the fact that we have come to know the Good Shepherd, and we enjoy the safety and provisions of His loving care.

Because of our unconscious identification with the ninety and nine, we miss the point of the parable. We become apathetic and indifferent with regard to the lost sheep, which is out in the darkness of the night.

Without intending to, we become brothers to the elder brother who enters the picture toward the end of this chapter. We forget the grace of God that reached out to us, and we become self-righteous and cold-hearted.

II. The lost sheep.

It is not the ninety and nine but the lost sheep which is under consideration in this parable. The lost sheep is the symbol of man without God. Man without God is out in the darkness and danger of a midnight where there is no light, no joy, and no safety.

Christ as the Good Shepherd came into the darkness of our world to reveal the concern God has for us.

III. The searching shepherd.

The shepherd had concern in his heart for the welfare of the lost sheep when he discovered that it was not present with the others. Because of his concern for the welfare of the sheep, and because of his love for each one, he went out into the darkness and danger and loneliness of the night, seeking and continuing to search until the lost sheep was found and restored. He experienced great joy upon finding the lost sheep, and he lovingly carried it to the safety of the fold.

IV. The Good Shepherd continues to seek the lost sheep.

A. *Our Lord wants to use the church in the world today to seek the lost.*
   1. He wants to use the pastor in this quest.
   2. He wants the deacons to participate in the search.
   3. The Good Shepherd needs good Sunday school teachers to teach the Word and enlist people in Bible study.
   4. The great Shepherd of the sheep, through the Holy Spirit, has bestowed upon the individual members of the church the gifts they need to be effective in searching for the lost sheep.

Conclusion. Do we really care about those who are not enjoying the safety of the fold?

Are we willing to take a spiritual inventory to see whether or not we are like the scribes and Pharisees who had no concern for the nonbelieving and irreligious people about them? Are we willing to be honest with ourselves and with God at the point of measuring the concern in our hearts for those who do not yet know Him? Jesus was doing something more than telling an interesting story about a shepherd and a lost sheep. He was trying to say something about God's individual and personal care for persons. He would lead us to have the same kind of concern. This parable tells us that God is a sheep-counter. If one sheep is outside the safety of the fold, it concerns the heart of the Father God. If you are outside the safety of the fold, be assured that God is concerned. Christ is seeking you through the church and through your Christian friends. Christ is seeking you. He wants to find you and to receive you. He wants to restore you to the Father. He wants you to experience the safety of belonging to the Father God.   —*TTC*

* * *

SUNDAY EVENING, MARCH 4

TITLE: Ezekiel—Individual Responsibility

TEXT: **"O house of Israel, I will judge you every one after his ways"** (Ezek. 33:20b ASV).

SCRIPTURE READING: **Ezekiel 33:1–20**

Introduction. Having served as a priest in the temple in Jerusalem, and not being fitted by either training or experience for any other work, Ezekiel found himself somewhat out of place among the captives in Babylon. What could he do? Surely there was something better than to surrender to the situation. He sat down by the river among his fellow captives with his thoughts. Here, as He had found Moses in the wilderness of Midian, God found His sorrowing servant. The result was tremendous. There came to Ezekiel a new revelation, a new concept of God.

God cares for His people as individuals. God has no pleasure in the death of the wicked. God longs for His people to repent so that He can forgive and restore them. With this new message, which would put new heart into his people, Ezekiel went out to minister. This erstwhile priest had entered into that select circle of God's noblemen called the prophets.

The Prophecy of Ezekiel may be divided into two parts: chapters 1–32, predicting the overthrow of Jerusalem, and chapters 33–48, predicting Israel's restoration to her own land. During the first period his message seems to have been little heeded by the people, but during the latter, Ezekiel is a man of great influence.

Our Scripture lesson, forming a transition between the two parts, deals with the oustanding contribution of Ezekiel, the doctrine of individual responsibility, from three points of view. We want to look at each of these, and then, in closing, at the dangers of this doctrine in the context of our own times.

I. The prophet's responsibility for individuals (vv. 1–9).

A missionary to the Gbeapo people in Liberia was seeking a word in their language for *prophet*. She could not use their words for either "soothsayer" or "diviner" because they were not exact equivalents and because these people looked upon them as fakes and charlatans. But she noticed that morning and evening the official representative of the chief of the village went down its streets delivering instructions, the message of the chief, and announcing events to come. This was the word she used, "God's town crier." And such is a prophet.

The figure Ezekiel uses, that of a watchman on the wall, is very similar. He is to warn the people in time of danger. In verses 1–6 the illustration is given; in verses 7–9 it is applied to them as individuals. Ezekiel took his task seriously. God had called him to this task (vv. 1, 2a, 7a), and God had defined his duties specifically. He was to watch for the enemy and to blow the trumpet when he came. He was not responsible for the response of the people. No words in the Bible are more solemn than Ezekiel's application of this figure of the watchman to himself (vv. 7–9).

In a very real sense all of God's own people *are* prophets, for every Christian has received the Holy Spirit (Rom. 8:9). To every Christian God says, "I have set thee a watchman." We must give the warning from Him.

II. God's concern for individuals (Ezek. 33:10–11).

Some knowledge of Israel's theological beliefs and of their secular history will help us understand these verses. The Israelites believed in group morality: that the group was responsible and that God would deal with them as a nation and not as individuals. As a corollary to this, they believed that they would suffer in a moral sense for their fathers' sins. Thus it was that when Jerusalem fell, their attitude was: "Our transgressions and our sins are upon us, and we pine away in them; how then can we live?" (v. 10b ASV).

One of Ezekiel's great contributions was to show the Israelites that this was not true and to teach them the doctrine of individual responsibility. Ezekiel's message was this: As individuals there is hope, if, as individuals, you repent.

A. *God is concerned that individuals know their own sinfulness* (v. 10). Unless a man is convicted of his own sins, he will die in them. These people were conscious of their sins to the point of despair, saying, "How then can we live?"

B. *God is concerned that individuals know that God yearns to restore and not destroy* (v. 11). The prophet is to convey the most tender solicitations for their best welfare. He pledges the integrity of God on this: "As I live, saith the Lord, Jehovah" (ASV).

C. *God is concerned that individuals know that restoration is possible.* "I have no pleasure in the death of the wicked; but that the wicked turn from his way and live" (v. 11b ASV). This is a foretaste of what Jesus later clearly taught. As a Father, God knows and loves each individual soul. A father does not love his family in general: he loves each child in particular. "God so loved the world" (John 3:16) is but one side of the coin. The other side is this: "There is joy in the presence of the angels of God over one sinner that repenteth" (Luke 15:10). Restoration is possible for every man.

D. *God is concerned that individuals turn from their evil ways and live* (v. 11c). "Why will ye die?" Every word of this question is dramatically emphatic. That question sings its way through the New Testament and all of Christian history.

III. The individual's responsibility for his own destiny (vv. 12–20).

Every individual is ultimately responsible for his own destiny. This is at the core of true religion. This is religion's full and final answer to those who would subordinate the person to the group, the individual to society. Every person must either accept or reject for himself or herself God's offer of pardon and salvation. Each soul is free and accountable; therefore, repentance is necessary for every individual.

Centuries before Ezekiel made this doctrine of personal accountability so clear, Moses hinted at it and warned against any individual's attempting to hide his wickedness behind the group (see Deut. 29:18b–19). Moses was warning that it is folly to suppose that identification with Israel and participation in the formalities of religion would protect a man in his sin.

Historically, we can see the timeliness of this doctrine, for the old idea of national repentance was impossible. The nation was no more.

The prophet's concern for individuals, God's concern for individuals, and the individual's responsibility for his own destiny—all of this is clearly set forth and expanded in the New Testament. It is the priceless heritage of the Christian.

But how does this doctrine fare in the context of today?

IV. Some dangers to the doctrine of individual responsibility.

At the minimum there are two dangers to the doctrine of individual responsibility in our time.

A. *There is the danger that we can so emphasize individualism that we will forget the responsibility angle, both to God and to our fellow-man.*

Soren Kierkegaard tells of a peasant who came to the capital city to sell his firewood. So much did he have to sell and such a price did he receive that he was able to buy his first pair of shoes and a pair of long stockings with enough left over for a glorious drunk. Trying to find his way home, he fell asleep in the middle of the highway. When a wagon came along, the driver, not wishing to get down, shouted, "Get up, or I'll drive over your legs." Aroused at last, the still drunken peasant, not recognizing his own legs by reason of the new shoes and stockings, shouted back, "Drive on! They are not my legs!" This is the essence of individualism. This is one danger.

B. *There is the danger that this doctrine of individual responsibility will perish from the earth, that it may vanish from men's minds.* What are some of the dangers, the threats?

1. The rise of anti-God political philosophies poses a grave threat. Denying outright the very existence of God, they hardly promote the belief of man's accountability to Him. Certain nations committed to these views were defeated in war, but these views live on.

2. The increasing trend toward mass generalization in our world poses another grave threat. Modern industrialization with its cult of mass production has tended to crush our interest in the individual. We think of crowds, groups, and classes.

3. The tremendous social pressures toward mass conformity pose another threat. They leave no room for individual responsibility and run counter to man's desire to be an individual.

4. The growing trend away from personal evangelism in favor of clever schemes of social redemption also threatens the doctrine of individual responsibility. Highly commendable but often misplaced efforts at social reform miss the boat many times because they short-circuit the one thing—individual conversion—that can bring about true reform.

5. The wholesale neglect of personal religion is the gravest threat of all. When people do this, they forget that they were created in God's image, that they have the capacity for fellowship with their Creator, and that they are accountable to Him.

Conclusion. This then is the doctrine the great prophet Ezekiel teaches. This our Lord died to make possible. This the apostle Paul also declares, "So then each one of us shall give account of himself to God" (Rom. 14:12 ASV). There is no more certain fact in all the world than that.   —*WTH*

* * *

WEDNESDAY EVENING, MARCH 7

TITLE: The Habit of Giving

TEXT: "Give, and it will be given to you; good measure, pressed down, shaken together, running over, will be put into your lap. For the measure you give will be the measure you get back" (Luke 6:38 RSV).

SCRIPTURE READING: Matthew 6:19–21

Introduction. Jesus had the habit of being a giver at all times. If we would truly be His disciples, we must see life as an opportunity to give.

Giving is not instinctive. We are instinctively and naturally acquisitive. Giving is a habit that must be learned either by observing the actions of givers or by receiving instructions from those who have discovered that the highest possible happiness comes not to the receiver, but to the giver.

Frank B. Gilberth has said, "We're worn into grooves by Time—by our habits. In the end, these grooves are going to show whether we've been second-rate or champions, each in his way in dispatching the affairs of every day. By choosing our habits, we determine the grooves into which Time will wear us; and these are grooves that enrich our lives and make for ease of mind, peace, happiness—achievement" (*The Forbes Scrapbook of Thought on the Business of Life* [New York: Forbes Incorporated], p. 80). How different life would be if we had the habit of facing each situation with the question "What can I give?" rather than "What can I get?" Jesus saw life as an opportunity to give rather than to receive.

I. Jesus saw God as the great Giver (cf. John 3:16).

Nowhere in all of the Scriptures is God pictured as a "getter." Instead God is the great Giver. Because God is by His very nature a giver, it follows that He loves in a special way those who develop the grace of giving (2 Cor. 8:7). God is not enriched by the gifts of men, nor is He threatened with poverty by the stinginess of men. The very nature of God's love is shown in that He is a giver. If we would be the true sons and daughters of God, we must let His disposition lead us to become givers.

II. Christ was a great giver.

John describes the Savior as being "full of grace" (1:14). This means that everything Jesus did was done without a price tag being attached to it. He was moved with the adequacy and the sufficiency of God to meet the spiritual needs of a bankrupt humanity. He was not looking for profit or gain. He was moved to be a giver for the good it could do and because of the joy it could bring to His own heart (Acts 20:35).

Jesus declared, "It is more blessed to give than to receive," because giving does bring more happiness, excitement, fulfillment, and satisfaction than does the accumulating, the hoarding, and the keeping of material substances.

III. Jesus encouraged His disciples to be generous givers.

"You received without paying, give without pay" (Matt. 10:8 rsv).

Jesus encouraged His disciples to go out as the bestowers of the gifts of God upon those to whom they would have the privilege of ministering.

It is tragic that many of us think that the only gifts we have are monetary. There are other gifts that can enrich the hearts and lives of others far greater than a gift of money.

A. *We can give the gift of ourselves to those about us in a manner that will be helpful to them.*

B. *We can give the gift of affirmation to others.*

C. *We can give the gift of encouragement to others.*

D. *We can give the gift of forgiveness to those who have mistreated us.*

E. *We can give the gift of appreciation and praise to those who are worthy.*

F. *We can give the gift of friendship to those who feel alienated and who have experienced embarrassment.*

G. *We can give the gift of kindness, which is a language that even the blind can see and the deaf can hear.*

H. *We can give the gift of our Christian testimony to the world about us.*

Conclusion. We can literally become an artesian well of God's love if we will accept the philosophy of life that "it is more blessed to give than to receive."

Jesus had the habit of being a giver. This is a habit that you and I can develop as well.

Make good habits, and your habits will make you good.   —*TTC*

* * *

SUNDAY MORNING, MARCH 11

TITLE: Searching for Silver Treasures

Text: "Or what woman, having ten silver coins, if she loses one coin, does not light a lamp and sweep the house and seek diligently until she finds it?" (Luke 15:8 rsv).

Scripture Reading: Luke 15:1–10

Hymns: "Joyful, Joyful, We Adore Thee," Van Dyke
 "Though Your Sins Be As Scarlet," Crosby
 "Whosoever Will," Bliss

Offertory Prayer:

Father God, thank You for affirming our worth as persons in sending Your Son Jesus Christ to minister to us and to die for us on a cross. Thank You for every indication of Your divine concern for our welfare. Thank You

for placing within our hearts a concern for others. **We come bringing tithes
and offerings in the name of our Lord to the end that others may experience
Your mercy and come to know the good news of Your love through Jesus
Christ. Amen.**

Introduction. Luke 15 contains the parable about lost things. It tells the stories
of a lost sheep, a lost coin, and a lost son.

This parable reveals God's sorrow over lost things, God's activity in the
interest of lost people, and God's joy when the lost are found.

This great parable contains a picture of a needy, suffering world that needs
to be rescued and restored to its Shepherd, its Owner, and its Father.

This great parable gives to us a portrayal of God's purpose for the church. It
reveals an excellent purpose for each Sunday school class. It tells us why the
choir should lead the congregation in singing the Good News. This parable gives
a board of deacons their reason for being. Each individual needs to place himself
right in the middle of this parable and identify with each section of it.

This parable reveals to us that God is a sheep-counter. When one out of a
hundred is lost, God is aware of it and concerned.

This parable also reveals that God is a coin-counter. When one coin is lost,
He is concerned.

**I. Christ came into the world in search of lost coins—the coin of a human
soul.**

A. *Human beings before they come to know Jesus Christ are lost and away
from God like the lost coin was away from the woman who once owned it.*

B. *Human beings are lost from themselves and from their higher selves
until they find their true identity with God.*

C. *Human beings are lost from each other until they become the sons and
daughters of God through faith in Christ.* Man by nature experiences alienation
and loneliness, and, oftentimes, real despair.

D. *The lost coins—the lost souls of this world—are lost valuables to God.*

II. The woman and the lost coin.

A. *To the woman the silver coin had security value.* It was one-tenth of her
possessions.

B. *To the woman the silver coin may have had a great sentimental value.* In
the Middle East in those days, a headdress with ten silver coins attached often
signified that the woman wearing it was married. It would have value comparable
to a wedding ring with ten diamond insets. Perhaps this was the coin that the
woman in the parable lost.

I knew of a woman who lost a diamond from a ring. She and her husband
were distressed until they had exhausted every possibility of finding it and suc-
ceeded. God is concerned to the extent that He sent His Son to rescue men from
perishing (John 3:16).

III. The woman's search for the lost coin.

A. *She lighted a lamp in order to search her house for the lost coin.* Let
each of us put himself into the midst of this parable and make a personal
application. We are to be the light in the world, shining in a dark place so that

those about us can find the way to God through our testimony (Phil. 2:14–16). We are to illuminate the way *to* God and the way *of* God. We are to demonstrate the difference that Jesus Christ makes in one's life.

B. *The woman sought carefully and diligently for the lost coin.* She swept the floor. Each of us who has experienced the love of God in Jesus Christ needs to have personal concern for those about us who do not yet know Him.

C. *The woman was persistent in her search: "until she finds it."* Giving up or quitting in this matter of trying to communicate to others the love of God should not be an option for us.

IV. Notice the joy of finding lost treasures (Luke 15:9–10).

A. *Consider the joy of the woman when she found the lost coin.* Consider the joy you can experience when you are used by the Holy Spirit to help find and rescue a lost soul.

B. *Consider the joy of the neighbors* (15:9). Not only did the woman rejoice, but her neighbors also rejoiced over the recovery of the lost coin. Everyone rejoices when someone comes to know God's love and mercy.

C. *God experiences His greatest joy when a person is born into His family through the miracle of the new birth as a result of receiving Jesus Christ as Lord and Savior.*

D. *Consider the joy of the angels* (15:10). Even the angels of God rejoice when someone is saved.

E. *Are the redeemed in heaven able to rejoice at the moment that one is converted?* We cannot be certain, but we could infer such by the statement that "there is joy before the angels of God over one sinner who repents" (v. 10 RSV). It is possible that this is a reference to the joy of the redeemed when someone makes the decision to become a Christian.

Let us consider the joy of the lost coin that regains its value. While a coin is lost, it is valueless. It has value only in the hands of someone who can use it as a medium of exchange. Have you ever known anyone yet who came to know Jesus Christ as Savior who did not experience great joy as he or she was restored and had the experience that brought him or her to know God?

Conclusion. From this parable we need to recognize that each one and everyone is of supreme value to God.

Each one can be of great value to others.

God is a sheep-counter. God is a coin-counter. You can be saved today because God wants you to experience your full potential value. You can do so through faith in Jesus Christ and faithfulness to Him. Decide now to let Him be Lord in your life.　　　　　　　　　　　　　　　　　　　　　　—*TTC*

* * *

SUNDAY EVENING, MARCH 11

TITLE: Barnabas—the Layman

TEXT: "For he was a good man, and full of the Holy Spirit and of faith: and much people was added unto the Lord" (Acts 11:24 ASV).

SCRIPTURE READING: Acts 9:26–30; 11:19–26

Introduction. Devoted, disciplined, and trained laypersons who will follow Christ's called servants in the work are the key to conquest in the kingdom. Many churches recognize this. In West Germany there is the "Kirchentag," an annual conference which brings together half a million laymen from all over Europe. Roman Catholics have the Christopher Movement to encourage religious activity of all believers. Lutherans have the Lutheran Layman's League; and Southern Baptists have an organization called "Baptist Men," whose purpose is to support the "total program of the church."

Behind all these organizations is the realization that the tasks confronting the modern church are too great to be undertaken by religious professionals alone. If preachers are the heavy artillery, laymen are the infantry; and heavy artillery never won a battle without infantry support to do hand-to-hand combat with the enemy. To be effective, every church must have a great group of active laymen taking Christ into all areas of life. Too often the modern church gives the impression of a paid quartet attempting to render the glory and majesty of Handel's *Messiah*.

When the Book of Acts was written, the distinction between clergy and laity had not clearly appeared; but there was a clear distinction between the apostles and disciples. Every believer was a disciple, but only the Twelve were considered apostles. Barnabas was not an apostle in this technical sense, but he fulfilled the role of a layman in so many ways we may designate him as "Barnabas—the Layman." Notice five things suggested by our text and its context.

I. Barnabas had the moral quality that made him effective.

The last part of our text is explained by the first. "And much people was added unto the Lord." This wonderful result is explained by the fact that Barnabas "was a good man, and full of the Holy Spirit and of faith." He was a good man. This is the most desirable quality anyone can have. Goodness in a person's life cannot be explained by his economic condition, his educational attainments, his profession, or his physical surroundings. Whence comes goodness?

A. *Goodness is begotten out of a consciousness of having been forgiven.* One of the most famous letters in the archives in Washington, D. C., is a letter taken from the body of a deserter whom President Lincoln had pardoned and sent back to his regiment. Written across the face of that letter are the words, "Taken from the body of R. McIntyre at the Battle of Five Forks, Virginia, 1865." That was the last cavalry action of the war. McIntyre fought to the end.

Anyone who knows the experience of having been forgiven understands the motives that could so remake a pardoned deserter. The consciousness of being pardoned sinners is a tremendous motive for moral excellence among Christians. It was for Barnabas.

B. *Goodness is learned from the example of others who are genuinely good.* This is well demonstrated in the experience of the apostles who, in spite of conspicuous limitations in other ways, became good men chiefly as a result of their association with Christ. Goodness can be contagious at long range. The life of our Lord may have an effect upon us today much as it did on Peter, James, and John and others of long ago.

II. Barnabas had the Spirit-given grace which enabled him to be a generous contributor to his church.

A. *Barnabas gave liberally of his material possessions.* At the time when many members of the Jerusalem church were in need, Barnabas, like many others, "having a field, sold it, and brought the money and laid it at the apostles' feet" (Acts 4:37 ASV). The generosity of Barnabas flowed from the activity of the Holy Spirit. He was "full of the Holy Spirit" (11:24). Most of the financial problems of the modern church may be traced to a dearth of the Holy Spirit. Where He is in control, people give liberally.

B. *Barnabas gave liberally of his time.* The investigative trip to Antioch took time. He willingly gave it. His preaching in Antioch, his journey to Tarsus to seek Saul, his part in helping solve the Judaizing controversy—all these took time. No church can go forward in Christ's work without many laypersons who give willingly of their time.

C. *Barnabas gave willingly of himself.* He gave not only money and time, but his energy, his influence, his insight. Barnabas' mind, heart, and will, his all, were on the altar in the service of the Lord.

III. Barnabas had the spiritual insight which enabled him to see leadership qualities in others.

Spiritual insight in one facet of faith. You cannot see the potentialities in other people unless you have faith in God and faith in other people. Barnabas did see potential in people because he was a man of faith.

A. *Barnabas saw great potential in Paul.* He stood up for Paul before the Jerusalem church when all others were suspicious of him. He so trusted Paul that he staked his good name in Jerusalem and all his influence with the apostles on the genuineness of Paul's conversion (see 9:26–28).

B. *Barnabas saw great potential in John Mark.* It was probably upon Barnabas' suggestion that Mark went with Barnabas and Paul as their helper on the first mission tour since Mark was Barnabas' cousin (Col. 4:10). When Mark deserted them at Perga in Pamphylia, Paul found this difficult to overlook and refused to take him on the second mission tour. Barnabas and Paul went separate ways in their work because of this, but later events proved Barnabas right and Paul wrong. Paul later used Mark as a helper (Col. 4:10; 2 Tim. 4:11a). Mark is the author of the Gospel that bears his name. Barnabas' faith in him was vindicated.

IV. Barnabas had the spiritual quality of loyalty which gave him stability.

In the contention with Paul over John Mark, Barnabas revealed a virtue scarcely mentioned in the New Testament—that of loyalty. The absence of loyalty makes traitors; its presence, heroes.

Churches have always needed loyal laymen like Barnabas, but never more than today. Even in this era of ecumenicity, loyalty to one's own church is not a vice. Loyalty to one's own denomination gives a cutting edge to faith in a secular world that wants to destroy all distinctions, all lines, all differences.

V. Barnabas had the gracious humility of spirit which enabled him to play a support role.

Many people cannot do this. They do not have the humility of spirit. They must be "lead mule" or they won't pull. We have at least two illustrations of Barnabas' humility of spirit.

A. *Barnabas sought Paul's help in the work at Antioch* (Acts 11:25). Think what that meant for Barnabas. It meant, for one thing, the admission of the fact that he was over his head in the work at Antioch. It takes real humility to admit such a thing. Few can. It meant, moreover, that he would no longer be the leader at Antioch. Paul would be. Barnabas knew this. To have the heart to discover a more talented person than yourself and then to have the grace to enlist him at the cost of demoting yourself to second place takes grace. Barnabas had such grace.

B. *Barnabas played a support role to Paul on the first mission tour.* In their call to mission the Spirit said, "Separate me Barnabas and Saul" (13:2b). In Acts 13:7 the writer speaks of Sergius Paulus' calling unto him "Barnabas and Saul." But in verse 13 Luke speaks of "Paul and his company." Barnabas knew this would be the case before they ever set foot in a boat to begin the journey. This takes humility of spirit.

Conclusion. Great preachers are needed in the work of the kingdom. But no preacher can accomplish much without great laypersons supporting his leadership. Peter, John, and Paul occupy center stage in the New Testament, and rightly so; but Barnabas deserves an important place on that stage too, "for he was a good man, and full of the Holy Spirit and of faith."   *—WTH*

* * *

WEDNESDAY EVENING, MARCH 14

TITLE: The Habit of Forgiving

TEXT: **"For if you forgive men their trespasses, your heavenly Father also will forgive you; but if you do not forgive men their trespasses, neither will your Father forgive your trespasses" (Matt. 6:15–16 RSV).**

SCRIPTURE READING: **Matthew 18:21–35**

Introduction. Our precious Lord developed and maintained the habit of being forgiving toward those who mistreated Him on all occasions. This was supremely demonstrated by His words from the cross in which He offered forgiveness and prayed for the forgiveness of those who were crucifying Him. This prayer for forgiveness was not the impulse of the moment, but rather it was the expression of a permanent principle by which Jesus lived.

If you and I would be true followers of Jesus, we must adopt His basic fundamental attitudes and then engage in the same kind of activities in which He participated.

I. Jesus taught that we should seek forgiveness and also grant forgiveness (Matt. 6:8).

It is significant in the Model Prayer that our Lord would teach His disciples to be forgiving in the same breath in which He taught them to pray for forgiveness.

Our Lord taught that if we would experience forgiveness, we must be forgiving. To forgive others is not a price we pay in order to receive forgiveness; it is a condition we must meet in order to obtain forgiveness. There is a difference between paying a price and meeting a condition.

II. Jesus taught that we must be forgiving (18:21-22).

It was common practice in the days of Jesus that forgiveness should be granted three times. When Peter inquired concerning the giving of forgiveness seven times, he was being very generous. Jesus shocked His disciples by telling them that they must not place restrictions upon forgiveness: "I do not say to you seven times, but seventy times seven" (v. 22 RSV).

Behind our Lord's command to practice unlimited forgiveness, there is His divine desire to deliver us from attitudes and actions that are self-destructive. He recognized that to harbor hate within the heart is to create an acid that will destroy one's capacity to be loving and helpful.

Our Lord recognized that all of us will experience mistreatment and injustice in one form or another. In His own experience, He developed the habit of always practicing forgiveness rather than responding with hate, bitterness, and hostility. He never resorted to retaliation. Retaliation of evil for evil will destroy our homes, our families, and our fellowship.

The apostle Paul indicates that Satan seeks to prevent us from practicing forgiveness in order that he might gain an advantage over us (2 Cor. 2:10-11). The most expensive luxury anyone can have is a grudge that he carries around against a brother or a sister.

Conclusion. A forgiving spirit prevents the devil from establishing a beachhead in our minds and thought processes.

A forgiving spirit delivers us from becoming involved in a vicious cycle of self-destructiveness.

A forgiving spirit prevents the acid of hate from collecting in our hearts.

A forgiving spirit brings healing to the broken heart and the injured spirit of another as well as to ourselves.

A forgiving spirit permits us to reveal the love of God as we have experienced it through Jesus Christ.

A forgiving spirit enables us to experience God's continuing miracle of forgiveness.

Let each of us develop the habit of being forgiving rather than being vindictive and retaliatory toward those who mistreat us.   *—TTC*

* * *

SUNDAY MORNING, MARCH 18

TITLE: Living in the Far Country at Our Address

TEXT: **"Not many days later, the younger son gathered all he had and took his journey into a far country, and there he squandered his property in loose living" (Luke 15:13 RSV).**

SCRIPTURE READING: **Luke 15:11-32**

HYMNS: **"This Is My Father's World," Babcock**
       "I Will Arise and Go to Jesus," Hart
       "Only Trust Him," Stockton

OFFERTORY PRAYER:
    Father God, we come to Your house today that we may sit at Your table and enjoy the banquet of Your grace. Thank You for being so generous to

us. Thank You for providing for us so abundantly. Today, from that which we have earned, we come bringing tithes and offerings. Bless these gifts to the end that Your name shall be honored and lifted up and that people will come to know Your love and Your purpose for their lives. Through Jesus Christ our Lord we pray. Amen.

Introduction. Our Lord spoke words of stern rebuke, but in a discrete manner, to the religious leaders of His day when they found fault with Him because He was associating with nonreligious people. He responded to their charge by giving this parable of the seeking shepherd, the seeking woman, and the waiting but compassionate father. Very little attention is given to the elder brother whose attitude toward the returning brother portrayed the attitude of religious people of that day toward the return of sinners to God. Before we find ourselves too critical of those people, we need to examine our own performance record to see if we have unintentionally acted like we were the twin brothers of the elder son.

I. We exclude ourselves from this story.

The average professing Christian who reads this story usually does so with some degree of pious self-satisfaction. We think of the parable as the "parable of the prodigal son," when in reality it is the parable of the brokenhearted father who yearns for the return of a foolish and self-destructive son. We fail to identify with this parable for a number of reasons.

A. *We have never demanded our inheritance from our parents before their death like the prodigal did.*

B. *Neither have we applied for a passport into a foreign country that we might get away from the restraints of home.*

C. *Most of us who read this parable are not living in illicit sex outside of wedlock; and, consequently, we miss the point of this parable.*

D. *Most of us who read this are not working in a pigpen, nor are we bordering on starvation, so we do not see ourselves at all in the parable.* In fact, most of us who read this parable are bothered by excess weight rather than being starved.

E. *Most of us do not even have a prodigal brother, and so we do not even identify with the elder brother.*

We come to the conclusion that this powerful parable has no application or message for us individually and personally. How sad to think that we could be so insensitive to what our Lord was trying to communicate.

II. Are we twin brothers of the elder brother?

A. *Do we find it easy to be satisfied with ourselves as we are because of a negative kind of righteousness?*

1. Most of us can rejoice over the fact that we have never killed anybody.

2. Many of us have never taken up the habit of smoking.

3. Some can boast of the fact that they have never taken one drink of alcohol, much less been in danger of becoming an alcoholic.

B. *Do we find it easy to be judgmental toward those who have brought injury and poverty upon themselves because of self-inflicted wounds?* It is easy to be hasty and harsh in arriving at judgments concerning others.

C. *How long has it been since you have enjoyed a feast with God because of the return of a prodigal?* When the prodigal returned, the father sent word to all that they should come and enjoy the feast. Some of us live so far away from where salvation experiences are taking place that we don't even know that a feast with God is a present possibility for those who are helping Him rescue people from the far country.

III. Where is the far country?

The late Dr. Ellis A. Fuller said concerning the far country, "It is anywhere that a man tries to live without God." The far country is just one step away from the will of the Father God.

The far country is so close that all of us are familiar with it, and yet some of us do not recognize that we are either living in the far country or right on its border.

A. *The far country begins when we demand our freedom to do what is contrary to the Father's good will.*

B. *The far country begins when we see life as an opportunity to be selfishly happy.*

C. *The far country begins for a person when he or she shows absolutely no concern to improve the quality of his or her spiritual vitality or effectiveness in communicating the great love of God for those who are in sin.*

IV. Are we twins of the prodigal who returned?

Some may be identical twins of a prodigal while others of us bear at least some similarities to him.

A. *Have we departed from where we once were in the Father's house?*

B. *Have we wasted our time, talents, and treasures in selfish pursuits?*

C. *Have we found our hearts hungry and thirsty for the food and fellowship of God's home and family?*

    1. The desire for selfish freedom leads to the far country.

    2. Neglecting to nourish our souls upon the food of God can lead us to the far country.

    3. Greed for material possessions can cause us to drift into the far country.

    4. Unresolved resentment can lead us to the far country.

    5. Some of us allow trouble to cause us to drift away from God.

D. *Have you found life to be a fruitless rat race that brings no satisfaction to your heart?* It could be that you are in the far country without being aware of it.

Conclusion. The prodigal acted as an irresponsible and self-destructive person for a period in his life. However, just because one acts irresponsibly on one occasion doesn't mean he has to remain that way always.

    1. The prodigal came to great want.

    2. The prodigal came to himself and evaluated himself.

    3. When the prodigal decided to return to his father, he came at once. He came as he was.

    4. The prodigal discovered that he was met a great way off. He found that provisions had already been made for his return. He experienced great rejoicing.

If you have been living in the far country, even at your address, it is time to come home to the Father God. —*TTC*

* * *

SUNDAY EVENING, MARCH 18

TITLE: **Paul—Marks of a Well-adjusted Personality**

TEXT: **"I can do all things in him that strengtheneth me" (Phil. 4:13 ASV).**

SCRIPTURE READING: **Philippians 3:3–4:20**

Introduction. Can it be that in this personality-adjustment business we have started at the wrong place and proceeded in the wrong direction? Introducing the chapter of Romans where he describes salvation as reconciliation, Paul says, "Being therefore justified by faith, we have peace with God through our Lord Jesus Christ" (5:1 ASV). That is the starting point: "peace with God." Man can never be adjusted to life—to his vocation, his fellowman, his past, his present, or his future—unless and until through Christ he has been remade into a new creature (2 Cor. 5:17).

This was true of Paul. Before he met Christ on the Damascus road, he was, according to his own testimony, a maladjusted man. Out of that experience, and as a result of the growth stemming from it, he became one of the greatest men in history.

Our passage is rich in autobiographical insights into Paul's mind and heart. Below are five marks of a well-adjusted personality as illustrated in his life and experience.

I. A man with a well-adjusted personality has the right attitude toward his worldly status (Phil. 3:3–8).

There are two ways in which a man may have an elevated worldly status: by right of inheritance and by virtue of his own attainments. Paul had both.

A. *As to his heritage Paul names four things:*
1. Circumcised the eighth day" (v. 5a). He was no proselyte but an Israelite by birth, having by heredity and the sign of the covenant his part in the covenant promises.
2. "Of the stock of Israel" (v. 5b). Paul's parents were not proselytes, but were themselves Hebrews by birth.
3. "Of the tribe of Benjamin" (v. 5c). This was the tribe which gave Israel her first king and which remained true to the Davidic throne when the other tribes broke away from Judah.
4. "An Hebrew of Hebrews" (v. 5d ASV). Although living at Tarsus, Paul's parents adhered to the Hebrew language and customs. He was no Hellenist by upbringing, but a Hebrew. This was an impressive pedigree.

B. *As to his own personal attainments, Paul names three things:*
1. "As touching the law, a Pharisee" (v. 5e). By his own choice he had embraced the party that took the strictest view of the law.
2. "As touching zeal, persecuting the church" (v. 6a ASV). Paul was not merely a Pharisee, he was a zealous Pharisee, a relentless persecutor of all heretics.

3. "As touching the righteousness which is in the law, found blameless" (v. 6b ASV). So far as the observance of all formal rules, precepts, and practices of the law were concerned, Paul measured up to all requirements. As far as worldly status was concerned, Paul could outboast almost anybody (v. 4b).

C. *As to his attitude toward his worldly status, Paul's scale of values had undergone a radical revision* (vv. 7–8).

Something had happened when he became a Christian to revise all his former standards. The new power in Paul's life was utterly devastating to his old views. Henceforth his attitude toward worldly status was, "What things were gain to me, these have I counted loss for Christ" (v. 7 ASV). His motive? "That I may gain Christ" (v. 8d ASV).

II. A man with a well-adjusted personality has continuing aspirations for his own developing Christian life (3:8b–16).

A. *He aspires to righteousness* (vv. 8d–9).

A Christian has two kinds of righteousness: the good works of his own life for which he was created in Christ Jesus (Eph. 2:10), and the righteousness of God imputed to him by faith (2 Cor. 5:21) upon the basis of the atoning work of Christ. It is the former which gives him his standing as a Christian before the world; it is the latter which gives him his right standing before God. The latter is in Paul's mind here.

B. *He aspires to fuller Christian knowledge* (Phil 3:10–11).

The resurrection of Christ is mentioned first here. It was the victorious Christ who met Paul on the Damascus road; and when he had met Him, the sufferings of Christ came to have a meaning for Paul. This is the knowledge he desires, that the great facts of Christ's life might be reenacted in his own.

C. *He aspires to maturity as a Christian* (vv. 12–15).

As we seek to make progress as Christians Paul gives three simple rules for striving.

1. Concentration. "One thing I do," said Paul (v. 13b). He was saying, "I have one purpose, one thought, one goal." Here is our weakness. We give the Lord, among other things, a little time, a little place, a little effort, a little thought.

2. Direction. "Forgetting the things which are behind, and stretching forward to the things which are before, I press on" (vv. 13c–14a). The direction is forward, and forward only.

3. Perseverance (v. 14), "I am not already there," Paul is saying, "the goal is still a long way off, but I am pressing on."

D. *He aspires to stability* (v. 16).

The word here translated "let us walk" means to walk in a straight line. We might translate this verse, "Whatever be the stage of development, let us keep to the line. Let us not stray to one side or the other." In situations where spiritual endurance is demanded and where many weaken, there still remain a few Christians who stand fast. These God can use.

III. A man with a well-adjusted personality has high hopes for the church (3:17–4:7).

A. *He has high hopes for the church here and now.*

1. He hopes they may have a Christlike walk (3:17–4:1). Walking is a favorite figure of Paul's as he enjoins a worthy Christian life (*see* Eph. 4:1).

2. He hopes they may have an unbroken fellowship (Phil. 4:2–3). Reading between the lines, apparently Euodia ("fragrant") and Syntyche ("fortunate") were at odds. Painfully impartial as he addresses them, Paul says, "Help these women." The touchstone is "the mind of Christ" (2:1–5).

3. He hopes they may be joyous and gentle witnesses for Christ (4:4, 5). In Philippians the theme of joy comes to the surface five times (1:18; 2:2, 17; 3:1; 4:4). In the word translated "forbearance" is the idea of gentleness. People charged with the ministry of reconciliation must not allow an overbearing spirit to cripple their efforts.

4. He hopes they may be a praying church (4:6). Four things are necessary to prayer: freedom from anxiety, an attitude of worship, a spirit of thanksgiving, and specific requests.

5. He hopes they may have inward peace (4:7). This is a peace independant of circumstances which springs from our union with Christ. This is a gift of Christ (*See* John 14:27).

B. *Paul has high hopes for the church hereafter* (Phil 3:20–21).

1. The nature of the church prefigures what shall be. He says, "Our citizenship is in heaven." As a Roman colony, the big events for Philippi were the visits of the emperor. A church is a colony of heaven on earth, and one day her King will come.

2. The nature of the resurrection body is a pledge of Christ's final triumph when every knee shall bow and every tongue confess Him (*see* 2:10–11; 3:21).

IV. A man with a well-adjusted personality has a disciplined mind (4:8–9).

We are in large measure the fruit of our thoughts; and therefore what we think is most important (Prov. 23:7a). The first law of the mind is that we can concentrate on only one thing at a time. Paul is saying, "The true, the honorable, the just, the pure, the lovely, the well reported—think on these things" (*see* Phil. 4:8).

But this takes discipline. If we ask Him, God will garrison (a military term) our minds as well as our hearts, but He will not close the door on the guests we welcome. A disciplined mind takes practice.

V. A man with a well-adjusted personality has the right philosophy toward material things (vv. 10–20).

Paul's Epistle to the Philippians is in reality a "bread and butter" letter; and here in this last section Paul gets around to thanking them. Here is the Christian philosophy toward material things.

A. *This right philosophy includes gratitude for material things* (v. 10). The failure to be grateful for gifts of material things will make material things our master.

B. *This right philosophy includes contentment in our material circumstances, whether much or little* (vv. 11–13). Though using the Stoic's word for "content," Paul disclaims mere self-sufficiency (*see* 2 Cor. 3:5). He elaborates his manly independence of material circumstances and says that he has been initiated into the happy secret of independence (Phil. 4:12) which he longs to share with others. In verse 13 Paul is saying, "I am a match for all circumstances through the One whose inflow of power enables me."

C. *This right philosophy includes fellowship in the use of material things* (vv. 14–16). Not only does he commend their last gift to him as their fellowship with his affliction, he also cites their past record as further proof of the fellowship they enjoyed with him in the matter of giving and receiving.

D. *This right philosophy discerns the sacramental nature of giving* (vv. 17–20). The highest scriptural appeal for giving is the fruit that increases to the account of the giver.

Conclusion. All of these marks of a well-adjusted personality stem out of a most important presupposition: a saving experience with Jesus Christ whereby one becomes in Him a new creature. Before Paul met Jesus, he was a learned, zealous, sincere man; but his life was being consumed by the inner fires of tension and discontent. After he met Jesus, he was at peace with God, at peace about the past, alert to the opportunities of the present, and unafraid of the future. Through Christ, all this can be yours as well.   —*WTH*

* * *

WEDNESDAY EVENING, MARCH 21

TITLE: The Habit of Seeing the Good

Text: "He brought him to Jesus. Jesus looked at him, and said, 'So you are Simon the son of John? You shall be called Cephas' (which means Peter)" (John 1:42 rsv).

Scripture Reading: John 1:35–42

Introduction. Dr. Ralph W. Sockman has said, "Habit must play a larger part in our religious life. We worship when we feel like it; we pray when we feel like it; we read the Bible when we feel like it. Leaving our religious exercises to the promptings of impulse, we become creatures of impulse rather than soldiers of Christ. An army made up of creatures of impulse would be only a mob." Jesus not only had great inward attitudes, but He had great habits that always expressed themselves in outward conduct. As followers of Christ, we need to identify His inward attitudes and adopt His methods of relating to others. Jesus had the habit of always seeing the good that was potential in the people about Him.

I. Jesus saw the potential for good in Simon (John 1:42).

Jesus saw this impulsive, unstable man as one who could become as solid as a rock. Jesus, while knowing that Peter had the potential to deny Him three times, could also see the potential for this man's standing like Gibraltar on the Day of Pentecost to proclaim the meaning and significance of what God was doing through the gift of the Holy Spirit.

Jesus had the habit of seeing good in others.

II. Jesus saw the potential for good in Matthew, the tax collector (Matt. 9:9).

Tax collectors were not very popular among the Jewish people of Jesus' day. They were the despised representatives of a foreign government, which was guilty of tyranny and oppressive taxation. As Jesus passed by, He saw this man and invited him to become one of His followers. So far as we know, this man brought only his pencil with him. This man had the capacity to become the writer of the first Gospel known as the Gospel of Matthew.

Jesus had the habit of seeing the good in others.

III. Jesus saw the potential for good in the woman of Samaria (John 4:1-39).

If there was ever a hopeless case to come across the pathway of Jesus, it would appear that this woman of Samaria was such. She had experienced the heartbreak and tragedy of rejection and the shame of having five failures in marriage. She was worthless in the eyes of others. She was now living with a man outside wedlock. She was considered by all as a worthless reject. It is impossible for us to imagine the despair that must have filled her heart and life.

It was not within the realm of possibility for her to realize the potential of what was beginning to take place when she came to the well that day at the noon hour to draw water. Jesus saw her. He loved her. Wisely He requested a favor of her. He offered to her the gift of living water, and then He opened a spiritual conversation in which He revealed to her that He could give to her the gift of living water. The end result of this dialogue with a destitute woman was that she became a powerful witness for God. The Scriptures tell us, "Many Samaritans from that city believed in him because of the woman's testimony" (John 4:39 RSV).

Jesus had the habit of always seeing the good in others.

Conclusion. Most of us, if we will be honest with ourselves and with God, will have to admit that we often see the potential for bad in others. We are hypercritical. We notice the flaws in others. We observe their deficiencies and their lacks. To the degree that this is our pattern, we find ourselves in contradiction to the character and the conduct of our Savior.

Let us cultivate the attitude of looking for the good in others. Let's develop the habit of our Savior of always looking for good in others.   —*TTC*

* * *

SUNDAY MORNING, MARCH 25

TITLE: **Bringing Joy in Heaven and on Earth**

TEXT: **"Just so, I tell you, there will be more joy in heaven over one sinner who repents than over ninety-nine righteous persons who need no repentance" (Luke 15:7 RSV).**

SCRIPTURE READING: **Luke 15:1-7, 10, 22-24**

HYMNS: **"God, Our Father, We Adore Thee," Frazer**
"There's a Glad New Song," Fisher
"Since Jesus Came Into My Heart," McDaniel

OFFERTORY PRAYER:
Father God, we thank You today for all of the blessings that are associated with our earthly life. By faith and with hope we would thank You for all of the blessings that will be associated with our heavenly life in the hereafter. Today we come bringing tithes and offerings to express our grat-

itude to You and our desire to see others hear the gospel and come to know Jesus Christ as Savior. Bless these gifts to that end. We pray in Jesus' name. Amen.

Introduction. What does it take to fill your heart with joy?
What does it take to fill the heart of a child with joy?
What does it take to bring joy to your parents?
What does it take to bring joy to the heart of your companion?
To what degree do you bring joy to others?
During the past week did you do anything that was designed to produce joy for others?

When the Christ child was born, the angel announced His birth with these words, "Be not afraid; for behold, I bring you good news of a great joy which will come to all the people; for to you is born this day in the city of David a Savior, who is Christ the Lord" (Luke 2:10–11 RSV).

To some, happiness is a toy. To the student, happiness is a good grade. To the athlete, happiness is a victory. To young people in love, happiness is marriage. To the farmer, happiness is a good harvest. To the young graduate, happiness is a job. Someone has said the best way to spell the word *happy* is with the letters H-O-M-E.

Our Scripture for today tells us that it is possible for us to bring joy to those who are in heaven as well as to those who are on earth.

God also invites us to find the joy of being the means whereby the lost may experience salvation.

This parable tells us that God needs our faithful cooperation in finding the lost sheep and thus bringing joy to the heart of the Shepherd and to all of those associated with Him.

I. There can be joy in heaven and on earth when a sinner repents.

This parable of the lost sheep, the lost coin, and the lost son provides us with a picture into the heartbreak of God over lost things.

A. *God sees the lost world and the sheep that have gone astray.* Satan has been saying to humanity from the dawn of human history that God is not good and that He should not be trusted. People have listened to these lies and gone astray.

B. *God sees us as lost values.* We are of supreme value to God because He so loved us that He gave His Son to die for us.

C. *God sees a lost world as lost sons and daughters bent on a pathway of self-destructiveness and ruin.*

Satan would lead everyone to believe that there is something better than the Father's will and the Father's home, and many have believed these lies as well.

D. *God sees all of us as those who need to repent.* Repentance in the mind and heart is the human response that brings joy in heaven and on earth.

Repentance is a religious word that needs to be better understood by modern man. Repentance is more than sadness for sin. Repentance is more than reformation. Repentance is more than a simple decision to walk a straight and narrow path.

Repentance is a deep inward change of mind that results in a different kind of life and conduct.

Repentance is a change of attitude toward God, toward sin, toward self, toward others, and toward things. Repentance is a change of attitude and direction on the part of man that produces joy in heaven and on earth.

We are able to repent—that is, to come to a new attitude toward God—when we hear the good news of how He loves us in and through Jesus Christ.

II. The joy of heaven and earth.
There is joy on earth when one repents.

A. *There is joy in the heart of the sheep that is found.*
1. Forgiveness is experienced.
2. Spiritual cleanness is enjoyed.
3. Acceptance by God is a fact.
4. New relationships are formed.
5. A new nature is received.
6. An appetite for spiritual things develops.
7. Assurance of a heavenly home brings joy.

B. *There is joy in the family of God when a person repents.*
1. The church rejoices.
2. A larger circle of friends rejoice.
3. Everyone in the family circle rejoices.

C. *There is joy in heaven when one repents.*
Jesus speaks of the fact that, "There is joy before the angels of God over one sinner who repents" (Luke 15:10 RSV).
1. God the Father rejoices.
2. God the Son, our Savior, rejoices.
3. God the Holy Spirit rejoices.
4. The angels of God rejoice.
5. It is highly possible that all of the redeemed of God rejoice.

III. What can we do to produce joy in heaven?
We need to let genuine Christian compassion come into our hearts. We need to let the love that God has for sinners invade our total being. We need to recognize the supreme value of spiritual values.

A. *We must aggressively proclaim the good news of a God who is good to the lost sheep, to the lost coins, and to the lost sons who are out in the world.*

B. *We as Spirit-filled followers of Jesus Christ must be good models so as to serve as lights in a dark place and as the salt that creates thirst.*

C. *We must cooperate together as the church in ministries of outreach and mercy and helpfulness.*

D. *We must personally obey the Great Commission of our Lord in our individual worlds.*

E. *We must trust in the Holy Spirit of God to take our testimonies and use them to bring about faith in the hearts of those who need to come to Jesus Christ.*

Conclusion. How long has it been since you did something to bring joy in heaven?

You brought joy to heaven when you trusted Jesus Christ as your own personal Lord and Savior.

You have produced joy in heaven if you have helped someone else to trust Jesus Christ as Lord and Savior.

You can bring joy in heaven if you will aid someone to return to the Father's house with an attitude of trust and commitment.

God the Father hungers to see the lost found, restored, and renewed by His Holy Spirit.

Let us rejoice in the opportunity that is ours to produce joy both in heaven and on earth.

If you have not yet received Jesus Christ as Savior, you can bring joy in heaven and on earth today by receiving Him now.   —*TTC*

* * *

SUNDAY EVENING, MARCH 25

TITLE: Demas—The Quitter

TEXT: **"For Demas forsook me, having loved this present world, and went to Thessalonica" (2 Tim. 4:10a** ASV**).**

SCRIPTURE READING: **2 Timothy 4:9–18**

Introduction. Paul's second Roman imprisonment was quite a contrast to his first. This time he was not in his own hired house, but in the dread Mamertine prison, a miserable dungeon reserved for the condemned, with the sentence of death hanging over his head. The prisoner there never knew when his sentence would be carried out—such was Roman "justice."

Paul's greatest need was human fellowship. He was tired and old and sick; but above all he was lonely. Time was running out, and he knew it. This made Demas' desertion all the more painful. Demas, Crescens, and Titus had all gone away. Demas, in contrast to those "that have loved his appearing" (4:8b ASV), loved instead "this present world" and thus deserted Paul to enter secular pursuits in Thessalonica. It is unjustified reading between the lines to say that Demas fell from grace, or that he was a traitor, or that he was apostate. He was just a quitter. When the pressure became too great, he deserted.

We ought to read of his experience with sympathy and compassion, for too often our own picture is in this frame. Demas is a legitimate example to suggest a sober theme: "The Quitter." Applying this personally, there are three affirmations I wish to make, and then raise a question in closing.

I. There are times when we ought to quit.

A. *When one realizes he is going in the wrong direction, he ought to quit.* The prodigal son in Jesus' story did this (Luke 15:17–18a). An unknown poet has said:

> The man who once most wisely said,
> "Be sure you're right, then go ahead,"
> Might well have added this, to wit,
> "Be sure you're right before you quit."

B. *When one realizes that his actions and profession do not tally with his convictions, he ought to quit.* After three years as a ministerial student in a denominational college, a student appeared before the ministers' group and said,

"I believe in a God-called ministry; but I do not now believe God has called me. This being true, I cannot continue as a ministerial student." He had deep convictions, and he quit. Now forty years later, he is a successful businessman, a consecrated and useful layperson, and no pastor ever had a more devoted friend among his laypeople.

There are times when we ought to quit, but we must be sure about it.

II. There are times when we think we have ample provocation to quit.

A. *Sometimes we are treated unjustly and feel like giving in to our feelings and quitting.*

It is difficult to be impressed with the religion of those who withdraw their total support from their church to indulge a personal pique at someone. They quit with a vengeance that grieves the Lord and delights the devil.

B. *Sometimes we feel we are too tired to go on, so we decide to quit.*

Motivation is so important! A speaker who had been on the "Death March" off Batan Peninsula in May, 1942, in the Second World War, said, "You would be amazed how far you can go after you're so tired you think you must quit, when you know that if you do, you'll get a bayonet through your back or a bullet through your head."

Elijah was exhausted, but God was patient with him until he regained his strength. Never make a major decision when you are physically exhausted or mentally depressed.

C. *Sometimes we feel that our efforts are not appreciated, so we decide to quit.*

How prompt we are to criticize, how slow to express appreciation. Many jobs people do are necessary but altogether thankless. It takes a lot of butter to keep some people going. You have to "butter them up" all the time. We neglect those faithful, appreciation-starved workhorses who keep on going, bruises, saddle sores, and all. And yet, if one of these faithful does quit, just a bit of kindness or a word of appreciation may get him going again.

D. *Sometimes the one on whom we had reason to depend—on whom we did depend—lets us down and we want to quit.*

A faithful pastor with fifty years experience said, "I have resigned only five times in my whole ministry, and each time it was to go to another work. But," he said, "I must have resigned to my wife forty-seven times on Monday morning."

Other provocations could be mentioned, and quitters are plentiful.

III. There have been times when God has used men who were tempted to quit, but wouldn't, to bless the world.

A. *Moses suffered as no other leader ever suffered.* At one point he got so low he asked God, "Have I conceived all this people? have I brought them forth, that thou shouldest say unto me, Carry them in thy bosom, as a nursing-father carrieth the sucking child, unto the land which thou swarest unto their fathers?" (Num. 11:12 asv). He even asked God to kill him if such were the case, but he did not quit!

B. *Samuel was thoroughly put out when the people demanded a king to reign over them.* But God said to him, "They have not rejected thee, but they have rejected me, that I should not be king over them (1 Sam. 8:7b asv). And Samuel did not quit!

C. *Elijah got so low that he confessed, "I am not better than my fathers"*
(1 Kings 19:4d ASV). He pled with God that he was the only true follower left and
that he was a fugitive (v. 14). But Elijah did not quit!

D. *Jeremiah was often tempted to quit.* Called the "weeping prophet," no
servant of God ever suffered more anguish of soul than he. He thought about
quitting (Jer. 9:2). He tried to quit, but the "burning fire shut up in [his] bones"
(20:9) would not permit it. Jeremiah did not quit!

E. *Of Columbus someone once said, "If Columbus had turned back, no one
would have blamed him; but no one would have remembered him."* But Columbus did not quit!

F. *There are great lessons to be learned from these people and others like
them:*

1. The margin between success and failure is often very thin. Try one
more time. Maybe this time you'll make it. After many failures with an experiment, the great Edison's young assistant said, "Just think, Mr. Edison, all that
work and nothing to show for it."

"Don't say that," Edison replied. "Now we know thirty-seven things that
won't work." Experiment number thirty-eight did it!

2. Our commision is not to succeed, but to be faithful. Perry F. Webb,
Sr., once said, "I would rather fail in a cause destined ultimately to win, than to
succeed in a cause destined ultimately to fail." So would all of God's great people!

3. God can use dedicated failures, as well as glowing successes, on the
part of those who are true. By every test the world knows Jeremiah to be an
abject failure. He never carried anything through to victory. But he was true to
God; and when God's Son walked this earth in the body of our flesh, men said of
Him, "This is Jeremiah." No prophet was ever more honored.

Conclusion. Consider this question in closing: "What if a person has quit? What
does he do? What can he do?" He can begin again. He can ask God to forgive
him, get back into the harness, and go on. John Mark quit, but the record shows
he began again. Barnabas was right in insisting he be given another chance. Paul
was wrong, as he tacitly admits in 2 Timothy 4:11b.

What about Demas? Dr. Barclay has a plausible conjecture. Demas is the
shortened form of Demetrius. In 3 John the writer says, "Demetrius hath the
witness of all men, and of the truth itself: yea, we also bear witness; and thou
knowest our witness is true" (v. 12 ASV). It is heartwarming to think that "quitter" was not the final verdict on the life of Demas.   —*WTH*

* * *

WEDNESDAY EVENING, MARCH 28

TITLE: The Habit of Witnessing

TEXT: **"I must preach the good news of the kingdom of God to the other
cities also; for I was sent for this purpose"** (Luke 4:43 RSV).

SCRIPTURE READING: Luke 4:40–44

Introduction. Jesus was literally the good news about God for men in His
person as well as in His performance. Everything that Jesus said and did was a

means of communicating His personal testimony concerning the nature and character of God.

I. Jesus wants us to be witnesses for Him (Acts 1:8).

II. The Holy Spirit will bless with great power our personal testimony (Acts 4:33).

III. Jesus has commanded us to give our personal testimony (Matt. 28:19–20).

The imperative in this Great Commission is in the verb translated "make disciples." There is no way we can do this without utilizing our personal testimony regarding faith in Jesus Christ. Each of us who knows Jesus Christ as Savior can give a testimony of what has happened in our life.

In the business community the testimony of a satisfied customer is highly prized. Often the testimony of an expert is required. Many times the testimony of casual observers can be very helpful as well. Jesus wants us to give our own individual and personal testimony of what God means to us.

Conclusion. Without our personal testimony, the world will not know about what Jesus Christ means to us.

Without the personal witness of believers today, the Holy Spirit cannot show to the world what Jesus Christ can do in their lives if they will but trust Him.

Without our personal witness, others cannot receive the gift of faith and come to know Jesus Christ as Savior.

Our Lord had the habit of being a good witness for God by the life He lived, by the deeds He performed, and by the words He spoke.

Each of us who is a true follower of Jesus needs to develop this habit of giving the continual testimony of a satisfied customer.

Let us give our witness personally.
Let us give our witness boldly.
Let us give our witness with humility.
Let us give our witness with expectancy.
Let us give our witness for Christ joyfully.   —*TTC*

* * *

SUGGESTED PREACHING PROGRAM
FOR THE MONTH OF APRIL

Sunday Mornings

The purpose of the ministry of John the Baptist is the suggested theme for this series of messages that lead up to Easter and close the month with a message on the living Christ. That theme is "That All Might Believe Through Him."

Sunday Evenings

A series of messages based on the prophecies of the Book of Ezekiel is suggested. God came to Ezekiel during very difficult times and gave to him a message that was good for Ezekiel and for the exiles. The suggested theme is "The Prophet's Message for Stressful Times."

Wednesday Evenings

We begin a series of studies based on Paul's Epistles to the Church at Thessalonica. The suggested theme is "Let the Apostle Paul Speak to Your Needs in the Present."

* * *

SUNDAY MORNING, APRIL 1 *(used this in the fifth st)*

TITLE: The Blessing of Believing

TEXT: "There was a man sent from God, whose name was John. He came for testimony, to bear witness to the light, that all might believe through him" (John 1:6–7 RSV).

SCRIPTURE READING: John 1:43–51

HYMNS: "Come, Thou Fount of Every Blessing," Robinson
"'Tis So Sweet to Trust in Jesus," Stead
"Have Faith in God," McKinney

OFFERTORY PRAYER:
Thank You, Father God, for giving to us the gift of faith that we might see and respond to Jesus Christ affirmatively. Thank You for Your graciousness and Your faithfulness that causes our faith in You to grow. We come today with tithes and offerings, eager that they might be used to help others come to have faith in Jesus Christ. Bless these gifts to that end we pray. In His name. Amen.

Introduction. The apostle John declares that the controlling motive which guided him in his writing of the Fourth Gospel was the desire that people might "believe that Jesus is the Christ, the Son of God, and that believing you may have life in his name" (20:31).

John describes the purpose behind the ministry of John the Baptist as being "that all might believe through him" (1:7).

The writer of the Book of Hebrews declares that faith is essential if we would find ourselves pleasing to God and if we would experience the rich reward that can come from Him (11:6).

Paul ascribes both the goodness and the greatness of Abraham, the father of the faithful, to the fact of his great faith in both the person and the promises of God (Rom. 4:9–21).

To believe in Jesus means that we accept Him to be all that God claims for Him and intended Him to be. To really believe in Jesus is to be open to Him and responsive to His instructions and suggestions. To really believe in Jesus is to follow Him as Lord and Teacher and Guide. To really believe in Jesus is to agree with Him and to cooperate with Him in His work in the world.

There are rich blessings that come to those who truly believe in Jesus.

I. Through believing in Jesus we become the children of God.

A. *Most of the contemporaries of Jesus robbed themselves of the privilege of becoming true sons and daughters of God* (John 1:11). Those who did recognize Him and respond to Him affirmatively as Savior enjoyed the privilege of becoming God's children (v. 12).

B. *We become the children of God through faith* (Gal. 3:26; John 3:14–16). The faith that makes a full commitment to Jesus Christ is that which brings us into a child's relationship to the Father God. Baptism, church membership, and a life of spiritual growth and ministry grow out of and result from this basic relationship that is established through believing in Jesus Christ as the Son of God.

II. Through believing in Jesus we avoid the death that sin brings (Rom. 6:23).

God spoke words of warning at the dawn of human history regarding the penalty of eating the forbidden fruit: "You may freely eat of every tree of the garden; but of the tree of the knowledge of good and evil you shall not eat, for in the day that you eat of it you shall die" (Gen. 2:16–17 RSV). Adam and Eve did sin and die spiritually. They cut themselves off from the life of God and from fellowship with Him. From that day until this, the human race has lived under the sentence of spiritual death until a new birth takes place which imparts the gift of eternal life (John 3:16; 5:24).

Through believing in Jesus as the One whom God has sent to be our Savior, we regain the life of God that was lost because of sin.

III. Through believing in Jesus we receive the removal of the condemnation of sin (3:17–18).

God takes no pleasure in the death of the wicked. The consequences which sin have brought on the human race break the heart of God. The Bible is a record of God's redemptive activity, seeking to make provisions that will make possible the removal of condemnation for sin and the restoration of life and the fellowship that was lost in the Garden of Eden.

John declares that God did not send Jesus into the world to condemn the world but that the world through Him might be saved. He also affirms that those who put faith in Jesus Christ as the Savior experience the removal of condemnation, and this means they receive the blessing of acceptance into the family of God (3:18).

These great verses of Scripture declare that God is for us rather than against us. God is far more eager to be gracious and forgiving than He is to be just and judgmental.

Many have negative feelings about God, but when these are analyzed, it is often discovered that they are but the results of our own guilty consciences. God is more eager to accept us than He is to reject us. Through Jesus Christ we can experience the joy of His acceptance.

IV. Through believing in Jesus we are granted God's full self-disclosure (1:51).

John's gospel opens with the declaration that Jesus Christ is the living Word of God who came to earth to be God's language, speaking to us of His love, His nature, and His purpose for us. The writer of the Book of Hebrews declares that Jesus Christ is God's final revelation of Himself to mankind (1:1-3). In John 1:51, Jesus makes an amazing claim in terms that we can understand today. He claims to be the stairway by which God comes down to men and by which men can ascend to be with God.

To appropriately understand what Jesus was saying, we need to be familiar with the experience of Jacob's great dream at Bethel in which he saw a ladder set up on the earth with the top of it reaching to heaven.(He saw the angels of God ascending and descending, and the Lord stood above it. The God of Abraham and of Isaac revealed Himself to Jacob in the loneliness of that night experience. God appeared to him with promises and encouragement. He recognized that experience as being "the house of God and the very gateway of heaven" (Gen. 28:10-17). It is one thing to experience the presence of God in the starry skies above or in the beauty of nature about us. It is another thing to come to know God personally through faith in and faithfulness to Jesus Christ.

Conclusion. We need to believe in Jesus Christ as the Son of God. We need to believe in Him because of who He is, because of what He accomplished, and because of what He can do in our lives today. It is through believing in Him as the Christ of God that we experience the peace of God (Rom. 5:1). We experience these great blessings of believing not because of human connections nor because of the accumulation of vast amounts of knowledge. We receive these blessings not because of the money we might possess or the achievements we might accomplish. We receive these great blessings through believing in Jesus Christ as the Son of God who came to be our Savior. Through believing in Jesus we find the way to the Father (John 14:6). Believe in Him today for the good of your own heart and life and for the good of those about you.   —*TTC*

* * *

SUNDAY EVENING, APRIL 1

TITLE: Before You Talk, Listen

Text: "**Son of man, go, get thee unto the house of Israel, and speak with my words unto them**" (Ezek. 3:4).

Scripture Reading: Ezekiel 2:8-3:21

Introduction. Few people, perhaps no one, have ever been ushered into God's service with such a vision of the Almighty as Ezekiel experienced. While still a young lad, the one who became a great prophet was carried to Babylon in 597 B.C. during the second invasion of Jerusalem. When he became thirty years of age, he had a vision of God, recorded in chapter 1, which scholars find difficult to reproduce for the edification of readers. The point of the vision was that God is everywhere, even in Babylon where the people were captive. He "stands within the shadow and keeps watch above his own" even when they are in difficult and dangerous places. What a blessing this must have been to the young man being called into God's prophetic ministry!

So overwhelmed was Ezekiel after the vision of divine glory that he fell on his face. The Spirit of God entered into him, however, and set him upon his feet. A voice informed him he was being sent to the rebellious children of Israel. Whether they heeded him or not, they would know that a prophet had been among them. The events that follow point out some basic considerations for one who feels called into God's service either "full-time" as a paid person serving as pastor, full-time evangelist, missionary, or on a church staff, or one who remains a layman and serves the Lord on a non-paid basis. The works may vary somewhat, but the basic things needed at the outset remain the same.

I. A "Thus saith the Lord."

God gave Ezekiel a book which symbolically contained the message He had for His people. Ezekiel was told to absorb it completely. When he did, it became in "my mouth as honey for sweetness" (3:3).

A commission from man is often disappointing because no power is given to carry it out. God, on the other hand, never lets His workers go without full resources. He is prepared to supply all their needs. Ezekiel, of course, lived before the Bible as we know it was compiled. Today, we have both the Old Testament for guidance and the New Testament as our complete and final authority. In addition, we have the Holy Spirit to aid us in interpreting the message. Although the Scriptures have come through many translations, we can with confidence accept most of the present versions as containing the truth of God for our lives. When we go out armed with the Sword of the Spirit, proclaiming it to a lost world, people will be saved. When we hold high the standards of righteous living for regenerated people, we can with confidence and assurance know that God will bless His efforts. If someone asks us what Zedekiah asked Jeremiah during the Jerusalem crisis, "Is there any word from the LORD?" (Jer. 37:17), we can reply that there is and we have it. The Bible contains the mind of God, the state of man, and the way of salvation. We can preach it if we have made it a part of our lives. Let us appropriate and use the resources God has made available for us.

II. A courage because of selflessness.

What makes a person bold? Is it not because, since he is committed to his ideals and convictions, he has no selfish goals or ambitions? Thus, he is not afraid of rejection because his pride is not at stake. He wishes only to do what is right as he understands it.

God gave Ezekiel a difficult job. He was called upon to preach to people who had become disenchanted and, therefore, rebellious. Their frustration caused them to vent their problems and discouragements upon God and thus upon anyone who came in God's name. Such an assignment is no easy task. One must, in accepting such a mission, forfeit all claim to personal attainment, finding his joy and fulfillment in doing what he feels to be the will of God for his life.

A missionary to a desolate and disease-ridden country in Africa was once told, "You will not live three years if you stay here." He replied, quietly, "I died the day I came." Courage means dying to self. Paul said, "I die daily" (1 Cor. 15:31). This is true selflessness and, therefore, genuine courage. A person, armed with this spirit, can accept the fact that whether the people hear or not, they will know that a prophet has been in their midst!

III. An identification with the people.

Before one can meet the spiritual needs of people, he must understand them. Often when we remain where people are for a while and see their problems, we react as Ezekiel did—silence, astonishment, and amazement come to us dramatically.

Ezekiel was told to "sit where they sit" before he was sent to preach. Unless a pastor "goes in and out" among the people, he does not know how to preach to them adequately.

One great preacher of another generation was "called on the carpet" by a committee because his preaching was deemed unsatisfactory. One man in the church defended him, saying, "I don't know whether his preaching is like it ought to be, but I know one thing. He stayed with me all night long when my wife was passing through a health crisis. He can preach any way he wants to. I love him for what he's meant to me as a pastor." Of course, this represents an overreaction from a person who had been helped greatly. Preaching is certainly important, both the content and the manner in which the message is delivered; but the point is certainly worthy of strong emphasis that until pastors live with their people and share their problems, they are not really prepared to preach to them.

IV. Now, it's time to preach.

At last the order came! God had made Ezekiel a "watchman unto the house of Israel" and commanded him to speak to the wicked with a word of warning. Living with the people does not mean that we soft-pedal our message. Far from it! A preacher must comfort when it is time to comfort, but he must condemn sin when it's time to condemn sin. God made it clear that the prophet's task is not to be successful, but rather to deliver the message. We are, of course, to be as winsome as possible and use our personalities in pleasing ways even when we bring before the people their guilt. Our ultimate reward, however, is not whether they respond, but whether we have declared God's Word faithfully.

Conclusion. To preach, we must first of all have something to preach. This involves listening to God. A woman spent a long time giving her new cook instructions. She said, "In the time it takes me to tell you what to do, I could do it myself!" The cook replied, "Yes, and in the time it takes me to listen, so could I." Listening does take time, but not as much as some folks think. The average person can listen faster than he talks, but the average person also enjoys talking more than listening.

Ezekiel listened and became a great prophet. So did Isaiah and Jeremiah! So will every Christian, whether a "preacher" or a layman who wishes to witness! Let us learn to listen in order that we may have the message when it comes our time to speak!

—*FMW*

* * *

WEDNESDAY EVENING, APRIL 4

TITLE: The Church at Thessalonica

TEXT: "Paul, Silvanus, and Timothy, To the church of the Thessalonians in God the Father and the Lord Jesus Christ: Grace to you and peace" (1 Thess. 1:1).

SCRIPTURE READING: 1 Thessalonians 1:1–10

Introduction. First Thessalonians is one of the earliest letters written by Paul, possibly the first. Although brief, it is an important revelation from the Lord. The Book of Acts provides background material in understanding Paul's relationship to the church. Paul went to Thessalonica from Philippi; and his brief stay, probably no longer than a few months, was marked with much success. Some unconverted Jews in the city became jealous and tried to seize Paul and Silas (Acts 17). They fled the city for Berea and then Athens where similar incidents occurred.

While in Corinth Paul received a report about Thessalonica from Timothy. Some in the church were confused about the Lord's return and had quit working. Divisions had erupted in the fellowship. Paul writes to strengthen the young congregation and reestablish his relationship. The letter is also a challenge to remain faithful during persecution. The first verse is in the form of a traditional greeting, but the words are carefully chosen and full of truth about the church.

I. The church's position in the world.

A. *The church gathered:* ". . . the *church* of the Thessalonians." The word *church* is the Greek word *ekklesia,* which means a "called-out assembly." The church exists for a special purpose; it consists of believers who have been called out of sin into holiness (1 Peter 2:9). The call came because of the Father's love and was brought to us by the Lord Jesus Christ. In worship the church celebrates the gift of life and prepares for ministry in the world.

B. *The church scattered:* ". . . the church *of the Thessalonians.*" The redeemed are called from sin to live for Christ in a particular place. The Thessalonian Christians faced a tremendous challenge. Their city was a cosmopolitan commercial crossroads. Pagan religions and materialism abounded. It was possible for them to fulfill the Great Commission in their own city for people of many nations traveled through Thessalonica.

Every church of the Lord has been called to serve and witness. We are "in the world but not of the world." What about the church in our city? Are we obedient where we are? Tal Bonham wrote of two kinds of churches— "uttermost only and Jerusalem only. . . . A church cannot justify a low profile in local evangelism by claiming to be a 'great mission church' on the basis of money given. . . . A New Testament church has the world on its heart— beginning at its own front door."

II. The power of the church.

The church is a divine body, and the power to accomplish her mission rests in God the Father and in the Lord Jesus Christ. This implies an experiential encounter with Christ, who builds the church with people who acknowledge His lordship. Paul affirmed he could do "all things in him who strengthens me" (Phil. 4:13). The degree we are "in Christ" will determine our impact on the world. Our zeal in witnessing, our coping with persecution, our relationships with people, and our victory in temptation are all derived from abiding in Christ. The success of the Thessalonian church was because they were "in the Lord."

III. The person the church exalts.

The church exists to exalt "the Lord Jesus Christ." He is the cornerstone; the church is the body of Christ. Paul notes three things about Jesus:

A. *Lord.* This is the Greek equivalent to the Old Testament name "Jehovah." Jesus is God! As Lord we are to make Him first in our lives. He is Lord of the church and Lord of each life.

B. *Jesus.* The angel said to Joseph, "Thou shalt call his name JESUS: for he shall save his people from their sins" (Matt. 1:21). Jesus is our Savior— forever adequate for the sin problem.

C. *Christ.* He is the Messiah, the fulfillment of Israel's hope. Jesus is God's Anointed One. Peter confessed Him as the Christ, but Jesus clarified the meaning of the messiahship when He talked about the cross (Matt. 16:13-27).

Conclusion. What one decides about Jesus is the crucial decision. When a church loses the distinctive message of "the Lord Jesus Christ," she has lost what the world most needs and cannot expect the Lord's power to bless her efforts.

—BW

* * *

SUNDAY MORNING, APRIL 8

TITLE: Why Did God Send His Son Into the World?

TEXT: "For God sent the Son into the world, not to condemn the world, but that the world might be saved through him" (John 3:17 RSV).

SCRIPTURE READING: John 3:14-21

HYMNS: "Have Faith in God," McKinney
"'Tis So Sweet to Trust in Jesus," Stead
"Whosoever Will," Bliss

OFFERTORY PRAYER:

Father in heaven, we thank You for the privilege of being able to come to Your house to join with others in prayer and praise and proclamation of the Good News. We thank You that we can unite our offerings together to make a significant offering that the good news of Your love can be published not only in this community, but to the ends of the earth. Bless these tithes and offerings to that end; we pray in Jesus' name. Amen.

Introduction. John, the beloved apostle, specifically reveals to us the controlling motive that guided him in the selection of both events and the words of our Lord as he wrote his gospel (John 20:30-31). He was seeking to encourage and assist people in believing that Jesus was the Christ and that through believing in Him they could receive the gift of eternal life. John's motive was evangelistic.

A ministerial student was given an assignment to talk with successful people concerning the essentials for success. A professor of psychology in a Christian college gave him a good suggestion. She said, "Make the plan of salvation very simple and repeat it often." John the apostle writes in order to make the plan of salvation easily understood, and he repeats it often throughout his gospel.

Our text speaks of the primary purpose of God for sending His Son Jesus Christ into the world. John makes two statements, one negative and one positive. The negative statement is that God did not send His Son into the world to condemn it. The positive statement is that God sent His Son into the world that the world might be saved through Him.

I. God sent His Son into the world to reveal His all-inclusive love.

A. *Some thought that God loved only the chosen people of Israel.* They believed that all others were under the condemnation of God. Jesus came to reveal that both Jews and Gentiles were included in the love of God. It was necessary that Jesus use some restraint in revealing how broad the love of God was lest He alienate people who had narrow views of God's love. It remained for the apostles, particularly Peter and Paul, to be used to show that God's love also extended to other people.

B. *Some people thought that God loved only the very successful who kept the law perfectly.* The Pharisees were in this group. They were prominent and influential. They were the religious leaders of that day. They had a narrow concept of the love of God and believed that all who fell below the standard of perfect obedience to the law were outside the concern of God.

C. *John tells us that God did not send Jesus Christ into the world to criticize, to cut off, to condemn, or to put down.* God sent His Son into the world that the world might be saved through Him.

II. God sent His Son into the world to save men from perishing.

A. *Christ came to save us from ignorance of the true nature of God.* He came to reveal that God is love, that God is merciful, and that God is gracious. He came to reveal that the Holy God comes to us with the offer of forgiveness and cleansing.

By His coming Jesus revealed the nature of man as God meant for it to be.

By His coming Jesus revealed life as a qualitative experience spent in service to God and to others as God meant for it to be.

B. *Christ came into the world to save us from the stupidity of the self-destructiveness of sin.* The Prodigal Son is a classic illustration of those who neglect to believe or who refuse to believe that God is good and that the best place for us is in the Father's house and in His will.

Sin is a form of moral insanity. It is a road that leads to self-destructiveness in every area.

C. *Christ came not only to save us from the consequences of our sin in the past, but He also came to save us from the power of sin in the present.* He came also to save us from the presence of sin in the future.

D. *Christ came into the world to save men from perishing in both the present and the future.* Jesus speaks of a place called hell more than any other New Testament character. He came in order that we might be saved from this terrible fate. He did not want us to die and spend eternity away from God. He came that we might find the way to the Father (John 14:6). By deciding to become children of God, we avoid spending eternity in the place prepared for the devil and his angels (Matt. 25:41).

III. God sent His Son into the world to provide a simple way of salvation:

". . . that whosoever believes in him should not perish but have eternal life" (John 3:16).

If we would find the way to God, we will not find it through obedience to a law or through outstanding efforts to achieve our highest and best. We will find it only through faith in Jesus Christ.

A. *To experience salvation we must believe with all our hearts that Jesus Christ is God's Son.* Jesus was more than just one of the children of God. He was the unique and only begotten Son of God. He was the only one of His kind. He was the eternal God with a human body and a human face. He came on a mission from heaven to earth.

B. *To experience salvation we need to believe with all our hearts that God is as Jesus declared Him to be.* We need to recognize and respond to the revelation of the Father God in and through Jesus Christ. As we believe that God relates to us as a loving Father, we find that we can commit ourselves to Him with joy and confidence. Only as we relate to Him in a faith relationship can we experience the lifting power of His great love for us.

C. *To experience salvation, we need to believe with all our hearts that God will do for us what He has promised to do.* The New Testament contains many promises from God to His people. We need to recognize and to claim these promises.

The men and women of God through the ages who have experienced inward joy and who have achieved significantly in service to others have been those who believed that God was dependable and reliable.

Conclusion. The great Charles Haddon Spurgeon said that there are at least three essential elements in the faith that saves. These elements are knowledge, mental assent, and trust.

1. You need to *know* something significant about God in order to be able to really believe in Him. To get this information about God, we need to study the Word of God. The faith that saves is based on information that we have about God that comes to us through the Holy Scriptures.

2. The second element of this faith that saves is *mental assent*. There must be a willingness in the mind to give consent and assent to the truth about God, man, and life as it is revealed in the New Testament.)

3. The third and final element in this saving faith is *trust*. This means commitment and dependence upon God. It means to place confidence in. It means to make the leap of faith and to pin your hopes on Jesus Christ as the One who came to be your Savior.

The faith that saves is a decisive decision made by an individual in response to Jesus Christ. John wrote his gospel to help you have that kind of trust in Jesus Christ. "For God sent the Son into the world, not to condemn the world, but that the world might be saved through him."   —*TTC*

* * *

SUNDAY EVENING, APRIL 8

TITLE: **We Are Responsible for the Lost**

TEXT: **"When I say unto the wicked, Thou shalt surely die; and thou givest him not warning . . . his blood will I require at thine hand" (Ezek. 3:18).**

SCRIPTURE READING: **Ezekiel 3:17–21**

Introduction. Returning for a moment to the message of last Sunday, we see that God compared Ezekiel's duty to warn the wicked as that of a "watchman unto the house of Israel." In days when alien armies wandered ruthlessly through the land and came upon both walled and unwalled cities without warning, the watchman was of supreme importance. Taking his place in an elevated tower, he saw the enemy coming and immediately sent an urgent message to the community nearby.

The figure of speech is clear! The watchman's duty is to warn; the people's duty is to heed the warning. So it is with the one who speaks for God. He cannot make a sinner repent but can only warn of the judgment in store for one who insists upon living in rebellion to God.

I. People without the Lord are lost.

Turning for a moment to the New Testament, we can pour its content into this passage from Ezekiel, giving it a spiritual meaning. The person without Christ is not only a sinner, for all have come short of God's glory; but he is lost and doomed to an eternity of punishment. Jesus spoke often of hell and told one story of a man who went there while one whom he knew and mistreated upon earth went to heaven, illustrated by the familiar Jewish symbol of "Abraham's bosom." Jesus spoke of hell as a place where the "worm dieth not and the fire is not quenched"; John pictured it as a lake of fire.

II. God commands Christians to care.

The New Testament counterpart to Ezekiel's figure of speech is that of the Christian going out to witness concerning the work of Christ and the necessity for people to repent. To do this, we must have the kind of compassion that Jesus had when He looked at the multitudes and saw them as sheep without a shepherd. Two specific occasions stand out in the post-resurrection days of Jesus concerning the importance of telling others about the Savior. On a mountain in Galilee, Jesus told a group (probably the "above five hundred brethren" mentioned by Paul [1 Cor. 15:6]) that they were to "teach all nations" concerning His redemptive work (Matt. 28:19). On a mountain outside Jerusalem only a moment before He ascended to heaven, Jesus told His disciples that they were to be witnesses for Him "to the uttermost parts of the earth" (Acts 1:8). These two incidents put the responsibility squarely on Christians to warn others of the fate in store for those who will not receive the message of salvation. Of course, the job is big. A discouraged person of another century said to the Duke of Wellington, "Are Christians really obligated to tell the message of Christ to all the world?" He replied, "What were the marching orders of your Commander?" He replied, "Oh, that's easy. He told us to take the message to everyone." The military man responded, "If those are the marching orders of your Commander, you have no alternative."

III. To fail is a serious thing.

In Ezekiel's day, the watchman was guilty of blood if he failed to warn the people of coming danger. The prophet made it clear that if the messenger fails to warn the wicked, God will require his blood at the watchman's hand. This same principle applies in the New Testament. To be indifferent to the spiritual needs of our fellow-man and fail to tell him the gospel story is a serious thing. The New Testament is not clear as to how far God would go in requiring a lost person's blood at our hands, but no Christian should want that responsibility on his shoulders. A man who had spent many years in sin was converted late in life but fell terminally ill. He had no doubt of his own salvation, but as death approached he was haunted by the fact that he had won few, if any, people to the Lord since his new birth. He wrote a haunting song:

> Must I go, and emptyhanded?
> Must I meet my Saviour so?
> Not one soul with which to greet Him;
> Must I emptyhanded go?
>
> Not at death I shrink nor falter,
> For my Saviour saves me now;
> But to meet Him emptyhanded,
> Thought of that now clouds my brow.

Conclusion. Although the Scripture in Ezekiel does not emphasize rewards except to say that the faithful watchman will "deliver his soul," other passages speak of great joy that comes to those who are faithful in proclaiming God's Word. A later prophet (Dan. 12:3) spoke of those who "turn many to righteousness" shining "like the brightness of the firmament," which indicates God approves of those who seek to be helpful in bringing people to Christ. Jesus spoke of the "peacemakers" who He says shall be called "children of God."

In a sense, the joy of leading another to Christ is sufficient reward, but God holds out other good things for the one who makes believers of others. Recently, this writer had the joy of having as a visitor on a Sunday morning a young man whom he had led to Christ twenty-seven years earlier but had lost touch with over the years. The joy of talking with this young man and his wife and finding they were active Christians was fulfilling.

While emphasizing the seriousness of not witnessing, we also should stress the delight and ecstasy that comes in seeing one, led to Christ by our own efforts, blossom into a full-grown Christian and return at a later time to bless us. Let's be good watchmen, accept our responsibility, and leave the rewards to God!

—*FMW*

* * *

WEDNESDAY EVENING, APRIL 11

TITLE: **Grace and Peace**

Text: **". . . Grace to you and peace"** (1 Thess. 1:1c RSV).

Scripture Reading: **1 Thessalonians 1:1; 1 Corinthians 15:9–10**

Introduction. Paul's greeting to the Thessalonian Christians included two words traditionally used by Greeks and Hebrews when they greeted each other.

Paul's use is much deeper, for these two words describe the entire work of Christ. The greeting goes to individuals and to the whole church. Peace flows from grace; where grace is at work, peace will be present.

I. Grace for individuals.

Many ideas are embodied in the word *grace*. It is used for prayer at the table as well as to describe personalities. Lofton Hudson wrote a book entitled *Grace Is Not a Blue-eyed Blonde*. In the New Testament grace primarily means God's gift.

A. *Grace that saves*. In our sin God graciously seeks us and forgives us. Salvation is the work of God's grace from the beginning to the end (Rom. 3:23-24). Paul told the Ephesians, "By grace are ye saved through faith; . . . it is the gift of God: not of works, lest any man should boast" (2:8-9). If someone asked Paul what he meant by grace, he would probably say, "That which encountered me on the Damascus Road."

Saving grace brings peace. "Therefore, since we are justified by faith, we have peace with God through our Lord Jesus Christ" (Rom. 5:1 RSV). There is no more enmity brought on by sin.

B. *Grace that sustains*. James Moffatt said, "Grace is more than pardon; it is power which makes a man efficient for all the challenges . . . of life." It was God's grace that enabled Paul, the zealous Pharisee, to love Gentiles. Grace enabled him to cope with his "thorn in the flesh." Paul affirmed, "By the grace of God I am what I am. . . . I worked harder than any of them, though it was not I, but the grace of God which is with me" (1 Cor. 15:10 RSV).

Sustaining grace brings peace. We are admonished to commit our problems in prayer to the grace of God. The result will be "the peace of God, which passes all understanding" (Phil. 4:7).

II. Grace for the church.

A. *A church where grace is manifest*. Paul desires the Thessalonian church to be a fellowship where God's grace works in a mighty way, a place where people are being saved. Such a church possesses the deepest peace and the strongest unity. Petty problems are quickly overlooked when sinners are being saved. A contagious spirit of enthusiasm prevails in a church where grace is at work.

B. *A church sustained by grace*. The Thessalonian Christians were facing persecution. God's grace is sufficient. Jesus promised, "I will build my church; and the gates of hell shall not prevail against it" (Matt. 16:18). His grace at work in the church is more powerful than the forces of evil outside.

Conclusion. Grace and peace to you! These were not just words passing through the apostle's lips. They describe his deepest longing and the desire he also expressed to the Colossians, Philippians, Ephesians, Galatians, Corinthians, and Romans. He yearned for grace and peace to rest upon Philemon, Titus, and Timothy. These gifts are still available to each Christian and every church.

—*BW*

* * *

SUNDAY MORNING, APRIL 15

TITLE: The Weeping King

TEXT: "'Blessed is the King who comes in the name of the Lord! Peace in heaven and glory in the highest!' . . . And when he drew near and saw the city he wept over it" (Luke 19:38, 41 RSV).

SCRIPTURE READING: Luke 19:28–44

HYMNS: "Crown Him With Many Crowns," Bridges
"Great Redeemer, We Adore Thee," Harris
"I Will Sing the Wondrous Story," Rowley

OFFERTORY PRAYER:

Father, You have given us the power to get wealth, and we rejoice in the fruits of our labors. Today we come bringing a portion of the income You have blessed us with, and we would dedicate it to Your service. Accept these gifts as life in crystallized form, and use them for the advancement of Your kingdom in this community and to the ends of the earth. Amen.

Introduction. The first inquiry concerning Jesus Christ brought the request, "Where is he that is born King of the Jews?" The last formal introduction of Jesus Christ before His death on the cross was worded in the superscription that was placed upon that cross: "Jesus of Nazareth, the King of the Jews."

In His temptation experience, Jesus was offered the kingdoms of this world on the devil's terms. He rejected kingship on that basis.

In the Sermon on the Mount Jesus described the nature of His kingdom and the characteristics of the citizens of His kingdom.

Throughout His ministry Jesus demonstrated kingly authority over the demonic, over disease, and over death.

There were times when His disciples wanted to make Him a king. They were thinking of His being a nationalistic and political king, who would reestablish the sovereignty of the nation of Israel as a political force in the world. Jesus rejected that kind of kingship.

In His triumphal entry into Jerusalem at the beginning of Passion Week, our Lord boldly and compassionately offered Himself as the King of love and grace.

The triumphal entry, which is recorded in all four of the Gospels (Matt. 21:1–11; Mark 11:1–11; Luke 19:29–44; John 12:12–19), was Jesus' bold declaration of His messiahship and His claim to be the Christ of God. He came into Jerusalem, not to assert His sovereign rights to the throne of David's political kingdom, but to declare His kingship in the hearts of those who would trust Him and follow Him. William Barclay has described this most beautifully and significantly: "He came lowly and riding upon an ass. We must be careful to see the real meaning of that. In western lands the ass is a despised beast; but in eastern lands, the ass could be a noble animal. Often a king came riding upon an ass; but when he came upon an ass, it was the sign that he *came in peace. The horse was the mount of war! The ass was the mount of peace.* So when Jesus claimed to be king, He claimed to be the king of peace. He showed that He came, not to destroy, but to love; not to condemn, but to help; not in the might of arms, but in the strength of love" (*The Gospel of Matthew,* Vol. II [Philadelphia: Westminister Press], p. 267).

Luke describes one experience in connection with the triumphal entry that is not recorded by the other apostles. Luke records, "And when he drew near and saw the city he wept over it, saying, 'Would that even today you knew the things that make for peace! But now they are hid from your eyes'" (19:41–42). Here we see the King weeping over the city.

The King was not weeping for Himself. These were not tears of self-pity, remorse, or personal failure. They were the tears of a King suffering for His people.

I. The King was weeping because of the compassion of perfect knowledge.

His heart was filled with compassion for His people. He was experiencing the pain of a shallow acceptance, which did not deceive Him into believing that the people were willing to accept a King of love, grace, mercy, and righteousness.

He had a perfect knowledge of the situation as it was in the past, in the present, and in the future; and this caused His heart to break with compassionate concern.

II. The King was weeping because of the blindness and deafness of the city.

Throughout His earthly ministry Jesus restored sight to the blind and made it possible for the deaf to hear on many occasions. He did this in order to help the people see the need to really use their eyes for seeing and their ears for hearing.

Jesus sought to minister to a group of people whose minds were filled with conceit and complacency. They had a feeling of spiritual superiority when they considered those about them. They were preoccupied with their own ways and goals and were unwilling to open up their minds to new truth about God as Jesus was trying to communicate it.

They were spiritually and morally blind and deaf and would not permit themselves to see and hear. This caused the King to weep on their behalf.

III. The King was weeping because the city was passing up its opportunity forever.

Once opportunity comes to us, if it is not recognized and seized, we miss it and it is gone forever.

Jesus knew in a way that we can never know what His people were missing because of their unwillingness to believe and to respond to Him as the Messiah of love. He wept because they were passing up their unique opportunity.

IV. The King was weeping over the city because it was on a collision course with disaster.

Jesus could forsee that the nation was on a collision course with political disaster. He describes this in Matthew 24, in which He foretells the destruction of the temple and the calamity that was to befall the city. His predictions became reality by A.D. 70 when Titus the Roman general captured and destroyed the city.

V. The tears of a weeping King provide us with an index to His character.

Jesus came to reveal the nature and character of God to man. He came to reveal that God is not cold, distant, removed, and unconcerned. He came to reveal that God loves and wants to save man from his self-destructiveness.

A. *Paul describes the compassion of this King who, though He existed in the form of God, did not hold on to the prerogatives of that position, but poured*

Himself out into the form of a man in order that He might come and rescue man from sin (Phil. 2:5–8).

B. *This God-appointed King submitted to the humiliation and the pain of crucifixion in order that He might reveal the heart concern of God for His people* (Matt. 27:32–44). The tears of the King reveal the heartbreak of God.

V. The tears of the weeping King reveal the divine helplessness.

A. *The King was omnipotent in creation.*

B. *The King is omnipotent in keeping the machinery of the universe in perfect coordination.*

C. *The King has no omnipotence in human hearts until He is invited to come in and take the place of authority.*

Conclusion. It is easy for us to be critical of those who rejected the claims of the King during His earthly ministry. Before we condemn them, however, we need to inquire as to whether or not we have rejected or ignored the kingly claims of Him who conquered death and the grave and who will someday come back as the King of Glory.

When we look at the world and see how few have even heard the good news of the Christ, we must admit that we have either rejected or ignored the command of the King to carry the Good News to the ends of the earth.

As His disciples, we need to recognize that we have robbed ourselves of the promise of His kingly companionship when we have neglected to recognize His authoritative command to evangelize the world (Matt. 28:19–20).

Jesus was born to be our King. We need to make Him the Lord of our lives. We need to let Him be the Lord of love in our homes. We need to let Him be Lord in our vocations. We need to let Him be the Lord in our decision-making processes.

He would have us do the good will of God in the present even as it is done by the angels in heaven. Let us crown Him King in our hearts today.   *—TTC*

* * *

SUNDAY EVENING, APRIL 15

TITLE: God Accepts No Proxy Religion

Text: "As I Live, saith the Lord God . . . the soul that sinneth, it shall die" (Ezek. 18:3–4).

Scripture Reading: Ezekiel 18:1–4

Introduction. Proverbs have a way of weaving themselves into the fabric of a country's heritage. The prophets and poets of Israel and Judah appropriated sayings that had been used by others and incorporated into their sermons and poems. More than we sometimes realize, this is done in today's religious world also.

The Jews had a saying that seems to have dated back many centuries. It goes like this: "The fathers have eaten sour grapes, and the children's teeth are set on edge" (Ezek. 18:2). It may have had some variations, but the basic idea was the same. One does not suffer for his sins. The punishment is postponed until another generation. This may have been a perversion of understanding the words from

Moses in the Ten Commandments, "I the LORD thy God am a jealous God, visiting the iniquity of the fathers upon the children unto the third and fourth generations of them that hate me" (Exod. 20:5). Both Jeremiah and Ezekiel confronted this philosophy head on and insisted that God does not operate that way. From the words of Ezekiel, some thoughts come to stimulate our minds and bless our hearts.

I. Sometimes it seems to be true.

Someone has spoken of a "golden rule" for the expositor, and this chapter illustrates that idea. We should interpret others the way we wish they would understand us. We should bear in mind that when a new idea comes, one often cannot introduce it without seeming to disparage previous truth. For instance, we *do* suffer for the sins of a previous generation, and generations after us will suffer for our sin.

For instance, if one generation is immoral, another generation will suffer for it. Some physical deformities are due to indiscretions on the part of the parents. Medical science is warning expectant mothers in strong terms today concerning their eating and drinking habits during the period they are carrying the baby in the womb. Personal hygiene is of utmost importance both before and after the conception of a child. A generation can spend money unwisely and hopelessly mortgage those who are to follow. Solomon, for instance, left his nation with a great problem because he lacked integrity in several areas of his life and reign. The prophet knew this truth well, but this was not his point!

II. We suffer ourselves.

Although there is a "human solidarity" whereby each generation commits those who come after it, there is also an individual responsibility we cannot escape. The natural sequence of cause and effect is used by God in order to discipline our own lives; and, in this function, He sees to it that the individual receives a due reward for his deeds. God does not hold a man responsible for the circumstances into which he was born but only what he does with them after he comes to this world. God cuts a straight path of personal accountability through the "tangled undergrowth" of our personal heredity. We are not hopelessly trapped. We can and must assume an obligation for the world into which we come.

III. How can we adjust the seeming inconsistencies?

One who wishes to refute the contentions thus far may say, "But how do you explain the prosperity of the wicked? Some never get their deserved punishment. They die prosperous even as they have lived in affluence. Also, what about good people who never receive the rewards of their lives? They die without reward. Is God fair? Does this principle really hold?"

This is why there is a need for a heaven and a hell. As the Christian farmer said to the non-Christian farmer who boasted that his crops were better at harvest than his neighbor's though he worked them on Sunday, "God does not settle all His accounts in October." Neither does God give final rewards on this earth. In a sense, of course, the one who lives the righteous life finds that the laws of the universe, given by God, cooperate with Him and produce a stable and successful operation. But when things don't work out that way, we should remember there are both a heaven and a hell. All things are adjusted in eternity.

One evangelist said there were three reasons why he knew there was a heaven. First, fairness told him so; second, feeling told him so; and third, faith told him so. The first point is particularly well taken. God is fair and, therefore, even when the principle of goodness being rewarded does not work out on earth, there is another world in which the accounts can be adjusted and balanced.

IV. Salvation is not by works.

In stressing this interpretation, we need to remember that salvation does not come by doing more good things than bad things. Receiving Jesus as Savior makes one a new creature and assures a place in the heavenly home. One does not become a righteous person by doing righteous deeds but rather by accepting the atoning work of Christ, who is our righteousness.

All of us are sinners; and if God gave us what we deserve, none of us would go to heaven but all would end up in hell. We should not confuse personal salvation by faith in Christ with the rewards of good deeds in a life to come. Both are true, but we need to keep our thinking straight. The application of this principle that every person must suffer for his own sin, and the logical counterpart that every person will be rewarded for his own deeds, was used by the prophet to stress the importance of the individual in God's sight.

V. A further truth.

God's Word is so full that many "side lessons" come to us in addition to the main teaching of a verse. Here, we have a basic concept that has shaken the world with the truth implicit within it. The individual is of utmost importance. Jesus enlarged upon this and brought it to full fruition in His teachings. The Christian faith has stood for it through the years.

What is this truth? Every individual is competent to stand before God and, therefore, *must* stand before God. God will accept no proxy in religious life. A parent cannot accept Jesus for his child. Neither can a child accept Jesus for his parent. We can bring influences to bear, but the decision remains with the individual.

Conclusion. How wonderful to find that centuries before Christ ever came, God was working. Indeed, the Old Testament Scriptures speak of Him often and His message continuously. In Ezekiel we see a prophet in captivity speaking to rebellious people, but he projects to them one of the most profound truths ever to come from the heart of God.

Are you utilizing your abilities to their fullest? Are you trying to be yourself rather than someone else? God does not call upon you to be or to do that of which you are incapable. Neither will He let you do for another what that person can do for himself. Proxies are accepted in stockholders' meetings, but heaven is not carried on by a board of directors. God loves every individual; but, even more, God demands that every individual choose for himself!   —*FMW*

* * *

WEDNESDAY EVENING, APRIL 18

TITLE: I Hope So? Or I Know!

TEXT: "For we know, brethren beloved by God, that he has chosen you" (1 Thess. 1:4 RSV).

SCRIPTURE READING: 1 Thessalonians 1:2–10

Introduction. Ask the question, "Are you certain of eternal life?" and the answer is likely to be one of three responses: "No"; "I hope so; no one can know for certain"; or "Yes, I am sure!" An insecure Christian is susceptible to evil. An uncertain Christian spends time working to stay secure rather than glorifying Christ and reaching others. Paul was confident of the Thessalonians' salvation—"We know . . . that he has chosen you." Jesus said it was possible for all men to know "that you are my disciples" (John 13:35). How can we know? Paul cites three assurances of salvation.

I. Source of salvation.

A. *Beloved by God.* "See what love the Father has given us, that we should be called children of God; and so we are" (1 John 3:1). Imagine a young man giving his fiancée a diamond ring with the stipulation, "If you happen to lose that ring, it's all over." Genuine love is complete and unreserved, "for better or for worse." Marital love is an earthly pattern of God's love. Our salvation is secure because it rests on the eternal love of God. The Roman Christians were reminded that nothing "shall be able to separate us from the love of God, which is in Christ Jesus our Lord" (8:39).

B. *Grounded in the Word, communicated by the Holy Spirit.* "Our gospel came to you not only in word, but also in power and in the Holy Spirit and with full conviction" (1 Thess. 1:5 RSV). H. A. Ironside said, "Faith rests on the naked Word of God; that Word believed gives full assurance." The Holy Spirit utilizes the Word of God to convict us of sin, judgment, and the righteousness of Christ.

We can be sure of our salvation because the source is the love of God, communicated by the Holy Spirit through the Bible and leaving us with the assurance we have done what the Word requires.

II. Response to salvation.

Paul had confidence in the Thessalonians' relationship with God because they had "received the word" (v. 6). Two elements are involved in that response.

A. *Repentance.* "You turned to God from idols" (v. 9). Repentance means to turn in a new direction. Thessalonica was located fifty miles from Mt. Olympus, considered to be the home of the gods. The Thessalonians had renounced dead idols for the living Lord. Authentic conversion is a change of loyalty and lifestyle.

B. *Faith.* Repentance turns us away from sin, and faith turns us "to God." Faith is the individual's response to God's love. "To all who received him, who believed in his name, he gave power to become children of God" (John 1:12 RSV).

III. Results of salvation.

Jesus said, "You shall know them by their fruits" (Matt. 7:16). Paul noticed the results evident in the lives of the Thessalonian believers.

A. *Example.* They followed good examples (v. 6) and "became an example" for others (v. 7). Practice backed up their profession.

B. *Witness.* "The word of the Lord sounded forth from you" (v. 8 RSV). The phrase uses the illustration of a trumpet blast or roll of thunder—bold, excited, confident witnesses. How different this is from the mild, timid, and tepid witness given by some believers.

C. *Anticipation.* "To wait for his Son from heaven" (v. 10 RSV). No dread or fear fell over them as they faced the future with uncertainty because of persecution. A song expresses the Christian's confidence: "Many things about tomorrow I don't seem to understand, but I know who holds tomorrow and I know He holds my hand."

Conclusion. Five days before Pulitzer Prize writer William Sarroyan died, he wrote, "Everybody has got to die, but I have always believed an exception would be made in my case. Now what?" The confident Christian knows what is beyond death.   —*BW*

* * *

SUNDAY MORNING, APRIL 22

TITLE: Guess Who Came to Church This Morning?

TEXT: **"Then I turned to see the voice that was speaking to me, and on turning I saw seven golden lampstands, and in the midst of the lampstands one like a son of man. . . . 'For where two or three are gathered in my name, there am I in the midst of them'" (Rev. 1:12; Matt. 18:20 RSV).**

SCRIPTURE READING: **Revelation 1:9–20**

HYMNS: **"Hallelujah! Christ Is Risen," Wordsworth
"Christ the Lord Is Risen Today," Wesley
"He Lives," Ackley**

OFFERTORY PRAYER:
Father God, we come to the church of the living Lord today that we might bow in worship before Him. We come bringing tithes and offerings, portions of our lives in crystallized form, that we might dedicate ourselves to Him in His service. Accept these gifts and use them to publish the good news of His death for our sins upon the cross and His victorious resurrection from the dead. We pray in Jesus' name. Amen.

Introduction. This is Easter Sunday. Guess who came to church this morning? As you look about you, you see some faces that are familiar. They are here every Lord's Day. You can also see the faces of friends who moved away but who have returned for this special time of the year. In our joy of greeting and welcoming guests, we need to be cautious lest we overlook the presence of our special Guest this morning.

This is Easter Sunday. This is the one day out of the year in which we celebrate in a special way the resurrection of Jesus Christ from the dead. It is altogether proper that many people come to the house of prayer and worship on this day. It is most appropriate that we should have many guests with us today. If a person could attend church on only one Sunday out of the year, we would not be surprised if they would choose Easter Sunday for that significant experience.

Easter tells us that the death of Christ on the cross was not a disaster. Easter tells us that love is stronger than hate and that in God's heart life is stronger than death. Today we would recognize that it was Easter which gave to us a living Christ, who is to be with us in our hearts all of the time; and He is to be with us in a special way when we come together for worship. He made that promise to His disciples when He said, "For where two or three are gathered in my name, there am I in the midst of them" (Matt. 18:20).

As the years stretched into decades following the resurrection of our Lord, there were those who became disillusioned and even depressed; particularly this happened as they experienced persecution and great suffering because of their loyalty to the lordship of Jesus Christ. The Book of Revelation was given to John the beloved apostle while he was in exile on the Isle of Patmos. He records, "I was in the Spirit on the Lord's day" (1:10) and there came to the eye of his soul a vision of the living Christ: "in the midst of the lampstands, one like a son of man" (v. 13). The word which is translated "in the midst" is the same word found in Matthew 18:20. Today we need to recognize and to respond to the promise of this living Lord to meet with His people when they come together for prayer, for praise, for proclamation, and for the purification that comes as a result of cleansing through confession.

Have you experienced the presence of this living Lord in this service today? He is here. May you have ears to hear and eyes to see the spiritual reality of His presence.

I. Our Lord is alive from the dead.

Jesus Christ is not merely a historical personage to whose great deeds we look back with admiration. He is alive, and we call Him Master. He is alive and has authority over death and the grave. We speak of Him as One who was, but He is also the One who *is*. His residence upon the earth was only one incident in His existence. His life did not begin in Bethlehem, nor did it conclude when He died on the cross. He is essentially the Living One.

John saw our Lord "in the midst" of the churches. In the person of the Holy Spirit, He came to abide with us and within us. He is not removed by an immeasurable space from where we are living and laboring. He is in the midst of us, quite near to us; He is accessible every hour. He is observant of our every action. In the fullest sense He is "with us."

John saw Him in the midst of the churches as the ruling Lord. He is described in terms indicating His sovereignty. During His earthly ministry He exercised authority over disease, the demonic, death, and natural events. Today we need to recognize the sovereignty of our Lord who manifested Himself as love, and we should become the channels for that love to reach others.

II. Our living Lord came to church today.

As we read the seven letters to the churches of Asia Minor which were recorded by John following His vision of the living Lord, we can discover the purpose Christ has for coming to church today.

A. *Christ came to church to commend us.* Christ wants to commend you in every area in which you are seeking to be and to what is good. He wants to affirm you and to encourage you. He sees and knows about your faithfulness and endurance, your generosity and kindness and helpfulness.

B. *Christ came to church to correct us.* He wants to correct us, not to condemn us. "God sent not his Son into the world to condemn the world; but that the world through him might be saved" (John 3:17). All of us need to check our road map. We need to make adjustments in our attitudes, ambitions, and actions. Jesus wants to help us do so.

C. *Christ came to church to cleanse us.* From time to time Jesus not only offered forgiveness, but granted forgiveness to those who came making confession. Every time we come to God's house we need to do some heart searching and put forth a sincere effort to confess and to turn from our every sin. Jesus is more eager that we experience the joy of cleansing than we realize.

D. *Christ came to church to complain.* Though He came to complain, He is not a complainer. He complains if we fail to be our best. He comes to complain if we are disobeying God. He comes to complain if we are mistreating others. He has a right to exercise authority over our lives. He wants to use us for the glory of God.

E. *Christ came to church to comfort us.* Some of us are greatly discouraged today. Some of us are lonely. Some of us are experiencing the pain of grief. Jesus Christ would comfort us today if we would but listen to Him.

F. *Christ came to church to commission us.* He has work for us to do. He has ministries for us to render. There is a needy world out there that needs to know about the love which took our Savior to the cross and the power that raised Him from the dead.

Conclusion. Yes, Christ came to church today. If you have not yet trusted Him as Lord and Savior, He is here to come into your heart and to bring you the gift of forgiveness, the gift of new life.

If you have already trusted Him as Savior, He is here not only to minister to you, but to use you in ministering to others.

This living Christ who has been with us today will go with us when we leave. Recognize Him, respond to Him, let Him be to you all He is able to be.

—*TTC*

* * *

SUNDAY EVENING, APRIL 22

TITLE: Whatever Comes, Serve the Lord

TEXT: "So I spake . . . in the morning: and at even my wife died; and I did in the morning as I was commanded" (Ezek. 24:18).

SCRIPTURE READING: Ezekiel 24:15–18

Introduction. To dissolve earthly ties is difficult. Perhaps the hardest of all to do is with a companion whom we have come to love and depend on through the years. Jeremiah had no wife and hence he never knew an experience such as that of Ezekiel. Hosea's domestic tragedy took another form. His wife left him for another lover. Ezekiel, however, lost his wife at a single stroke through death.

God came to Ezekiel with a strange command. He was to show no grief but continue "business as usual." Was God cold-hearted? Not at all! The people were in exile and needed an object lesson of one who could handle his grief and still be true to God. Ezekiel was the man, and his demonstration must have meant much to those who heard him.

I. A good woman is a choice gift of God.

Look at history and you will discover that most men who have achieved greatness had the help of a good companion.

Sometimes we forget to love those who mean much to us, or at least we fail to express our appreciation to them. Thomas Carlyle, that rugged individualist, neglected his wife and failed to let her know how much she meant to him. If you go to the old Abbey Kirk at Haddington, you can read over the grave of Jane Welch the first of many regretful tributes he paid to her: "For forty years she was a true and loving helpmate of her husband, and by act and word worthily forwarded him as none else could in all worthy he did or attempted. She died at London the 21st of April, 1866, suddenly snatched from him, and the light of his life is gone out." Someone has said that the saddest sentence in the English literature consists of those words written by Carlyle in his diary: "Oh, that I had you yet for five minutes by my side that I might tell you all." If you are a careless person, dealing carelessly with loved ones, acting as though you would have them always, hear these solemn words of warning from Carlyle: "Cherish what is dearest while you have it near you, and wait not till it is far away."

II. Death comes to all.

For the true believer in Jesus, death is a blessed and glorious event, the most wonderful experience that could ever come to anyone. Paul said, ". . . to die is gain" (Phil. 1:21). To the unbeliever, death is a nightmare. One skeptic of another generation said on his deathbed, "Until this moment I thought there was neither a God nor a hell. Now I know and feel there are both, and I am doomed to perdition by the just judgment of the Almighty." Whatever our attitude toward Christ, death is certain.

III. Life must go on.

Every human being has a work to do, even if his dearest friends leave him. A sense of duty pursues us always, omnipotent like God Himself. Daniel Webster said, "If we take to ourselves the wings of the morning and dwell in the uttermost parts of the sea, duty performed or duty violated is still with us, for our happiness or our misery. If we say the darkness shall cover us, in the darkness as in the light, our obligations are yet with us."

Ezekiel, being dedicated to God, continued his work though he did not understand why his companion was taken away. So often we do not have the answers as to why a painful thing happens. We must grope blindly in the darkness of uncertain light and pray that dawn will ripen into the day. Thomas Carlyle said, "Do the duty which lieth nearest to thee which thou knowest to be a duty. Thy second duty will already have become clearer."

IV. Sorrow can motivate.

The record does not tell us why God took Ezekiel's wife from him. Neither does it tell the end result of his bereavement. We can, however, be almost certain of one thing. When sorrow comes, we often become more tender and more useable in the Lord's service. Someone has said that suffering either makes us bitter or better. If we recognize God's wisdom in all things, we can learn great lessons from suffering and use them to serve the Lord more faithfully.

Jean Paul Richter said, "Sorrows gather around great souls as storms do around mountains; but like them, they break the storm and purify the air of the plains beneath them." He continues, "Has it never occurred to us, when surrounded by sorrows, that they may be sent to us only for our instruction, as we darken the eyes of birds when we wish them to sing.'' Lord Byron once wrote, ''Grief should be the instructor of the wise.'' Unless pain conquers us, it is not evil. Phillips Brooks once said, ''Wherever souls are being tried and ripened, in whatever commonplace and homely way, their God is hewing out the pillars for his temple.''

Conclusion. To give pious clichés is easy and we should refrain from doing so. On the other hand, everyone, pastor or layman, who has been a Christian a long time has seen examples of how suffering has made one more mellow. Ezekiel refused to resign from the human race because suffering came. He looked at his grief but he also looked at his God and decided that the latter was bigger than the former. He brushed his tears away and found his comfort in his work. So does everyone who follows his example!   —FMW

* * *

WEDNESDAY EVENING, APRIL 25

TITLE: How to Win Friends and Influence People—for Christ!

TEXT: **"So, being affectionately desirous of you, we were ready to share with you not only the gospel of God but also our own selves, because you had become very dear to us" (1 Thess. 2:8).**

SCRIPTURE READING: **1 Thessalonians 2:1–20**

Introduction. Dale Carnegie offers a popular self-improvement course designed to build self-esteem and strengthen relationships. The Bible is a book on developing and maintaining friendships—influencing people for Christ's sake. First Thessalonians 2 is a good demonstration of these biblical principles. Paul had great success in Thessalonica, partly attributable to the way he related to people. The key to Paul's approach is found in verse 8: ''You had become very dear to us.'' *Very dear* is the Greek word *agape*—God's love. This chapter describes the vital nature of love which Henry Drummond said was ''the greatest thing in the world.'' Four qualities of love are found in the chapter.

I. Authentic (vv. 3–5).
    Paul's day was noted for roaming philosophers, sorcerers, and other peddlers who used tricks to impress their audiences. Paul approached them with honesty and an absence of deception, deceit, and manipulation. He was honest, direct, and decisive.

II. Gentle (v. 7).
    The image is a mother breast-feeding her child—a picture of tenderness and selflessness. ''Love is patient and kind'' (1 Cor. 13:4). Part of the fruit of the Spirit is gentleness (Gal. 5:23), which involves patience, empathy, and merciful comparison. This quality is essential to win friends and influence people for Christ.

III. Firm (vv. 11–12).
    Paul shifts his image to that of a father who ''exhorted, encouraged, and charged'' his children to be all they could be. Love is not gullible, nor does it

ignore situations and evil which threaten "a life worthy of God." The father Paul has in mind cares for each one of his children and is personally involved to help each one toward maturity. Love is never effective at long distance.

IV. Current (vv. 13–19).

These verses refer to ways Paul sought to keep his love up-to-date. His love was deepened through daily prayer for the Thessalonians. He corresponded with them and "endeavored . . . with great desire to see you face to face." Paul was not too timid to say, "I love you." Possibly some of the inactive members in our churches have become that way because love from other members has not remained current. Outreach for Christ would be more effective if we expressed His love at times other than a special evangelistic effort.

Conclusion. How is your love life? is an important question for the Christian. Is your life characterized by love for people which is authentic, gentle, firm, and current? We cannot expect to win friends and influence people for Christ without love.   —*BW*

* * *

SUNDAY MORNING, APRIL 29

TITLE: Both Lord and Christ

Text: **"Let all the house of Israel therefore know assuredly that God has made him both Lord and Christ, this Jesus whom you crucified" (Acts 2:36 rsv).**

Scripture Reading: **Acts 2:32–36**

Hymns: **"All Hail the Power of Jesus' Name," Perronet**
"Christ the Lord Is Risen Today," Wesley
"Crown Him With Many Crowns," Bridges

Offertory Prayer:

Father in heaven, thank You for the power of the lordship of our living Lord. Today as we bow before Him with our gifts of tithes and offerings, bless them to the end that others shall come to know Him in His love and forgiveness and power. Amen.

Introduction. The resurrection of Jesus Christ was a great shock not only to those who put Him to death, but even to His beloved disciples.

The resurrection revealed that in a mysterious and miraculous way the purposes of God were at work in the substitutionary death of Jesus Christ on the cross for our sins.

It was only over a period of time, under the strong leadership of the Holy Spirit, that the disciples of our Lord came to understand that Christ was indeed a High Priest of good things to come and that by His death on the cross, He had offered Himself as a sacrifice for the sins of a guilty human race (Heb. 9:11–15). He became the Mediator of the new covenant and thus made it possible for God to be both just and merciful in dealing with our sins.

By raising Jesus Christ back to life, the eternal God was appointing Him to a position of authoritative lordship as well as recognizing His redemptive work on the cross. In our text Peter declared on the Day of Pentecost that "God has made him both Lord and Christ, this Jesus whom you crucified" (Acts 2:36). There is probably no other word in our religious vocabulary which has experienced greater robbery of meaning than the word *Lord*. This is a word which slips glibly off our tongues as if it were nothing more than a given name. In reality it is a title that carries with it great authority. If we use it merely as a given name, we misrepresent its meaning.

We need to understand the meaning of this title in order that we might both recognize and respond properly to the Christ who conquered death and the grave on that first Easter.

The word *kurios* is a word which has a rich variety of meanings in the New Testament. As we understand this we can better understand the manner in which we should relate to the Christ who conquered death and the grave. *Kurios—lord—*was the normal word of personal address to one who was respected. It is similar to the word *sir* in English, *herr* in German, *monsieur* in French, and *se*ñor in Spanish. It is a *mister* of respect rather than mere formality.

I. "Kurios"—Lord—was a title recognizing authority.

Chief executive officer in the business world or *boss* is a title everyone would understand, and this is the implication of the position to which God appointed Jesus Christ following His resurrection.

This term *kurios* was used of one who had the right to command. It would signify the authority of a captain of a ship or the commanding officer of a military base. It would be comparable to the authority of a chief of police.

If we would respond to Jesus appropriately, we need to do so other than on a sentimental basis. We need to recognize His sovereignty and His right to be our "boss." *Kurios—lord—*is a title used to describe absolute possession or ownership.

A. *The owner of the vineyard was a "kurios" —lord* (Luke 20:13).

B. *The owner of the colt upon which Jesus rode was a "kurios" —lord.*

God appointed Jesus Christ to be our Owner and Possessor as His disciples. This means He has the right to requisition our time, our talents, our energies, our everything.

II. "Kurios"—Lord—was a term used to describe one who served as a guardian.

In the ancient world women were denied legal rights. If children or women were to engage in business, they had to do so through the services of a guardian. This guardian could be a husband, a father, a brother, or some other relative. By means of a guardian the helpless enjoyed a great degree of protection.

God has appointed Jesus Christ to be our Protector. He wants to give us strength to overcome the Evil One. He wants to protect us from death and the grave and from the possibility of spending eternity away from God.

III. "Kurios"—Lord—was the regular title that was given to Roman emperors.

A. *By means of this title the emperor was recognized as the ruler of the empire.*

B. *By means of this title the emperor asserted authority.*

In a world which resents authority and rebels against the establishment, we need to beware lest we fail to respond properly to the lordship of Him who came because of the love of God for us.

IV. In the Greek translation of the Old Testament, the word *Kurios*— Lord—was the word regularly used as the name for Israel's God.
God was powerfully declaring the deity of Jesus Christ by raising Him back to life again. This was no mere demonstration of power. This was a divine authentication of the God-man, Jesus Christ.

Conclusion. The question Saul of Tarsus put to the Voice which interrupted his mad career of persecution on the road to Damascus would be appropriate for all of us: "Lord, what will You have me to do?"

He deserves all of the respect that we could pay to the finest person we know. Because of His authority we need to relate to Him in a submissive but loving relationship.

Since He is our Owner we need to acknowledge that we belong to Him in totality and entirety.

Since He is the One whom God has anointed to be our Guardian, we should be grateful to Him.

Since He is the One who serves as the Emperor in the realm of the spiritual, we should give to Him our loyalty and faithfulness.

Since He is the God-man we should bow before Him in worship as did Thomas and the other apostles. —*TTC*

* * *

SUNDAY EVENING, APRIL 29

TITLE: Can a Dead Thing Really Live Again?

Text: "And he said unto me, Son of man, can these bones live? And I answered, O Lord God, thou knowest" (Ezek. 37:3).

Scripture Reading: Ezekiel 37:1–11

Introduction. As Ezekiel came toward the conclusion of his ministry, the Lord revealed a number of things concerning the future of His people, Israel. He had chosen them as instruments through which to bring Jesus into the world, and He would not forsake them until their mission was accomplished. They may have suffered temporary setbacks, one of which was in effect while they were captives in Babylon, but God purposed to bring them back to their homeland and reveal to Ezekiel the certainty of His intention.

— As is often true in Scripture, certain principles stand out in a context and have application far beyond the original scriptural setting. This is true in this story of what has been called the "valley of dry bones." God can make dead things live. The nation Israel seemed to be dead, but the nucleus was still there, and God would fulfill the promise of Isaiah that a "remnant shall return" and carry on God's work in the future. Many other things in our ordinary living seem dead sometimes, but with God's help new life can come.

I. A dead home can live again.

As a pastor I learned many years ago the importance of Christian homes. The first home was in a garden. God's presence was there, and we call it Paradise, which is a name we also use for heaven. A happy home is indeed "an early heaven"; and where God reigns within a home, we have a foretaste of our heavenly mansion.

Sin, however, can destroy the happiness of our homes as sin destroyed the first home, driving a wedge between man and his Maker and then between members of the family. A broken home is a terrible thing. One of our Old Testament prophets tells us that God hates divorce (Mal. 2:16); and even though conditions sometimes seem to justify it, everyone suffers to some extent when a husband and wife sever relationships. Since a new home is established at every marriage, a home dies when divorce comes. In fact, love and happiness may die many times in a home even though divorce never takes place.

Can a dead home live? Yes! In my own ministry I've seen it happen. I have remarried several couples who have divorced and wanted to start over again with each other. It has always been a delightful experience. Homes that are dead in other ways can be "born again" when Jesus Christ is received as the unseen Guest and the complete Lord of life in that home.

II. A dead church can live again.

A small community had a church which had existed and "died" several times. A pastor came who determined that he would help that church to "live again." Times were tough for a number of years, but today that community is thickly populated, and a lovely church building houses an enthusiastic congregation of believers.

Of course, some churches are almost dead though they have the name of being alive. John wrote to the church at Sardis, "I know thy works, that thou hast a name that thou livest, and art dead" (Rev. 3:1). Is there hope for these churches? Yes! When a congregation of believers catch a fresh vision of Jesus, great things can take place in a church.

> If you want to work in the kind of a church
> Like the kind of a church you like,
> You needn't slip your clothes in a grip
> And start on a long, long hike.
>
> You'll only find what you left behind
> For there's nothing that's really new.
> It's a knock at yourself when you knock at your church.
> It isn't your church, it's you.
>
> Real churches aren't made by men who're afraid
> Lest somebody else go ahead.
> When everybody works and nobody shirks
> You can raise a church from the dead.
>
> So, if while you make your personal stake
> Your neighbor can make one, too.
> Your church will be what you want to see.
> It isn't your church, it's you.

III. Dead sinners can live again.

One who does not know Jesus Christ as Savior is described by the Bible in a number of ways but none more graphically than "dead in sins" (Eph. 2:5).

Therefore, it is only logical that the Christian life should be described as a resurrection.

Christ's death on the cross was to set us free from sin's dominion. He fulfilled every prophecy and symbolism of the Old Testament. Only through His redeeming work can a lost person find forgiveness and deliverance. When one has come to know the power of Jesus in his life, he can appreciate the words of the one who wrote,

> Down in the human heart, crushed by the tempter,
> Feelings lie buried that grace can restore.
> Touched by a loving heart, wakened by kindness,
> Chords that are broken will vibrate once more.

New life is possible in Jesus because He gave His life for us.

Conclusion. Never give up on anyone! As long as there is breath there is hope! Dead things can come to life when Jesus, God's own Son, comes to them. Broken lives can be mended and unhappy people can find joy. Dead bones can live but only through God's power.   *—FMW*

* * *

SUGGESTED PREACHING PROGRAM
FOR THE MONTH OF MAY

Sunday Mornings

The period of time from Mother's Day in the month of May until Father's Day in the month of June provides the pastor with an appropriate opportunity to emphasize truths relating to marriage and family life. The suggested theme for the Sunday morning messages is "Good Housekeeping." Hopefully each pastor will be able to secure some of the excellent books on this topic that have been published in recent years. They would prove helpful in preparing a series of messages using a theme such as the one suggested here.

Sunday Evenings

The prophet Daniel lived in a time of great stress. His was a faith that allowed God to strengthen and use him significantly in those times. The suggested theme for a series of messages based on his life is "The Prophet's Message for Stressful Times."

Wednesday Evenings

Continue the studies based on Paul's epistles to the church at Thessalonica, using the theme "Let the Apostle Paul Speak to the Present."

* * *

WEDNESDAY EVENING, MAY 2

TITLE: How to Handle Trouble

TEXT: "That no one be moved by these afflictions" (1 Thess. 3:3 RSV).

SCRIPTURE READING: 1 Thessalonians 3:1–13

Introduction. Paul's journey to Thessalonica took him through several cities where heated opposition was expressed. The gospel's success in Thessalonica brought persecution against the young church. Paul had his own troubles in Corinth, the city from which he was writing. This letter calls his friends to renewed courage. His desire for them is disclosed in verses 3 and 8—"that no one be moved by these afflictions . . . stand fast in the Lord." This chapter contains some important words on how to handle trouble.

I. Expect trouble.

We live in a world of freedom where the possibility for both good and evil will bring some trouble. "You yourselves know that this is to be our lot" (v. 3). Jesus sent the disciples out "as sheep in the midst of wolves" (Matt. 10:16). The way of the Cross brings some trouble. We live in a world where trouble comes because of sin. Trouble is inherent in life, and we ought to live with that realistic attitude.

II. Refuse Satan an entrance through the door of trouble.

Paul expressed his concern for the Thessalonians "that somehow the tempter had tempted you and that our labor would be in vain" (1 Thess. 3:5 RSV). Our adversary will use trouble to make us bitter, angry toward God, or cause us to withdraw from others. Recall what Jesus said to Peter as He faced the troubling hours near the cross: "Simon, Simon, behold, Satan demanded to have you, that he might sift you like wheat, but I have prayed for you that your faith may not fail; and when you have turned again, strengthen your brethren" (Luke 22:31–32 RSV).

III. Face trouble with prayer.

Paul and the Thessalonians were linked in intercessory prayer. The apostle was in the habit of "praying earnestly" for his friends, and he in turn was strengthened by their fervent prayers. The only way trouble should get us down is down on our knees in prayer. Lloyd Ogilvie said, "Courage is fear which has said its prayers." Paul promised the Philippians that the result of delivering our anxieties to God was the possession of His peace which passes all understanding (Phil. 4:6–7). If we maintain through prayer our fellowship with the Lord, we will experience the promise of the psalmist: "Call upon me in the day of trouble; I will deliver you, and you shall glorify me" (50:15 RSV).

IV. Reach through trouble to others.

Paul prayed that these persecuted pilgrims would "increase and abound in love to one another and to all men" (1 Thess. 3:12 RSV). It was impossible for Paul to wallow in self-pity while he reached out in love to the Thessalonians. The words of this song challenge us:

> Reach out and touch a soul that is weary,
> Reach out and touch a stranger in despair,
> Reach out and touch the heart that is seeking . . .

Our own troubles become smaller as we minister to others in love.

V. Be patient.

Paul refused to look at his troubles only in the present tense. He looked to the future and realized God was not finished. The rest of the story would be told "at the coming of our Lord Jesus with all his saints" (v. 13 RSV). This was the perspective Paul shared in Romans 8:18–25. He could go through present sufferings with patience because of the glory that is to come.

A preacher was asked what he regarded as the most comforting verse in the Bible. He answered, "And it came to pass." Told that that was just the beginning of a verse, the preacher replied, "Still those are the most comforting words in the Bible to me. It didn't come to stay—it came to pass." Be patient in trouble.

Conclusion. Out of his own experience Paul has given us these five ways to handle trouble. As we implement these, may the Lord see us unmoved by trouble and standing fast in the Lord.   —*BW*

* * *

SUNDAY MORNING, MAY 6

TITLE: **Living at Home During the Storm**

TEXT: **"Every one then who hears these words of mine and does them will be like a wise man who built his house upon the rock; and the rain fell, and** the floods came, and the winds blew and beat upon that house, but it did not fall, because it had been founded on the rock" (Matt. 7:24-25 RSV).

SCRIPTURE READING: Matthew 7:24-27

HYMNS: "O Jesus, I Have Promised," Bode
"God, Give Us Christian Homes," McKinney
"Moment by Moment," Whittle

OFFERTORY PRAYER:
Loving Father, after whom all the families of earth are named, we thank You for the gift of family life and love. Tell the cloud of witnesses in glory of our love and deep gratitude for their sacrifice and influence. Strengthen us to face the problems of our world and make our homes a powerful testimony of Your way, truth, and life. Help us to give in realization of all that has been given to us. Use these gifts to change individuals and build Christian homes. In Jesus' name we pray. Amen.

Introduction. The destruction of a house by flood or other natural calamity is a sad loss. Yet a greater loss is the breakup of a family. The words of Jesus' parable appropriately describe the condition of many a home—"great was the fall of it" (Matt. 7:27e). The forecast for the family is 100 percent chance of storms. These are turbulent days for family life.

The storm that lashes out at home life is illustrated by the rising rate of child and spouse abuse, higher incidence of alcoholism among youth and women, and one million teenage runaways each year. The raging storm hits the home with permissive morality, materialism, and egotistical individuality. One of the most dangerous assignments for a police officer is settling family quarrels. One newspaper called the home "one of society's most violent places."

How can we live at home during the storm? Remedies and alternatives abound—no-fault divorce, trial marriage, living together, swapping, and swinging. Proposals now come with multiple-choice response: "Darling, will you be my husband, wife, soulmate, roommate, first mate, second mate, none of the above?" What a storm rages around the home! How can we live at home during the storm?

I. Be convinced of and committed to the home's significance.

A sound, secure, spiritual family life will come only when we are convinced that the home is crucially significant for the welfare of our world and the work of the Lord.

A. *A concern of the Lord.* Home and family life is of vital interest to the Lord. The home was created before the state, church, or any institution. Much biblical teaching is expressed in the language of the home. God is "our Father," and Christ came in the context of family life. The first churches were in homes. If a Christian neglects his family, he is "worse than an infidel" (1 Tim. 5:8). The home is significant to our Lord, and it should be to us.

B. *Significant to you?* Where is your home in your priorities? Home has been defined as "the place you go to from the garage." Robert Frost said, "Home is the place, where when you have to go there, they have to take you in." Youth sometimes say, "I guess I'll go home; there is no place else to go." The significance of home is measured by the time we invest with the people who form our families. A counselor said he frequently hears this comment from women following a divorce: "He spends more time with the children now than he did before the divorce." That same commitment of time and involvement could preserve many families and deepen every relationship.

II. Cultivate the commitment of love.

A. *A growing love.* The love that brought two people together into a home must be nurtured. Love must grow and mature as people grow and encounter new experiences. Look for new challenges; don't let stagnation set in. Allow freedom and individuality. Kindle the spark and fan the fire. Otherwise love may die.

B. *A Christlike love.* It is said, "They fell in love," and it sounds like a ditch they stumbled into. Love involves commitment, and at its deepest it reflects the nature of Christ—"love . . . as Christ loved the church and gave himself up for her" (Eph. 5:25 RSV). This kind of love "bears all things, believes all things, hopes all things, endures all things" (1 Cor. 13:7 RSV).

III. Continue until the conclusion.

A. *Till death do us part.* It seems few people really believe that phrase of the marriage vow. To approach marriage and family life with a back-door-exit mentality is to sow the seed of ruin at the very beginning. Enter marriage determined to stay on board until the end of the journey. Choose a partner you can stay with.

Suzanne Britt wrote in *Newsweek:* "I'm grown up. I have responsibilities; I am in the middle of a lifelong marriage. I am hanging in there, sometimes enduring, sometimes enjoying. For some reason we assume that people can't stay married for life, but we make no such assumption about staying on the same job, keeping the same religion or voting the same ticket" (June 11, 1979, p. 27).

B. *Be realistic.* Christian homes are not immune from problems. Jesus' family had problems, and Mary and Martha experienced friction. The rain, the floods, and the wind hit both houses in Jesus' parable. The storms will come wherever we are. Determine to ride out the storms and have the joy of better days.

IV. Center the home in Christ.

Jesus said the "wise man" built his house on the rock. The wise person listens to Christ's Word and is obedient to it. A homebuilder had a slogan: "I can build you a house but you will have to make it a home." Christ can make a home. He provides security, stability, strength. "Except the LORD build the house, they labour in vain that build it" (Ps. 127:1). Is Christ the interest center in your home?

King Hezekiah welcomed visitors from Babylon into his home. Isaiah inquired, "What have they seen in your house?" (2 Kings 20:15 RSV). What do others see in your home and family? Are faith, love, and ministry evident? Is Christ present?

Conclusion. These are difficult days for home life. A bride pondered her future: "Am I boarding a sinking ship?" Sometimes it is stormy, but it is possible to live at home during the storm. Commit yourself to the grand task of building a Christian home. Cultivate and nurture the love that created your home. Determine to continue until the conclusion. With Christ as Lord it is possible to have a home like a haven of peace in a stormy world.   —*BW*

SUNDAY EVENING, MAY 6

TITLE: **Come Drink From God's Fountain**

TEXT: **"And it shall come to pass . . . every thing shall live whither the river cometh" (Ezek. 47:9)**

SCRIPTURE READING: **Ezekiel 47:1-12**

Introduction. In the verses we read, the prophet climaxes his picture of the temple area by describing the sacred stream that flows south of the altar and the east gate down to the Dead Sea. Although no tributaries support it, the stream grows deeper as it goes forward. In a short time it is uncrossable and freshens the Dead Sea. Nourishing evergreen and everbearing trees on its bank, the waters serve as a beautiful picture of God's grace and saving power through Jesus Christ.

I. Source.

Although the water comes through the temple, the blessing produced by it does not originate there but is conveyed from a source invisible and far off. Likewise, in God's great gospel plan to restore the fallen race, there exist both instrumental and efficient agencies. God has appointed means and a divine way to infuse those means with life. Those who love the river from the temple are the most likely, while walking on its banks, to receive the water as it comes from the source. Likewise, those who stay near the means of spreading the gospel are the most likely to receive the Good News and be blessed by it. We must remember, however, that the waters have their spring in the everlasting hills.

Likewise, the source of the gospel power is God. Through Jesus, our Savior, who has ascended on high, God has sent forth His Spirit, who lives on earth and inspires every good thought, but, even more than that, convicts lost people of their need for salvation.

II. Progress.

The prophet saw the water, first ankle-high, then knee-high, next to the loins, and finally a river too deep to be forded or even for swimming. The flow did not cease and the waters did not ebb. Rather, they moved gradually and constantly in the ever-deepening stream.

The gospel of Jesus Christ has certainly moved forward through the centuries. This does not mean the Scripture teaches that the world will continue "to get better and better," but that the gospel has constantly gone out into areas where people have not known of Jesus. The early preachers, some of whom were only fishermen, moved against all the power of the Roman Empire with the gospel. The Caesars conspired to strangle it and armies marched out against its people, but the gospel triumphed marvelously.

Of course, there have been periods when faith was eclipsed and corruptions blemished the bride of Christ, but the gradual progress of the gospel did not cease. Even today, in spite of our shortcomings and limitations, Jesus Christ stands as the central figure in the world. We should be encouraged by this thought, but we should also be challenged with our tremendous responsibility to be used in spreading the message by our own efforts.

III. Effectiveness.

Everywhere the river comes, the dead live! How true of the gospel! Not only every person, but every part of every person is changed by the gospel. No one who ever came to Jesus has been turned down or disappointed. Paul says, "For I am not ashamed of the gospel of Christ: for it is the power of God unto salvation to every one that believeth" (Rom. 1:16). In addition, the regenerating power of the Holy Spirit changes one in such a way that he becomes a new creation in Christ Jesus. The gospel is the most effective agency known in this world for motivating and changing the course of a person's life. We should remember, however, that it is not a set of rules or even a system of doctrine that saves, but Jesus Christ who personally enters the sinner's life with His transforming power.

Conclusion. Our responsibility in heeding the message of this Scripture is twofold. First, if we have never been saved, we need to come to the Water of Life and drink freely. The last invitation in the Bible reminds us of this life-giving stream in Ezekiel. John said, "And the Spirit and the bride say, Come. And let him that heareth say, Come. And let him that is athirst come. And whosoever will, let him take the water of life freely" (Rev. 22:17).

If we have already received Jesus as Savior, we are to tell others of this great and glorious gospel. The Book of Ezekiel, which begins in the early chapters with a captive people longing for God's presence, concludes with a temple from which come life-giving streams not only for Israel but, through Christ, for all the world. What a glorious gospel is symbolized in this Old Testament prophet's message and later personally enters history in Jesus Christ.   —*FMW*

* * *

WEDNESDAY EVENING, MAY 9

TITLE: A Sanctified Person

TEXT: "For this is the will of God, your sanctification" (1 Thess. 4:3 RSV).

SCRIPTURE READING: 1 Thessalonians 4:1–12

Introduction. In giving me directions to a certain family's home, a man said, "They live near that sanctified church." The phrase indicates how a good biblical word has come to describe a denominational group which overemphasizes one aspect of the faith. What is sanctification, which is declared by Paul to be God's will for us? The Greek word is *hagiasmos*—holy, holiness, set apart, consecrated, belonging to God.

Holiness produces anxiety for many people. One concept is embodied in the self-righteous "Holy Joe" type. Holiness is seen also as a certain appearance in dress or a withdrawal from the world. The biblical concept of holiness is to become like Christ, distinctively different individuals consecrated to Christ. The concept of holiness runs throughout the Bible (Exod. 19:5, 6; Lev. 19:2; Deut. 7:6–9; Rom. 12:1; Col. 3:12; 1 Peter 2:9). Paul takes this aspect of God's will out of the realm of theology and into specific categories of life.

I. Consecrated personal life (vv. 3–8).

God's will is to "abstain from immorality" (v. 3 RSV). The Christian is set apart to live a morally pure life. This was a radical message in the morally decadent first century. Pagan temples in Thessalonica had prostitutes, and God's gift of sex was debased and exploited. Paul affirmed the principle that all sexual misuse of the body violated God's will. "Shun immorality. . . . Do you not know that your body is a temple of the Holy Spirit . . . glorify God in your body" (1 Cor. 6:18–20 RSV). This is an extremely relevant word in our society where sex is considered the key to sell everything from toothpaste to movies.

II. Consecrated relationships (vv. 9–10).

Thessalonica was a selfish and lustful city with many people committed to getting ahead in business and commercial affairs. "Love of the brethren" was an uncommon virtue in the city. The presence of the church—a fellowship of brotherly love—was a testimony to God's power. Sanctification involves an ever wider and deeper love for people—"do so more and more" (v. 10). Jesus said, "By this all men will know that you are my disciples, if you have love for one another" (John 13:35 RSV).

III. Consecrated employment (vv. 11–12).

Evidently some of the Thessalonian believers misinterpreted Paul's teaching on the return of Christ. They quit their jobs, sat down, and waited. Without any work to do, they became busybodies, loafers, and fanatics. Paul reminds them of God's will while waiting for Christ's return—honorable work.

Holiness is reflected in our work relationships. Honest work will strengthen our Christian witness (v. 12). A Christian cannot separate witness from work; we witness by the way we work. Other significant words on work are found in Ephesians 4:28 and 6:5–9.

Conclusion. Some people might measure holiness by church attendance or faithfulness in the devotional life. The sanctified person has made a commitment to live a different life. Human sexuality, family, church, and work relationships are all consecrated to the Lord. Life is lived "to please God," who has called us to be holy even as He is holy.   —*BW*

* * *

SUNDAY MORNING, MAY 13

TITLE: A Great Woman

TEXT: **"And it fell on a day, that Elisha passed to Shunem, where was a great woman; and she constrained him to eat bread. And so it was, that as oft as he passed by, he turned in thither to eat bread" (2 Kings 4:8).**

SCRIPTURE READING: **2 Kings 4:8–26**

HYMNS: **"Praise to the Lord, the Almighty," Neander/Winkworth**
"Gracious Saviour, Who Didst Honor," Shirreff
"O Blessed Day of Motherhood!" McGregor

OFFERTORY PRAYER:

We thank You, Father, for godly women who, like Mary, have responded to Your will by saying, "Be it done unto me as you say." We are grateful for the strength and stability Christian mothers have brought to our community, church, and nation. On this day of recognition may these mothers experience a special blessing of grace and peace. We thank You for mothers who taught us to be faithful stewards of life. May our giving reflect those truths and bear witness of the positive and lasting influence of Christian mothers. We pray in Jesus' name. Amen.

Introduction. Michael Novak wrote in *Harper's Magazine* (April, 1976): "We live in curious times. Choosing to have a family used to be routine. But so many, so varied and so agressive are anti-family sentiments in our society today that choosing to have a family has become an act of courage. To love family life . . . is to be marked today as a heretic." Curious times indeed! Did you think you would live to see the day when two lesbians would be permitted to adopt a child? Extremist leaders in the feminist movement have made mothers feel they have missed life. In many homes a child is regarded as an intrusion instead of an inspiration. The lifestyle that prompted the words of an old hymn, "If I could hear my mother pray again," is nearly an endangered species.

Unfortunately, too many mothers find it easier to play golf than to pray with their children. For some it is more exciting to hold a crystal cocktail glass than cuddle a child. Others are wise about disco and ignorant about the wiles of the devil. The words of Proverbs 31 are being fulfilled: "Who can find a virtuous woman? for her price is far above rubies" (v. 10).

In these curious times an inspiring example is needed for mothers—an example of courage and commitment, a pattern with which today's mothers might cut a new lifestyle from the fabric of life. The Shunammite woman, whose story is told in 2 Kings 4, is such an example. God pays her a sublime compliment—"a great woman." The brief vignette of her life reveals that the compliment was more than justified.

I. Focused priorities.

Our priorities show who we are. Jesus said, "Where your treasure is, there will your heart be also" (Matt. 6:21). Our priorities mold our living. The priorities on which this Shunammite woman focused made her great.

A. *Spiritual perception.* She said of Elisha, "I perceive that this is an holy man of God" (2 Kings 4:9). She was interested and became involved in the things of God. Jesus said, "Seek ye first the kingdom of God, and his righteousness" (Matt. 6:33a). Stronger homes will never come as long as the Home Box Office gets a higher rating than the family altar.

The Shunammite woman's concern for spiritual life is evidenced by her hospitality for the prophet of God. The current condition of the family can be measured by the uneasiness many feel about the preacher visiting in their home.

B. *Service to people.* She was willing to get involved in another's life. Jesus said, "Whosoever will be great among you, let him be your minister . . . your servant" (Matt. 20:26–27). The community has many service clubs which do many good things. Often the approach is to raise money and write a check. Money is always needed, but it can be a cold substitute for compassionate personal involvement. Personal service always involves a risk.

C. *Satisfied with her position.* Elisha asked what he could do for her and she gave no indication of a particular request. She was not complacent about life but contented. We have so much more now than in the days of the Great Depression, but are we any more contented? "Godliness with contentment is great gain" (1 Tim. 6:6). A world in need, a lost world without the Savior, will never be reached unless we reach the place where we can say with Esau, "I have enough, my brother" (Gen. 33:9).

II. Family partnership.

This woman's greatness is also seen in the way she coped with her family relationships.

A. *Positive attitude*. For many years she suffered the "curse" of barrenness. Other women considered her inferior, and most thought she was guilty of some sin. Evidently she did not become bitter, nor turn inward and feed on her problem. Neither did it become a total barrier between her husband and herself. Their relationship at first was characterized by communication and cooperation: "Let *us* make . . ." (v. 10).

You may have experienced many problems in your life. These may not have been of your own making, but it is in your power to determine how these problems will affect you. They can be liabilities or assets.

B. *Struggle with irresponsibility*. Not all was as it should have been in this home. In later years when their child became ill, the father said, "Carry him to his mother" (v. 19). Does this indicate an attitude on the part of the father that the work in the field was his responsibility, while the child was his wife's domain? Some families may have a man in the house, but he isn't much of a father. "*Fathers*, provoke not your children to wrath; but bring them up in the nurture and admonition of the Lord" (Eph. 6:4). With only 16 percent of American homes having the husband as the sole provider, there is certainly a need for shared responsibility in every aspect of home life and family care.

When their child died, his mother prepared to go see Elisha. Her husband questioned, "Why will you go to him today? It is neither new moon nor sabbath" (2 Kings 4:23 RSV). Did this reflect a shallow interest in the things of the Spirit? Why go to church in the middle of the week? You may have a spouse with little interest in spiritual concerns. You may have to carry the spiritual load. This woman did not always have a true partnership; she had to go the second mile. That is why the Bible calls her a great woman.

III. Faith's persuasion.

The most significant element of the Shunammite woman's inspiring life was her faith. What a tremendous declaration of faith she made! With her only child dead at home, she said, "It is well" (v. 26). Faith gives stability in the storm. Faith supplies the foundation on which to rebuild when things have fallen in ruins. Faith believes that "in all things God works for the good of those who love him" (Rom. 8:28 NIV).

"A woman that feareth the LORD, she shall be praised" (Prov. 31:30). You might be praised for your pastry, poise, political persuasiveness, or pretty face. Will God praise you at the last day—"Well done, thou good and faithful servant"? Can you join with Paul to say: "I am persuaded, that neither death, nor life, nor angels, nor principalities . . . nor any other creature, shall be able to separate us from the love of God, which is in Christ Jesus our Lord" (Rom. 8:38–39).

Conclusion. Is is well with your life today? Do you have eternal life in Christ? Are your priorities pleasing to God? Are you living by faith, serving others, and responsibly fulfilling your Christian calling in your home and the community? This is an opportunity for these crucial areas to be made well in Christ. —*BW*

* * *

SUNDAY EVENING, MAY 13

TITLE: Personal Purity Pays

TEXT: "And at the end of ten days their countenances appeared fairer . . . than all the youths that did eat of the king's dainties" (Dan. 1:15 ASV).

SCRIPTURE READING: **Daniel 1:1–21**

Introduction. The first invasion of Jerusalem by Nebuchadnezzar in 605 B.C., recorded only in Daniel 1:1, served as the vehicle for deporting a young man, Daniel, seemingly already a respected leader, and his three friends: Hananiah, Mishael, and Azariah.

In order to incorporate the best of Jewish life into his political system, the king gave orders that some of the young men who showed particular aptitude should be given special instruction and, therefore, should be served the typical food of that day which was not God honoring or body building. The subsequent events may be described in three simple sentences: Daniel purposed, Daniel persevered, Daniel prospered.

I. Daniel purposed.

How thrilling to see young people with strong convictions concerning moral and spiritual matters. Daniel stands near the top in all generations of those who have been willing to take a stand for personal purity even if it costs them favored positions and the possibility of a forfeited life. He insisted that he would not "defile himself" with the food that was opposed to his religious training. When the one in charge of him and the other three protested that to grant the request could endanger his own life, Daniel pleaded for a ten-day test.

Daniel must have already been an exceptional young man with a winsome personality, for the Babylonian official agreed to his proposition. Not knowing the outcome, he was so impressed by the fine spirit of this Jewish lad that he laid his own life on the line. What a wonderful testimony to the fact that the secular world is indeed impressed when godly people take a stand for what is right. A number of years ago a young man attended a party, not knowing alcoholic beverages would be served at the table. He had been taught not to indulge; but when he saw his friends, one by one, let the drink be poured in their glasses, he wondered what he should do. He decided to base his decision on what one young woman whom he admired and respected, did when she was offered the drink. With a smile, she turned her glass upside down, and it was easy for him to do the same when the pourer came to him. That man, well known among most Christian musicians today, was B. B. McKinney, writer of many wonderful songs about the Lord.

II. Daniel persevered.

An old cliché says, "If at first you don't succeed, try, try again." Brought over into the Christian context, we might say that to live the Christian life requires more than one decision to live for Jesus. Though that initial decision is important, we must decide day by day and sometimes even minute by minute to serve Christ and to hold our standards high. Sometimes this involves insisting to others, as Daniel did, that we be allowed to live our Christian life and worship our God regardless of the rules and regulations which prevail in an institution. Perhaps the best translation of verse 11 is that Daniel "kept on saying" to the stewards, which means he had to repeat his request several, perhaps a number of times. In the New Testament, the proper translation of the Greek verbs in the Model Prayer is: "Keep on asking and you will receive, keep on seeking and you will find, keep on knocking and it shall be opened to you." Paul spoke of "pressing onward" for the prize of the high calling of God in Christ Jesus, suggesting that the accomplishment of his Christian goal meant perseverance. Living the Christian life is not easy and seems to get even more difficult as the world becomes more secularized.

III. Daniel prospered.

At this point we must be very careful! Certainly one cannot expect automatic promotions or pay raises every time he does a good deed for the Lord. If this were true, Christianity would be merely a good insurance policy rather than a spiritual experience. We must do right because God wants us to do right and because we love Him. Jesus told us to do our good deeds not even expecting a reward.

On the other hand, rewards do come. Sometimes, as in the case of Daniel, God rewards us openly and quickly. When we live in harmony with the moral and spiritual laws He has established in the universe, we are cooperating with God, and success is inevitable. Daniel was true to the things God had set forth for him to obey; and therefore he prospered greatly. So will we! One poet said:

> I know that right is right;
> It is not good to lie;
> That love is better than spite,
> And a neighbor than a spy.

> I know that conscience needs
> The leash of a sober mind;
> I know that each good deed
> Some sure reward will find.

> In the darkest night of the year,
> When the stars are all gone out,
> That courage is better than fear,
> That faith is truer than doubt.

> Fierce though the fiends may fight,
> And long though the sun may hide,
> I know the truth and right
> Have the universe on their side.

Daniel was rewarded quickly, but some of us often have to wait for a long period of time to be vindicated. Let us develop patience when our rewards do not come as quickly as we wish. By all means, however, let us stay in tune with God and live according to His will.

Conclusion. Lives of such men as Daniel bless the world. Such people are a part of the "militant minority" who dare to be different for the sake of the Lord. They serve as a creative force for the world. They are salt to preserve it and light to shine through the darkness. Will you dare to be a Daniel?   —*FMW*

WEDNESDAY EVENING, MAY 16

TITLE: **Whether Awake or Asleep**

TEXT: **"For God has not destined us for wrath, but to obtain salvation through our Lord Jesus Christ, who died for us so that whether we wake or sleep we might live with him" (1 Thess. 5:9–10 RSV).**

SCRIPTURE READING: **1 Thessalonians 4:13–5:11**

Introduction. Paul had been with the Thessalonians only a short while. While there he taught them about the triumphant return of Christ. Some questions went unanswered; people were concerned that their departed loved ones would miss the glory of the Lord's return. Paul wrote to comfort these believers. His message contains powerful truth about death and life. Imagine the Thessalonians as they look in four directions.

I. Looking down.

The Thessalonians stood looking down at the graves of departed loved ones. They were encouraged not to "grieve as others do who have no hope" (v. 13 RSV). This passage gives two New Testament views of death.

A. *The last enemy.* Death entered the world because of sin; and death is the last enemy to be destroyed. The reality of death's defeat came when Jesus died. Paul said, "We believe that Jesus died," in reference to His death on the cross (v. 14). "The wages of sin is death" (Rom. 6:23); and on the cross Jesus paid the consequences of our sin. Jesus experienced all the horror of death; and, as a result, death for the Christian becomes the transition into the presence of the Lord.

B. *Asleep in Jesus.* A common New Testament description of death is "sleep." This does not refer to "soul-sleeping" but reflects an absence of fear in the Christian's attitude toward death. The grave becomes the beginning of a new life. It is entrance into eternal life with Jesus Christ. What a contrast between the ways a Christian and an unbeliever face death. The unbeliever has "no hope"; the Christian is with Jesus. "Absent from the body, . . . present with the Lord" (2 Cor. 5:8).

II. Looking up.

Because of Jesus Paul urges the Thessalonians to turn their eyes from the grave to the sky. "God will bring with him those who have fallen asleep. . . . For the Lord himself will descend from heaven" (1 Thess. 4:14, 16 RSV). Alexander Maclaren said, "We are not looking for the undertaker but the upper-taker, for a cleavage in the sky instead of a hole in the ground." This hope is declared "by the word of the Lord" (v. 15), who does not lie.

A. *The Lord's descent.* "The Lord himself" will return. The disciples watched the Lord ascend into glory and were told "this Jesus, who was taken up from you in heaven, will come" (Acts 1:11 RSV). The word for His "coming" is *parousia,* used in the Greek for the parade of the returning King. What a great day! Jesus will return to climax His plan for mankind.

B. *The Lord's victory.* Jesus will come "with a cry of command" (1 Thess. 4:16 RSV). This is the word an officer shouts to his troops. Christ will return as Conqueror. We will "meet the Lord in the air" (v. 17) where Satan has ruled as prince. Christ will have complete victory over evil.

III. Looking in.

A. *Beware of speculation.* There is "no need" to try and calculate the time of the Lord's return. Plotting a prophetic calendar is a waste of time, because the Lord will return suddenly, "like a thief in the night" (5:2 RSV).

B. *Be ready.* The New Testament usually couples the Lord's return with an emphasis on preparation (2 Peter 3:11–12). We are to walk in the light and be ready whenever the Lord comes. Be ready with faith, love, and salvation (1 Thess. 5:8). The hope of Christ's return purifies the Christian (1 John 3:3).

IV. Looking out.

A. *Win the lost.* The Lord's coming is delayed in order that more might be ready. God's will is for all to "obtain salvation through our Lord Jesus Christ" (1 Thess. 5:9 RSV). While we wait, we are to work in the fields which are white unto harvest.

B. *Encourage the saved* (v. 11). This interim between Christ's ascension and His return is a time to build up the church. Look out for others in the fellowship.

Conclusion. Jesus has put a new face on death and has given us abundant life. While we wait for His victorious return, we will work to win the world. —*BW*

* * *

SUNDAY MORNING, MAY 20

TITLE: Is It OK to Be Single?

Text: "Let every one lead the life which the Lord has assigned to him, and in which God has called him . . . keeping the commandments of God" (1 Cor. 7:17, 19b).

Scripture Reading: Matthew 19:10–12; 1 Corinthians 7:7, 17–35

Hymns: "God of Our Fathers, Whose Almighty Hand," Roberts
"O Master, Let Me Walk With Thee," Gladden
"Because He Lives," Gaither

Offertory Prayer:
Loving Father, we are grateful for Your call to us through Christ— "Follow me, and I will make you to become. . . ." Thank You for grace toward our sin, patience with procrastination, and courage to overcome our fears. We pray for persevering power so that we may not miss all that You have in store for us.

Thank You, Lord, for the privilege of serving You through the church. Open our eyes that we may see the opportunities all about us. We present this offering in an effort to "redeem the time" and bring people to Christ.

We love You and pray in Jesus' name. Amen.

Introduction. Each person in a group session was asked to introduce himself and tell something about his life. One woman told her name and said, "I'm just an old maid!" The comment seemed to reflect the put-down of a society that has thought it less than O.K. to be single.

Statistics indicate that over one-third of the adults in America are single. In Dallas, Texas, alone there are about 315,000 singles. Political analysts, economists, community leaders, and churches are giving more attention to this significant segment of society. Yet many single people experience the feeling they have a disease or are a disgrace or a disaster. Is it O.K. to be single? The Bible says yes!

I. Jesus' lifestyle and teaching.

. A. *Jesus' lifestyle.* The lifestyle of our Lord Jesus is an affirmation of singleness. The Incarnation was secured in the context of a family. Could God not also have decided for Christ to fulfill His ministry in the setting of a marriage? He could have, but He chose not to do so. Should we then think it weird or impossible for someone today to have meaningful and powerful life as a single person?

B. *Jesus' teaching.* Matthew 19:10-12 are the closing comments of some teaching Jesus gave on divorce and the continuity of marriage. The disciples noted the high standard established by the Master and said, "It is not good to marry" (v. 10). Jesus responded: "That [not marrying] is something which not everyone can accept, but only those for whom God has appointed it. For while some are incapable of marriage because they were born so, or were made so by men, there are others who have themselves renounced marriage for the sake of the kingdom of Heaven. Let those accept it who can" (vv. 11-12 NEB).

Jesus also said, "In the resurrection they neither marry, nor are given in marriage" (22:30). This indicates eternal life to be the highest goal and relationship for now and forever. Whether by choice or by circumstance, it is O.K. to be single. Jesus' lifestyle and teaching affirm singleness as an acceptable alternative lifestyle.

II. Paul's affirmation.

Although the immorality of Corinth and the expected return of Christ are the background for his thoughts, Paul also offers an affirmation for singleness: "I wish that all were as I myself am" (1 Cor. 7:7 RSV). It is possible to live as a single and realize it is a "special gift from God" (v. 7 RSV). "To the unmarried and the widows I say that it is well for them to remain single as I do" (v. 8 RSV). This was a radical statement for Paul's time. The Old Testament does not have a word for *bachelor*. An early Jewish document mentions seven types of persons who would be excommunicated from heaven, and the list begins with "a Jew who has no wife." In a society where marriage was prevalent and anything else considered less than normal, Paul said it was O.K. to be single.

III. Acceptance and opportunity.

A. *Acceptance.* Paul's focus is on accepting one's circumstance and accentuating the unique opportunity. "Only, let everyone lead the life which the Lord has assigned to him" (v. 17 RSV). The most important issue is "keeping the commandments of God" (v. 19 RSV). Whether single or married obedience to the will of God is desired.

The most important issue for an unmarried woman is not, "How can I find a husband so that I may be happy?" It is, rather, "How can I live out the creative life that God intended in love for all men and women to have?" This is neither to say that we repress any hope for marriage in God's gracious will nor that we refuse to face the agonizing problems inherent in the unmarried state. Rather it is to affirm that both our natural desire for marriage and all of our problems in not being married are under the control of a compassionate Lord" (Ada Lum, *Single and Human* [Downers Grove, Ill.: InterVarsity Press, 1977], p. 23).

This also means that those who are married must accept and affirm those who are single, and we should not give them our feelings of inferiority or stigma. Let all say to them by word and deed, "You're O.K.!"

B. *Opportunity.* A single person, especially one without children, has a unique opportunity to serve Christ through the church and in the community. "The unmarried man is anxious about the affairs of the Lord, how to please the Lord; but the married man is anxious about worldly affairs, how to please his wife, and his interests are divided" (vv. 32b–34a rsv). A single person does not have the responsibilities of a married person. This gives no support for lax service by the married, but it does encourage singles to greater utilization of a unique opportunity.

Conclusion. Is it O.K. to be single? Yes! The best affirmation is found in the salvation we receive in Christ. "You were bought with a price; do not become slaves of men. So, brethren, in whatever state each was called, there let him remain with God" (vv. 23–24 rsv). Are we faithful where we are? Are we keeping the commandments of God?

Ada Lum concludes her helpful little book with these words: God doesn't intend in the slightest for us singles to live second-rate lives. Neither does he intend that our own lives should be lived out simply as dull reflections of some kind of so-called sublimated, compensating life. If we're living life God's way, we're not substituting for marriage. We are living in the very best way that he has lovingly planned for us all along (Ibid., p. 81).   —*BW*

* * *

SUNDAY EVENING, MAY 20

TITLE: God Has His Hand on History

TEXT: **"And . . . shall the God of heaven set up a kingdom, which shall never be destroyed: and the kingdom shall not be left to other people, but it shall break in pieces and consume all these kingdoms, and it shall stand for ever" (Dan. 2:44).**

SCRIPTURE READING: **Daniel 2:1–49**

Introduction. Nebuchadnezzar had a dream. However, not only did he not know what it meant, neither could he remember it. His advisors could not tell him what the dream was, much less what it meant. Finally Daniel was summoned and did both. Four great kingdoms were decreed, including Babylon, and after that would come an everlasting kingdom that would consume the others and stand forever.

In this message we shall not go into the controversial interpretations but rather confine ourselves to one great spiritual teaching which emerges and which all people, regardless of eschatological position, must agree on—God has His hand on history. Someone has said that the correct rendering of the word should be "His story" for this is what history truly is—the record of how God deals with nations and, of course, individuals.

I. Civilizations have a way of decaying.

Survey the centuries and you will discover a great truth. Man, left to his own devices, simply cannot make it. He does not have the moral control nor the inner resources to live in such a way as to guarantee longevity or perpetuity. Dictators arise and strut across the page of history, but they pass into oblivion. The nations and empires they establish suffer the same fate.

The reason for this is, of course, that they lack the moral consistency that comes with a godly life; people turn away not only from high standards but from any standards at all. Charlemagne, though he seemed to possess some Christian principles, was a cruel and ruthless person. When he was buried, he was placed in a vault, and a statue of him was set up with a sword in hand. At the base was an open Bible. Years later, on entering the vault, men discovered that the sword had fallen and the point of it, coincidentally or perhaps providentially, rested on the New Testament verse that says, "For what is a man profited, if he shall gain the whole world, and lose his own soul?" (Matt. 16:26).

II. God always works toward a goal.

The Greeks taught that history traveled in cycles. They felt that which has been is that which shall be and that which shall be is that which has been. The Hebrews, on the other hand, guided by divine inspiration, felt that history moved toward a goal. Actually, of course, both are true. History does indeed move in cycles, but as it does so, it also moves toward a goal.

God, when He saw the world once more become sinful after the Flood, decided on a different approach. Rather than destroy the world this time, He would choose a person from it and through his seed bring redemption to the world. Abraham was his choice, and Jesus came through Abraham's seed. While it is not correct to say that God literally "turned His back" on the Gentile nations during Old Testament days, it does seem safe to say that God worked in a unique way with the Jewish people, giving them a fuller revelation of Himself and producing the Savior through them. Now Christianity is a worldwide religion, and all people may come directly to Christ. The glorious gospel is for everyone! This was, of course, in the mind of God from the beginning!

III. God's kingdom will never die.

Since Jesus has come, a new era has been inaugurated in the world. We are now living in the light of the glorious gospel of Christ. Jesus said that no one could come to the Father except by Him (John 14:6). Not only is it impossible to know what God is like without Jesus, we cannot have forgiveness without coming to the old rugged cross where the Lamb of God was slain, who also rose again from the dead. Nothing will ever defeat nor destroy the fresh movement that began in Jesus.

Conquerors have come and gone. The Caesars, Alexanders, and Sennacheribs have come and gone, but the Lord Jesus Christ still lives. People have tried to stamp out the Bible, God's Word, but the anvil of His truth has worn out the hammers of skepticism. One poet put it beautifully:

The kingdoms of the world go by
In purple and in gold.
They rise, they triumph, and they die,
And all their tale is told.

One kingdom only is divine;
One banner triumphs still;
Its king a servant, and its sign
A cross upon a hill.

Conclusion. The panoramic view of history presented to Daniel in his vision says to us that God has the "whole world in His hand" and will never abdicate His rule. Someone has said that the wisest thing a person can ever do is to find out where God is going and go with Him!

To think in terms of national history, however, is not enough. The main question is, Where do you as an individual fit into God's program? God doesn't save nations, but He does save individuals. God doesn't consign a nation to hell or heaven, but He does determine the fate of individuals in the world to come upon the basis of what each one has done with the Savior. Of course, each nation deteriorates or prospers in line with what the nation as a whole does with God; but the point is that, when Joshua said to the people, "Choose you this day whom ye will serve" (Josh. 24:15), he used the second person singular pronoun. Each person is responsible for his own choice!   —*FMW*

* * *

WEDNESDAY EVENING, MAY 23

TITLE: Body Life

Text: "Always seek to do good to one another" (1 Thess. 5:15b rsv).

Scripture Reading: 1 Thessalonians 5:12–15

Introduction. Ray Stedman has an excellent book on the church entitled *Body Life*. His title is appropriate for this section of Thessalonians in which Paul gives some practical but profound guidelines for life in the body of Christ. Guidance is given for the church as an organization and as an organism.

I. The church organized (vv. 12–13).

A. *Respect for leaders.* An important part of life in the body of Christ is the relationship toward church leadership. David Hubbard wrote, "Spiritual anarchy is as repugnant to God as political anarchy." God's gift to the church is spiritual leadership (Eph. 4:11). Church leaders deserve respect because they labor for the Lord. This respect comes easily when love for Christ is present.

B. *Leaders who labor.* Implied in Paul's word is the assumption that church leaders will lead in the spirit of Christ, who "loved the church." Lyle Schaller coined the phrase about the minister who "pays the rent" to describe a leader who is faithful in his expected responsibilities. Such a minister has earned the respect of the congregation. "Let the elders who rule well be considered worthy of double honor, especially those who labor in preaching and teaching" (1 Tim. 5:17 rsv).

C. *Peace must prevail.* "Be at peace among yourselves" (1 Thess. 5:13).

Is this primarily related to relationships with leaders? It is certainly true that strife, rivalry, argument, and gossip are destructive to effective leadership. Openness and honesty are essential. Conflict can be constructive but must never become a barrier to fellowship.

II. The church as organism (vv. 14–15).

A. *Each member a minister*. The challenge to minister is issued to the entire fellowship: "We exhort you, brethren." Each member is to admonish, encourage, help, and be patient with others. Church leaders are called to equip the members of the body "for the work of ministry" (Eph. 4:12 RSV). Each member bears responsibility for the health of the body.

B. *Minister to special needs*. The Thessalonian congregation had some special situations which called for ministry. Our church has some of these— "idle . . . fainthearted . . . weak." The strong are to help the weak (Rom. 14). We need to be sensitive to needs and minister to them.

C. *Minister without retaliation*. "See that none of you repays evil for evil" (1 Thess. 5:15 RSV). This is in harmony with Jesus (Matt. 5:44). Since we believe God works in all things for the good, we leave every difficulty with Him.

Conclusion. Church leaders and other members best fulfill their responsibilities in the church when they seek the highest good in Christ for others.   —*BW*

* * *

SUNDAY MORNING, MAY 27

TITLE: The Covenant of Marriage

TEXT: ". . . the Lord was witness to the covenant between you and the wife of your youth, to whom you have been faithless, though she is your companion and your wife by covenant" (Mal. 2:14 RSV).

SCRIPTURE READING: Malachi 2:10–16

HYMNS: "Come, Thou Almighty King," Anonymous
"O Happy Home Where Thou Art Lord," Spitta/Findlater
"O Perfect Love," Gurney

OFFERTORY PRAYER:
Heavenly Father, we affirm that this is Your world and that we are tenants here. We acknowledge that You give us the power to get wealth. Remind us again that life does not consist in the abundance of possessions. Convict us of selfishness, and free us to be liberal with our possessions so that the world might know You. Help us to focus on people, and strengthen our relationships with family and church. Accept our gifts as an expression of love. Use them to bless our fellowship and extend the kingdom. We thank You for Jesus' sake, in whose name we pray. Amen.

Introduction. The message of the prophet Malachi opens with the people's expression of doubt about God's love. Wrong views of God and false forms of worship inevitably lead to fractured social relationships. The situation in Israel demonstrated this reality. Marriage is one of the first places affected by a wrong relationship with God.

The prophet pronounces God's displeasure on two practices: marriage with heathen women (vv. 10–12) and the prevalence of divorce (vv. 13–16). His remarks express the Lord's hope for marriage and the crucial role it has in God's work in the world.

I. Marital choice can mar God's covenant.

A. *The priority of faith.* Israel is told they have "profaned the covenant" (v. 10) because of marriage to "the daughter of a foreign god" (v. 11 rsv). Exodus 19 describes the covenant established between Israel and the Lord. Exodus 34 forbade marriage with pagans; the practice of other religions in the home would provide temptation to break faith with God. "Can two walk together, except they be agreed?" (Amos 3:3).

It is disturbing to witness the trend of marriages which relegate faith and relationship to the Lord to a low priority. Differences in religion or the absence of any commitment to God is pushed into the background with the remark, "We love each other and so this will work out." Love Christ first; give priority to faith; and then choose a mate.

B. *A partner with faith.* The best solution is to choose a spouse who shares your commitment to Christ. Ideally this individual should come from your same Christian heritage. Certainly the person should be a saved and certain believer. To do less is to weaken your own covenant relationship with the Lord.

Many qualities and attributes strengthen marriage. Choose a partner with whom you share a vital relationship to Christ. The wrong marital choice can mar God's covenant.

II. The character of marriage.

Malachi offers an amazing description of marriage, closely akin to the spirit of Jesus and definitely in tune with all God's hopes for marriage. If you decide to marry, what does God expect of the marriage? The prophet cites four characteristics of a godly marriage.

A. *A covenant and not a contract.* "The Lord was witness to the covenant between you and the wife of your youth . . . she is . . . your wife by covenant" (v. 14 rsv). It has become fashionable to enter into marriage with a contract. A covenant implies commitment and faith; a contract implies convenience and fear. A covenant relationship declares that two have agreed to discover God's will together and work together to do that will. A contract stipulates what one will do *if* the other does certain things. A covenant declares we will achieve and fail together, laugh and cry together. In a covenant one is constrained from doing anything that would endanger the love of the other (Ernest Mosley, *Priorities in Ministry* [Nashville: Convention Press, 1978], p. 87).

B. *Companionship.* "She is your companion . . ." (v. 14). The Lord God said, "It is not good that the man should be alone" (Gen. 2:18). David Mace wrote, "Parenthood, therefore, may enrich marriage, but it will not sustain marriage. Neither will sex. There is much more in marriage than the physical love-making. In the daily living together of husband and wife amid all the changes and accidents of human life, what will matter most of all is that they are true and trusty friends" (David Mace, *Whom God Hath Joined* [Philadelphia: Westminster Press, 1953], p. 24).

C. *Creation.* "What does he desire? Godly offspring" (Mal. 2:15 rsv). The command to Adam and Eve was to "be fruitful, and multiply, and replenish the earth" (Gen. 1:28). Part of God's purpose for marriage is to provide the best possible environment for the growth and development of a child. Mace notes that procreation means "creation for and on behalf of another" (Ibid., p. 20). For two Christians parenthood is a way of sharing in the creative work of God. Adoption and foster parenthood are avenues open to those who are unable to have children.

D. *Continuity.* It takes time to build a covenant relationship. Time is involved in deepening companionship; time is required to see the results of creative parenting. God's ideal is for marriage to last. "I hate divorce" (v. 16 rsv). Jesus said, "What therefore God has joined together, let no man put asunder" (Mark 10:9 rsv). Although the Lord still loves the divorced individual, He hates divorce; it violates His ideal. He enables one to overcome the grief of divorce, but the ideal must be maintained.

Too many approach marriage lightly, thinking that divorce is available to them if necessary. Yet divorce is not always a happy solution, for 59 percent of second marriages fail. Divorce should be regarded as the last recourse rather than the first option. The trend will not be reversed until individuals committed to Christ accept their duty and privilege to set the example of devotion and fidelity.

Conclusion. Decisions involved in marriage are crucial for personal and community well-being. The strength of the church is also affected. Marriage should honor the covenant relationship with God. The choice of a nonbelieving spouse can mar that covenant. With a Christian mate determine to maintain a covenant marked by love, companionship, and creativity. As the union continues until death, it will be blessed by the Lord.   *—BW*

* * *

SUNDAY EVENING, MAY 27

TITLE: Trust God and Take Your Stand

Text: "If it be so, our God whom we serve is able to deliver us from the burning fiery furnace . . . we will not serve thy gods, nor worship the golden image which thou hast set up" (Dan. 3:17–18).

Scripture Reading: Daniel 3:1–30

Introduction. Your religious faith may lead you into the fires of affliction and tribulation. But, if it does, it will lead you safely through to the other side. Daniel's three friends learned this truth, and the recording of it through God's divinely inspired messenger has blessed the world for centuries. More than a story from the dim past, this account of Shadrach, Meshach, and Abednego is as relevant as tomorrow's sunrise. As long as selfish men with large portions of personal pride and ambition try to dominate faithful servants of the Lord, this story will speak its message afresh.

I. Dedication.

Nebuchadnezzar comes across as a strange character. One would think he had learned his lesson from two previous encounters with Daniel, but apparently he soon forgot the lessons he had learned concerning the simple food the Hebrews ate and the dream Daniel had interpreted.

The king had a gold statue made ninety feet high and nine feet wide and set it up in the Plain of Dura. He then gave orders for all his leaders to come together to dedicate this statue. The decree was sent forth that when the music started, everyone was to bow down and worship this golden monstrosity that Nebuchadnezzar had established. Moreover, anyone who refused to do so would be thrown into a blazing furnace.

II. Dilemma.

For a short time, Daniel's three friends, who had remained faithful to their God even in a foreign land, faced the choice. What would they do? No doubt they did not debate long. They realized at the very first where their loyalties lay; and with a good spirit, but also with firm conviction, they refused to honor the king's request.

In today's world, only a few people are called on to face such a traumatic choice, although the number does seem to be growing in certain areas; but we are often faced with the responsibility of taking a personal stand for God though it means a certain kind of oppression. To be ostracized socially or to be discriminated against economically can hurt a lot! Those who suffer such tribulation must often feel they could stand the physical torture more easily than peer pressure or financial hardship. We all have our "fiery furnaces" regardless of our station in life.

Faith, however, is able to triumph over every difficulty and trial. The same principle that enabled Moses to suffer affliction with God's people rather than enjoy the pleasures of sin for a season caused these exiles to rise above the fear of a fiery furnace.

Of course, these willing martyrs—committed to God's will for their lives—must also have been aware that it may not be God's purpose to deliver them from the perils of death. If not, they reasoned that it would be far better to be carried heavenward on the fiery chariot of martyrdom. The words *and if not* are among the most sublime words ever written or spoken. They represent the conviction that one who trusts God must hold to the very end. Another great man of God, likewise, affirmed his faith when he said, "Though he slay me, yet will I trust in him" (Job 13:15). Such triumphs of faith over adverse circumstances stand as glorious achievements, attained through the help of God's Holy Spirit. Possessing clear insight into the truth that the voice of duty must be obeyed will lead one to defy every combination of opposing forces.

III. Deliverance.

A foretaste of what would happen came when those who put the three men into the furnace were burned themselves because of the exceedingly hot flame. Although the death of these executioners seems to have attracted no special notice, the fact that the flames did not immediately consume Shadrach, Meshach, and Abednego must have held some promise of a favorable outcome.

The miraculous story reached its climax as the people saw four persons rather than three in the furnace. Looking at the story from this side of Calvary, we have no problem identifying the visitor. He was more than a "son of the gods," as some translations render it. He was the second member of the Trinity. We have here a brief preincarnate appearance of Jesus Christ, our Lord and Savior.

Only one choice was available for the king. He must investigate and act on the evidence. The deliverance was followed by a royal decree. How long Nebuchadnezzar's resolution lasted is not the question. The point is that God protects His own and turns the wrath of sin to His glory. Throughout history, this drama has been reenacted in various forms as people have dared to stand firmly and without fear. These three men had faith and were delivered. Faith is not trying to believe in spite of the evidence but rather daring to do in spite of the consequence. An element of the first may be present, but the essential part of faith is complete commitment. Only then is it saving faith.

Conclusion. Although many lessons may be gleaned from the story, one stands out supremely. God never forsakes His faithful followers.

> There is an eye that never sleeps
> Beneath the wing of night.
> There is an ear that never shuts
> When sink the beams of light.
>
> There is an arm that never tires
> When human strength gives way.
> There is a love that never fails
> When earthly loves decay.
>
> That Eye unseen still watcheth all;
> That Arm upholds the sky;
> That Ear doth hear the sparrow's call;
> That Love is ever nigh.

One Christian of another generation said when he faced a great crisis in his life, "My head is resting sweetly on three pillows—Infinite Power, Infinite Wisdom, and Infinite Love." God gives us strength to solve our problems when this is the need; but when they are too big for us, He intervenes miraculously and delivers. In the fiery furnace, God showed His great power by performing a supernatural act to bring salvation. He also performed such a deed at Calvary because man was not able to atone for his own sin. Trust God always and do what is right. He will never leave one of His loved ones, nor force him to walk alone. —*FMW*

* * *

WEDNESDAY EVENING, MAY 30

TITLE: God's Will for You

TEXT: **"Rejoice always, pray constantly, give thanks in all circumstances; for this is the will of God in Christ Jesus for you" (1 Thess. 5:16–18 RSV).**

SCRIPTURE READING: **Philippians 4:4–7; 1 Thessalonians 5:16–18**

Introduction. Young and old alike are sometimes puzzled about the will of God. "It is not the will of my Father . . . that one of these little ones shall perish" (Matt. 18:14 RSV), but then what? Paul shares three specific aspects of God's will for individuals. J. B. Phillips' translation of our text is vivid: "Be happy in your faith at all times. Never stop praying. Be thankful, whatever the circumstances may be."

Paul frequently shared this trilogy—Romans 12:12; Colossians 4:2; Philippians 4:4–7.

I. These three are for you.

A. *Rejoice.* An excited, enthusiastic attitude toward life is contagious. Try the approach of the psalmist: "This is the day the LORD has made; let us rejoice and be glad in it" (Ps. 118:24 NIV). If one will "rejoice always," he will never have to worry about quenching the Spirit.

B. *Pray.* Prayer should be the door through which we approach each day and the door we close on the day. Prayer must also permeate the day—"pray constantly." Rosalind Rinker has defined prayer as "a dialogue between two persons who love each other." Prayer needs to be moved from a structured speech of theology to conversation with a loving Father. Instead of just a Sunday ritual, it must become a daily experience.

C. *Give thanks.* A blind person told me, "I don't think about what I have lost. I'm thankful for what I still have." Thanksgiving has become a seasonal expression. The grace of gratitude has remarkable power to overcome depression and give new direction to life. "Count your blessings. Name them one by one."

D. .*Daily experience.* A theme is repeated in this trilogy—"evermore . . . without ceasing . . . is everything." Make these attributes a daily experience; put them to work in everything that happens.

II. Tested and approved by Paul.

Paul was not writing sweet words empty of power. Examine his life; he practiced what he preached.

A. *Thorn in the flesh* (2 Cor. 12:1–10). Whatever this burden, he was not allowed freedom from it. He prayed about it and found God's grace to be sufficient.

B. *Imprisonment* (Phil. 1). He let God use his confinement for "the futherance of the gospel" (v. 12). While in jail he "prayed, and sang praises unto God" (Acts 16:25). He rejoiced always.

III. Offered in Jesus Christ.

A. *In Jesus.* It is possible to approach life with these three attributes. Life in Jesus includes all three dynamics. Jesus came to give abundant life.

B. *For you.* This is God's will for you as an individual. Are you in Jesus? Does the sin of personal rebellion or selfishness block the joy Jesus wants to give? The prayer of repentance and faith will enable Him to impart a new nature. With His help you can face every circumstance. You have not been lost in the crowd. Christ's love is for you. Will you accept it?

Conclusion. It is inconceivable that one should trust Jesus for life beyond the grave and fail to rely on Him for the experiences of daily living. God's will is salvation for time and eternity. While on the way to glory He wants us to rejoice, pray, and be thankful.   —*BW*

* * *

SUGGESTED PREACHING PROGRAM
FOR THE MONTH OF JUNE

Sunday Mornings

We continue with the general theme "Good Housekeeping," giving attention to some of the basic needs within marriage and family living.

Sunday Evenings

We continue the series of messages based on the prophesies found in the Book of Daniel. The suggested theme is "The Prophet's Message for Stressful Times."

Wednesday Evenings

We conclude the studies based on Paul's Epistles to the Church at Thessalonica, using the theme "Let the Apostle Paul Speak to the Present."

* * *

SUNDAY MORNING, JUNE 3

TITLE: Do You Know Where Your Children Are?

TEXT: ". . . the boy Jesus stayed behind in Jerusalem. His parents did not know it, but supposing him to be in the company they went a day's journey, and they sought him among their kinsfolk and acquaintances; and when they did not find him, they returned to Jerusalem, seeking him" (Luke 2:43–45 RSV).

SCRIPTURE READING: Luke 2:39–52

HYMNS: "Friend of the Home," Lewis
"I Think When I Read That Sweet Story," Luke
"O God, Who to a Loyal Home," Fosdick

OFFERTORY PRAYER:
O Father, revealed to us in Jesus Christ, we rejoice in knowing You are touched with the feeling of our infirmities. We know that you understand the tension that sometimes exists between parents and children. Give wisdom and patience to our families in these difficult days. Lord, we pray for the ability to discern what is best among the good. Give us courage to maintain Christian priorities in a society often apathetic to Your values. May this offering make us aware that the best values cannot be preserved without sacrifice. Thank You for the sacrifice of Jesus, in whose name we pray. Amen.

Introduction. Each evening prior to the late news, a certain television station had the practice of stating the time and asking, "Do you know where your children are?" That was the question Mary and Joseph had to answer that first night away from Jerusalem on their return home from the Passover celebration. They probably traveled in a caravan with other pilgrims. The women usually left first and the men followed; the children played and visited among friends and relatives. When evening came and all gathered for the meal, Jesus was not present. Imagine their anxiety and agony for they did not know where He was.

Do you know where your children are? The question needs to be asked in three ways—literally, physically, and spiritually.

I. Literally—do you know where your children are?

This is probably the primary intention of the television question, and it raises the problem every parent faces. Parents must face the tension between control and permissiveness, guidance and freedom. There are dangers with extremes in both directions. Mary and Joseph supposed "him to be in the company" (v. 44), but they really didn't know.

Today's parents face the challenge of creatively directing their youth or letting them roam and "find themselves." It is easier to let neighborhood or peer groups rear them, but the risks are higher. We are "conceived in iniquity," and the tendency toward sin calls for guidance to do what is right.

Do you know where your children are—the movies they see, the books they read, the friends they make? Parental dictatorship is not needed, but creative parental involvement is essential for any child to mature.

II. Physically—do you know where your children are?

Are you aware of where your child is as a maturing individual? This aspect calls for an awareness of needs at any given age. Some children are pushed into relationships before they have the maturity to cope with them. A teen-ager related, "I didn't want to date so early, but mom said that other girls were. 'They'll think you're not popular.' When my boyfriend and I started going steady, I wanted mom to say, 'No—you're too young.'" Later the girl struggled with the dilemma of breaking a relationship that had become too involved.

Another tendency is to regard young people as less mature than they are. This is reflected in a lack of trust or a continuation of very strict guidelines long after they are needed. A parent's cautious and secretive way of approaching sexuality illustrates a misunderstanding of a child's maturity.

A strong temptation also exists for a parent to make his child become what he himself never was. The pressure begins in Little League, where many angry parents may ruin a child's play. The pressure is in the classroom, where the push for academic excellence may cause a child to fail in needed social development. The pressure is on the future, trying to mold a young person into a vocation a parent may have desired for himself but was unable to achieve.

Mary and Joseph searched two days before they located Jesus,, and it seems the last place they looked was in the temple. Jesus asked, "How is it that you sought me? Did you not know that I must be in my Father's house?" (v. 49 RSV). They were ignorant of His maturity, interests, and desires. Do you know where your children are?

III. Spiritually—do you know where your children are?

Just as each child will unnaturally respond to evil, every child, because he is made in the image of God, has a natural attraction toward good and God. Do you know where your children are spiritually? Many youth are more atune to the voice of God than their parents. Mary and Joseph were "astonished" at Jesus' response in the temple (v. 48).

A parent has an awesome responsibility regarding the spiritual welfare of children. Fathers are admonished to "bring them up in the discipline and instruction of the Lord" (Eph. 6:4 RSV). Jesus warned about causing the little ones to stumble (Matt. 18:6).

It is in the home where spiritual foundations are laid. It is a miracle of God that some find Christ and have a strong relationship with Him when they were never exposed to the faith at home. A strong spiritual environment of Christian love and faith is the best heritage to impart to a child. "Train up a child in the way he should go: and when he is old, he will not depart from it" (Prov. 22:6).

Conclusion. Do you know where your children are? It is a good question and one that every Christian parent eventually answers in hope—"I hope and I have faith they are where they will honor Christ." The father of the prodigal son did his best and then let his son go. Love and faith triumphed for that family. Is the love of God our Father and faith in Christ the Son the most important part of your life? Such a commitment is needed by parents and their children.

One of you here today may be struggling with your relationship to the Lord. You realize you need Jesus, His forgiveness, and a new start on life. You can receive all that and more by confession and rejection of sin and total trust in Jesus alone as Lord and Savior. For Heaven's sake, do it! For the sake of your family, do it!   —*BW*

* * *

SUNDAY EVENING, JUNE 3

TITLE: Learn the Lesson God Wants to Teach

TEXT: **"Now I Nebuchadnezzar praise and extol and honour the King of heaven, all whose works are truth, and his ways judgment: and those that walk in pride he is able to abase" (Dan. 4:37).**

SCRIPTURE READING: **Daniel 4:1–37**

Introduction. Nebuchadnezzar stands as one of the strangest men who ever ruled an empire. He seems to make a fresh start at different times to serve the true God, but somewhere along the way he slips back. We certainly must admire the way he treated Daniel and his three friends concerning the food they were given to eat. Also, he seems to have accepted Daniel's God after the Hebrew lad revealed the secrets of the king's dream. We cannot condone his throwing the Hebrew children into the fiery furnace, but he "repented" and made a decree that forbade anyone to speak anything against the God of Shadrach, Meshach, and Abednego.

To say that Nebuchadnezzar was completely dishonest and hypocritical seems unfair. On the other hand, however, he certainly did not remain true to the vows he made. He loved prosperity, with all the amenities that accompany it, and refused to exercise the personal discipline necessary for a life that honored and pleased the God whom Judah worshiped. The story before us has some elements of a flashback, as we are given many details of Nebuchadnezzar's past conduct, although the story opens and closes in the present tense.

I. A testimony based on an experience.

Patrick Henry is reported to have once said, "The only way I can predict the future is by looking at the past." How true! Every generation, however, must learn for itself that the stove is hot. Someone went so far as to say, "Experience is not the best teacher. It is the only teacher." As Nebuchadnezzar begins the story, he looks backward. Something had happened to teach him a great lesson. He was ready now to give testimony concerning it.

Those of us who are Christians can identify with this king, though he lived many centuries ago and never embraced either the Christian faith or Judaism. He was, however, influenced by the monotheism and the high moral standards that are a product of it. Everyone who lives today in a Christian land is both influenced and benefited, to some extent, by the Christian faith. Someone said once that anyone who lives in a Christian land without identifying personally with Christianity is actually a parasite, because he enjoys the blessings but refuses to accept the responsibilities of the Christian faith.

II. A look backward.

Nebuchadnezzar was living comfortably and enjoying great prosperity when a dream frightened him. He called for his staff of fortunetellers, magicians, wizards, and astrologers, but they could not explain the dream to him. Finally, he called Daniel. We wonder why Nebuchadnezzar did not call Daniel first, since he had made him chief of the fortunetellers and had great confidence in his ability. Perhaps the king used Daniel only on special occasions and felt his lesser staff members could handle this situation.

The dream consisted of a huge tree in the middle of the earth that grew bigger and bigger until it could be seen by everyone and was loaded down with enough fruit for the entire world to eat. Wild animals rested in its shade, and birds built their nests in its branches. Various animals ate from it. The king then saw an angel who gave orders to cut the tree down and chop off its branches, stripping its leaves and scattering its fruit. The command, however, ordered the destroyers to leave the stump, with a band of iron and bronze around it, in the ground. He then ordered dew to fall on the man in the dream and let him live with the animals and plants for seven years, having the mind of an animal rather than that of a human being.

Daniel explained that the dream applied to the king himself, who had grown tall and strong so that his power extended over all the world. Daniel told Nebuchadnezzar that the supreme God had decreed that he would be driven away from human society to live with wild animals, eating grass like an ox and sleeping in the open air where the dew would fall on him, for seven years. After that, he would confess that the supreme God of the universe controls all kingdoms. The angel ordered the stump to be left in the ground because Nebuchadnezzar would become king again when he acknowledged the God that rules the world. Daniel then told Nebuchadnezzar that if he changed his way of living, he would continue to be prosperous. Although Daniel did not say it, the implication is that if he failed to do this, the dream would come true.

Nebuchadnezzar did not obey the prophet! A year later, while walking around on the roof of the royal palace, he boasted how great the city of Babylon was and took credit for building it in order to display his own power, might, glory, and majesty. Before the words were out of his mouth, God spoke from heaven, told him he would be driven away from human society, and then enumerated the very things that were present in the vision. The words came true, and Nebuchadnezzar suffered the fate Daniel had predicted in interpreting the dream. The king's hair grew as long as eagle feathers and his nails as long as bird claws. Fortunately, at the end of seven years, the king repented and was restored.

He sang praises to God when his captivity was removed and he was put back on the throne. This is the background for the king's testimony in the first few verses of this chapter.

III. Don't learn the hard way!

Nebuchadnezzar went through a virtual hell on earth before he learned about God and yielded to Him. Some people are so strong-willed and bent on sin that they must suffer many things before they finally yield to the Savior. If it takes this to lead someone to Christ, God has a way of bringing it upon a person. Others, however, do not have to go this far in sin. They give their hearts to the Lord in the tender years of their lives. The hymnwriter sang,

> Early let us seek thy favor,
> Early let us do thy will,
> Blessed Lord and only Saviour
> With thy love our bosoms fill.

The foreign mission board of a major denomination ran a survey recently and found that the conversion experiences of the missionaries appointed by the board that year took place at an average of less than nine years of age. We can go deep into sin and be delivered by the grace of God, but how much more wonderful to commit ourselves to the Savior before the evil days set in upon us. You see, even when the grace of God saves us from sin and hell, scars often remain, and somehow we cannot be as equipped for service in the Lord's work as we might have been if we did not have the years of sinning.

Conclusion. Where are you today? If you are out in the wilderness with Nebuchadnezzar, turn to the Lord. You do not have to wait seven years as he did! You can come to Jesus now! If, on the other hand, you are young but old enough to understand you are a sinner, you do not have to wait for a sin-soaked life to be yours before claiming the blessings of God's grace. All are sinners, and thus all must be saved by Jesus; but look at yourself now and in whatever state of sinful deterioration you find yourself, come to Jesus now before the sin gets worse and the decision becomes more difficult! —*FMW*

* * *

WEDNESDAY EVENING, JUNE 6

TITLE: Three Essentials for a Growing Church

TEXT: **"Brethren, pray for us. Greet all the brethren with a holy kiss. I adjure you by the Lord that this letter be read to all the brethren"** (1 Thess. 5:25–27 RSV).

SCRIPTURE READING: **1 Thessalonians 5:23–28**

Introduction. Paul closes his First Letter to the Thessalonians with three practical admonitions. They are essential for a church that desires to grow.

I. Prayer.

"Brethren, pray for us" (v. 25). Paul will repeat himself when he writes again (2 Thess. 3:1). His experience only deepened his commitment to prayer as an essential ingredient to a vibrant faith and a growing church. It was a note he sounded to other congregations as well (Rom. 15:30; Eph. 6:18; Col. 4:3).

Paul, like other apostles, knew the value of intercessory prayer (James 5:16). Jesus said, "My house shall be called a house of prayer" (Matt. 21:13). Good programs are nothing without prayer. Prepared preaching is powerless without prayer. A church that makes little of prayer will not grow.

II. Fellowship.

"Greet all the brethren with a holy kiss" (1 Thess. 5:26 RSV). This common greeting in the early church expressed their oneness in Christ and their spiritual affection as members of the family of God. This custom has largely vanished, but the essential element must remain—authentic Christian love. Growing churches are known for their warmth of fellowship and genuine concern for people. Jesus said, "Love one another as I have loved you" (John 15:12). He was unafraid to share His life with others.

The church is called the family of God. Is our congregation a family others want to be a part of because they are loved?

III. God's Word.

"I adjure you by the Lord that this letter be read to all the brethren" (1 Thess. 5:27). The Thessalonians were commanded to read Paul's letter, which the Holy Spirit inspired. A growing church gives priority to God's Word. The centrality of preaching and Bible study are essential for a growing church. When a publisher announced the publication of a condensed version of the Bible, I thought, "Many people and churches already have one. They take what pleases them and ignore what they do not like."

Conclusion. Many elements have been stressed to insure a growing church— adequate facilities, trained staff, good materials, finances, vision. If prayer, · fellowship, and God's Word are missing, a church might grow, but it will not be the church Jesus is building.   *—BW*

* * *

SUNDAY MORNING, JUNE 10

TITLE: **Honor Within the Home**

TEXT: **"Children, obey your parents in the Lord, for this is right. 'Honor your father and mother' (this is the first commandment with a promise), 'that is may be well with you and that you may live long on the earth.' Fathers, do not provoke your children to anger, but bring them up in the discipline and instruction of the Lord" (Eph. 6:1–4 RSV).**

SCRIPTURE READING: **Exodus 20:12; Ephesians 6:1–4**

HYMNS: **"I Am So Glad That Our Father," Bliss**
        "Jesus Loves Me," Warner
        "O God in Heaven, Whose Loving Plan," Martin

OFFERTORY PRAYER:

Our Father, may this worship experience honor and glorify Your name. We acknowledge our trust in You whom we have come to know in

Christ. Cleanse our hands and purify our hearts and receive these gifts in deep gratitude for Your merciful forgiveness. In Jesus' name we pray. Amen.

Introduction. "David considers leaving town with Chris and kidnapping Dottie. Billy Clyde meets Phoebe, who thinks she can use him to help break up Donna and Chuck's marriage. After Chuck throws Billy out of his apartment, Billy vows revenge. Chuck believes Donna is pregnant. In defending her love of Mark to his mother, Ellen realizes how much she does love him, and the couple goes to bed. Brooke gets Danny to skip work in order to take her out. . . . His divorce from Nancy final, Frank asks Caroline to marry him. Erica plans to plant pot on Claudette, and she tells Nick that Claudette is now on probationary parole." Thus went one week's chronicle of a television soap opera. Is this what faces "all my children"? The Scripture's help in parent-child relationships is desperately needed. The fifth of the Ten Commandments remains a very relevant word—"Honor your father and your mother."

This commandment is a bridge between the first four commandments, which focus on God, and the last commandments, which relate to other people. The pivotal position of this commandment illustrates the significance of the family. What happens in the home determines our understanding of God and our understanding of people. If we lose ground on this commandment, the other nine are severely threatened. The word *honor* also stresses this fact. *Honor* is used to describe the nature and presence of God. Here it is applied to the home. Glorify the home! Lift it up with respect and reverence.

I. A word to children.

This commandment was originally addressed to adult males in a time when parents lived with their married children. Honor, respect, and reverence are to be given to parents—always! Our Lord's own example as a youth (Luke 2:51) and on the cross (John 19:25–27) indicates that He accepted this guide for life in the family.

A mother in a geriatrics center said to me, "We get lonely." The sadness of her words were deepened when I realized her children, who lived in the town, rarely came to visit. It will not be well for children who fail to honor their parents.

One of the characteristics of the last days will be disobedience to parents (2 Tim. 3:2). Children are to obey their parents "in the Lord, for this is right" (Eph. 6:1 RSV). This principle remains and is clearly enunciated in both Old and New Testaments.

II. A word to parents.

Parents are to be worthy of honor. Can much honor come to a parent who is not honorable? The inspiration comes from parents and the return is honor from children. Two options are noted in Ephesians 6:4: "Fathers, do not provoke your children to anger, but bring them up in the discipline and instruction of the Lord" (RSV). Parents can provoke or provide. The choice is between a harsh, negative, and oppressive presence or a patient, positive, gentle, Christlike involvement.

Many rebellious young people are acting out their anger toward parents whom they resent for harsh treatment or they are trying to seek attention from neglectful parents. "Nurture and admonition" are positive attributes which describe education by deed, discipline toward the right, and encouragement. A careless and indifferent parental response will reap tragic consequences, as the example of Eli testifies (1 Sam. 3:13).

What a calling it is to be a parent! The challenge is to "bring them up" rather than break their spirits, insure their maturity rather than our mastery. Children want and need this from parents. A little girl was involved in one misbehavior after another, interspersed with meaningless scoldings by her mother. She finally plopped herself in a chair and declared, "I wish daddy would come home and make me behave."

III. Relationship centered in Christ.

The basis for honorable home relationships is in Christ. Children are asked to respond "in the Lord"; parents are admonished to rear children "of the Lord." Both parent and child must find themselves "in the Lord" and with His help develop the relationship He has given them. The same responses we make to Christ are needed in the home—repentance, confession, forgiveness, love. John Claypool had defined a family as a "covenant of caring . . . responsible love within a fellowship of forgiveness and reconciliation." Is Christ your Lord?

James Dobson's father prayed at his son's wedding: "It is also our earnest prayer for them, not that God shall have a part in their lives, but that He shall have the preeminent part; not that they shall possess faith, but that faith shall fully possess them both; that in a materialistic world they shall not live for the earthly and temporal alone, but that they shall be enabled to lay hold on that which is spiritual and eternal" (James C. Dobson, *Straight Talk to Men and Their Wives* [Waco: Word Books, 1980], p. 56).

Conclusion. Jesus did not come to destroy the law but to fill it full of meaning. In Jesus this commandment of honor within the home can find its deepest meaning. Responsibility rests on the entire family. With Christ as the tie that binds, the home can be the best place on earth.　　　　—*BW*

* * *

SUNDAY EVENING, JUNE 10

TITLE: **Do You Weigh Enough?**

TEXT: **"Thou art weighed in the balances, and art found wanting"** (Dan. 5:27).

SCRIPTURE READING: **Daniel 5:1–31**

Introduction. So many lessons may be gleaned from the story of Belshazzar's feast that one scarcely knows in which direction to move in giving an exposition or preaching a sermon from the story. The climax, of course, comes when Daniel makes the stern pronouncement to the king that, in God's sight, he falls short. We will focus on that truth but seek also to give an overview of the entire story.

I. Revelry.

When Paul cataloged "the sins of the flesh" in his letter to the Galatians, he concluded with "drunkenness" and "revellings." These two sins of indulgence signify unbridled license that produces degrading conduct. In Paul's day such activity often began with a band of friends accompanying a victor in an athletic contest. Laughing and dancing, they sang praises to him. Such activity often was a part of the devotees of Bacchus, the god of wine. Nocturnal and riotous mobs of half-drunken and frolicsome people paraded the streets with music and torches in honor of Bacchus or some other depraved deity, singing and playing before the houses of their friends with drinking parties that lasted until late into the night.

Such conduct characterized Belshazzar's feast, but a dimension was added to it that introduced blasphemy against the Hebrew God, Yahweh, who was holy and refused to be insulted. The king gave orders to bring in the gold and silver cups and bowls which his father Nebuchadnezzar had brought to Babylon from the temple in Jerusalem. The people, including his concubines, drank intoxicating beverages from these utensils and engaged in riotous and degrading conduct.

When people surrender themselves to the passions of their lower nature, they lose all self-control. Sin piles on top of sin as they seek to outdo each other in immoral and filthy behavior. Belshazzar's feast must have been this type of folly. Ignoring all principles of decency, they participated in the grossest sins with animallike behavior.

II. Revelation.

God can stand only so much of man's sin and no more! In the New Testament, Paul speaks of how "God also gave them up to uncleanness through the lusts of their own hearts" and "gave them up unto vile affections" and "gave them over to a reprobate mind" (Rom. 1:24, 26, 28). In the midst of the banquet hall, God suddenly appeared and wrote upon the wall of the king's palace a message that no one could read.

After all earthly resources were exhausted, God's prophet, Daniel, was summoned. The king offered him gifts to read the message, but Daniel refused them, although he agreed to read and interpret the words. His message was simple. God had dealt with Nebuchadnezzar when he became proud, stubborn, and cruel, disciplining him in the wilderness. Although Nebuchadnezzar repented and acknowledged the supreme God, Belshazzar had not profited by the example. The present king was, therefore, ripe for judgment.

What did the message mean? God had numbered the days of Belshazzar's kingdom. He had been weighed on the scales and by divine measure was too light. His iniquities so far exceeded his good points that he was in trouble, deep trouble. This was God's Word and there was no appeal from it.

III. Retribution.

The mills of God sometimes grind slowly, but at other times they work quickly. In Belshazzar's case, judgment came the same night that Daniel proclaimed it. The Persians were already "casing the joint" and planning to attack. They made their move shortly after Daniel startled the king and his leaders with the shocking warning.

Two differing accounts, from nonbiblical sources, tell us how the feat was accomplished. One says the Persians diverted the water of the Euphrates River, which flowed through the main part of the city of Babylon, and came in the dry riverbed. Another source says the people were so disgusted with the rule of Belshazzar that they revolted and opened the gates of the city, allowing the Persians to enter virtually unopposed. Of course, both versions could be true. Belshazzar was wicked enough to incur the wrath of even a pagan empire!

Judgment always comes. The moral law of sin and retribution is written into the universe. We are not only punished *for* our sins, we are punished *by* our sins. Sin itself pays us off. The Scripture does not say, "Be sure your sin will be found out," but rather, "Be sure your sin will find you out" (Num. 32:23). Sometimes we say that sin doesn't pay, but the bitter truth is that sin does pay—it pays in currency that is minted in the coffers of hell.

Conclusion. If you were placed on the scales of God's righteous judgment, how would you rate? Would you register "sixteen ounces to the pound" or would you fall short of the standard?

On one thing we must be careful. The New Testament makes it clear that we are not saved by doing more good deeds than bad deeds. We are saved by faith in Jesus Christ, by repenting of our sin and trusting Jesus as our personal Savior. On the other hand, nowhere does the Bible, either in the Old Testament or the New, minimize righteous deeds. We produce fruit according to what kind of tree we are, and the good tree cannot produce bad fruit any more than a bad tree can produce good fruit. Jesus told us that we can know people by their fruits.

What if Belshazzar had fallen down at Daniel's feet, repenting of his sin and pleading for mercy? What if Judas had come to Jesus and begged for forgiveness? God would have saved either one of them at the last minute, working whatever miracle was necessary, if they had come with sincerity and genuine repentance. Most likely, you have not gone nearly as far in sin as Belshazzar or Judas, but you still need to be saved. The only way you can "weigh enough" on God's scales is to accept the substitutionary death of Jesus as the atonement for your sin. Will you do it?   —*FMW*

* * *

WEDNESDAY EVENING, JUNE 13

TITLE: When the Lord Is Revealed

Text: ". . . when the Lord Jesus is revealed from heaven . . ." (2 Thess. 1:7 rsv).

Scripture Reading: 2 Thessalonians 1:3–12

Introduction. Every chapter of 1 Thessalonians concludes with a reference to the triumphant return of Jesus Christ. Paul expands that theme in his second letter. The certainty of the Lord's coming is reflected in the word *when—when* the Lord is revealed." Only a matter of time and He will come. His return will be a revelation; all will be made clear.

I. The Lord's coming provides perspective on present problems.
This passage was written to people undergoing persecution. Some were probably asking if Christ cared. They came to realize the life of Christ did not exempt them from trouble. In Him they discovered a new power to cope.

A. *An experience of growth.* The Lord, our present help in trouble, enables us to experience growth, which prepares us for His return. It happened to the Thessalonians—"Your faith is growing abundantly" (v. 3b rsv). Some things we will never discover without the test of adversity.

B. *Deepens our dependence on others.* ". . . the love of every one of you for one another is increasing" (v. 3c RSV). Problems often reveal true friendships and make us aware of our need for others.

II. The Lord's coming will reveal eternal destiny.

A. *Separated from glory.* Those who have refused Jesus Christ "shall suffer the punishment of eternal destruction and exclusion from the presence of the Lord and from the glory of his might" (v. 9 RSV). Instead of annihilation, unbelievers will spend an eternity dying. The reality is worse than the description. Those who remain "short of the glory" (Rom. 3:23) will be forever separated from the glory.

B. *Glory for the saints.* "When he comes . . . to be glorified in his saints" (2 Thess. 1:10 RSV). Jesus restores the glory lost by sin. When Jesus returns, we will be glorified and He will receive glory. As someone said, "We get Him and He gets us."

III. Today's decision determines tomorrow's destiny.

Eternal destiny is involved in individual response to "the gospel of our Lord Jesus" (v. 8). The gospel asks everyone to repent and believe. Jesus warned, "Except ye repent, ye shall all likewise perish" (Luke 13:5).

The Lord's return will be a glorious experience to "all who have believed." To believe in Jesus is to acknowledge sin, turn from it, and trust Jesus alone for salvation.

Jesus is the way, the truth, and the life. He is the only way to heaven (John 14:6). Today's decision about Jesus determines eternal destiny. Are you ready to meet Him?

Conclusion. On a stretch of Tennessee highway approaching the Kentucky state line, a number of billboards advertise businesses that sell fireworks. Some of the signs boldly note, "Last Chance." Yet a little farther will be another such establishment. Eventually a traveler will come to the "Last Chance." Just beyond is the state line beyond which fireworks cannot be legally purchased. Today might be someone's last chance. When the Lord comes, the time to decide will be gone. The time of Christ's return is classified information, known only to the Father, but He is coming. We may go before He comes. None of us knows how far down the road of life we have traveled. The line between now and eternity might be close at hand. Be ready! —*BW*

* * *

SUNDAY MORNING, JUNE 17

TITLE: Daddy, How Do You Spell Love?

TEXT: "Beloved, let us love one another; for love is of God . . . In this the love of God was made manifest among us, that God sent his only Son into the world, so that we might live through him" (1 John 4:7a, 9 RSV).

SCRIPTURE READING: 1 John 4:7–16

HYMNS: "Christian Hearts, in Love United," Zinzendorf/Foster
"Love Is the Theme," Fisher
"Love Lifted Me," Rowe

OFFERTORY PRAYER:

Lord, we rejoice in the gift of Your love. No greater love can be found than that manifested in the death of Jesus. Realizing His sacrifice we are convicted of our unworthiness. Empower us to love without limits, to live in His strength, and to lay all at His feet. Accept these gifts, a portion of Your creation, and use them to hasten the day when the kingdoms of this world shall become the kingdom of our Lord. We pray in Jesus' name. Amen.

Introduction. One Saturday afternoon while a father was cutting the grass, his four-year-old daughter came to the back door and shouted, "Daddy, how do you spell love?" He gave her the four letters, which with her newly found skill of printing she placed on a drawing she later proudly presented to those she loved.

How do you spell love? It is more than a matter of putting four letters of the alphabet together in correct sequence. We spell it as we express it and live it and in the way we fulfill our personal relationships. In that way love may be the most misspelled word in the vocabulary of our lives.

There is abundant evidence of the disastrous consequences of a misdirected and inadequate love:

• the teen-ager whose parents have given her everything but the gift of their presence and love.

• a battered spouse victimized by one who had earlier said, "I pledge to you my love."

• a church torn by jealousy and misplaced priorities.

• the words whispered in the ear of a date as the car stops in front of a motel—"You love me, don't you?"

How do you spell love? Our children are asking. A world desperately in need of Christ's love is watching and waiting for our response, which will make the difference in the quality of life now and forever. I suggest we spell love with trust that accepts the risks, with an involvement that is willing to share, and with commitment that stays until the finish.

I. Trust, involvement, commitment.

A. *Trust.* There can be no genuine love without trust—trust that accepts the risks of sharing with another your life, thoughts, goals, and dreams. It is not love that keeps a child tethered to a parent unwilling to trust that young person to make some decisions for life. Nor is it love that motivates a husband to grill his wife about friendships. Jealousy leaves no room for trust and risk. The apostle Paul said, "Love believes all things." That does not mean love is gullible or blind, but it does mean love possesses the attitude of complete trust.

B. *Involvement.* Love is also involvement that is willing to share. Folksinger Joan Baez was married to David Harris. David was sent to jail for refusing to serve in the army; while he was incarcerated, Joan was always singing about David, telling of the love between them. David wrote a book about their relationship—how much he missed his wife and was looking forward to the day when he could be united with her and with his child. A few months after David's release he said, "Living together is getting in the way of our relationship." They decided to separate—long-distance love is much easier. Some who are legally married live like singles. She is on the Civic Club circuit; he is on the golf course. He mows the yard; she mops the floor. Each is doing his own thing—no involvement, no commitment, no sharing. Their "first love" goes unnourished until, afflicted with emotional and spiritual malnutrition, it finally dies in the cold, sterile environment of what might have looked like a "perfect marriage."

C. *Commitment.* Love is also commitment that never gives up. Paul said, "Love endures all things . . . never ends . . . abides." It has a commitment quality that is willing to persevere and fine tune the relationship. This should prevail in all our relationships—husband-wife, parent-child, employer-employee, pastor-congregation. At every level of relationships, love is not blind emotion; it is an act of the will, a decision of commitment.

II. Two biblical examples.

Two examples from Scripture illustrate this kind of love.

A. *A father and his daughter.* The Old Testament Book of Esther describes the relationship between a father and his daughter. Esther won the Ms. Kingdom Pageant and became queen. Haman, elevated to power by King Ahasuerus, issued an edict that everyone should bow before him. He became furious when Mordecai, Esther's adopted father, refused to obey the order. In his fury, Haman issued an order to annihilate all the Jews.

Esther, who had not seen the king in some days—and that tells us much about their marriage, the lack of involvement, communication, and trust—was encouraged by Mordecai to intercede on behalf of her people. To do this meant a possible death sentence. Esther said, "I will go to the king, . . . if I perish, I perish" (4:16 RSV). What a risk! What involvement! What commitment! Esther had come to know this love through her adopted father Mordecai.

Some of you have never been fathers in the flesh, but perhaps you have been a better father to some than their natural fathers. You have related to a niece, nephew, or youth in the church as a father. You have been a spiritual father, willing to trust, accept risk, and involve yourself because you loved. Esther and Mordecai knew trust, involvement, and commitment. They faced the risks and won!

B. *A father and his two sons.* Luke 15 is the second example of love. The younger son asked for his share of the coming inheritance that he might go out on his own. Dad gave it to him—no fuss, no fighting. He had loved his son and reared him, and then let him go, risking him to the far country. The father never gave up and later reaped the reward of renewed and deepened love. He had a commitment that stayed until the finish and later saw the boy's return. He did not meet the boy with, "I told you so!" but "My son, welcome home!" He wrapped his arms around him with a love that had never really let go.

III. The Father's love.

The crucial thing about love is that it can only be spelled with help from the Father. Just as the daughter asked, "Daddy, how do you spell love?" so must we come to God in order to know the true meaning of love.

The apostle John said, "Love is of God . . . ; See how he has shown his love among us." We cannot know what love is outside of a relationship with the Lord. In creation God has shown His love for the entire world, over which we were called to "have dominion." What a risk! In Christ, God "became flesh and dwelt among us." In Christ our Lord became involved with the full dimensions of our lives—temptation, suffering, joy, death. He was willing to share it all in order to give us life. At the cross He demonstrated commitment of the deepest

kind (Rom. 5:8). Facing the cross, John noted the commitment of love—
"having loved his own who were in the world, he loved them to the end" (John
13:1 RSV). Through the church He loves us still; He has trusted us with the
ministry of reconciliation. He risks the mission of winning the world to the likes
of us. He isn't finished yet (Phil. 1:6; 1 John 3:1–2)!

Conclusion. "Daddy, how do you spell love?" The Father tells us to spell it
with trust, involvement, and commitment. In his letter to the Ephesian Christians, Paul prays that we may know the dimensions of Christ's love and be rooted
and grounded in it. He begins the prayer with the hope "that Christ may dwell in
your hearts by faith . . ." (3:17). There can be no love until Christ is first
accepted into our hearts by faith. We must be willing to acknowledge our sin and
failure and accept Christ's death for sin. This is trust. We risk it all for Him. We
are willing to become involved. We make a commitment. Then we can know the
love of God.   —*BW*

* * *

SUNDAY EVENING, JUNE 17

TITLE: Believe in God, He'll See You Through

TEXT: **"So Daniel was taken up out of the den, and no manner of hurt was
found upon him, because be believed in his God" (Dan. 6:23).**

SCRIPTURE READING: **Daniel 6:1–28**

Introduction. On the pages of scriptural history, Daniel is pictured as a great
and nearly faultless man. During his first years in Babylon, while Nebuchadnezzar was king, he attained prominence and position. The Babylonian Empire had
passed off the scene, and Persia now ruled the world. Daniel, however, was still
a respected leader, one of the three top men in the empire. When an "excellent
spirit" is in a person, his abilities are almost always recognized and rewarded.

I. Jealousy.

How terrible is envy and what awful things it does to people! Daniel's peers
and subordinates conspired to find fault with him in order that they might bring
an accusation to the king. Finding none, they sought to "set him up" by a subtle
scheme. Appealing to the pride and ego-centeredness of the Persian ruler,
Darius, those who wished to discredit Daniel suggested that he establish a law
saying that whoever asked a petition of any god or man for thirty days should be
cast into the den of lions. Not recognizing that they wished to entrap one of the
most trusted servants in the empire, Darius signed the decree; and, according to
the law of the Medes and Persians, it could not be altered.

Love of self and an exalted opinion of our own importance causes us to do
many strange and foolish things. At the conclusion of a sermon, a woman went
down the aisle on profession of faith during the invitation hymn. After the service
was dismissed, the preacher asked the woman, "What was it that I said in my
sermon that caused you to make this decision?" She replied, "Frankly, I didn't
hear much of what you said tonight. But I was thinking of my spiritual needs and
saw a woman across the aisle from me. I knew she was praying for me because

she had been talking with me earlier about my need for the Savior. Her godly life and the many wonderful things she has done to help me with various problems kept bearing upon my mind as you preached. I came to the Savior because, of course, of my need; but I came because of her personal influence, not something you said." Pride produces envy, and together they cause us to think more highly of ourselves than we ought to think.

II. Jeopardy.

Those who practice the presence of Christ are not intimidated by either ridicule or threats. We gain the impression from the scriptural account that as soon as Daniel heard of the edict, he deliberately went into the house to pray, thus showing his contempt for such human efforts to oppose God. Whether he did it in deliberate defiance or not, he continued his usual custom of praying three times daily in his private devotions.

As we read the Scripture, we notice that the king was greatly upset when he learned one of his most loyal servants stood in jeopardy and must be imprisoned. People who have a good relationship with God make good "employees"; and wise employers realize they are valuable assets to the company. Many years ago, a young man was told by his employer that he must work on a Sunday morning. He refused, insisting he went to God's house for worship on Sunday mornings. In rage and hate, the boss fired him. Later, the employer was having dinner with one of his peers and was asked, "Do you know of a good young man that I could put to work in my company? I need one who is trustworthy in every way." He said, "Yes, I do," and gave him the young man's name. The friend replied, "But I thought you fired him several weeks ago." He said, "Yes, I did, but let me tell you why." He gave the reason and said, "I guess I have too much pride to hire him back, but I can recommend him to you completely."

No doubt, Darius would have loved to have excused Daniel, but he could not do so. He was entrapped in his own decree and cast him into the den of lions. The Scripture says, however, that the king "set his heart on Daniel to deliver him: and he laboured till the going down of the sun to deliver him" (6:14).

III. Justification.

The king slept little during the night! He arose early and hurried to the den. Shouting to Daniel he said, "O, Daniel, servant of the living God, is thy God, whom thou servest continually, able to deliver thee from the lions?" (v. 20). Daniel replied affirmatively. The Scripture says that Daniel was "taken up out of the den, and no manner of hurt was found upon him, because he believed in his God" (v. 23).

As a result of Daniel's faithfulness he was personally saved from death; but, even more, the influence of this event caused Darius to issue a decree throughout his empire that the God of Daniel "is the living God, and stedfast for ever, and his kingdom that which shall not be destroyed" (v. 26). The concluding verse in the chapter speaks graphically: "So this Daniel prospered in the reign of Darius, and in the reign of Cyrus the Persian" (v. 28).

Conclusion. None of us ever knows how great his influence is and how much effect we have on others by the way we live. A college president once said to a group of ministerial students, "Do you know when you will preach your greatest sermon? It will not be when you stand in the pulpit some Sunday morning and the sanctuary is packed. You will preach your greatest sermon when you walk down the street of the town where you serve, and someone at a distance will point to you and say to the person with him, 'That man is our preacher. He's a good man. He not only preaches the gospel, he lives it.'" This is what being a Christian is, and we should never forget it! Trust God. He will work things out, either by taking the burden from us or by giving us the strength to bear it!   —*FMW*

* * *

WEDNESDAY EVENING, JUNE 20

TITLE: The Man of Sin

Text: **"Let no one deceive you in any way; for that day will not come, unless the rebellion comes first, and the man of lawlessness is revealed"** **(2 Thess. 2:3 RSV).**

Scripture Reading: 2 Thessalonians 2:1–12

Introduction. Apparently some of the Thessalonian Christians interpreted Paul's message about the Lord's "sudden" return to mean "immediate." He now writes to clarify that two events will precede the Lord's return—the rebellion and the revelation of the man of sin. Jesus predicted a time when many would turn from the faith adhered to in a merely formal way (Matt. 24:10–13). This apostasy will have a leader—"the man of sin."

I. Revelation.
Who is this man of sin? He is not Satan, but he comes with Satan's blessing. Verse 9 is most accurately translated, "the coming of the lawless one by the activity of Satan" (RSV). Neither does this refer to the Roman Emperor or a particular religious body. The man of sin appears to be an individual, the same person John called the antichrist. In him will be embodied all opposition to God's way. His coming will be accompanied by power and wonderful signs (v. 9). He will exalt himself above all that is sacred and recognize only one god—himself!

II. Restraint.
In verses 6–7 Paul notes that the principle of lawlessness is now being restrained. The Holy Spirit at work in the world is the restraining power. Each Christian is sealed against the awesome power of evil. The powers of the evil one are limited by the protecting ministry of the Holy Spirit. What chaos would reign in the world if the Spirit of God were removed!

III. Requiem.
The death song for the evil one can begin. ". . . the Lord Jesus will slay him" (v. 8 RSV). The Victor in the conflict is assured. The man of sin will be slain and his plan destroyed. Jesus Christ's appearance will be enough.

Conclusion. Dark days are coming. The conflict of the ages is on the horizon. Whose side are you on? With the man of sin are those who "refused to love the truth and so be saved" (v. 10 RSV).   —*BW*

* * *

SUNDAY MORNING, JUNE 24

TITLE: Good Things That Make a Bad Marriage

TEXT: "Therefore a man leaves his father and his mother and cleaves to his wife, and they become one flesh" (Gen. 2:24 RSV).

SCRIPTURE READING: Genesis 2:18–25

HYMNS: "God, Our Father, We Adore Thee," Frazer
"Jesus Is Lord of All," McClard
"Happy the Home When God Is There," Ware

OFFERTORY PRAYER:

We bow before You, loving Father, to ask a blessing of grace and peace upon these gifts and each life who presents them. Convict and change those who have not discovered the joy of giving toward the work of the Lord. Enlarge our vision, deepen our compassion, stir up our zeal, and increase our resources. May many be brought to Christ our Lord, in whose name we pray. Amen.

Introduction. It would be difficult to find a relationshp with as many possibilities for good but in as much difficulty as marriage. The continuing increase in divorces testifies to the problem faced in marriage. There are as many recipes for a successful marriage as couples who have experienced good marriages. Every marriage needs to find the right ingredients, blend them with the needed seasonings, and keep it at the proper temperature for an enjoyable result which blesses God and man.

A butterfly became trapped inside a car. It possessed the wonderful gift of flight, but the more it flew around in the car, the closer it came to death, the fragile wings damaged by the hard glass. The driver stopped the car and gave it freedom to enjoy the good gift of flight. There are many good things that make a good marriage. However, sometimes these good things contribute to a bad marriage.

I. Individuality.

David Mace has called marriage a "partnership of equals" (*Whom God Hath Joined* [Philadelphia: The Westminster Press, 1953], p. 60). The truth of Galatians 3:28 is to be realized in marriage: ". . . there is neither male nor female; for you are all one in Christ Jesus." Husband and wife are called to respect each other as individuals and treat each other as equals. Kahlil Gibran wrote in *The Prophet:*

> Love one another, but make not a bond of love:
> Let it rather be a moving sea between the shores of your souls. . . .
> And stand together yet not too near together:
> For the pillars of the temple stand apart,
> And the oak tree and the cypress grow not in each other's shadow.

A partnership of equals is more difficult to maintain than a relationship between tyrant and slave. A democracy demands more of its people than a dictatorship. Marriage must have partners skilled in teamwork, cooperation, and a willingness to change roles if needed. A high degree of trust and open communication is crucial. The good quality of individuality makes for a bad marriage when these other elements are missing. When rights are stressed more than responsibility and the relationship is marked by demands and domination, the marriage is in grave danger. That kind of individuality makes a bad marriage.

II. Sex.

Sexuality is a gift of God—"male and female he created them. . . . And the man and his wife were both naked, and were not ashamed" (Gen. 1:27; 2:25 RSV). An old rabbinic saying states, "The man is restless while he misses his rib that was taken out of his side; and the woman is restless till she gets under the man's arm, from whence she was taken." A healthy sexual relationship is a good part of marriage. "Do not refuse one another except perhaps by agreement for a season, that you may devote yourselves to prayer; but then come together again, lest Satan tempt you through lack of self-control" (1 Cor. 7:5 RSV).

However, sex characterized by lust, desire out of control, can ruin a good relationship. "Each one of you know how to take a wife for himself in holiness and honor, not in the passion of lust like heathen who do not know God" (1 Thess. 4:4–5 RSV).

Sex void of love can bring the downfall of a good marriage. A survey of women noted the third highest problem causing depression was the absence of romantic love in marriage. "The husband . . . shall cheer up his wife which he hath taken" (Deut. 24:5). The emotional well-being of a wife is the specific responsibility of her husband. The courting should not stop when the vows are said. Sex without love which is "patient and kind . . . not jealous or boastful . . . arrogant or rude" will always make a bad marriage. Sex with the love "which bears all things, believes all things, hopes all things, endures all things" will enrich the marriage and "two shall become one."

III. Commitment.

Good marriages call for commitment—individuals committed to each other. "For this cause shall a man leave father and mother, and shall cleave to his wife" (Matt. 19:5).

Marriage partners must be committed to integrity, hard work, purity in thought, word, and deed, and committed to church and community. Yet over-commitment can make a bad marriage. James Dobson says, "Overcommitment is the number one marriage killer. We lack the discipline to limit our entanglements with the world, choosing instead to be dominated by our work and the materialistic gadgetry it will bring. And what is sacrificed in the process are the loving relationships with wives and children and friends who give life meaning" (*Straight Talk To Men and Their Wives,* [Waco: Word Books, 1980], pp. 136, 139).

Marriage requires quality time. It is impossible for "two to become one" without a qualitative investment in each other's lives. Overcommitment will ruin a good marriage.

Conclusion. Individuality, sex, and commitment are ingredients for a good marriage. Pervert these gifts into domination, lust or absence of love, and over-commitment, and the result will be a bad marriage. With Christ's help the good can become better. A prayer written by David Mace expresses the direction we must take: "May we so value our homes and loved ones, O God, that for their sakes no toil will seem too hard, no sacrifice too great, no offering too costly. As

husband and wife, may we discover that because we love each other we can work
the better, and because we work together we can love more truly" (Mace, *Whom
God Hath Joined*, p. 80).   —BW

* * *

SUNDAY EVENING, JUNE 24

TITLE: The Wisdom of Winning

TEXT: **"And they that be wise shall shine as the brightness of the firmament;
and they that turn many to righteousness as the stars for ever and ever"
(Dan. 12:3).**

SCRIPTURE READING: **Daniel 12:1–4**

Introduction. Lyman Beecher, the great preacher, was once asked the question,
"What is the greatest thing that a person can do in this world?" He immediately
replied, "The greatest thing that a person can do is not to be a doctor—as
important as that might be—nor to be an attorney—as equally important as that
might be—nor a professional person of any kind. Rather the most important
thing that one person can do is to bring another person to Jesus Christ."

The last seven chapters of Daniel differ greatly from the first six. Whereas
the former contain stories of Daniel and his three friends, and are relatively easy
to understand and interpret (with the possible exception of chapter 2), the latter
part of the book deals with prophetic material that has become controversial
among biblical expositors. At the close of the book, however, Daniel spoke of a
resurrection, followed by a tremendous statement of the blessings God has in
store for those who "turn many to righteousness" or, as we would say today, are
"soulwinners." Whereas Ezekiel warned the people of his day concerning the
danger of not being a good watchman and failing to warn people when the danger
comes, Daniel spoke in a more positive way of the good things God has reserved
for those who are faithful in telling others about the Lord, causing them to change
their ways and live according to God's standards.

I. Resurrection reality.

Regardless of how we interpret the prophetic material of the preceding
chapters, one things stands clear. God revealed to Daniel that there will be a
resurrection. This is one of the most plainly taught truths in the New Testament,
and even in the Old Testament passages abound concerning the reality of a
resurrection. As Christians, we need to have our minds deeply and permanently
impressed with the irrefutable statements that the dead will rise again. That
which Job posed as a possibility, in Jesus became historical fact.

Life beyond the grave is a subject that has fascinated the best thinkers
through the years. Even the philosophers arrived, in their speculations, to believe
in a kind of immortality; but it remained for Jesus to make so explicit the grand
and glorious truth of a bodily resurrection that Christians can be bold in believing
it. Resurrection is more than a bare dogma of immortality of the soul or the
survivor of some vague and intangible essence. Resurrection promises the rees-
tablishment of personal life on the other side of the grave. Such hope has inspired
faith that the total personality, the recognizable man or woman invested by God's
gift with a perfect organism, enters beyond death on a richer and fuller existence.

Could a finite thing created
In the bound of time and space
Live and grow and learn to love thee,
Catch the beauty of thy face
Fade, and I be gone forever,
Have no being, know no place?

No, my soul will not believe it;
Thou art in me and I in thee,
I will listen to the message
That my own soul speaks to me;
Shamed that faith should ask a token,
Doubt her own eternity.

As Benjamin Parson said when facing death, "My head is resting very sweetly on three pillows—infinite power, infinite wisdom, and infinite love."

II. A significant difference.

Daniel made it clear that two classes of people will emerge from the grave. He spoke of those who would awake "to everlasting life" and those who would, on the resurrection day, face "shame and everlasting contempt." Elsewhere in the Scriptures, especially in the New Testament, one's eternal destiny after resurrection is spoken of as either heaven or hell. We shall not at this point attempt to deal thoroughly with these two places, but note only that they do exist. Although Jesus was kind and tenderhearted, He warned the people often about the danger of passing from this life to the next without adequate preparation for meeting God.

Many reasons can be found for heaven and hell even if we did not have it so plainly taught in the Scripture. Unless there is a separation at the end, God is not just. To allow the wicked and righteous, the saved and unsaved, to remain with each other throughout eternity would be an indictment against the holiness of God as well as His fairness. If the death of Christ on the cross says anything, it shouts loudly that people need to be saved from the penalty of sin. Jesus bore the punishment we deserve for sin when He died on the cross. His resurrection from the grave was God's way of saying that He approved of everything Jesus did on Calvary. Both the eternal fires of hell and the glorious beauties of heaven give unmistakable testimony that God has decreed a separate place throughout eternity for the two classes of people who live on this earth. One who has committed his life to Jesus as personal Savior can be certain of a future heavenly home and, in the light of that certainty, serve the Lord with courage and confidence.

III. Help others to have a better resurrection.

To lead others to Christ is not an elective in the curriculum of life. In the New Testament, Jesus spoke often of the necessity for believers to be witnesses. Standing on a mountain outside Jerusalem Jesus gave His disciples their marching orders. They were to be witnesses in every area imaginable—Jerusalem, Judea, Samaria, and the uttermost part of the earth. Nothing should stop them. The fields were white unto harvest but the laborers few.

Although living a life of Christian character and attempting to develop in maturity are important, they can never serve as substitutes for leading others to the Lord. A great servant of God of another generation, who possessed many gifts, spent his ministerial life in a small church in a small town. When his eloquent tongue was silenced by the government and he was exiled to Aberdeen, his homesick heart still dwelt among the people he had left and whom he could not forget. He wrote:

> Oh! if one soul from Anwoth
> Meet me at God's right hand,
> My heaven will be two heavens,
> In Emmanuel's land.

In addition to being soulwinners ourselves, we should seek to train others in what L. R. Scarbrough used to call "the finest of the fine arts." Charles Spurgeon felt keenly the importance of this labor and wrote:

> He who converts a soul
> Draws water from a fountain;
> But he who trains
> A soulwinner
> Digs a well
> From which thousands
> May drink to eternal life.

A pastor can reproduce himself many times by training others to become soulwinners. Years ago, a pastor who knew the art of soulwinning visitation assisted a pastor in a revival meeting who did not know how to win the lost. Saturday morning the visiting preacher skipped the service to go home but returned for the evening meeting. He was greeted by an excited pastor who told his visiting friend, "I went out this afternoon, did what you taught me, and won three people to the Lord."

Conclusion. A great pastor who became a "secretary of evangelism" and then a seminary president sat in the car with his wife and two daughters watching the Fourth of July fireworks in a large city. When they were over, he said to his daughters, "Let me teach you a little lesson tonight. A few minutes ago you saw the beautiful fireworks that made the sky beautiful for a short time, but they are gone, never to return. Now let me tell you about your grandmother who has gone to be with the Lord. She was a person who led many people to Jesus. Her life lives on through those whom she won to the Lord." He then recited the words of our text, "and they that be wise shall shine as the brightness of the firmament; and they that turn many to righteousness as the stars for ever and ever." He said to his daughters, "You must decide whether your lives will be like the fireworks that glitter for a brief time and pass away or like your grandmother's life that shines for generations to come, even forever." —*FMW*

* * *

WEDNESDAY EVENING, JUNE 27

TITLE: The Lord Is Faithful

TEXT: "But the Lord is faithful" (2 Thess. 3:3).

SCRIPTURE READING: 2 Thessalonians 3:1–5, 16

Introduction. Writing from Corinth, a wicked city with few Christians, to the persecuted Thessalonians, Paul closes his letter by focusing on the faithfulness of God. In changing times we can be secure in the Lord, who is the same yesterday, today, and forever. He can be trusted to take us through every difficulty and accomplish His purpose. Paul later said this to the church at Corinth (1 Cor. 1:9).

Paul may have been like many preachers who say "finally" and then introduce additional material. Significant issues concerning church fellowship are addressed (2 Thess. 3:6–15) but these are to be seen in light of God's faithfulness. He will not let a few individuals destroy the work of the church.

God's faithfulness is expressed through four prayer petitions.

I. The Lord is faithful to bless His work (v. 1).

A. *The work of the Word.* "Pray for us, that the word of the Lord may speed on and triumph" (v. 1). These are athletic terms and express the apostle's confidence that the Word of the Lord will have ultimate success. The prophets were often misunderstood, but the Lord's promise kept them faithful: "So shall my word be that goes forth from my mouth; it shall not return to me empty, but it shall accomplish that which I purpose, and prosper in the thing for which I sent it" (Isa. 55:11 RSV). The living Word is actively at work in the world (Heb. 4:12).

B. *Our work with the word.* Notice how the Word is strategically placed between "us" and "you." The greatest triumph for the Word comes when a committed disciple shares it with others and helps lead them into discipleship. The Thessalonians were a prime example of Paul's work with the Word. Since "faith comes by what is heard" (Rom. 10:17), the primary work of the church is to share the Word with a waiting world.

II. The Lord is faithful to deliver from evil (2 Thess. 3:2–3).

Whenever the Word is faithfully declared, it will be met with resistance. The Lord is faithful to deliver His people from evil.

A. *The attack of evil.* Resistance to the Word comes from "wicked and evil men" (v. 2) and also from "the evil one" (v. 3 ASV)—Satan. The personality of Satan is manifest in personalities we encounter within and outside the church. "Not all have faith." The Lord who taught us to pray, "Deliver us from evil" (Matt. 6:13), is "able to keep you from falling and to present you without blemish before the presence of his glory with rejoicing" (Jude 24 RSV).

B. *The Lord's defense.* Because of the Lord and the Word, although we experience evil's attack, those same two realities are our defense. "*He* will strengthen you and guard you from evil" (2 Thess. 3:3). "He who is in you is greater than he who is in the world" (1 John 4:4). Jesus met Satan's temptation with the written Word (Luke 4:1–13). "Thy word is a lamp to my feet and a light to my path" (Ps. 119:105).

III. The Lord is faithful to direct His people (2 Thess. 3:4–5).

While we fight against evil, we are directed by God into a more mature relationship with Him. We are strengthened within to wage war with evil.

A. *The love of God.* God's love, "a still more excellent way," was the help Paul offered to the confused Corinthian church (1 Cor. 12:31). Only His love could turn the Thessalonians from fear to faithful witnessing.

B. *The steadfastness of Christ.* Some of the believers have turned their eyes from Jesus and given up their work. "Consider him who endured from sinners such hostility against himself, so that you may not grow weary or fainthearted" (Heb. 12:3 RSV).

William Hendriksen wrote concerning this verse: "When the love which God has for the Thessalonians and which he is constantly showing to them becomes *the motivating force* in their lives and when the endurance exercised by Christ in the midst of a hostile world becomes their *example*, then they will do and will continue to do whatever God through his servants demands of them" (*New Testament Commentary, Thessalonians, Timothy and Titus* [Grand Rapids: Baker Book House, 1979], p. 197).

IV. The Lord is faithful to bestow peace (2 Thess. 3:16).

Paul closes his letter with the request he expressed at the opening of each letter. His deep desire is that this church experience the peace of God. Similar to other passages in Scripture, peace is defined in both vertical and horizontal dimensions.

A. *Peace in the Lord.* "May the Lord of peace himself give you peace" (v. 16 RSV). The peace we need can only be received from Christ (John 14:27). A right relationship with the Lord brings peace of mind and opens the channel for peaceful relationships.

B. *Peace in the world.* "Peace at all times in all ways." When the Lord is "with you," this becomes a reality. One can know "the peace of God, which passes all understanding" (Phil. 4:7) and go through any experience.

Conclusion. Thomas Chisholm's hymn echoes Paul's prayer:

> Great is Thy faithfulness!
> Morning by morning new mercies I see;
> All I have needed Thy hand hath provided—
> Great is Thy faithfulness, Lord, unto me!

The Lord is faithful and awaits our fervent prayers for Him to bless the Word, deliver us from evil, direct us down the path of closer communion, and bestow His blessed peace.   *—BW*

* * *

SUGGESTED PREACHING PROGRAM
FOR THE MONTH OF JULY

Sunday Mornings

Using Genesis 3 as the scriptural base for the messages, we use the theme "Updating the Garden of Eden to the Contemporary World." Modern man faces many of the challenges and options faced by the pair who dealt with the Serpent in the Garden of Eden. Genesis 3 has a contemporary application when studied perceptively.

Sunday Evenings

The suggested biblical passage for these messages is the Book of Jonah. The theme is "The High Cost of Disobedience to the Clear Will of God and the Chastisement Which Always Follows." The Book of Jonah is much more than ancient history. It takes the form of a divinely inspired "short story," which contains practical suggestions for the people of God today.

Wednesday Evenings

Psalm 23 has not only been a source of comfort in times of grief, but it has provided encouragement and motivation for the people of God as they face the various pressures of life. "With the Lord As My Shepherd, I Shall Not Suffer the Lack of Anything That I Need" is the suggested theme for these devotional messages, which will continue for thirteen Wednesday evenings.

* * *

SUNDAY MORNING, JULY 1

TITLE: False Promises

TEXT: **"You will not surely die," the serpent said to the woman. "For God knows that when you eat of it your eyes will be opened, and you will be like God, knowing good and evil" (Gen. 3:4 NIV).**

SCRIPTURE READING: **Genesis 3:1–10**

HYMNS **"All Creatures of Our God and King," Francis of Assisi**
"Great Is Thy Faithfulness," Chisholm
"My Faith Has Found a Resting Place," Edwards

OFFERTORY PRAYER:
Heavenly Father, we bow before You to acknowledge that You are the One who called us into being and the One who sustains us each day of our existence. May we ever be open to Your voice. Like the sheep of Your pasture, may we ever know Your voice and be able to reject those false voices which would call us from the path of fellowship with You. Accept our praise as well as our offerings as expressions of our desire to follow You and to share that blessing with others in our land and around the world. In the name of Jesus we pray. Amen.

Introduction. The young woman was upset. She had tried to get rid of the roaches in her apartment for weeks to no avail. It seemed that two roaches

176

replaced every one she killed. One evening while listening to her radio, she heard an advertisement for a new method guaranteed to eliminate the insects she battled every day.

In only a few days, the postman brought her miracle product. Eagerly she unwrapped the package, then stood astonished as her eyes fell on two one-inch pieces of board. A mimeographed sheet gave directions: "Place the roach in middle of bottom board, then firmly press down on the roach with the top board."

What the young woman received was not at all what she had expected. She had been duped by misleading advertising, an experience known too well by some of us here this morning. But misleading advertisements or false promises are not new. They have been around since the beginning of time when the Serpent, identified in later Christian writing as Satan, made false promises to Eve. The Serpent had no concern for Eve's well-being. She was only a tool in the ongoing battle by Satan to lure people away from fellowship with God.

All of this is part of the story of Genesis 3:1–10.

I. Promises of Satan.

A. *Penalties won't come true.* Most of us obey rules and regulations because we understand they are devised for our own benefit. For example, at a crosswalk there are signs telling us when it is safe to walk and when it is unsafe. We obey those signs because we do not want to be hit by a car and be injured or killed.

Occasionally, as we wait for the light to change, someone will walk out into the street. Cars slow down; some even stop. Our minds begin to tell us we don't have to obey the walk and don't-walk signs. We conclude that the cars will stop for us anyway. A matter of personal safety becomes nothing more than a game of bluff to see who will stop first, the cars or the pedestrians. Once the penalty of disobedience is removed, it is easier to disobey the rules.

B. *"Your eyes will be opened."* The same kinds of promises surround us today. Those trying to live a Christian life are constantly bombarded with messages claiming the power to introduce one to "the real life." The appeals of drugs, alcohol, and sex are widely known. Find a "high" by participating in these; use them as avenues to know what life is really like, we are told.

Other people use power, money, or authority to make themselves feel important at the expense of others.

The promise is the same. "Think of yourself first; use other people; eat, drink, and be merry; then your eyes will be open to what life is about."

C. *"You will be like God"*—*an appeal to the ego.* All of us feel a little uncomfortable with ourselves. There are always those who are more talented or more attractive than we. Hear Satan promise that by ignoring God, Eve will be like the One who cares for her and her husband, the One who fellowships with them each evening. Equality with God—that was the promise, and for Eve it was something to be grasped.

D. *You will know good and evil.* The force of the Hebrew word is not knowing good as opposed to evil. Rather, it is to know good at one end of the spectrum, evil at the other end, and all things in between.

"Eve," says Satan, "not only will you not die from eating the forbidden fruit, you will end up being just like God. You will know all there is to know. You will be in on life for the very first time."

That is quite a line. The price for this promised transformation was disobedience to God.

II. Process of sin.

Often I have approached this passage and seen only the defiant, rebellious act of disobedience. Yet disobedience does not spring up full-grown without roots to support it. Disobedience is the climax of the process, the fruit of the plant.

A. *Seeds of doubt.* The seeds were the doubts planted in Eve's mind, doubts about God and about His care for her.

B. *Plant of disbelief.* The doubts sprouted, and a plant of disbelief sprang up. The plant was fertilized by the false promises of the Serpent and watered by Eve's own experiences. The tree offered her food; the food was pleasant to the eye, and eating it appealed to her pride—she would be like God.

C. *Fruit of disobedience.* Only then did disobedience occur. The process was complete. Eve bought the false promises of Satan with her disobedience to God.

III. Results of disobedience.

What she and Adam got was something very different than the promise to be like God and to know all things.

A. *Personal shame.* Adam and Eve had purchased shame at who they were personally. They looked at themselves and were embarrassed. They wanted to hide themselves, so they made fig-leaf aprons to hide behind.

B. *Altered relationships.* Adam and Eve also purchased an altered relationship with each other. Before their sin they lived in an idealistic state where they were helpers for each other. They were one in every sense of the word and without shame. Now, however, their sexual identity caused them to recognize differences for the first time. The oneness was replaced by separate physical identities.

Instead of standing together, now each was out for himself; for when God confronted them with their disobedience, Adam blamed Eve for his sin, and Eve blamed the Serpent.

C. *Broken fellowship.* Their relationship with God was changed. Instead of being like God, Adam and Eve were now frightened by His presence. Instead of fellowship with God, Adam and Eve hid from Him. Their disobedience had cost them the joyful presence of the One who called them into being and who sustained them day by day.

In one act of disobedience Adam and Eve changed forever their relationship to themselves, to others, and to their God. Satan had promised more than he could deliver. His promises had been false. Adam and Eve had only been tools in the Great Deceiver's war with God.

IV. Wars of today.

That war continues today.

A. *Private lives.* It continues in our private lives as we repeat the struggles of Adam and Eve. Will we believe God and live in obedience to His commands, or will we believe the devil and disobey? Daily this is the question we face in our family lives, in our business lives, in our political lives, in our spiritual lives. The pursuit for personal righteousness by God's people is a never-ending quest. At its core is the single question of obedience to God or believing the false promises of Satan.

B. *Public lives.* In our public life, the question is the same. Will we seek first the kingdom of God and His righteousness or will we go after other things? Our world is full of voices, some of them well-meaning, who attempt to equate the kingdom of God with some political state. Others declare that the work of God is dependent on preserving a particular type of economy. At the altar of patriotism we are asked to bend our knees and worship.

Yet God's kingdom has thrived under dictators as well as democracy. It has survived monarchies and anarchy. The sun has set on many empires, but the sun has yet to go down on the kingdom of our God and His Son, our Savior.

All of us love our country. We sing its national anthem with pride. Its achievements in the world are our achievements, and its shortcomings cause us grief just as they do for our leaders. Yet to bow the knee at any other altar than the altar of our God is idolatry.

As Christians we hear the false promises of our public life, and we must declare that our first allegiance is obedience to our God. To do any less would result in the same tragedy that disobedience brought to Adam and Eve.

Conclusion. Thankfully, the Scripture does not end in tragedy for the disobedient, Adam and Eve, or you and me. Rather, the story holds out the promise of a restored relationship between God and man. Once that relationship is restored, barriers between brothers can be removed, and man can once again find peace within himself.

The promise of Genesis 3:15 was fulfilled with the coming of Jesus of Nazareth, God's Son. Through faith in Him we too can become God's children. Through faith in Him our disobedience can be forgiven. Through faith in Him our hopelessness can turn to hope both for the present and for eternity.

If you are tired of buying the false promises of Satan, then today accept these gifts of God to all who will believe and obey.   — *BST*

* * *

SUNDAY EVENING, JULY 1

TITLE: The Easy Road of Resistance

TEXT: "**The word of the LORD came to Jonah son of Amittai: 'Go to the great city of Nineveh and preach against it, because its wickedness has come up before me**" (Jonah 1:1–2 NIV).

SCRIPTURE READING: **Jonah 1:1–3**

Introduction. The marvel of God's Word lies in the fact that it is always relevant to the needs of people, regardless of the time in which they live. Even though the Book of Jonah has been the plaything of atheist and agnostic alike, along with other critics of the Bible, it remains one of the most relevant books in the Bible for the present time. It speaks to the twentieth-century church in general and to individual Christians in particular, in plain and piercing terms.

For the most part, the church as a whole, as well as individual Christians, has rebelled against the will of her Lord in regard to her mission in the world. Many Christians have discreetly turned aside from the issues in their society which were once addressed with fearless and positive confrontation by the church. In this sense, the story of Jonah is clearly relevant to our generation.

For the next five Sunday evenings, we shall deal with the Jonah story under the theme "How God Deals With Rebellion." In this first study we shall see "the easy road to resistance" by examining the directions God gave Jonah, the dilemma which all of this posed for that reluctant prophet, and finally the decision Jonah made.

I. The directions God gave to Jonah (1:1).

A. *Jonah is referred to also in 2 Kings 14:25, along with his father.* His hometown, Gath Hepher, located about four miles north of Nazareth in Galilee (the modern Arab town of el-Meshed), is also named. We know nothing about Jonah's life, other than the reference in 2 Kings, where he was God's messenger of mercy to Israel during the reign of King Jeroboam II, and his experience in Nineveh, and the incidents related thereto. So here we see the sovereign will of God in choosing Jonah, an unknown, to do a job for Him. The Word of the Lord came specifically to Jonah. God knew exactly whom He was looking for and where to find him. It is both wonderful and frightening to know that God is equally aware of who and where *we* are!

B. Then, *"the word of the Lord"* came to Jonah. Whenever God speaks, there is substance and content. He does not waste words. He does not engage in superfluous chatter. God's Word is serious business; and when we read or listen to its message, we are inescapably responsible before God for what we have heard.

And these words were directed specifically to Jonah. He could not take comfort in that they might be for someone else. Along with these words came the fact that God knew Jonah—both his strengths and his weaknesses. He knew Jonah's potential.

And certainly this is true in God's relationships with us. We are prone to forget that God sees the end from the beginning. When we learn to cooperate with Him, we do not fail.

II. The dilemma (v. 2).

A. *As we noted earlier, God had already used Jonah in the past.* He had ministered, we know, during the reign of King Jeroboam II. We can assume that he had been God's spokesman on other occasions in Israel. But up until now, he had lived and ministered among his own people, God's chosen people. Like any other Israelite, Jonah felt great security and pride in his identity with Israel. Jehovah was *his* God and the God of *his* people. So it was "business as usual" with Jonah. Then all of a sudden God broke into Jonah's secure and comfortable lifestyle. We can imagine that Jonah thought, "Why *me*, Lord? Why not one of those prophets who live in the big cities, who have been exposed to the ways and personalities of pagans? I am just a country preacher, out here in the boondocks of Galilee. This simple, rural lifestyle is all I know. Not *me*, Lord! Isaiah, Amos, Hosea—*they* could do it far better than *I* could, Lord!"

B. *Why Nineveh?* Nineveh was a pagan city, whose people, through the generations, had been enemies and persecutors of God's people. Nineveh would never have been on Jonah's itinerary, nor even on his prayer list. God may ask *you* to do something which doesn't make any sense at all. We do not always know why God picks certain places to do things. You do not know why you were born where you were, rather than in another country with different parents, and on a different date in history. Likewise, God may be directing you in a certain way that you don't understand.

So you are saying, "I can't do it. It's too big for me. I am afraid; I cannot go in that direction. Besides, I just can't understand why God would say to *me*, 'Do that!' " One of the thrilling things about our God is that He is full of surprises. We never really know what He is going to do next. But we can take comfort in the words the angel spoke to Mary concerning her conception of Jesus, "With God nothing shall be impossible" (Luke 1:37).

III. Jonah's decision (v. 3).

A. Jonah had said, "Not Nineveh, Lord! Anywhere but Nineveh!" When Jonah deliberately turned his back on God's will for his life at that time, that *might* have been the end. For God dealt far more stringently with His disobedient children in those days before this marvelous age of grace, which our Lord Jesus ushered in for us. Thus, when Jonah paid the fare on the ship in order to go to Tarshish, in the opposite direction from Nineveh, that *could* have been the end for him.

B. Sometimes, through our disobedience, we force God to "finish with us" before He would like to. When we persist in saying no to God concerning something He wants us to do, something we *know* He wants us to do, sometimes He says, "All right, have it your way. I'll use another!" And He *does* choose someone else to do the job He had planned for us.

But that was not the end of the story for Jonah, as we shall see in the studies to come. God stayed with Jonah. Jonah thought he had settled the matter once and for all. But just as God knew where Jonah was when He called him in the little village of Gath Hepher, He knew where he was when he boarded that ship at the port of Joppa.

Conclusion. It is an easy road that leads down to "Resistance Harbor." It is downhill all the way! Just as Jonah found a ship already there, ready to sail in the opposite direction from Nineveh, so Satan sees to it that the means of *our* resistance toward God are easy and available.

According to Jonah's experience, we can be sure of one thing: If we are God's children, we are not our own. We belong to Him. We are His children, and He is our heavenly Father. That means He is going to deal with us as disobedient children when the need arises. But, O the joy that comes when we stop resisting His will for our lives and say, "Here am I, Lord! I can do nothing in my own strength. But 'I can do all things through Christ which strengtheneth me'!"

— *DLJ*

* * *

WEDNESDAY EVENING, JULY 4

TITLE: The Promise of God

Text: "The Lord is my shepherd; I shall not want" (Ps. 23:1).

Scripture Reading: Psalm 23:1–6

Introduction. A man of God was suffering with a bout of depression. One night while in a hotel room in a distant city and all alone, he became almost overwhelmed with his depression. During that episode he was seeking help the best he know how from God. In doing so, he started quoting the Twenty-third Psalm. That experience led to a much deeper study of the psalm than ever before, and the psalm came alive to him. The person who had this experience is the writer of these words. It is his hope that you will be helped also.

I. First, notice the brevity of the first verse and yet the profundity of it.

A. *The verse contains only nine words.*

Someone has said that the verses which compose this psalm would leave but a small blank on the page if blotted out. This would certainly apply to the first verse. But what a great loss it would be!

B. *These nine words are indeed profound.*

1. It is impossible to measure their influence. Just think of all the different translations into other languages, the references made to these words in literature, and the remembrances in human hearts.

2. It is also impossible to determine their usefulness. These words are as fresh as they would be if just written. They are always current. They make themselves at home in every language and have taught, inspired, and comforted for three thousand years. They have been repeated to the small child and been of comfort to the bereaved.

II. Verse 1 is an expression of human experience.

A. *It is the expression of weakness and trust.*

1. If it were angels who said, "The Lord is my shepherd," the words would not bring assurance to a frail and sinful heart.

2. If it were a voice from heaven saying, "The Lord is my shepherd," it would not have the effect it does coming from a weak and needy brother.

B. *It is the expression of a shepherd boy who knew by experience the care and tender affection of a good shepherd toward his flock.*

1. These words were spoken by someone of passions similar to ours; and they express faith, joy, and thanksgiving.

2. These words illustrate God's care for His people. He is the Shepherd of every need for every believer.

III. These are inspired words.

A. *They are the voice of God.*

B. *The thought is a continuity in both the Old Testament and the New Testament* (see Isa. 40; Ezek. 34; Luke 15; John 10; Rev. 7).

Conclusion. This passage suggests God's awareness of our needs, His ability and willingness to care for us, and our need of depending on Him.   — DRG

* * *

SUNDAY MORNING, JULY 8

TITLE: A Tree of Testing Or a Tree of Trusting

TEXT: "But God did say, 'You must not eat fruit from the tree that is in the middle of the garden, and you must not touch it, or you will die' " (Gen. 3:3 NIV).

SCRIPTURE READING: Genesis 3:1–10

HYMNS: "All Hail the Power," Perronet
"Faith Is the Victory," Yates
"He Leadeth Me," Gilmore

OFFERTORY PRAYER:

Heavenly Father, our hearts are made heavy when we reflect on our response to Your great love. Too often we have failed to seize the opportunities You placed before us. We have been untrue to our pledge to love You with all our hearts and all our souls and all our minds and all our strength. From You may we find forgiveness as we confess our sins and the liberty to share with others through this offering as You have freely shared Your greatest gift with us, even Jesus Christ. Amen.

Introduction. *Genesis* means "beginnings." On the pages of this book of the Bible are recorded the beginnings of the world, of mankind, of sin. The book is also about the beginnings of blessing, of grace, of covenant. The book itself is divided into ten stories. Last Sunday, and for the remaining Sundays of this month, we will examine parts of the first story, the story of heaven and earth.

In the past some people have tried to dismiss these early chapters of Genesis as unimportant. Yet again and again people return to them for an understanding of the nature of God, the nature of man, and the nature of sin; and for answers about man's relationship to himself, to others, and to God.

If one is grounded in the opening chapters of Genesis, other portions of the Bible become more understandable. Our focal point here is chapter 3:1–10. Yet, to understand the setting, one must remember the command of God outlined in chapter 2:15–17.

This morning we will explore the question of why God placed the tree of the knowledge of good and evil in the Garden of Eden. Was God simply setting up Adam and Eve for their ultimate disobedience? Is God really to blame for the fall of man, or was there another purpose served by the tree?

I. Necessity of the tree.

Let me contend with you this morning that the tree of the knowledge of good and evil was necessary because of the nature of God and because of the nature of man, as well as because of the nature of the gift God offered to Adam and Eve and continues to offer to each of us.

The setting of the story is in the Garden of Eden, an idealistic place where God had placed man. There God gave man purpose—to dress and keep the garden. Adam was invited to join God in the ongoing creation of God's world. Every need of man was tended to by God, even to the point of providing him a worthy companion in Eve.

Yet in the midst of this idealistic place, God planted the tree of the knowledge of good and evil and declared that "when you eat of it you will surely die" (2:17 NIV). This death is not to be understood as physical death. Rather, it is the death of relationship between God and His creation. That is an insight from this side of the story, not one known by Adam or Eve. Again the question, Why the tree?

A. *Nature of God.* To answer that question plunges us into the depths of truth about God and man.

When Genesis 1:26 records God's declaring, "Let us make man in our image. . . ," it is the declaration of a Being who finds His own existence too joyous to hoard. It is the declaration of a God who wants to share the quality and nature and eternity of His life with man. The words are not the description of a God who desires to have another plaything to manipulate. Rather, God is shown as One who at the very core is a giving, sharing Being.

God's gift to man is not damnation from a tree, even though the tree is central to the story. God's gift is and has always been Himself. Yet, to have God, there must be something like that tree in every person's experience.

B. *Nature of man.* Scholars have long debated the nature of man, and still the debate goes on. The balance between the sovereignty of God and the freedom of man is difficult to determine. Yet the prevailing Christian view is that man is a responsible being before God. He is not a puppet manipulated by strings on the fingers of a benign dictator called God. Man is free to respond to God, to accept His gift or to reject it. Just as God, at the core of His being, is loving, giving, and sharing; so man, at the core of his being, is a responsible being free to say yes or no.

C. *Nature of gift.* Added to the complexities of a sovereign God and a free man is the nature of gift. One of the desires of a teen-aged boy was to have a motorcycle. The weekend before his birthday his father took him shopping. They walked through the sporting goods section and passed a small motorbike called a moped. The father asked how he would like to have a moped. The son's response was sarcastic. "I wouldn't have one," he retorted. "I want a Cushman Eagle." The Cushmans were much bigger and more expensive. They walked on and finished their shopping, and it was some years before he learned that his father had saved his money and was prepared to buy him the moped as a birthday present if he would accept it, but he would not.

For a gift to be a gift, it must be freely given and freely accepted. If the giver is not free to give, then it is not a gift; it is extortion. If the receiver is not free to receive, it is dictatorial high-handedness.

II. Role of the tree.

How does one blend together God's giving, man's receiving, and the nature of the gift? The Genesis story does it with the presence of the tree of the knowledge of good and evil.

A. *Symbol of acceptance.* Man lived in the midst of God's perfect creation. To demonstrate that Adam and Eve freely accepted God's gift of Himself, God asked only obedience to one command: "But of the tree of the knowledge of good and evil, thou shalt not eat of it . . ." (2:17). In a word, man was to trust God and obey Him. To do so maintained the relationship of free gift. To disobey would be to reject God's gift, resulting in death.

Adam and Eve chose the course of rebellion against God and were driven from their perfect garden. Their relationship with God was broken when their bodies ceased to be the pure abode of the Spirit of fellowship with God. Their view of themselves was altered, and barriers were erected in their relationships with each other. Although they did not physically die, they perished nevertheless because of their disobedience.

Lest one believe that God rejoices in the fact that Adam and Eve or men and women of today perish, recall the words of 2 Peter 3:9, "The Lord is not slow about his promise as some count slowness, but is forbearing toward you, not wishing that any should perish, but that all should reach repentance" (RSV).

God does not revel in man's disobedience. Rather, He wishes for all to come to repentance. He wishes for all to freely accept His gift and to demonstrate that acceptance by living a life characterized by trust and obedience to God.

B. *Evidence of trust.* The dictionary defines trust as "assured reliance" or "confident dependence on the character, ability, and strength." Trust is something each of us lives with every day.

1. Between parent-child. If a parent says to a child, "Get out of the road; here comes a car," that parent does not want to debate the width of the road, the speed of the car, or the likely outcome if the child does not move. Every parent wants the kind of relationship with his or her child that evidences "confident dependence." If the parent says, "Get out of the road," the child trusts the parent and moves.

2. Between husband-wife. The same is true in marriage. Times come when spouses do not agree. At times it is necessary for one to say to the other, "I do not necessarily agree with all that you are saying, but because I trust you, I am willing to do this your way."

3. Through Christ. Ultimately we are talking about a trusting relationship with God through Jesus Christ. God's evidence of His desire for your repentance and mine was the gift of His Son. "For God so loved the world, that He gave His only begotten Son, that whoever believes in Him should not perish, but have eternal life" (John 3:16 NASB).

a. Adam-Eve. Adam and Eve were invited into relationship with God. Their trust in God was to be evidenced through avoiding contact with the tree of the knowledge of good and evil. Yet, they said no to God. They refused to obey Him. They would not accept His gift of Himself or participation in His very life.

b. Israel. Their decision to trust God or to disobey is the same kind of decision every man has faced. Deuteronomy 30:19 declares, "I call heaven and earth to witness against you today, that I have set before you life and death, the blessing and the curse. So choose life in order that you may live, you and your descendants" (NASB).

c. New Testament. In the New Testament, Romans 6:23 states, "For the wages of sin is death; but the gift of God is eternal life through Jesus Christ our Lord" (NASB).

III. Results of the tree.

Whether it be Adam and Eve, the children of Israel, or you and me, the decision is the same. Will we trust God and find life eternal or will we trust ourselves and reap death and the curse?

For those who have responded in a "confident dependence" to God through faith in Jesus Christ, hear also the words of Romans 8:14–15: "For all who are being led by the spirit of God, these are sons of God, for you have not received the spirit of slavery leading to fear again, but you have received the spirit of adoption, as sons by which we cry out ABBA, Father" (NASB).

Those who are the sons and daughters of God are to live each day in the same type of "assured reliance" on God. That does not mean we will always understand everything that God wants us to do. It means only that we will obey.

Conclusion. In Tennyson's famous poem "The Charge of the Light Brigade" are the lines, "Ours is not to reason why, ours is but to do or die."

To some extent those lines characterize the Christian's confident dependence or trust in God.

Into every life will come trees of testing. Hopefully our faithfulness will transform them into trees of trusting. *— BST*

* * *

SUNDAY EVENING, JULY 8

TITLE: The High Cost of Disobedience

TEXT: **"Then they took Jonah and threw him overboard, and the raging sea grew calm. At this the men greatly feared the LORD, and they offered a sacrifice to the LORD and made vows to him. But the LORD provided a great fish to swallow Jonah, and Jonah was inside the fish three days and three nights" (Jonah 1:15–17 NIV).**

SCRIPTURE READING: **Jonah 1:4–17**

Introduction. Sooner or later, every genuine Christian comes to understand fully and clearly what the apostle Paul meant when he wrote: "You are not your own; you were bought with a price" (1 Cor. 6:19–20 RSV). This means that we are the exclusive possessions of the almighty God. He who has all power in heaven, on earth, and under the earth *owns us.* Because of this, He is intensely concerned about how we live our lives. And His concern is such that he gets involved in our lives. Sometimes this involvement is positive—that is, He pours out blessings on us that we can hardly contain. But other times His involvement is negative—that is, He deals with us as loving parents deal with a disobedient child.

It is at this point that we have arrived in Jonah's story. His disobedience was not the result of thoughtlessness or carelessness. It was planned, calculated, intentional. Not only did he sharply disagree with God's assignment that he go and preach to the heathen Assyrians in Nineveh, he flatly refused to consider it at all! And so intense was Jonah's rejection of God's assignment that he did not just say no to God and remain at home in Gath Hepher. Rather he determined to put as much distance between himself and Nineveh, geographically, as he possibly could.

This often happens with disobedient Christians. Our "running from God" may not be geographical. There are many ways a person can "run from God." God is fully aware of this. Sometimes we "run down," and get tired of our evasive tactics, and return to God. Other times—and, I fear, most of the time—He must break into our little "game plans" and get our attention in rather abrupt and painful ways.

I. God's reaction to Jonah's disobedience (vv. 4–5).

A. *The text literally reads that God "hurled" a mighty wind and storm upon the sea.* And even though the sailors aboard the ship on which Jonah was a passenger were doubtlessly well accustomed to storms on the Mediterranean, they had never encountered a tempest like this one! The tragedy is that these men were being forced to suffer this fear *because of the sin of another!* Very often our disobedience toward God will cause other people to suffer, as well as ourselves. None of us lives to himself. Each of us has a sphere of influence; there are certain lives around us that we touch, either positively or negatively.

B. *But where was Jonah during this storm?* He was down in the hold of the ship, fast asleep. He had reached a second stage in his disobedience toward God. At first he was running, trying to find an escape route. The second stage was this false sense of security. At least on the surface of his consciousness, Jonah felt that he had successfully dealt with this troubling assignment from God. Disobedience in a Christian's life can progress to the point that one becomes insensitive to wrongdoing. He becomes comfortable, for a little while, in his sin. He feels, at least subconsciously, that he is "getting by" with his sin, that God is discreetly "looking the other way." Jonah was an existentialist, thinking, "What is happening right now is all that really matters."

II. God's instrumentality (vv. 6–16).

A. *Something happened which ought to have been the greatest embarrassment that could possibly have come to Jonah.* He had to be called to pray by a heathen! The captain of the ship, a Phoenician who worshiped false gods, awakened Jonah and implored him to call on his God. Apparently Jonah prayed some perfunctory prayer, for the storm did not lessen in its intensity.

B. *Now here is an amazing stroke of common sense displayed by these heathen sailors.* They came to the conclusion that there was someone on board who was guilty of some great crime, or else this terrible storm would not be beating down upon them. Their problem was to find out who the guilty person might be. They cast lots, and the lot fell on Jonah.

When this happened, they began to question Jonah. They did this not because they doubted the casting of the lots, but rather they wanted Jonah to confess whatever it was he was guilty of. This was unusually good and logical thinking on the part of these pagans.

C. *Jonah was in a corner.* He had no recourse but to make a full confession—which he did, *to these men,* but not to God! Jonah apparently told them the whole story. The sailors were terrified, for the violence of the storm breaking around them demonstrated the power of Jonah's God far better than Jonah could have. They asked Jonah what they should do to make the sea calm again. Jonah's answer shows the disobedient prophet in a better light than we find him anywhere else in the book. He said, "Pick me up and throw me into the sea, . . . and it will become calm. I know that it is my fault that this great storm has come upon you" (v. 12 NIV).

The sailors had more compassion for Jonah than he had for the people of Nineveh (v. 14). "Then they took Jonah and threw him overboard, and the raging sea grew calm. At this the men greatly feared the LORD, and they offered a sacrifice to the LORD and made vows to him" (vv. 15–16).

III. God's sovereignty (v. 17).

A. *Everything here is miraculous.* God's timing was a miracle. He arranged for the ship and the great fish to converge on course at that precise moment and at that precise spot. When Jonah was thrown overboard by these sailors, the fish was there with his mouth open!

The most important thing here is not the fish, but Jonah. Nothing pleases Satan more than for us to get sidetracked on the fish, and how it was possible for Jonah to live, physically, for three days and nights in the suffocating innards of that great fish. That can only be explained in terms of the miraculous. Jesus Himself called this a "sign" in Matthew 12:39, and we ought to leave it at that.

B. *There is a dual application here.* Jonah is a picture of Israel. Jonah, like Israel, was chosen of God to be a witness. Both were divinely commissioned. And both were disobedient. Likewise, Jonah is a type of the disobedient Christian.

Conclusion. And we can be certain of one thing: the cost of *our* disobedience toward God is high, and ultimately we must pay. May God help *us* to learn this lesson before it is too late. Jonah paid dearly for his disobedience.   — *DLJ*

* * *

WEDNESDAY EVENING, JULY 11

TITLE: The Presence of the Personal God

TEXT: "He leadeth me . . . thou art with me . . . goodness and mercy shall follow me . . . and I will dwell in the house of the LORD for ever" (Ps. 23:2, 4, 6).

SCRIPTURE READING: **Psalm 23:1–6**

Introduction. The Twenty-third Psalm is known and loved by many. We learn it early in life. To people in every walk of life, it is equally dear. It is in constant use in the home, funeral chapel, and in the sanctuary. In the time of joy, it brings gladness, and in the hours of darkness, comfort.

I. These verses suggest that our heavenly Father surrounds us.
He is before us, with us, and behind us.

A. *Fear comes from the unknown.*
In the text we are made to realize that no attack from the front or rear can reach us because our heavenly Father is there.

B. *One can apply this concept to several areas of life.*
1. Geography. He is wherever we are.
2. Time. In the morning, evening, or night, He is there. If applied to the calendar, the same is true.
3. Psychology or one's emotions. He is there in joy, sadness, love, and hate.
4. Experiences. He is involved in our vocations, our homes, and our religious experiences.

II. The words "Thou art with me" are often applied to death.

A. *To some, the approach of death is the valley of sunshine not shadow.* To some, it is a momentary passage.

B. *"The valley of the shadow of death" may stand for any crisis or danger.* The point is, there are no circumstances that come about where the Lord is not present.

III. The words "I will dwell in the house of the LORD for ever" teach the eternal presence of God.

A. *This verse teaches the truth of an eternal habitation in the presence of God.*

B. *This verse teaches the climax and reward of the earthly life with all its struggles.*

Conclusion. There are some truths for each person who reflects on these verses.

    1. The Lord's presence makes Him knowledgeable. He sees and hears.

    2. The Lord's presence indicates He is available to fight our battles.

    3. The Lord's presence is an indication of His love.

    4. The Lord's presence is a challenge to live courageously. — *DRG*

* * *

SUNDAY MORNING, JULY 15

TITLE: Why Eve?

TEXT: "Now the serpent was more crafty than any of the wild animals the LORD God had made. He said to the woman, 'Did God really say, "You must not eat from any tree in the garden"?'" (Gen. 3:1 NIV).

SCRIPTURE READING: Genesis 3:1–10

HYMNS: "Guide Me, O Thou Great Jehovah," Williams
          "When We Walk With the Lord," Sammis
          "He Hideth My Soul," Crosby

OFFERTORY PRAYER:

    Heavenly Father, thank You for the gift of life which You bestowed on us. Thank You for the gift of love evidenced in Christ Jesus and in this congregation of fellow believers. Thank You for Your written Word, the Bible, that helps us know You. And thank You for the presence of Your Holy Spirit, who guides us day by day. May we be faithful to the message of love, service, and obedience which these bring, and may we share the message with those about us through this offering and in every other way You make possible. In the name of Jesus we pray. Amen.

Introduction. The story is told of a traveler who, in the early days of our country, was wading across a river at one of its fording places. He was no more than a third of the way across the river when a group of five horsemen came splashing toward him. The horsemen stopped and the lead rider brusquely demanded of the young traveler where he was going. Standing knee-deep in water and facing five men on horseback, the young traveler told of his destination.

Then summoning up his courage, the traveler moved toward the middle rider and asked if he might ride behind him across the rest of the river. The horseman obliged, and the young man rode not only across the river but to the next fork in the road where the paths of the traveler and the five men on horseback parted. Before the parties went their separate ways, the lead rider privately asked the young traveler why he had asked only the middle horseman for a ride.

"Because his face said he cared and I thought he might help me" was the reply.

One kind face among five.

In nonverbal ways all of us send signals about ourselves. Some signals say good things about us. Others say things not so becoming. As we continue our study in Genesis 3:1–10, we want to ask ourselves what it was about Eve that caused the Serpent to choose her for his attack. Why didn't he begin with Adam? Was the woman somehow inferior? What signals did she send that indicated she was the easier target?

I. Eve encounters the Serpent.

Chapter 3 begins with the declaration of the Serpent as he approached Eve. His initial words indicate his evil purpose, for even this first utterance twists the command of God: "Did God really say, 'You must not eat from any tree in the garden'?" (3:1 NIV).

A. *Eve corrects the Serpent.* In verses 2–3, Eve corrects the misrepresentation of the Serpent with the true commands of God. But how did Eve know these commands? Chronology is vital to properly understanding the story. Genesis 2:15–17 records God's prohibition concerning the tree of the knowledge of good and evil. The creation of Eve does not occur until verses 21–22 of that chapter. Evidently Eve learned of the taboo on the tree in the center of the garden from her husband. Thus, when the Serpent approached, she could relate the Word of God she had learned from Adam.

B. *The Serpent beguiles Eve.* The Tempter would not be satisfied with one rebuff. Again he pressed Eve, but this time he attacked the character of God, and this time Eve succumbed to the temptation. Still unanswered is the question "Why Eve?" Perhaps it was precisely because she had secondhand knowledge about the tree of the knowledge of good and evil. Adam had lived the experience with God. That alone might have made him a more difficult target. With all of his subtlety, the Serpent went after the one who had to rely on the words of another rather than the one who personally lived out the experience.

II. We seek a firsthand experience.

Today many of us would like to have a firsthand experience with God. We long for an audible voice to speak out of the clouds or a bright light to overpower us, similar to what the apostle Paul experienced at his conversion. We seek the kind of experience that would drive away all lingering doubts.

A. *The miraculous will not satisfy.* The story of the rich man and Lazarus, recorded in Luke 16, is helpful here. Dives (a Latin term meaning "rich man") died and went to the place of the unrighteous dead called Hades. Lazarus, a beggar, also died and was taken into Abraham's bosom. When Dives saw Lazarus in Abraham's bosom, he asked if Lazarus could come and place just a drop of water on his tongue to help relieve the torture of Hades. Abraham declared it was impossible.

Dives then said, "I beg you, father, send Lazarus to my father's house, for I have five brothers. Let him warn them, so that they will not also come to this place of torment" (vv. 27–28 NIV).

"They have Moses and the Prophets; let them listen to them," was Abraham's reply (v. 29 NIV).

But Dives argued for the spectacular. "No, father Abraham," he said, "but if someone from the dead goes to them, they will repent" (v. 30 NIV).

Abraham's final answer is most interesting. "If they do not listen to Moses and the Prophets, they will not be convinced even if someone rises from the dead" (v. 31 NIV).

Even though we long for the spectacular, that irrefutable proof, God says that if we won't hear Moses and the prophets; if we won't hear the recorded, written Word of God; if we won't hear the testimonies around us; we will not believe even if we have the spectacular.

B. *Secondhand reports are enough.* Perhaps that is why God does not provide the spectacular for us.

1. Thomas. Again we turn to Scripture—John 20:19–25. The story is of our Lord's first appearance to the disciples following the Resurrection. Unfortunately, Thomas was not present. When the other disciples told him of the miracle of Jesus's appearance, Thomas declared that he would not believe until he put his fingers into the nail holes of Jesus' hands and his hand into the spear wound. Thomas would be satisfied with nothing less than a firsthand experience. The report of his fellow disciples was not enough.

In verses 26–29, the story of the next appearance of Jesus is recorded. This time Thomas was present, and the Lord invited him to fulfill his wishes, to feel the nail holes and the spear wound. At this Thomas cried, "My Lord and my God!" (v. 28).

Do not miss the response Jesus gave to Thomas. He said, "Because you have seen me, you have believed; blessed are those who have not seen and yet have believed" (v. 29 NIV).

Isn't that exactly where we are? We don't have the pillars of fire or giant clouds to direct us as did the children of Israel when they left Egypt. We do not have audible voices or blinding lights. Yet we do have the recorded Word of God, the Bible; and we do have the commendation of Jesus, "Blessed are those who have not seen and yet have believed."

2. Moses. In Old Testament times, the people feared to go before God, so they asked Moses to go in their behalf. Through Moses came the commands of God. The people believed this report and obeyed even though they did not have firsthand experience.

III. The Holy Spirit helps us hear.

The question must also be asked, How do we hear the Word of God? The answer is, Through His Holy Spirit.

A. *Work of the Spirit for non-Christians.* In John 16:5–16, Jesus declares that the Holy Spirit will convict the world of guilt in regard to sin and righteousness and judgment. This is the work of the Holy Spirit to those who do not know Christ as Lord and Savior.

B. *Work of the Spirit for Christians.* For Christians, the Holy Spirit will be the "guide . . . into all truth" (v. 13). As Jesus declared earlier, the Holy Spirit will "teach [us] all things" and cause us to understand all that He has said (14:26).

Conclusion. When God speaks to us through whatever instrument He chooses, our responsibility is to obey. Hebrews 3:7–8 is addressed to the "Holy brethren, partakers of the heavenly calling" (v. 7). Today we would call them Christians. The message is, "So, as the Holy Spirit says: 'Today, if you hear his voice, do not harden your hearts as you did in the rebellion, during the time of testing in the desert' " (vv. 7–8 NIV).

Rather, as verse 12 declares, "See to it, brothers, that none of you has a sinful, unbelieving heart that turns away from the living God."

A. *Eve was responsible.* Eve heard the commands of God, even though they came secondhand. She corrected the devil with her knowledge of God's commandments. She was responsible for obeying those commandments just as if God had said to her personally, "You must not eat from the tree of the knowledge of good and evil." But Eve hardened her heart. She chose to deliberately disobey God. Her secondhand knowledge of God's commandments was not enough.

B. *We are responsible.* You and I have the Word of God. We have the Word of God in Scripture. We have that ultimate Word of God in Jesus Christ, that Word which was made flesh and now lives in us because of our faith in Him. We have the Word of God's continuing presence in the form of the Holy Spirit, who guides us into all truth, who helps us know when God is speaking.

In Luke 11:28, Jesus declares, "Blessed are they that hear the word of God, and keep it." Hopefully, we will be found among those who do not have to have the miraculous but are satisfied with the Word of God available to us. From the standpoint of obedience to that Word, the signals we send must be certain signals about our faith in and commitment to Jesus Christ. Satan will find no easy targets among us, even if our reports are secondhand.   — *BST*

* * *

SUNDAY EVENING, JULY 15

TITLE: The Deep Agony of Chastisement

TEXT: "From inside the fish Jonah prayed to the LORD his God. He said: 'In my distress I called to the LORD, and he answered me. From the depths of the grave I called for help, and you listened to my cry. You hurled me into the deep, into the very heart of the seas, and the currents swirled about me; all your waves and breakers swept over me' " (Jonah 2:1–3 NIV).

SCRIPTURE READING: **Jonah 2:1–9**

Introduction. How does one classify Jonah in regard to his relationship with God? Either he was an apostate (one who has fallen away from the knowledge of God's truth, without hope of ever being restored) or a castaway (one who has been rejected for service) or what the New Testament calls an "overtaken" saint (the teaching that a believer can be "overtaken" in a fault—Gal. 6). Jonah was not an apostate—he was a genuine child of God and he was restored. He was not a castaway, for he *did* ultimately go to Nineveh and preach.

Jonah *was* an "overtaken" saint of God, a disobedient child of the King. He had deliberately refused to do that thing which he knew God would have him do. And God always has a chastening experience for the "overtaken" believer.

How long does it last? For Jonah, it lasted three days and three nights. For others, it may last a week, a month, a year, or even years.

In the face of this, let us examine the agony of Jonah in the midst of *his* chastening experience.

I. Jonah's distress (2:1–6).

A. *Though Jonah obviously recorded this prayer some time after the experience, God apparently had given him a "photographic memory" in regard to that event.* He had had time to reflect and to get all of the experience into perspective. The fact that Jonah called on the Lord in his distress (v. 2) is proof that he belonged to God, that he was a disobedient believer and not an apostate. For in spite of this terrible predicament in which Jonah found himself, he instinctively called on the Lord.

B. *Then Jonah said, "From the depths of the grave [or Sheol] I called for help"* (v. 2b NIV). Jonah did not mean that he thought he was dead, and that God would call him back from the grave and give him a second chance. Rather he was saying that the human impossibility of his situation was such that from every logical consideration, he was as good as dead. For this great sea monster had him securely in his innards; and like a giant submarine, he had carried him down to the depths of the sea.

We are amazed today at the sophistication of our means of radio communication in the space age. We can communicate with men even while they are on the surface of the moon! Well, Jonah found out how sophisticated *God's* communication system is. When he cried out to God from the belly of that fish in the depths of the sea, God heard him instantly. One of the most reassuring promises in the Bible states: "Before they call I will answer, while they are yet speaking I will hear" (Isa. 65:24 RSV).

C. *Then, Jonah came to realize something else.* This which had happened to him was no accident. He had not been swept off the deck of that ship by one of the great waves of the storm which was churning the waters of the Mediterranean. For he says, "You hurled me into the deep, into the very heart of the seas" (v. 3 NIV). Thus, in spite of Jonah's deliberate disobedience, his planned and calculated running from God, it is commendable that he was able to see God's hand clearly in all of this that was happening to him, and to call on God for help rather than curse Him because of the dilemma.

II. Jonah's reaction (vv. 6b–7).

A. *Where was Jonah's "pit"?* Physically, of course, it was this suffocating prison in the fish, with his head wrapped in seaweed, surrounded by all of the sea creatures the fish had consumed. But Jonah was submerged also in a "spiritual pit." It was that place of separation from God that one experiences when he sins as a believer. Now Jonah is isolated and alone with his own conscience in this fish. While he was aboard ship in the storm with the other sailors, he had company. But in the fish, it was just God, himself, and his sin of disobedience. That was far worse than the storm which had raged upon the surface of the sea.

B. *But what is thrilling about this is that even though his soul was overwhelmed by his circumstances, Jonah remembered the Lord* (v. 7). He didn't whimper and cry and wallow in self-pity. He saw God's hand in it all, and he began to pray. His prayer was not a ritual prayer, a memorized prayer. He wasn't worried about his choice of words and the sentence structure of his prayer. He simply poured out his soul to the Lord. He recognized the greatness and majesty of God. He admitted God's sovereignty in life in general, and in the lives of His children in particular. Then he confessed his sin of disobedience. He didn't blame his environment, the circumstances, or someone else. Jonah's reaction to his chastening experience was the kind that a true child of God will have.

III. Jonah's promise (vv. 8–9).

A. *The implication of Jonah's words here is that there are many who turn to a host of other sources for help when they find themselves in trouble.* He calls these other sources "worthless idols." Granted, there are times when our problems *are* physical. God has blessed the world with the miracles of medical science. He has endowed men and women with abilities and talents in this field, and He often cooperates with them in bringing us relief from these physical problems.

But other times our problems are spiritual, as was the case with Jonah. It is then that it is worthless to turn to "other sources" for help. When we do, these sources become as "worthless idols." They cannot help. They may treat symptoms, but they cannot touch the festering source of our trouble.

B. *Jonah discovered the source of his problem, and he turned to God for help.* That was the only place he could turn. "With a song of thanksgiving," he said that he did this. In spite of his agony in the fish, he could sing, for he believed that God was dependable and faithful to keep His promises. He knew that "help was on the way."

Conclusion. When we, as disobedient children of God, repent of our disobedience, the "frowning providence" of God which allowed our trial, our chastening, becomes the "smiling face" of God's marvelous grace.   *— DLJ*

* * *

WEDNESDAY EVENING, JULY 18

TITLE: The Providence of God

Text: **"He maketh me to lie down in green pastures: he leadeth me beside the still waters. . . . They comfort me. Thou preparest a table . . ."** (Ps. 23:2, 4–5).

Scripture Reading: **Psalm 23:1–6**

Introduction. The words *providence* and *provision* are similar in meaning, but in these messages on the Twenty-third Psalm, we will make a distinction between them. In this message, the word *providence* is used to refer to the overall workings of God.

I. The term *providence* points to preparation, care, and supervision.

A. *In these verses, it refers to infinite knowledge and power.*

B. *The doctrine of divine providence refers to God's preservation, care, and government which He exercises over all His creation in order that He may accomplish the ends for which He created them.*

II. The Twenty-third Psalm is a vivid picture of the spheres of providential activity.

A. *God exercises this care over the inanimate or physical universe.* The words in the text that suggest this idea are *pastures, waters,* and *food.* He prepares them, cares for them, and governs them. He knows where the waters and pastures are and leads to them.

B. *He exercises control over the animal world.* They are under His providential care. The words *sheep* and *food* are referred to.

C. *He exercises control over the rational world.* This refers to those who are possessed with the ability to reason—man. God loves and is concerned about His creation.

D. *He exercises control over the spiritual world.* This involves His redemptive plan and extends beyond time into eternity.

The Lord is mindful of the most minute want of the humblest person or the largest interest of the world-wide kingdom. The God of the Twenty-third Psalm is the Creator and Preserver of all things. He is a prayer-hearing and prayer-answering God.

III. There are some lessons to be drawn from these verses.

A. *God is a righteous ruler to be respected and adored.* He is also a tender, loving Father who is always thinking of and caring for His children.

B. *This psalm has the element of a messianic and Holy Spirit prophecy.* It tells of the Messiah and His work. Christ and the Holy Spirit lead and empower.

C. *This psalm emphasizes moral and spiritual blessings.* Such words as *obey, follow, dwell,* and *abide* indicate this.

Conclusion. In the Twenty-third Psalm, one finds the affirmation that God created a race of beings who should find their highest happiness by being in the highest degree holy. — *DRG*

* * *

SUNDAY MORNING, JULY 22

TITLE: God's Bad Reputation

TEXT: " 'You will not surely die,' the serpent said to the woman. 'For God knows that when you eat of it your eyes will be opened, and you will be like God, knowing good and evil' " (Gen. 3:4 NIV).

SCRIPTURE READING: Genesis 3:1–10

HYMNS: "Guide Me, O Thou Great Jehovah," Williams
"Grace Greater Than Our Sin," Johnston
"Nothing But the Blood," Lowry

OFFERTORY PRAYER:
Heavenly Father, we thank You for Your long-suffering love that seeks us when we go astray, that restores us from our fallen ways, that upholds us until this very day. We thank You for Jesus Christ, the clearest example of Your never-failing love, and for Your Holy Spirit who guides us day by day.

May our response be that of openness to Your Christ, our Savior, as He speaks in this hour; and may our service reflect our heartfelt gratitude to You as we give and as we go. In the name of Christ we pray. Amen.

Introduction. Have you ever been lied about? Do you know the pain of false rumors circulating about you or about something you supposedly did? If you have not yet experienced this phenomenon, you probably will. At some time or another all of us are the targets of rumor mongers.

I. The devil lies about God.

A. *Satan lied to Eve.* Although Satan directed his initial attack at Eve, the real target was God Himself; and the ammunition was words attributed to God. The Serpent contended that God had forbidden the couple to eat the fruit from any tree in the garden. Already the Serpent was lying about God.

1. Eve corrects the Serpent. But Eve knew the Words of the Lord. She knew that God had commanded that they not eat from only one tree, the tree of the knowledge of good and evil. Thus, armed with knowledge of the Word of God, Eve corrected the Serpent. She could speak from confidence born out of certain knowledge gained from learning the Word of God.

It is as if Eve was getting a foretaste of what Jesus would experience years later when He encountered the Tempter in the desert. Three times Satan tempted Jesus to sin, but each time the attempts were repelled when Jesus turned to the sure Word of God to declare, "It is written . . . ." Eve may not have had the written Word, but she had knowledge of the Word of God and with it resisted the first foray by her Enemy.

2. We can prove the nature of factual charges. One of the things that doubtlessly helped Eve was the nature of the charge against God. It was a factual charge. When Satan contended that God had said she could not eat from the various trees in the garden, Eve knew better. She could judge the truthfulness of the statement immediately.

3. God is your enemy. Satan would not be denied his goal of breaking the fellowship between God and man by only one rebuff. So he changed his attack and branded God as Eve's enemy. The words were, "You will not surely die, . . . For God knows that when you eat of it your eyes will be opened, and you will be like God, knowing good and evil" (3:4 NIV). One has only to look underneath the words to their meaning to grasp the violent nature of the devil's attack.

The very nature of the divine Creator was under attack. But then Satan went further. In the mind of Eve, he planted the notion of rebellion. Although unspoken, the suggestion is still present. The only way to care for oneself is to rebel against God. The only way to establish oneself is at the expense of others, namely God. If God is really my enemy, if He is really using me, Eve reasoned, then rebellion is the only course of action.

4. It is difficult to refute attacks on one's nature. Eve could handle the factual charges about what God said or did not say. She could not handle the attacks on the nature of God Himself. There is a lot of difference between saying John hit Joe and charging that John is greedy or Joe is lazy. It is difficult, even today, to refute charges about the character of another.

B. *We hear charges today.*

1. In families. Some charges are factual. They involve "so-and-so said" or "so-and-so did." These are the factual charges that, with enough time,

can be proved or disproved. But how does one correct charges about the nature of individuals?

2. In business. Frequently employees and employers scream at each other across bargaining tables and picket lines: "All you care about is yourself." Each brands the other enemy.

3. From misunderstandings. It has often been said that what you see depends on where you stand. What one marriage partner sees as expressions of love, the other may see as being "used." What the child sees as "lording authority," the parent may see as appropriate discipline. What the employer sees as acceptable working conditions, the employee may see as lack of concern by management.

Neither perspective may be entirely correct or entirely incorrect but the different perspectives cause unnecessary tensions.

II. Joys of sin for a season.

A. *Sin approaches in the most attractive garb possible.* Like an animal is lured out of the safety of its den by a tempting bait, so sin attempts to lure the Christian into its snare.

1. As Eve looked at the tree, the fruit appealed to her at the most basic level. It appealed to her survival needs for it offered her food. What could be more basic than doing those things which help one survive?

2. But the appeal was more than food. It appealed to Eve on the aesthetic level. It appealed to the eye. It was attractive.

3. And the fruit was still more. It offered the opportunity for what psychologists call "self-actualizing." Eve could be fulfilled personally because eating of the tree would make her like God.

On all the levels of need identified by psychologists, the tree of the knowledge of good and evil lured Eve toward sin.

B. *The Bible points to joy of sin for a season* (Heb. 11:25). Most of us can attest to the allurement of sin. It can be as practical as overeating when the mind runs wild imagining how delicious a particular dessert will taste. Momentarily our minds are captured by the passionate moments certain perfumes and after-shaves are supposed to produce. Even the teetotalers sing the jingles of the beer commercials and desire the "high country" experiences promised by the melodies.

C. *Sin lures out its prey.*

1. One can almost see Eve walk around the edge of the tree of the knowledge of good and evil. Every circle brings her closer and closer to the forbidden fruit. Yet, as she draws closer, nothing happens.

2. With jerky motions, Eve reaches toward the fruit only to draw back in fright of the promised consequences. Again she reaches toward the tree, and this time her fingers brush against the leaves and nothing happens. Now her doubts of God are growing. Her mind recalls God saying that if she touched the tree, she would die. Yet she feels no different than before the contact. Now, with defiance beating in her breast, she picks the fruit and nothing happens.

3. Eve lifts the fruit to her lips and bites into it and nothing happens. Only the juices from the sweetness of the forbidden fruit are on her lips. Now she is convinced that the devil is right. God is her enemy. With boldness she recruits her husband into her sin of rebellion.

D. *Sin has its payday.*

1. One can overeat and enjoy every mouthful, but there is a price to pay. Overeating is unhealthy. One must either exercise sufficiently to work off the extra calories or one grows fat. In light of the price of overeating, the extra bites are never as good as one imagines them.

2. The search for passion often results in unfaithfulness that destroys relationships and wrecks lives.

3. The "high country" experiences end up with one out of every seven drinkers captured by the bottle of alcohol. The toll in ruined lives is uncountable.

4. Adam and Eve found that God was right. They suffered the death of relationship with each other and brokenness before God. They believed the devil's lie about God, and they paid the price.

III. God's response to a bad reputation.

A. *By what you don't do.* Who would have blamed God had He called His experience with man a mistake and given Adam and Eve physical death as well as spiritual death? Thankfully, God did not respond in vengeance. Rather, despite Adam and Eve's buying into the lie about Him, God reacted in mercy toward the disobedient.

B. *By what you do.*

1. In Genesis 3:15, God took the initiative to reach out to an undeserving man and promised that reconciliation not only was possible but that it would occur.

2. In Genesis 12:1–3, God took the initiative and promised blessings to Abraham and his descendants, and through them, to the whole world.

3. In John 1:1–14, God offered Jesus Christ to do for us what none had been able to do for himself. Again, God reached out to undeserving mankind and offered Himself.

One can almost hear the words of Jesus on Calvary, with arms outstretched as he declares to the world, "Look, God is not your enemy. God is not against you. See how much He loves you." And Jesus died "that whosoever believeth in him should not perish, but have everlasting life" (John 3:16b).

Conclusion. Do not believe the devil's lie about God any longer. From the beginning God has reached out in mercy, grace, and steadfast love. He is reaching out even today. The Bible says, "Whosoever shall call upon the name of the Lord shall be saved" (Joel 2:32 NASB). Today you can be saved if you will turn your back on the bad reputation the devil is trying to give God and accept Christ as your personal Savior.   — *BST*

* * *

SUNDAY EVENING, JULY 22

TITLE: The Loving Patience of God

TEXT: "Then the word of the Lord came to Jonah a second time: 'Go to the great city of Nineveh and proclaim to it the message I give you'" (Jonah 3:1–2 NIV).

SCRIPTURE READING: Jonah 2:10–3:9

Introduction. What does the word *patience* mean to you? There are three definitions of this common term. Most people conceive patience in terms of a stoical endurance. It is the act of facing a situation with a dogged determination to "stick it out." Whereas we may admire such strength and determination, such an attitude usually deteriorates in time and resolves into self-pity and bitterness. A second kind of patience characterizes that person who is the eternal optimist, determined to "look for the silver lining" in a situation. Sometimes this person, as commendable as his optimism may be, only succeeds in hiding his head in the sand. He fantasizes and refuses to accept reality. His philosophy is that if you ignore a situation long enough, it will finally go away.

Then there is a third kind of patience which is rare indeed. It is the kind of patience God had toward Jonah and the kind of patience He has toward *us* at many points in our lives. It turns a seemingly impossible situation into a learning experience. Even though Jonah had some serious problems even after he had preached in Nineveh, still he learned some lessons about God through his experience with the storm and in the fish that he could never have learned anywhere else. Thus, we shall look at the "loving patience of God" toward His disobedient servant.

I. God's second call to Jonah (2:10–3:2).

A. *Does it surprise you that God "spoke" to this sea monster?* Why not? He made that creature! And He gave it a command that it clearly understood, for it "vomited Jonah onto dry land" (2:10).

However, before this spectacular event occurred, Jonah was convinced that there was nothing he could do about the situation. He had prayed, as we learned in our last study, but that was all he could do. Very often this is the way God deals with us. He brings us to the place where there is absolutely *no way of escape*. We come to a dead end. God brings us to the utter end of ourselves. Why does He do this? He does it so that we can see, beyond any shadow of doubt, that when He rescues us or delivers us from our impossible situation, it is totally His doing.

This was precisely the point to which God brought Jonah. Jonah came to accept the fact that he was totally helpless. He had hit rock bottom. God had Jonah's undivided attention.

B. *Then God spoke to the fish, and out Jonah came.* When God speaks, He liberates, He delivers, because His Word is truth. "Ye shall know the truth, and the truth shall make you free," said Jesus (John 8:32).

The first two verses of chapter 3 present to us the high point of the Book of Jonah. For we have here one of the most beautiful expressions in the Bible of God's love for His disobedient people. "The word of the LORD came unto Jonah the second time." There are other passages of Scripture that suggest the same truth (see Lam. 3:19–24). In Ephesians 2 Paul states that we by nature are "the children of wrath" (v. 3). Then he adds, "But God, who is rich in mercy. . . . has made us alive together (by grace are ye saved)" (vv. 4–5). Yes, God came to Jonah "a second time." He is the God of the second look.

II. Jonah's reaction to the fact that God gave him a second chance (3:3–4).

A. *Jonah learned an important lesson here—one that is just as timely for us today as it was for him in that ancient time.* He learned that *God's will does not change.* The first time God came to Jonah, He said, "Arise, go to Nineveh, . . .

and cry against it." God said, "Go," and Jonah said, "No." Jonah may have thought that if God had a little time to think about it, He would change His mind about Nineveh. So Jonah decided to take a Mediterranean holiday. But Jonah learned that God does not change His mind. God said, "Jonah, go to Nineveh" the *first* time; and He said, "Jonah, go to Nineveh" the *second* time!

B. *"Jonah obeyed the word of the LORD and went to Nineveh."* Jonah would have preferred that God had sent someone else to do the job He had asked him to do. But Jonah found out that *he* was the one God had chosen and called for this task. God selected Jonah to do a work nobody else could do as effectively. Likewise, God has something for you and me to do in His kingdom that no one else can do as effectively. And He will help us do it. Paul learned this lesson when he said, "I can do all things through Christ which strengtheneth me" (Phil. 4:13).

III. Nineveh's response (vv. 5–9).

A. *Jesus said that "Jonah was a sign to the Ninevites."* He meant that the account of all that had happened to Jonah because of his disobedience had reached Nineveh before the prophet arrived. They knew all about Jonah and that Jonah's God punishes sin. They also learned that He forgives and spares the sinner upon his repentance.

B. *The record gives us only five words of Jonah's sermon (in the original language).* In English, the phrase is longer: "Forty more days and Nineveh will be destroyed" (v. 4 NIV). Nowhere in the Bible or outside of it do we find where *one sermon* from a servant of God was used so greatly, for the whole city of Nineveh repented of sin and believed God.

Note that the people did not set their eyes on Jonah. He didn't become a national hero, an overnight sensation, or a household word. The account says that they believed *God*. And note also that the response of the people was so spontaneous that they did not wait for orders from the king. When Jonah's message reached their ears, they repented. And when the king heard it, he did exactly as the people were doing. And because of that, God spared the city. Their repentance automatically moved God's impending judgment away from them. God works the same way today.

Conclusion. The emphasis in this study concerns God's dealings with us when we are disobedient. He chastens us, disciplines us, corrects us—all in order to get our attention. He "comes to us a second time." He gives us a second chance.

— *DLJ*

* * *

WEDNESDAY EVENING, JULY 25

TITLE: The Provision of God

TEXT: **"He maketh me to lie down in green pastures"** (Ps. 23:2a).

SCRIPTURE READING: **Psalm 23:1–6**

Introduction. This psalm has, for more than three thousand years, been one of the most precious possessions of the church. Jews and Christians alike hold it dear. It brings God before each person in enduring character, and it gives a beautiful picture of the blessedness of God's people.

I. This text presents a picture of the needs of life.

A. *Green pastures are evidences of plenty even in a dry and barren land.* God is able to supply needs. The pastures look and taste good.

B. *Still waters provide refreshment in the dry and barren land.* These are the kind of waters of which the sheep can and will partake. They are not waterfalls that roar. They are still, and one can drink without fear.

II. There are some helpful comments one may consider in regard to the text.

A. *It is said that sheep refuse to lie down unless they are free of fear.* Sheep that are restless, discontented, agitated, and disturbed do not do well. This same thing can be said about people. Psalm 56:3 says, "What time I am afraid, I will trust in thee." First John 4:18 states, "Perfect love casteth out fear."

B. *It is said that sheep will not lie down unless they are free from friction with other sheep.* Where there is tension and rivalry, there is unrest. The shepherd's presence makes the difference in behavior. Jesus is the Christian's Good Shepherd. Paul pointed out what Jesus does for His children. "I have learned, in whatsoever state I am, therewith to be content" (Phil. 4:11).

C. *It is said that sheep will not lie down if tormented by parasites.* Only when they are free of such will they relax.

The Good Shepherd will use various means in order to rid the sheep of harmful insects. The Lord Jesus Christ removes from His children the many things that "bug" them. The Scriptures speak of the Holy Spirit, as symbolized by oil, by which the Lord brings healing, comfort, and relief from the harsh and abrasive aspects of life.

D. *It is said that sheep will not lie down as long as they feel the need of food.* It is imperative they be free from hunger. The provision of food is the responsibility of the shepherd. He does what is necessary to provide. The Lord Jesus—the Good Shepherd—does just this.

Conclusion. This is a message for the hurting, restless, and unsettled. Look to the One who has promised to supply all needs.   *— DRG*

* * *

SUNDAY MORNING, JULY 29

TITLE: Fig Leaves

TEXT: **"Then the eyes of both of them were opened, and they realized they were naked; so they sewed fig leaves together and made coverings for themselves" (Gen. 3:7 NIV).**

SCRIPTURE READING: Genesis 3:1–10

HYMNS: "He Lives," Ackley
        "At Calvary," Newell
        "I Stand Amazed," Gabriel

OFFERTORY PRAYER:

Heavenly Father, we come before You with praise in our hearts for Your work in our lives. You have granted us forgiveness from sin because of our faith in Your Son. Yet around us are many who are still loaded down with guilt and shame. You have given us peace that never fails. Yet the franticness of others demonstrates that many do not know this enduring peace. You have given us joy because we know You and are known by You. But the frowning faces around us testify that many have not accepted Your forgiveness and peace and joy. As we present these offerings, may they be used to lift up Christ Jesus so men and women near and far might be drawn to Him and might know the precious gifts we experience each day. In the name of Jesus we pray. Amen.

Introduction. What was the first thing Adam and Eve did after they rebelled against God? According to the text, their first act was to make themselves aprons of fig leaves because they realized they were naked. It is interesting that in the closing verse of chapter 2, the writer points out that Adam and Eve could live together without clothes and feel no shame. Yet, as soon as they ate of the forbidden fruit, they sought some kind of covering to hide behind.

Evidently, their sin brought with it a kind of embarrassment, a kind of shame. Adam did not want to be seen by Eve nor Eve by Adam, so they made aprons of fig leaves. "It is all right for you to see this outward apron, but it is not all right for you to see me as I really am," they were saying to one another. Behind this act was the unspoken admission that things were not all right on the inside, that a sense of shame had driven out the feeling of innocence of Genesis 2:25.

That feeling of Adam and Eve is no different than the feeling of people today who do not know Jesus Christ, nor is the act of hiding behind fig leaves any different than the acts of people today. What we may hide behind may not be actual fig leaves, but they serve the same purpose. They become something we hold up to people and say, "See these, but don't see me. Don't see what I'm really like on the inside."

What are some of these modern-day fig leaves? Let me suggest a few.

I. Possessions.

A. *Importance of possessions.* Some of us spend our lives pursuing possessions. That pursuit goes on until our possessions begin to possess us. We strive for the most expensive house on the block. We buy the car that tells the world that we are a success. We show off the labels in our clothes. We surround ourselves with luxuries of every type. Our possessions say something about us. They tell the world about our status in life, and status is important to us.

B. *Inadequacies of possessions.* But our self-images are fragile. There is always someone a little better off than we, always someone who was ahead of us in finding a new adult toy we wish we had. Eventually, our possessions can no longer sustain us. They cannot prevent us from knowing ourselves. From deep inside, feelings of inadequacy emerge. Our images of success can't stop the feelings of failure that pain us. Guilt and shame are once again our companions.

We cry to the world, "Look at my fig leaves. See them, but don't see me. Don't see what I am really like on the inside." We know ourselves too well, and what we know we do not like. We feel dirty on the inside. Madison Avenue has yet to make a soap that can wash away that kind of feeling.

II. Pleasure.

The Declaration of Independence of the United States of America declares that man has been given certain inalienable rights. Among these are "life, liberty and the pursuit of happiness." This generation seems to have rewritten that phrase to read, "life, liberty and the pursuit of pleasure." The 1970s have been described as the "Me Generation." We continue to live in a time characterized by the slogan, "If it feels good, do it." Self-indulgence is the expected, not the scorned.

A. *Public attitude.* Some of our nation's laws encourage this slothful attitude. Abortions are available on demand. As a result, the number of abortions reached 1.55 million in 1980 (Guttmacher Institute Report, May 5, 1982). That meant eighty abortions for every one thousand live births in the nation. In some places prostitution is legal. Where it is not, many officials speak of "victimless crimes." They say law-enforcement officers have more important things to do than enforce laws against prostitution where no one is really hurt. Gambling is now legal in thirty-three states through government-sponsored lotteries and/or parimutuel betting. Casino gambling is being discussed as a possible tax-raising device for several areas of the country, not just Las Vegas and Atlantic City. Americans spent $56.1 billion on alcoholic beverages in 1981 and consumed more than twice as much beer than any other nation (*Monday Morning Report,* Vol. 6, No. 15; Alcohol Research Information Service).

B. *Personal attitudes.* But the laws of a country and the civil attitudes only reflect the personal moral patterns of the people. Abortion rates and venereal disease epidemics must be judged in light of the promiscuity and infidelity of individuals. It is interesting that Americans cannot even buy toothpaste without judging it on the basis of its sex appeal. More people seem to live by the "Gospel of Schlitz" than by the gospel of Jesus Christ. Schlitz declares, "You only go around once in life, so grab all the gusto you can." People evidently believe that line and practice it.

The results are inevitable. Even the Hindu religion knows the tragic results of such license. The Hindus teach there are Seven Noble Paths to finding God. One of the paths is through pleasure. Hinduism says that after a time, the pleasure seeker will realize the futility of his or her search, that even the pleasures will lose their value, and the seeker will go after something higher in life.

For many, pleasures are losing their value and the results are tragic. People are finding they have been reduced to "things" rather than persons. People have become only toys to satisfy someone else and then be discarded. Relationships do not exist. Values do not exist. People end up used, broken, and alone.

Yet people pursue pleasure as if there were no tomorrow, as if they could hide behind the fig leaves of self-indulgence forever, as if there were no God.

III. A Christless religion.

Others take a different track. They believe in God but theirs is a Christless religion. According to a 1982 Gallup Poll, 98 percent of Americans believe in God. Yet only about two-thirds of Americans are affiliated with a church or synagogue. Only about 40 percent of Americans attend church or synagogue on a regular basis, Gallup says.

A. *"Man Upstairs."* This Christless religion could be called "the Man Upstairs" religion. These people acknowledge that some higher power exists, but they usually picture that power as a doddering old man with a long white beard who wants everyone to get along. The idea of God coming in the form of man to die for their sins is foreign to their thinking. God remains a far-off, unimportant figure with some sort of magical powers.

B. *Any religion.* Some in this group place more importance on sincerity of belief than in the truth of the belief. One can hear them say, "We are all headed toward the same goal anyway, so one religion is as good as another." The important thing, they will argue, is that one sincerely believe in whatever it is he or she believes in.

However, Jesus Christ declared, "I am the way, the truth and the life. No man cometh unto the Father except by me."

IV. Earn salvation.

Some people believe in God and in Jesus Christ. Yet they have trouble relating to God through Christ. This is true for some in the church as well as outside of it.

A. *Non-church members.* One non-church member once explained to me why he did not consider church participation important. He recounted how he worked two jobs to help care for his large family, was a moral man and an upright citizen. "I believe God will take all of that into consideration on Judgment Day," he declared. This man was treating God like He was part of a union negotiation. On one side was God and on the other was the nonchurchgoer. Between them, they would work out an acceptable plan for both parties.

Such an attitude is a repetition of Adam's sin. God set the standard. We either accept it or reject it. The terms are never changed.

B. *Church member.* Some church members have trouble finding God. Behind their anxious pursuit is the notion that they must earn God's love. Such people are driven by a compulsion that says, "If I can do just one more thing, God will have to love me." They sing in the choir, serve on several committees, attend every time the doors are open. They can never do enough. But instead of finding joy and fulfillment in their service, these folks end up anxious, frustrated, and scared that they have left something undone which must yet be accomplished before they can make God love them. Their efforts are as futile as Adam and Eve's trying to hide from God behind aprons of fig leaves.

V. The answer.

If all of these are nothing but fig leaves behind which one hides, what is the answer to knowing God, to finding forgiveness and cleansing? The Bible gives us that answer in Colossians 1:26–27.

There is no other hope than that which is built on Jesus Christ. Men and women continue to hide behind fig leaves, but God's remedy is plain. The remedy for man's spiritual ills is Christ Jesus. He alone provides the way to the Father. He alone brings forgiveness of sin. He alone cleanses us from all unrighteousness. He alone gives us purpose and meaning. He alone accepts us as we are. He alone is the Friend that sticks closer than a brother. He alone is our hope of glory.

Conclusion. You can know this Christ today. He can be yours and you can be

His. The Bible says, "Whosoever calleth on the name of the Lord shall be saved" (Rom. 10:13). This morning, in the name of Christ, we invite you to forsake whatever fig leaf you are hiding behind and come to Christ. Accept Him as your personal Lord and Savior, as your only hope of glory. — *BST*

* * *

SUNDAY EVENING, JULY 29

TITLE: The Continuing Battle With Rebellion

TEXT: "But God said to Jonah, 'Do you have a right to be angry about the vine?' 'I do,' he said. 'I am angry enough to die' " (Jonah 4:9 NIV).

SCRIPTURE READING: Jonah 3:10–4:10

Introduction. If you or I had been writing the story of Jonah, there is no doubt that we would have concluded it with the tenth verse of chapter 3. That is the logical ending. That would make it the kind of story we like to hear—the "lived-happily-ever-after" kind. But that is one of the unwavering characteristics of our Bible. It never glosses over the sins of the men and women whose lives it records. Rather it depicts these characters in their battle with temptation and sin. It reveals them at the pinnacle of strength and victory; but when they sink to the pits in their disobedience and sin, it records that, too.

So it was with Jonah. Certainly God was disappointed with Jonah's attitudes and reactions, but He never stopped loving him. God would much rather have demonstrated His love to Jonah by sending him blessings on top of blessings— just as He would with us. But there was a streak of rebellion in Jonah which, obviously, he had to fight all of his life. It is possible that Jonah *never* became a consistently obedient servant of God. He may have been stubborn and prejudiced all of his life. Consequently, God had to send His love to Jonah much of the time in the form of chastening and discipline.

Jonah found out—and we must never forget—that God will never leave His children alone. When we obey Him, He is going to be with us in blessing; when we disobey Him, He is going to be with us in rebuke and chastening. *If we are His children, we cannot escape Him.* Thus we come to our last study—Jonah's continuing battle with rebellion.

I. Jonah's displeasure (3:10–4:3).

A. *From every human standard, Jonah had been a success.* He had been God's spokesman in the great pagan city of Nineveh, and God had used his message in causing great conviction to come upon the people. They had responded positively and repented of their sin, from the lowliest peasant to the king on the throne.

A great sweeping reformation had come to that heathen metropolis. Apparently it had been a city of evil and sin comparable to that of Sodom and Gomorrah, or Tyre and Sidon. Its wholesale iniquity had risen like a stench in the nostrils of God. It was within forty days of total destruction. Its time was running out. But in His sovereign mercy, God extended a reprieve, *if* the people would repent and forsake their sin.

B. *Nineveh was so large that it took three days for Jonah to reach all of the major sections of the city with his preaching.* But in so doing, he reached everyone. All of the people came under the hearing of Jonah's message of warning and repentance. As we learned in our last study, the people listened carefully, and they believed Jonah's *God*, not just Jonah. And when Jonah's preaching mission was over, God had turned that great city right-side-up.

C. *But then we read this disconcerting statement: "But Jonah was greatly displeased and became angry"* (4:1 NIV). *Why* did Jonah become angry? Was he worried about his reputation back in Israel? Was he afraid that he would be the laughingstock of his people when he returned home? Would they think that Jonah was a turncoat?

Not really. Jonah simply begrudged the heathen Ninevites the abundant mercy of God! Jonah had gratefully received God's pardoning grace upon *his* repentance in the belly of the fish, but he was not willing for Nineveh to have the same pardon.

Then, with no apparent sense of shame or reluctance, Jonah laid bare his angry feelings toward God for what had happened. In his prejudice, he could not bear to see God show mercy and compassion to those whom he did not like. So a despondent, chargrined, angry Jonah set about to justify his running away from God in the first place. He dared to quarrel with God because He had spared Nineveh.

II. God's reaction to Jonah's displeasure.

A. *Jonah went outside the city walls of Nineveh and built himself a booth, a shelter, east of the city.* Some say that Jonah did this before the forty-day period of grace had expired. He was hoping, just perchance, that the repentance of the Ninevites was not genuine and that God would still destroy them.

In any event, after Jonah had built his booth, God caused a gourd vine to spring up with miraculous speed. Because of this shade that was provided for Jonah, he became "very happy" about the vine. And incidentally, this is the only place in the book where Jonah is said to have been happy or glad—and it was a selfish joy over his own comfort!

B. *God had a plan behind this.* That night, He singled out a worm who would have a special task to perform during its existence. It was to attack the tender stalk of that gourd vine; and overnight, the vine withered and wilted to the ground. When the sun rose the next morning, it was accompanied by a sultry east wind, which God also sent. And the combination of the blazing sun and the hot east wind almost caused Jonah to suffer a heat stroke. He became faint and begged to die.

Then God said to him, "Do you have a right to be angry about the vine?" And Jonah answered God with these unbelievable words: "I am angry enough to die." I do not think there is a picture in all of the Bible of an individual—one of God's children—who showed such stubborn rebellion as Jonah!

III. God's compassion (vv. 10–11).

A. *How great is God's wisdom and compassion!* What irresistible logic God used with Jonah, and what boundless love and pity He demonstrated to him! And notice the greatness of the city of Nineveh, as God describes it. Those who "cannot tell between their right hand and their left hand" are children who had not reached the age of accountability. And if we are to assume that these children represented even one-fifth of the total population of the city, there would have been some 600,000 inhabitants in Nineveh.

B. *Furthermore, we see the tenderness of God for His creation in the fact that He even mentioned the cattle in the city which were spared.* If God was willing and ready to spare Sodom if only *ten* righteous people could be found there, He surely wanted to have pity and spare 120,000 children, who had not reached the age of discernment and willful sin. Would to God that you and I could have just a tiny fraction of the compassion and concern of God for those in our world who are morally and spiritually destitute in their sin.

Conclusion. So, in this strange little Book of Jonah, we have an amazing account of God's mercy and concern for *all* people. And we have the disappointing picture of how God's own people can be guilty of such gross spiritual sins as prejudice and rebellion against God.

But we also see how we cannot escape God if we are indeed His own. He will never leave us in our disobedience—He will chasten us as children. Why? Because He is our heavenly Father, and we are His children. May God help us to learn the good lesson of obedience and submission to the Father's will, and thus know the joy of having Him release upon us the untold blessings of heaven.

— DLJ

* * *

SUGGESTED PREACHING PROGRAM
FOR THE MONTH OF AUGUST

Sunday Mornings

This series of messages will emphasize the place prayer should have in the life of each follower of Christ. The suggested theme for this series is "Waging Successful Spiritual Warfare With the Help That Comes Through Prayer."

Sunday Evenings

Four of Paul's epistles are suggested for the Sunday evening messages. A good theme would be "The Apostle Paul Speaks to Modern Churches Also."

Wednesday Evenings

Continue the devotional messages based on Psalm 23, using the theme "With the Lord As My Shepherd, I Shall Not Suffer the Lack of Anything That I Need."

* * *

WEDNESDAY EVENING, AUGUST 1

TITLE: The Provision of God (continued)

TEXT: "He leadeth me beside the still waters" (Ps. 23:2b).

SCRIPTURE READING: Psalm 23:1–6

Introduction. The Twenty-third Psalm has dried many tears. The provision of God is the heart of the psalm.

I. Some facts about sheep and water.

A. *It has been estimated that about 70 percent of a sheep's body is composed of water.* Water is necessary for a sheep to maintain normal body metabolism. It is the determining factor as to the sheep's vitality, strength, and vigor.

B. *The believer recognizes immediately that his Lord Jesus is the strength of his life.* He supplies all needs.

II. The right kind of water must be supplied.

A. *The water must be still or sheep will not drink.* That which is noisy is frightening and disturbing to sheep. Swift water is dangerous.

B. *The water must be pure or the sheep will pick up internal parasites and diseases.* Apart from the protecting hand of the shepherd, sheep will pause at puddles of polluted water. The Great Shepherd of the Christian leads His children to that which is pure and healthy.

III. The place of still waters is a resting place and a place of refreshment.

A. *The need of the human soul is described by the word* thirst (Matt. 5:6). The soul must be nourished by the right things. Each person must guard against taking in that which is harmful. The Shepherd directs in this matter.

B. *The thirst of the human soul is quenched by the One who gives the water which, when partaken of, causes the believer never to thirst again* (John 4:14; 6:35). This ''water'' takes many forms.

1. Dew. This makes the early morning a good time to refresh oneself spiritually.

2. Wells. This means labor for the shepherd. He must draw the water and make it available for the sheep.

3. Deep, quiet streams. The deep things of life are what count.

Conclusion. The Lord Jesus knows every need of the human heart. He has promised to meet each need. He provides whatever is necessary. *— DRG*

* * *

USFP 26.83
FBO

SUNDAY MORNING, AUGUST 5

TITLE: **Partnership in Prayer**

TEXT: **"And when he had considered the thing, he came to the house of Mary the mother of John, whose surname was Mark; where many were gathered together praying" (Acts 12:12).**

SCRIPTURE READING: Acts 12:1–19

HYMNS: **"Near to the Heart of God," McAfee**
"Sweet Hour of Prayer," Walford
"What a Friend," Scriven

OFFERTORY PRAYER:
Heavenly Father, thank You for Your promises to supply all the needs of soul and body. Forgive us for fears of our own security that keep us from giving to You for the spiritual needs of others as we ought. In faith and love we give this proportion this day. Use it to bring Your promises to others. We pray in Jesus' name. Amen.

Introduction. There is no more dramatic story in the New Testament concerning partnership and power in prayer than this record given us in the twelfth chapter of the Acts of the Apostles. In this story King Herod represents the subtle, fearful, and overwhelming power of the devil against the work of God. Over against this opposition, however, God puts a church or a fellowship at prayer. In other words, whenever Satan comes in like a flood, the Spirit of the Lord lifts up a standard against him (Isa. 59:19). The Enemy's single purpose in every age is to silence the voice of the gospel, but God's answer is always the mighty, working power of prayer. This is why this miraculous intervention is preserved for us. We can read it, study it, and learn the principles that determine victory over every attempt of Satan to thwart the redemptive purposes of God. Notice three important features about this particular prayer meeting.

I. The people at prayer.
Verse 12 is a simple statement of fact with eternal significance. As we have already seen, Satan had done his best to incarcerate Peter and to silence the message of life in the city of Jerusalem, but God responded by drawing together a

group of men and women to pray. Three classes of people were present at that prayer meeting.

A. *The "Mary" class.* It was "the house of Mary the mother of John, whose surname was Mark; where many were gathered together praying" (v. 12). Mary represented the influential people, for it appears that she was a woman of comparative wealth and influence. She had a commodious home, which was used as a meeting place for members of the church in Jerusalem. Thank God for the Marys of church history! Thank God for the Marys of today who make their homes available for Bible study, prayer, and Christian fellowship. No one can read the New Testament without observing the central place the home has had in the growth of the Christian church.

B. *The "Rhoda" class.* "As Peter knocked at the door of the gate, a damsel came to hearken, named Rhoda" (v. 13). Rhoda, whose name means "rose," represents the less significant people. Without question, she was but a familiar slave who kept the door. But what a fragrance her name and life have given the Christian church throughout the centuries. While God certainly uses the influential people, He never despises the less significant people. The prayers of Rhoda were just as effective and acceptable as the prayers of Mary.

C. *The "many" class.* We read that "many were gathered together praying" (v. 12). The "many" represent the inconspicuous people. These are the unnamed, common people who hear Jesus gladly, who respond to His message, and who become the members of His church, which is His body. Since the beginning of the church and down through the centuries, the preponderance of people in the church of Jesus Christ have been part of the "many" class, and this is how it will be until the church is complete and Christ comes back to receive His own.

II. The purpose in prayer.

We cannot read Luke's account here without being impressed with two aspects of prayer which constitute the elements of true purpose.

A. *Unity in prayer.* "Many were gathered together" (v. 12). Whatever differences might have separated the people involved were now completely lost in the unity of the purpose in prayer. This, undoubtedly, is the first secret of prevailing prayer. This is why Jesus declared, "If two of you shall agree on earth as touching any thing that they shall ask, it shall be done for them of my Father which is in heaven" (Matt. 18:19). And the psalmist reminds us that it is good and pleasant for brethren to dwell together in unity (Ps. 133:1), for there God pours out the precious ointment of His Spirit and distills the dew of His blessing.

B. *Urgency in prayer.* "Prayer was made without ceasing" (v. 5). The phrase "without ceasing" means that prayer was fervent and intense. This is the second secret of prevailing prayer. It is prayer of self-denial. It is the prayer that spells death to all who would interfere with the finding and fulfilling of God's purpose. When people are gathered to pray with this sense of urgency, they are also prepared to go through with God at any cost. This is "Calvary praying"; therefore it is victorious praying. When people pray like this, something is bound to happen.

III. The power of prayer.

Peter had been cast into prison. Previous to this, James had been beheaded with the sword. The Christians were apprehensive, so they prayed and they prayed and they prayed. God has so ordered it that the miracles that happen on earth are always channeled through the medium of prayer; and this case was no exception. The power of God was revealed.

A. *First, there was an unusual demonstration of power.* When Rhoda reported that Peter was alive and was standing outside the door, the participants in prayer claimed she was mad (v. 15). Without doubt, everyone imagined that Peter would be arraigned before the magistrate the next day, and then cautioned and released—all in answer to their prevailing prayers. But God always works far above all that we could ever ask or think. Therefore, the divine demonstration of power transcended the preconceived ideas of those faithful prayer warriors.

B. *Secondly, there was an undeniable demonstration of power.* "Peter stood before the gate" (v. 14). However unusual was the answer, it was undeniable.(Everyone in that fellowship knew that God had answered prayer and that prayer was a force, miraculous in its outworking.

(George Mueller said he never had any need for the orphans in his orphanage that God did not meet.(On one such occasion an orphanage ran out of milk. George Mueller prayed, and down the street came a farmer driving two milk cows. There is no limit to the power of prayer. R. G. Lee said, "Prayer can do anything God can do." When God hears prayer, the answer is both unusual and undeniable.

Conclusion. Are you involved in this partnership of prayer? God is looking for the Marys, the Rhodas, and the many who will learn the purpose of prayer and experience the unusual and undeniable power of prayer. Will you be such a person today? Do you not see the great need of the hour to unlock iron gates that hold prisoner those of our own generation? Will you not enlist in this great partnership of prayer today? — *GLS*

* * *

SUNDAY EVENING, AUGUST 5

TITLE: The Life of Christian Joy

Text: "Rejoice in the Lord alway: and again I say, Rejoice" (Phil. 4:4)

Scripture Reading: Philippians 4:4–7

Introduction. There are a lot of happy people in our world today, not withstanding what you may hear over radio or TV, or read in newspapers and magazines.

A poll was taken recently in a large city in which people were asked at random, "Are you a happy person?" Those conducting the poll were expecting a large percentage to say they were not happy. But to the pollsters' amazement, an unusually large percentage said they were happy people!

A Christian has the greatest reason of all to be happy. He knows the love and forgiveness of God through Jesus Christ.

Philippians is the loveliest letter Paul ever wrote. It has been called "The Epistle of Joy." Again and again the words *joy* and *rejoice* recur as a brilliant thread woven throughout the fiber of a beautiful piece of cloth.

We do well to remember that ours is meant to be a life of Christian joy—full of radiance and splendor.

I. The cause of Christian joy—the fellowship of believers (Phil. 1:3-8).

From what does a Christian derive the joy mentioned in Philippians 1:3-8? What was Paul's cause for Christian joy and what is ours? It is "the fellowship of believers."

That which brings joy to the Christian today is not the building in which he worships; it is not the program in which he participates; it is not even in the good that he does. If there is to be any real joy in his life, it comes from his own personal fellowship with other believers. The absence of this fellowship well explains the absence of joy in the lives of countless Christians today.

If ours is to be a life of "Christian joy," it must be a life lived in the fellowship of believers.

A. *The gratitude this fellowship shows* (v. 3). It is a lovely occurrence when remembrance and gratitude are bound up together. In our personal Christian relationships it is ideal to have nothing but happy memories, and that is how Paul thought of the Christians at Philippi.

B. *The growth this fellowship seeks* (vv. 9-11). Although everything was so wonderful, Paul was never satisfied—and neither is God. And although much may be wonderful, our fellowship seeks a growth yet to be realized. It seeks:

1. That profusion which is the measure of love: "that your love may abound yet more and more" (v. 9a). Here is a love that is unselfish in its concern for others. The picture is that of a bucket standing under a stream with the water pouring over on every side, overflowing to others.

2. That perception which guides the ministry of love (vv. 9b-10a). This is no sentimental love. It is a love which is guided by true knowledge and wise judgment.

3. That perfection which is the "must" of love (vv. 10b-11). Here is the standard that love sets—*perfection*. We are frightened by the word, but God isn't. And though we shall never achieve perfection in this life, we can at least aspire to it.

II. Joy and the place I'm in (1:12-26).

Paul had already spent about *two years* as a prisoner back in his home country. There had been the *long voyage* at sea. And there were added still *two more years* of captivity in Rome. Things weren't easy for Paul, yet, right in the middle of it all, he says, "I therein do rejoice, yea, and will rejoice" (v. 18c). Surely from this we learn that Christian joy is not dependent on the place we are in.

Three things may emerge from a difficult place that are worth considering.

A. *A bitterness that can spoil.* What was involved that *could* have made Paul an extremely bitter man? The following three things could have made Paul bitter; and, if allowed to enter your heart, they can make you bitter too!

1. The sheer unfairness of his bonds (v. 13a). It is not easy, is it, to sing when you have been treated unjustly and unfairly?

2. The subtle unfriendliness of his colleagues (vv. 15-16).

3. The seeming unfaithfulness of his Lord. This is not specifically stated here, but surely it must have been one of the weapons Satan would use to try and cripple this great warrior.

Paul refused to give in to a bitterness that can spoil.

B. *A blessedness that can surprise* (v. 12). Sometimes we are surprised at the blessings which come out of a difficult situation. Furtherance is the word used for the progress of an army or expedition. It describes the cutting away of trees and undergrowth and the removing of barriers which would hinder the progress of an army. So Paul's imprisonment, surprisingly enough, rather than being a barrier, removed barriers to the spread of the gospel!

C. *A boldness that can sing* (v. 18). Some of us sing so long as the sun shines; but the moment the clouds arrive, we begin to clam up and growl. We should remember that courage has its place in the Christian life.

III. Joy and the people I'm with (v. 28).

Some Christians do not have joyful lives because of the people they are with—or to be more accurate, because of their attitude toward the people they are with. Such a person is quite convinced that the only problem with society is other people.

Paul is acutely aware that the life of Christian joy and our attitudes toward people around us are vitally related. Because he is anxious that personal relationships should never disrupt the life of Christian joy, Paul gets down to the matter of "joy and the people I'm with." First of all there was:

A. *Opposition from without* (v. 28). "Your adversaries"—ceaseless pressure from without against the individual Christian and the church. There will be a continuous attack by Satan on the fellowship of the church, for it is the "cause of Christian joy" and Satan wants to remove any cause for our being happy Christians.

B. *Corruption from within* (2:3). How often disunity and therefore danger to the fellowship arises, not because of a retreat in the face of the enemy, but because of some personal advancement that is sought by a Christian here or there.

IV. Joy and the person I am (chap. 3).

In this third chapter Paul states a most disturbing fact—the person I am has everything to do with my living the life of Christian joy. He dares to suggest that the reason I am not living the life of Christian joy may well be explained by the person I am!

Three words in this chapter must characterize my attitude toward the person I am if I am to live the life of Christian joy.

A. *Bankruptcy* (v. 7). When Paul looks at his life—the rich tradition that was his and the triumphs that marked his service for Christ—he writes across it all in bold letters the word *worthless* and claims that he is utterly bankrupt in the presence of Christ. He seems to be saying something that Christ said earlier, "Happy are the *poor* in spirit, for theirs is the kingdom of heaven."

B. *Intimacy* (v. 10). The word translated "know" is not the "know" of the intellect; it is the "know" of intimacy. This verb indicates the closest, most intimate, and most personal knowledge of another person. So then, it is not Paul's aim to know *facts* about Christ, but to *know* Christ personally.

C. *Expectancy* (v. 14).

V. Joy and the good it does (chap. 4).

5   ''The life of Christian joy.'' Is this life worth the effort it takes to live? What good does it do? What have I to lose by going my own way, living my own life, and asserting my own will? What have I to gain by living in fellowship with God and His children?

These questions find their answer in this fourth chapter. It is here that Paul speaks of ''Joy and the good it does.'' If we have joy, all the good it does becomes our own.

A. *It makes Christ attractive to others* (vv. 2–8). When Paul spoke of his Lord, that which made Christ so attractive to others was neither Paul's physical appearance nor his eloquence, but it was the joy in which he spoke and lived. And if your life of Christian joy does nothing more than make Christ attractive to others, it is worth it all!

B. *It imparts grace to cope with life's problems* (vv. 12–13). Paul had more problems than most of us will ever know. But his life of Christian joy supplied him ample grace to cope with each problem in such a manner as to bring honor—not shame—to his Lord.

How often we are deceived by thinking that contentment is found in what one has. ''If only I had this or that I would be happy. I would find contentment!'' Then the day comes when we can afford our desire; but when we have obtained it, we discover that it does *not* bring joy or happiness. Then we become disillusioned, anxious, and frustrated because we have learned that contentment is not dependent on externals—however lavish they may be.

But the life of Christian joy imparts a grace that is content apart from externals. Whether we have much or little we have *Christ,* and this is what brings contentment, joy, and happiness!

C. *It instills new zest in the church* (vv. 20–23). Take a church that is half dead whose work is being carried on laboriously by spiritually anemic souls. Inject into its collapsed veins the stimulus of Christian joy, and in a few months you will hardly recognize it as the same church.

Conclusion. The new zest and enthusiasm which Christian joy imparts will not allow us to remain mute concerning our Lord. We must sing His praises! We must exalt His name! We must share His story! We must spread His joy!

For the ''life of Christian joy'' to do any real good, it must be shared with others.

There's a world out there that wonders if Christ really makes a difference. And your life of Christian joy alone can convince it.   — *JRM*

* * *

WEDNESDAY EVENING, AUGUST 8

TITLE: The Provision of God (continued)

TEXT: **''He restoreth my soul''** (Ps. 23:3a).

SCRIPTURE READING: **Psalm 23:1–6**

Introduction: A young woman had been badly injured in an accident. The prognosis was dim. The nurse was about to give the anesthetic when the young woman asked for permission to repeat something her mother had taught her as a child. She started quoting the Twenty-third Psalm. The nurse started to apply the anesthetic, but the doctor stopped her and requested the girl to finish. When she did, the doctor performed the surgery and it was successful.

This psalm does bring peace.

I. This verse assumes depression.

A. *Those in the Good Shepherd's care do need restoring at times.* David tasted defeat in his life and felt frustrated because of sin. He was acquainted with the bitterness of feeling hopeless and without strength in himself (42:11).

B. *There are many maladies that plague mankind, some of the worst of which are discontent, denial, destruction, and depression.* Depression is one of man's most bothersome ailments. Few people escape it.

II. The word *restore* in the text is the key thought.

A. *Restore means "to revive and invigorate when exhausted and weary of soul and spirit."* It is the renewing of strength when worn down and the bringing back after wandering.

B. *There are numerous biblical examples of restoration.* The thought is connected to restoring from disorder and decay (80:19). It is used in restoring from sorrow and affliction (Ruth 4:15). It is used in restoring from death (1 Kings 17:21–22).

III. The relation of sheep needing restoration and man's need of the same have a close parallel.

A. *Sheep are known to be cast down.* When a sheep lies on its back, it is extremely difficult, if not impossible, to turn over; but the sheep will not call for help.

The shepherd is responsible. He must keep close watch, as God does. He must know that all the flock are well taken care of. He must know the method of restoration and have compassion.

B. *Christians are cautioned about presumption* (1 Cor. 10:12).

1. Sheep will lie on an easy spot to their detriment. God's children are cautioned about looking for an easy way out.

2. Wool is a symbol of pride, but too much will endanger the sheep. So it is with the children of God becoming absorbed in their own desires.

Conclusion. There are many ways depression can be treated. One of the best is that of turning one's cares over to the Great Shepherd and letting Him restore.

— *DRG*

* * *

SUNDAY MORNING, AUGUST 12

TITLE: **The Pattern for Prevailing Prayer**

Text: **"Praying always with all prayer and supplication in the Spirit . . ."** **(Eph. 6:18).**

Scripture Reading: **Ephesians 6:10–17**

HYMNS: "O God Our Help in Ages Past," Watts
        "O Worship the King," Grant
        "Teach Me to Pray," Reitz

OFFERTORY PRAYER:
Our Father, make us grateful for the privilege we enjoy of worshiping You today. Make us grateful for the salvation we have in Christ our Lord. We bring our gifts out of hearts of gratitude and pray that You will bless and use them. We give them not because You need them but because we love and adore You. Let us rejoice in the blessedness of giving. In Christ's name we pray. Amen.

Introduction: A recently reprinted book by E. M. Bounds is entitled *Weapon of Prayer*. This title is based on Ephesians 6:18–20. It will help us to see the relationship of these verses to the whole section, verses 10–20, if we select certain key words from the passage: "Wherefore take unto you the whole armour of God . . . Stand therefore . . . Praying always." It would seem that Paul requires prayer to be cojoined with all the armor of God; and while he attempts no symbolism for prayer itself, it is certainly an essential aspect of the believer's preparation for spiritual warfare.

In the words of our text the apostle Paul gives us a pattern for prevailing prayer. As we study his words, we discover four marks that should characterize all of our intercession.

I. Perceptive prayer.

First, prevailing prayer is perceptive. According to Paul, we are to pray "in the Spirit."

We believe that the translators of the Authorized Version were quite correct in capitalizing the word *Spirit.* While conceivably Paul could be stressing the fact that all prayer must be the product of the renewed human spirit, I believe he is here stressing the fact that all prayer must be "in the Spirit," that is, "in the Holy Spirit."

But what does Paul mean when he exhorts us to pray "in the Spirit"? Some translations suggest that what he means is that we are to be energized by the Holy Spirit in our praying. This would then be equivalent to saying: "pray in the power of the Holy Spirit." That is certainly a vital and valuable observation with regard to prevailing prayer. We must be filled with the Spirit in the matter of effective prayer. The kind of prayer referred to by James, "The effectual fervent prayer of a righteous man availeth much" (5:16), is surely the expression of a person whose heart is controlled by the Spirit.

To pray with perception means not only praying in the energy of the Holy Spirit but praying in line with the Spirit's mind.

This simply means that we must examine ourselves in respect to the specific requests that we present to God in order to determine whether we are praying in harmony with the divine will. For this we have the Spirit's help, for Paul assures us in Romans 8:26–27 that "the Spirit also helpeth our infirmities: for we know not what we should pray for as we ought: but the Spirit itself maketh intercession for us with groanings which cannot be uttered. And he that searcheth the hearts knoweth what is in the mind of the Spirit, because he maketh intercession for the saints according to the will of God."

This is the first principle of prevailing prayer. We must seek to make our prayers perceptive and discerning, and for that we have the ministry of the Spirit of God.

II. Persevering in prayer.

But Paul teaches a second principle in these verses relating to intercessory prayer. We must be persevering in our praying.

This principle is indicated by Paul at two particular places in Ephesians 6:18-20—first, by the word *always* ("praying always"), and, second, by the words "watching thereunto with all perseverance and supplication."

A. *Let's look first at the word* always. Paul says we are to pray "always with all prayer and supplication in the Spirit." In other translations the word *always* is rendered "at all seasons," or "all the time," or "at every opportunity," or simply "unceasingly."

Prevailing prayer, therefore, is something that is to be maintained and sustained. We are to engage in this vital ministry all the time and at every opportunity. This requires that we have a constant sense of the conflict in which we are engaged. Are we not too prone to pray only at times when the reality of the conflict is brought home to us by a particular trial or temptation or by a specific kind of problem or pressure?

B. *The second way in which Paul enforces the fact that prevailing prayer should be persevering is found in verse 18:* "Praying always with all prayer and supplication in the Spirit, and watching thereunto with all perseverance and supplication." That is translated by Weymouth in this way: "Be always on the alert to seize opportunities for doing so, with unwearied persistence and entreaty."

That's what Paul really wants. We are to have a constant awareness of the conflict; and more than that, we are to lay hold of every opportunity of engaging in prevailing prayer.

We are being asked to take an inventory of our time. Each of us has twenty-four hours each day, no more, no less. We may have set times for prayer, and that is excellent. But what about the spare moments? Do we seize them for prayer? Time is always up for sale in the marketplace. Are we in there bidding for time, redeeming it for God?

III. Passionate in prayer.

Prevailing prayer is perceptive and persevering. It is also passionate. This aspect is latent in the words that Paul employs: "Praying always with all prayer and supplication in the Spirit, and watching thereunto with all perseverance and supplication for all saints." There cannot be that kind of praying without passion, without fervor and zeal (James 5:16). Prevailing prayer is kindled by fire from the altar of the Lord.

We must not confuse passion with noise and outward excitement. Passion is simply strong feeling. It is not to be identified with shouting and hand raising and clapping. These are not necessarily the proof of true passion and real spiritual desire. It is the shallow river that makes a noise.

But how can we make our prayers passionate? Let us not attempt it by artificial means—by trying to cultivate a particular tone of voice, or trying to whip up emotion and fervor.

The secret lies in the area of our spiritual desires. If we desire with all our hearts the object for which we pray, we shall automatically find ourselves praying with zeal and passion.

When a little child sets his heart upon a particular object, he will ask for that thing with great feeling and fervor. He will not try to imitate passion. He will be filled with a strong feeling toward that object. It is so also in the spiritual realm. As God's children, if we desire God's power and victory to be manifested on our behalf, we shall pray passionately and enthusiastically. Let us deal, then, with our desires. Out of the abundance of our hearts we pray.

IV. Particular praying.
Prevailing prayer is perceptive, persevering, and passionate. Finally we note that the prayer that prevails is the prayer that is particular. We are to pray always "for all saints; and for me."

A. *Notice that Paul exhorts us first to pray for all saints.* We are to remind ourselves of the fact that we belong to the body of Christ, and that our responsibility in prayer includes all fellow-members of that body. We shall pray for the church universal. That means the saints in China as well as in Canada; it means that we should pray for Christians in the U.S.S.R. as well as in the U.S.A.

Do we have this international outlook in our praying? Are we praying for all saints, those persecuted and imprisoned? Those in high places? Those preaching and teaching the Word of God? Just how universal are we in our prayer life?

B. *"But,"* you may respond, *"that is vague and too general.* I thought you said prevailing prayer is particular prayer." Well, look again at Paul's words. "Pray always for all saints; and for me." He asks prayer for himself.

Every Christian needs a prayer list that lists specific persons. We should know the needs of these people, and we should bring their needs daily to the Lord. Prayer is to be both general and specific.

Paul asks prayer that he might speak boldly. This is the whole purpose of spiritual warfare—the triumph of the gospel. It is for that reason that prevailing prayer must concentrate on the needs of those who are preaching and propagating the gospel throughout the world.

Conclusion. Let us engage in prayer, therefore, that is perceptive, persevering, passionate, and particular.

> Put on the gospel armour,
> Each piece put on with *prayer*.
> —George Duffield

— *GLS*

* * *

SUNDAY EVENING, AUGUST 12

TITLE: The Church Victorious

TEXT: "And he is the head of the body, the church: who is the beginning, the firstborn from the dead; that in all things he might have the preeminence" (Col. 1:18).

SCRIPTURE READING: Colossians 1:3–14

Introduction. The church has always stood at the threshold of being either the church victorious or the church defeated. At any given moment the church faces the choice of advance or retreat. It can be united by its concerted effort to reach out, or it can be divided by its obsession with petty differences within.

Obviously it is God's will that His church be the church victorious. But Paul feared that such might not be the case at Colosse. Wrong teachings, wrong attitudes, and wrong emphasis were threatening the unity and vitality of the church. In fact, William Barclay states that allowing these problems to develop unchecked might have been the ruination of the Christian faith.

Because Paul wanted the church at Colosse to become the church victorious he wrote this letter. And because God wants our church to become the church victorious, He has preserved this letter for us to read and to follow.

There are four important matters to be considered concerning the church victorious.

I. A prayer to be offered (1:3–14).

Prayer is a vital part of the church victorious. Without prayer there will be no victory in the church. In this passage Paul prays a prayer for the church at Colosse that indeed should be the prayer for every church!

A. *A prayer of thanksgiving* (v. 3). Paul likes to start a letter with thanksgiving. His eyes are open to all the blessings he sees. Prayer and remembrance should be tied together.

B. *A prayer for knowledge of God's will* (v. 9). Prayer starts with asking that we be filled with knowledge of God's will. The real object of prayer is to know the will of God. Prayer is not so much trying to make God listen to us as it is trying to make ourselves listen to God. In prayer we should not try to persuade God to do what we want Him to do. We should try to find out what He wants us to do.

C. *A prayer for Christian conduct* (v. 1:10a). Paul's prayer is that we may conduct ourselves in such a way as to please God. Nothing in this world is so practical as prayer. Prayer is not an escape from reality, nor is it a secluded meditation on and communion with God. Prayer and action go together. We pray, not in order to escape life, but in order to better face life.

D. *A prayer for productivity* (v. 10b). A growing Christian should be at work in some phase of his church's life. This fruitbearing is positive proof of our discipleship. "Increasing in the knowledge of God" can come only as we are "fruitful in every good work." God wants us to be productive.

E. *A prayer for spiritual strength* (v. 11). Long-suffering enables us to bear with people in such a way that their unpleasantness will never drive us to bitterness.

F. *A prayer for gratitude* (v. 12). Where there is gratitude there is graciousness. It is good therapy to express gratitude to God and man—especially within the church.

II. The power to be acknowledged (1:15–29).

The heart of Paul's letter is that Christ alone is the power to be acknowledged in the church. He is the Head. He is above all others and before all others. Christ is the undisputed head of the church victorious.

A. *Christ, the visible expression of God* (v. 15, PHILLIPS). When Paul wrote to the Colossians, he was not writing in a vacuum. He was writing to meet a specific situation. There was a tendency of thought in the early church which is known by the name *Gnosticism.* Its devotees were called *gnostics,* which means "the intellectual ones." These men were dissatisfied with what they considered the rude simplicity of Christianity, and they wished to turn Christianity into a philosophy. They reasoned that if the body is evil, then it follows that He who was the revelation of God could not have had a real body.

Paul asserts that Jesus perfectly represents God in a form which men can see and know and understand. He is not a sketch nor a summary of God. He is more than a portrait of God. In Him there is nothing left out. He is the complete and final revelation of God. Nothing more is necessary.

B. *Christ, the Creator of all* (v. 16). By Jesus all things were made, whether things in heaven or things in earth, or things seen and unseen. Paul is saying to the gnostics, "You give great importance to angels. You rate Jesus Christ merely as one of many angels. Not so; He created them."

C. *Christ, the Eternal Being* (v. 17).

D. *Christ, the head of the church* (v. 18). The church is the body of Christ. The body is the servant of the Head. The body obeys the Head's will. The body is powerless and dead without the Head. So Jesus Christ is the guiding and dominating mind of the church. Each word and deed of the church must be directed by Him. Without Christ the church cannot think the truth, act correctly, or determine direction.

E. *Christ, the Conciliator* (vv. 20–22). The purpose for which He came was reconciliation. He came to bring peace between man and God.

III. Perils to be avoided (2:1–23).

A. *The peril of pseudo-intellectualism* (v. 8).

B. *The peril of religious conformity* (v. 18). Other religions had hierarchies of divine beings to worship—so why not Christianity? Some were teaching that man is too unworthy to approach Christ directly. Christianity must avoid the peril of conformity if it is to maintain its purity and its power.

C. *The peril of folk religion* (vv. 16, 21). There was a tendency to insist on the observance of special days and rituals—festivals, new moons, and sabbaths (v. 16). Ritualism and the special observance of times and seasons was a feature of this folk religion. It laid down laws about food and drink (v. 16). Its slogans were: "Touch not; taste not; handle not" (v. 21). It is seen today in the religion of those who seek to impose their social patterns on others "in the name of the Lord." It is reflected in the mentality of some church members who insist that the *mechanics* of operating a church be carried out in a certain way rather than that the *message* of the church being carried to the lost.

D. *The peril of false piety* (v. 23). The Christian's freedom comes not from restraining desires by rules and regulations, but from the crucifixion of evil desires and the birth of good desires.

IV. Pattern to be followed (chap. 3).

The church is victorious only to the degree that each Christian experiences victory in his or her own life. Defeated Christians constitute a defeated church; victorious Christians constitute a victorious church.

A. *The pattern for personal behavior* (vv. 1:17).
  1. What to put off (vv. 1-2, 5, 8-9)
  2. What to put on (vv. 12-17)

B. *The pattern for family life* (vv. 18-31). What has family life to do with a victorious church? Everything! Much conflict and defeat in a church can be traced to an unhappy and unchristian family life.
  1. Husbands and wives (vv. 18-19)
  2. Children and parents (vv. 20-21)

C. *The pattern for employees and employers* (vv. 22-4:1). Christianity does not offer escape from hard work. Rather it makes a man able to work harder. The employee must do everything as if he were doing it for Christ. The employer must remember that he too has a Master—Christ in heaven.

D. *The pattern for relating to non-Christians* (4:5-6): "Be wise in your behavior toward non-Christians, and make the best possible use of your time. Speak pleasantly to them, . . . and learn how to give a proper answer to every questioner" (PHILLIPS).

Conclusion. You can make yours the church victorious by:

A. *Praying for your church.*

B. *Acknowledging the One who is the Power of your church.*

C. *Avoiding the perils that would defeat your church.*

D. *Following the pattern God sets for His church.* — JRM

* * *

WEDNESDAY EVENING, AUGUST 15

TITLE: The Provision of God (continued)

TEXT: "He leadeth me in the paths of righteousness for his name's sake" (Ps. 23:3b).

SCRIPTURE READING: Psalm 23:1-6

Introduction. The word *lead* is used frequently by Christians in their worship. Such statements as "lead in a decision" or "give direction to doctors" are often used in intercessory prayer. This text serves as a scriptural basis for such praying.

I. First, each person is asked to give some attention to a general interpretation of the concept.

A. *There are at least two interpretations that can be given to the idea of righteousness.*
  1. It can apply to the manner in which God leads. This is in accordance with the character and reputation of God.
  2. It can apply to the place to which God leads. This concept is seen in serenity and peace.

B. *The Good Shepherd leads and keeps within the bounds of good character and serenity.*

II. There are some parallels that can be made of sheep and humans that are brought out in this text.

A. *Consider some facts about sheep.*

1. They are creatures of habit. If sheep are left to their own will, they will follow their own trail until the ground becomes waste and becomes corrupt with disease.

2. They require careful handling. It is easy for their pastures to become overgrazed and impoverished; then erosion sets in.

3. They must be kept on the move. They cannot be left on the same ground too long. The shepherd has predetermined plans. He uses a rotation system.

B. *There are some facts about people that are similar.*

1. Isaiah 53:6 speaks of man following his own way. He clings to habit, does what he wants, and follows the crowd.

2. The Good Shepherd deals with His children as the shepherd does his sheep. He leads, protects, and takes care of them.

Conclusion. The wisest thing man can do is to acknowledge the Lord who directs his paths (Prov. 3:6).   — DRG

* * *

SUNDAY MORNING, AUGUST 19

TITLE: Intercessory Prayer

TEXT: "Let thine ear now be attentive, and thine eyes open, that thou mayest hear the prayer of thy servant . . ." (Neh. 1:6).

SCRIPTURE READING: Nehemiah 1:1–11

HYMNS: "What a Friend We Have in Jesus," Scriven
   "Tell It to Jesus," Rankin
   "Turn Your Eyes Upon Jesus," Lemmel

OFFERTORY PRAYER:

Heavenly Father, we praise You that You are the Father of our Lord Jesus Christ and that You have blessed us with every spiritual blessing in heavenly places in Christ Jesus. We acknowledge Your command to us to give, and we confess our lustful desires to get rather than give. Forgive us, and put within us the grace to give generously as You have prospered us. We gratefully commit ourselves and our gifts to You for Christ's glory. Amen.

Introduction. He is a wise man who in undertaking any work for God seeks to determine the need as it really exists. It is easy to become involved in that which is peripheral rather than that which is paramount and therefore primary.

In Nehemiah 1 we have a clear example of a man of God who sought to understand the need of God's people at Jerusalem. Nehemiah's method was to interrogate certain men who had been at Jerusalem and had seen for themselves the need as it existed. Nehemiah's investigation led to intercession and to personal involvement in the work of God.

Our text is the first of many texts recording the prayers of Nehemiah. In his book we find prayer offered before the work is undertaken, while the work is in progress, and after the work has been completed. Here is prayer in the quietness of his own room as well as amid the noise of the building of the walls of Jerusalem. Here is prayer offered both personally and individually.

Nehemiah's prayers were not all of the same nature. The prayer recorded in our text was intercessory in nature. By this we mean that it involved specific requests on behalf of God's people and Nehemiah himself. It is important for us to see the circumstances, characteristics, content, and consequences of Nehemiah's prayer.

I. Its circumstances.

Here is the prayer of a man who had not lost his love for the land and the faith of his fathers. Nehemiah's ancestors had been carried into captivity by the Babylonians. Seventy years had elapsed until the decree of Cyrus had permitted the Jews to return to their homeland. Initially only fifty thousand had responded, the majority choosing to remain in exile to enjoy their prosperity. For some reason, unknown to us, Nehemiah had remained in the service of the Medo-Persian king.

This prayer was also the prayer of a man who had been placed in the service of King Artaxerxes. It was not by chance that he was in this position but by providence. This position would become highly significant in the course of time.

As we further analyze the prayer, we note that this is a prayer of a man living in fellowship with God, the God of his fathers.

This man's prayer was filled with concern and compassion for others by the acquisition of fresh information about the plight of Jerusalem and its citizens.

The flame of his intercession burned brighter amid the darkness of his times as the fuel of information was placed on the altar of his heart.

II. Its characteristics.

Nehemiah's response to the news brought by his friends concerning Jerusalem gives to us the first characteristic of his prayer: humiliation and brokenness (v. 4). He responded "before the God of heaven." And this response was marked not by gladness but by grief, not by singing but by sorrow.

Closely allied to this aspect of humiliation and brokenness is Nehemiah's confession of sin. He recognized that the exile was caused by the sin of God's people. He confessed his own sin and his father's sins.

As we read Nehemiah's prayer we are impressed by his spirit of faith. Nehemiah prays in confidence, without wavering. He comes boldly to the throne of grace in order that he might obtain mercy and find grace to help in the time of need.

Finally, we note that Nehemiah's prayer is characterized by a reverence for God and a prayer expression of his own relationship to God. Listen to him pray: "I beseech thee, O LORD God of heaven, the great and terrible God, that keepeth covenant and mercy for them that love him and observe his commandments" (v. 5).

Let's examine our prayers. Do we come before God in humiliation and brokenness? Do we come confessing our sins and rebellion? Do we come in faith? Do we seek God's face, remembering that He is the Lord God of heaven and that we are His servants?

III. Its content.

Perhaps the most important aspect of Nehemiah's prayer is its content. The content may be summarized by three words found in 1:6, 8, and 11: *hear, remember,* and *prosper.*

A. *"Hear the prayer of thy servant"* (v. 6). Nehemiah understood that God was not deaf; he did recognize, however, that God will not answer the prayers of His people when they are not rightly related to Him in love and obedience.

Nehemiah drew attention to several aspects of his prayer to God. His prayer was *continual,* "day and night." His prayer was *definite* and *specific:* "for the children of Israel thy servants." His prayer was *contrite* and *repentant:* "confess the sins of the children of Israel, which we have sinned against thee: both I and my father's house have sinned." (v. 6).

B. *"Remember . . . the word that thou commandedst thy servant Moses"* (v. 8). Nehemiah probes the mind of God to remember His word, to keep His Word to His people. God had promised to punish, but He had also promised to prosper. Nehemiah pleads for that prosperity. Notice three important aspects of the ministry of intercession: the *man* of God believes the *Word* of God in order that the *work* of God might be accomplished.

C. The third request is found in verse 11: *"O Lord, I beseech thee, let now thine ear be attentive to the prayer of thy servant, and to the prayer of thy servants, who desire to fear thy name: and prosper, I pray thee, thy servant this day, and grant him mercy in the sight of this man."*

Hear. Remember. Prosper. Hear—for God is a living God. Remember—for God has spoken. Prosper—for God is a God of action.

IV. Its consequences.

Did God hear? Did God remember? Did God prosper? The remainder of the Book of Nehemiah answers these questions in the affirmative.

The secret of Nehemiah's success, then, lay not in his resources as one commissioned by Artaxerxes; it lay not in his ability and acumen as a man and as a leader. Rather, it lay in his power with God.

Conclusion. The secret of strong leadership is in the ability of the leader to be in touch with the great power of God. Nehemiah knew this power by personal experience. You can know this power by engaging in the great work of intercession.   *— GLS*

* * *

SUNDAY EVENING, AUGUST 19

TITLE: The Return of Christ

TEXT: **"But I would not have you to be ignorant, brethren, concerning them which are asleep, that ye sorrow not, even as others which have no hope"** (1 Thess. 4:13).

SCRIPTURE READING: **1 Thessalonians 4:13–5:22**

Introduction. At any given moment Jesus Christ may return. All prophecies have been fulfilled making possible Christ's return at any hour. This fact has been the hope of the church ever since Christ ascended and the angels promised, "This same Jesus, which is taken up from you into heaven, shall so come in like manner as ye have seen him go into heaven" (Acts 1:11).

Paul had shared this joyful news with the Christians in Thessalonica. His stay in the city was cut short by persecution. Driven from that city he went to Berea and then to Athens. He became anxious concerning the church at Thessalonica and sent Timothy to encourage the church and to report back to him.

Timothy brought word that the Thessalonian Christians were enduring their persecutions bravely; but some had died, and the others were puzzled to know how those who had died would get any benefit of the Lord's coming.

Paul then wrote this letter stating that those who had died would be at no disadvantage when the Lord comes.

Paul does not deal with all the events that will accompany Christ's return but rather speaks of what happens to Christians, living and dead, when Christ comes again. In so doing he answers many of our questions and strengthens our hope in and heightens our anticipation of Christ's return.

I. The return of Christ is not a hidden mystery.

There is a prevalent feeling that the return of Christ is shrouded in clouds of mystery which only a few can penetrate. This is not so! True, a few self-acclaimed experts on the Second Coming have added so many of their own ideas that the clear and simple doctrine of Christ's return is almost camouflaged.

But if you will limit yourself to what the Bible says, you will discover that the return of Christ is not a hidden mystery.

A. *Because you can know all you* need *to know about Christ's return* (4:13a). It is God's will that none of us be "ignorant" concerning the destiny of deceased Christians or the return of our Lord. The Bible tells us all we *need* to know about both. It may not tell us all we would *like* to know, but it does tell us all we *need* to know.

B. *Because Christ's return provides a basis for our hope* (v. 13b). Paul speaks of "that blessed hope, and the glorious appearing of the great God and our Saviour Jesus Christ" in Titus 2:13.

In 1 Thessalonians 4:13b, Paul tells them that they must not sorrow as those who have no hope. In the time of death pagans stood in despair. They met death with resignation and bleak hopelessness. Aeschylus wrote, "Once a man dies there is no resurrection." Third century B.C. Theocritus wrote, "There is hope for those who are alive, but those who have died are without hope."

But Paul states that in the return of Jesus Christ there is hope—hope for the living and hope for the dead.

II. The return of Christ is accompanied by the return of deceased Christians (4:14).

If a man has lived in Christ, even when he dies he is still in Christ. Between Christ and the believer there is a relationship which nothing can break (Rom. 8:35ff). It is a relationship independent of time and which overpasses death. Because Jesus Christ lived and died and rose again, so we shall live and die and rise again. Nothing in life or in death can separate us from Christ.

A. *Who have been with Christ since their death* (v. 14b). Jesus does not complete His sentence about the death of Lazarus until He speaks of Lazarus' being in heaven, "in Abraham's bosom."

B. *Whose resurrection is made possible by Christ's resurrection* (v. 14a). Paul clarifies this even further in 1 Corinthians 15:20, 23: "But now is Christ risen from the dead, and become the firstfruits of them that slept. . . . But every man in his own order: Christ the firstfruits; afterward they that are Christ's at his coming."

C. *Whose bodies and souls are reunited* (v. 16). In this moment our bodies share in our salvation. Man is both body and soul, and thus both participate in the resurrection.

III. The return of Christ results in our being changed (4:15).

Flesh and blood cannot inherit the kingdom of God and therefore we shall be changed and our corruptible bodies shall put on incorruption (1 Cor. 15:50–53).

But why shall we be changed? Because our earthly bodies are not capable of living forever and because our earthly bodies were participants in good and evil.

What kind of bodies will we have? The kind of resurrected body Christ had (15:20).

IV. The return of Christ provides us with a constant source of comfort (1 Thess. 4:18).

This is all that God considers we need to know about His return and the welfare of deceased Christians. And so He says, "Comfort one another with these words." In other words, "Be satisfied with what God has chosen to reveal to you."

V. The return of Christ challenges us to live the best life possible (5:1, 6, 22).

A. *By being prepared whenever Christ returns* (vv. 2–3). Paul uses two illustrations to stress the suddenness and unexpected nature of Christ's return—the coming of a thief and the birth of a child. The purpose of both illustrations is to challenge us to be prepared whenever Christ returns.

B. *This best life possible is a life of faith and love* (v. 8). Paul is warning the readers that they must not relax in godly living merely because they are not to expect Christ to come immediately. They must arm themselves against lethargy by putting on the breastplate of faith and love.

C. *A life of mutual support and help* (vv. 11–15).

D. *A life of joy* (v. 16).

E. *A life of prayer* (v. 17).

F. *A life of gratitude* (v. 18).

G. *A life of spiritual freedom* (v. 19).

H. *A life open to God's Word* (v. 20). Whatever God has to say, however He chooses to say it and through whom He may say it, we must be open to God's Word.

I. *A life of discernment* (v. 21). "But test everything that is said to be sure it is true, and if it is, then accept it" (Williams).

J. *A life free of even the appearance of evil* (v. 22). As we follow Paul's advice, we will be like lights in a dark room. We shall have joy within ourselves and power to win others to our Lord. It is then we shall know and live the best life possible!

Conclusion. Jesus Christ will come again. It could be today. Will you meet Him as Savior or only as Judge? The answer to that question rests in your own hands. Only you can answer it.   *— JRM*

* * *

WEDNESDAY EVENING, AUGUST 22

TITLE: **The Protection of God**

TEXT: **"I will fear no evil" (Ps. 23:4b).**

SCRIPTURE READING: **Psalm 23:1–6**

Introduction. There are many great and wonderful promises in this psalm. It is so rich that one can spend days meditating on the words and claiming the promises. The phrase "I will fear no evil" is one of the more outstanding and meaningful statements in the whole psalm.

I. The term *evil* is multiple in its application.

A. *It applies to death—the universal evil.* "O death, where is thy sting?" (1 Cor. 15:55).

B. *It applies to physical harm.* This is especially true as one considers the application of shepherd-sheep relations. Sheep are susceptible to falling from cliffs, being caught in underbrush, and being infected with disease. The shepherd protects his sheep from such evils. In the same way, each person has his dangers, and the Good Shepherd guards His sheep.

C. *It applies to economic security.* "My God shall supply all your need according to his riches in glory" (Phil. 4:19).

D. *It applies to temptation.* "For in that he himself hath suffered being tempted, he is able to succour them that are tempted" (Heb. 2:18). "There hath no temptation taken you but such as is common to man: but God is faithful, who will not suffer you to be tempted above that ye are able; but will with the temptation also make a way to escape, that ye may be able to bear it" (1 Cor. 10:13).

E. *It applies to disappointment, frustration, and discouragement.*

II. The text says, "I will fear no evil."

A. *Fear is a devastating emotion.* Webster defines fear as "a distressing emotion aroused by impending pain, danger, evil, etc., whether real or imaginary." Fear is somewhat synonymous with anxiety, which begets tension and can produce heart attacks. Fear has been described in various ways as being anything from thief to murderer. It has been called a liar, cheat, and a cruel, unrelenting antagonist of reason and soundness of mind. It is an unholy taskmaster.

B. *Fear has some horrible effects.*

1. It can kill outright. Many people associate this text with death, but it states that man is not to fear death. For the Christian, death is a deliverance from pain, sorrows, and cares.

2. It can paralyze. This has been referred to as conversion hysteria.

3. It can convulse. In fear, one may hyperventilate and go into convulsions.
4. It can immobilize.
5. It can incapacitate.

C. *There are at least four dimensions to fear:*
1. Intensity
2. Length or duration
3. Breadth—real or imaginary
4. Relativity—time and circumstances

D. *Fear is universal.*

III. The text states that fear can be conquered.

A. *To conquer fear, it must be understood.* The Holy Spirit is present to illuminate and interpret.

B. *Fear can be controlled through the presence of God.* This is done by loving God and having faith in God.

Conclusion. There are fewer more profound or meaningful statements than "I will fear no evil." — *DRG*

* * *

SUNDAY MORNING, AUGUST 26

TITLE: The Answer to Our Disturbing Situation

TEXT: "Then he answered and spake unto me, saying, This is the word of the LORD unto Zerubbabel, saying, Not by might, nor by power, but by my spirit, saith the LORD of hosts" (Zech. 4:6).

SCRIPTURE READING: Ephesians 6:10–20

HYMNS: "Break Thou the Bread," Lathbury
"Teach Me to Pray," Reitz
"Footsteps of Jesus," Slade

OFFERTORY PRAYER:
Our Father, as You are forever giving good gifts to us, enable us to share Your joy as we give cheerfully and generously to Your cause and kingdom. It is for this purpose that we dedicate ourselves and our gifts to You. In the name of Your Son, Jesus, Your greatest gift to us, we pray. Amen.

Introduction. Zerubbabel was a key man in the community of those Israelites who returned to Palestine from Babylon in response to the generous and enlightened policy of Cyrus the Great. Born and raised in Babylon, Zerubbabel was a descendant of the house of David; and although he was never allowed to be a king of Israel, he did serve as the civil governor. Along with Joshua, the high priest and religious leader, this man gave leadership to the struggling community.

In the decree of Cyrus liberating the Jews to return from exile, there was permission for them to rebuild the temple of God at Jerusalem. This temple had been ruthlessly razed to the ground by the Babylonians. "The stones of the sanctuary," lamented Jeremiah the prophet, "are poured out in the top of every street" (Lam. 4:1). Accordingly, when the exiles returned home, the first concern was the rebuilding of the temple of their God. Ezra records the jubilation of the people "when the builders laid the foundation of the temple of the LORD" (3:10–11).

When Zechariah and his companion, Haggai, appeared on the scene, things were not going well for the returnees. Opposition was present on every hand. It is always the case that when God's people say, "We will arise and build," that the devil's crowd says, "We will arise and destroy."

This was a time of defeat, discouragement, and depression for the people of God. Where could the leaders of God's people find the answer for such difficult days? Where can the church find the answer for its problems today? The secret is found in our text; and the key to unlock the truth of that secret and make it available is prayer.

Zechariah had a personal message to the ruler Zerubbabel from the Lord. His personal message is our text and lives up to the prophet's name: Zechariah—"Jehovah remembers." Notice that God remembers and gives the solution to allay every fear and solve every problem.

In seeking to grasp the point of God's message to Zerubbabel we must remind ourselves first of the disturbing situation confronting the civil leader of God's people. The circumstances that Zerubbabel faced were made up of a number of factors. Let's examine four of them.

I. An unfinished project.

First, Zerubbabel faced an unfinished project, the rebuilding of the temple of the Lord. There can be no doubt that the task of rebuilding was part of the divine plan for the Israelites. Indeed, God raised up Cyrus to enable His people to rebuild the temple, prophesied by Isaiah before the death of that great king (44:28).

In the same way God has assigned us a divine project to undertake and complete. We refer to the building of that spiritual temple, which is the church of the living Christ. It is never right for work on that building to come to a standstill. There is always work to be done in the construction of that spiritual house.

Honesty demands that we confess to the times when we become discouraged and give up our part of the work of our Lord. Yet we must never forget that God has called us to the work and that it is His will that the work should be carried through to completion. It was an unfinished task that was faced then as well as now.

II. An unrelenting pressure.

Secondly, God's people faced an unrelenting pressure, the opposition of the enemies of God's people. Let's look at the design of the enemy.

A. *First, the enemy weakened the hands of the people of Judah.* How this was done is not clear. Perhaps they cut off supplies. They could have made surprise attacks against the people. Whatever form this opposition took, it resulted in weakened hearts and hands.

The amazing thing about the enemy of the people of God is that he uses the same basic battleplan more than once. Right now he is seeking to cut you off from your Source, the Lord God Himself. He is seeking to take you by surprise. He looks for ways to intimidate you to prevent you from completing the task God gave you to do. He constantly turns the pressure on your life and on the life of the church.

B. *Judah's enemies weakened the hands of the people.* They also troubled them. The root of this word means to cause to palpitate, and thus to terrify! God's people were scared into stopping their work on the temple of the Lord.

The devil is a master at terrifying people into quitting. He knows every argument to paralyze God's people into inactivity. He can stir up the storm clouds of discouragement so that God's people will retreat to the safety of the storm cellars of life and never accomplish the task God has given them.

C. *Finally, we note that the enemies of the people of Judah hired counselors against them to frustrate their purpose.* They didn't mind spending some money if as a result they could quench the zeal of God's people and crush the building project at the outset.

We are dismayed as we read the account at the success of the enemy over God's people. "Then ceased the work of the house of God which is at Jerusalem" (Ezra 4:24). This was the disturbing situation facing Zerubbabel.

III. An unspiritual people.

Again Zerubbabel faced an unspiritual people. This was a new problem. In another day as they returned from Babylon, they did so with hope and inspiration. They began the work with great confidence in the Lord—until they ran into opposition.

When they started focusing upon the enemy they ceased to focus upon the Lord. They became idle and inactive. This gave way to humanistic thinking that led to outright carnality.

We are experts at rationalizing our failures. We have a hundred and one alibis to explain why we are not engaged in the work of the Lord, but most of them are just feeble excuses.

IV. An unwelcomed prospect.

The final factor in the disturbing situation was the unwelcome prospect. Namely, that since Zerubbabel did not have the remedy for his people's discouragement or the resources to change defeat into victory, there was nothing he could do under the circumstances. The opposition he and his people faced loomed up like a huge mountain before them. Would he ever be able to finish the project God had given him to do? The prospect was grim indeed.

When our way seems darkest, when God seems to have forgotten, when resources are all dried up, we need to remember His divine solution.

God gave the assurance to His leader that there was no prayer too hard for Him to answer, no problem too difficult for Him to solve, no promise that He would not keep.

The same assurance is given to us today. But we must remember that it is not by our power nor our might but by His Spirit that we can overcome the opposition. You may ask, "But how do I receive this power? How may I be led by the Spirit?" The apostle Paul answers this for us in Ephesians 6:18: "Praying always with all prayer and supplication in the Spirit, and watching thereunto with all perseverence and supplication for all saints." Prayer is the answer to our disturbing situation.

Conclusion. Are you disturbed over some situation where the enemy has defeated you? Do you at this moment feel distressed because you have not completed the work God has given you to do? Have you tried prayer? Face your failures the way Zerubbabel did in the power of the Lord.   *— GLS*

* * *

SUNDAY EVENING, AUGUST 26

TITLE: Seven Things You Should Know About Christ's Return

TEXT: **"Now we beseech you, brethren, by the coming of our Lord Jesus Christ . . ." (2 Thess. 2:1).**

SCRIPTURE READING: **2 Thessalonians 2:1-3**

Introduction. The fact that Christ is coming again can be a source of comfort or a cause for confusion. It can unite us in a concerted effort to win people to Christ or it can divide us in an effort to win converts to our particular point of view.

Because the return of Christ is future and because each detail is not spelled out in Scripture, this blessed hope has often been confusing. Such was the case in the church at Thessalonica.

The idea of imminence of the Lord's return was so emphatic in the minds of many believers that some fell into serious error in their application of the teaching. Paul related what he said in chapter 2 to his statement in 1 Thessalonians 4:13-17 regarding the coming of the Lord and the resurrection. He put himself in the class of those who would be living when the Lord returned.

It appears that many of the Thessalonians were disturbed. They believed that the Lord's coming was so imminent that they had stopped working and were making themselves busybodies in the Christian fellowship (2 Thess. 2:2; 3:6-12). It was necessary for Paul to explain that he did not mean to emphasize the coming of the Lord in such a way as to disturb the Thessalonians. So he sets forth seven things we should know about Christ's return.

I. Tribulation to His opposition (2 Thess. 1:6-9).

The Christians at Thessalonica had suffered persecution. Paul assures that when Christ returns the scales of justice will be balanced and God will "recompense tribulation to them that trouble you."

A. *The people who will experience tribulation.*

    1. Those who persecute Christians (v. 6b). Paul says when Christ returns those who have persecuted Christians will themselves experience tribulation—a tribulation not of man but of God's justice.

    2. Those who refuse to know God (v. 8a). They could have known God. They heard the same gospel and had the same opportunity others had but they chose not to know God. Earlier, in Romans 1:21, Paul had spoken of such people.

    3. Those who reject the gospel of Christ (v. 8b). The Williams translation reads, "Those who *will not* listen to the good news of our Lord Jesus."

B. *The pattern of tribulation.* "These will receive the punishment of eternal destruction as exiles from the presence of the Lord and his glorious might" (v. 9).

II. Glorification of His person (vv. 10–12).

A. *The object of glorification* (v. 10).

On March 23, 1743, when *The Messiah* was first performed in London, the king was present in the great audience. It is reported that all were so deeply moved by the "Hallelujah Chorus" that with the impressive words, "For the Lord God omnipotent reigneth," the whole audience, including the king, sprang to its feet, and remained standing through the entire chorus. From that time to this it has always been the custom to stand during the chorus whenever it is performed. With spontaneous joy the soul stands to salute him who "cometh in the name of the Lord." He is "king of kings, and Lord of lords" and to him we pledge allegiance.

B. *The avenue of glorification.* Verse 10 states, "to be glorified *in his saints* . . . to be admired *in all them that believe."*

III. Stabilization of His church.

"And now, what about the coming again of our Lord Jesus Christ, and our being gathered together to meet Him? Please don't be upset and excited, dear brothers, by the rumor that this day of the Lord has already begun. If you hear of people having visions and special messages from God about this, or letters that are supposed to have come from me, don't believe them. Don't be carried away and deceived regardless of what they say" (2:1–3a LB).

A. *What needs to be stablizied?*

1. The content of our minds. "Do not let your minds be easily unsettled" (v. 2a Williams).

2. The conduct of our emotions. "Please don't get upset and excited" (v. 2b LB). We must never allow our particular view of Christ's return to cause us to get "upset or excited" either within ourselves or toward others. After all, our commission is not to win converts to a particular view of eschatology but to win people to Jesus Christ, who is the center of eschatology.

B. *Why do we need to be stabilized* (vv. 2b–3a)? There were some in the church at Thessalonica that had become so disturbed by what they heard from some people that they quit work and were passively awaiting Christ's return.

IV. Revelation of His enemy (2:3–12).

A. *First, there will be "a falling away."* Jesus had spoken of times of turmoil which His followers would face. When this epistle was written many Christians had turned away. Other such experiences would come. Paul knew that the cause of Christ was destined to suffer great reversal and that many would forsake it.

B. *Second, "that man of sin be revealed, the son of perdition."* Jesus used this same term in reference to Judas, "and none of them is lost, but the son of perdition" (John 17:12).

Satan is described in 2 Thessalonians 2:4 as one who opposed all that is called God; he exalted himself in opposition to God, even setting himself up as an object of worship. Satan-worship and all forms of the occult are evident everywhere today.

This one was destined to be revealed (that is, exposed for what he really is) in his own time. This one (who is called "the mystery of lawlessness") was already at work (v. 7). Paul stated in verse 5 that he had discussed these matters with the Thessalonians when he was with them. In verse 8 he mentioned that this lawless one was destined to be destroyed by Christ when He returned.

The "man of sin" is Satan and the "one who restrains him" is the Holy Spirit.

V. Jubilation for his work (2:13–14).

Paul is saying that the return of Christ should bring joy and thanksgiving to us. We shall not experience the tribulation that will come to his opposition at his appearing. Nor shall we share in the destruction of Satan when he is exposed for all he really is at Christ's return. Rather, we have been: (1) "chosen to salvation"; (2) set aside, "sanctified by the Spirit"; (3) "called" by God; and (4) assured of sharing in the "glory of our Lord Jesus Christ."

What cause for jubilation! What great work He has done for us and to us. We have no fear but only joyous anticipation of His return!

VI. Continuation in His Word (2:15–17).

Williams translates verse 15 in this manner: "So then, brethren, stand firm and keep a tight grip on the teachings you have received from us (me)." These are the teachings Paul gave first in his preaching, then in his first letter, and now in this one. "Stand firm." Swerve not to the right or the left however much false teachers may try to disturb you.

VII. Separation from his disorderly followers (3:6–15).

The disorderly (vv. 6–15) were lazy people who took advantage of the charitable disposition of the church (see 1 Thess. 4:9–10). They used their expectation of the immediate return of the Lord as an excuse for abandoning their ordinary occupations. They claimed the right to be supported by other Christians.

Although Paul was an ardent advocate of charity toward those who were really in need, and though he spent a good deal of time gathering offerings of money for the poor, he spared no words in condemning the able-bodied who could, but would not, work. He definitely forbids the church to support such people. Paul even commands the church to withdraw fellowship from them.

Conclusion. Paul has given us seven things we *should* know about Christ's return. But there is one thing you *must* know, and that is, Christ will return!

The big question we must ask ourselves is, "Am I ready this very moment should Christ return?"

As a Christian I must ask, "Am I ready . . . ?"

As a lost person you must ask, "Am I ready? Am I ready to meet Christ and give an account for all my sins?"

You can be ready. You can get ready now!

— *JRM*

* * *

WEDNESDAY EVENING, AUGUST 29

TITLE: **The Provision and Protection of God**

TEXT: **"Thy rod and thy staff they comfort me" (Ps. 23:4c).**

SCRIPTURE READING: **Psalm 23:1–6**

Introduction. The text for this message combines some subjects of previous messages on this psalm. These subjects are provision and protection. One of the truly great thoughts presented in God's Holy Word is comfort. He is a God of comfort.

I. *Comfort*—this is the provision.

A. *Comfort is a universal need.* This need arises from many sources, but the two most common are physical and emotional. The lesson in the text is that the Lord is always equal to the occasion.

B. *The word* comfort *means to cheer and to encourage.* It affords the power of calm endurance of affliction.

C. *The word* Comforter *in the New Testament* (John 14:16, 26; 15:26; 16:7) *literally means "called to one's side for help" and refers to the Holy Spirit.* Thus, the Comforter is Helper, Guide, and Teacher. He is also the believer's Advocate.

II. *Rod* and *staff*—this is the protection.

A. *The more acceptable idea is that the two terms refer to one and the same instrument.* The shepherd's crook is used to describe, in a poetic way, the rod or club with which he defends his sheep; and he uses the staff on which to lean. The instrument described by the two names was used both to beat off predatory animals and to direct the sheep.

B. *This instrument is not only one of care and protection, but also an emblem of compassion and concern.*

III. A detailed study of the instrument.

Even though the "rod" and "staff" have been referred to as one and the same instrument, they are now being separated for discussion.

A. *The rod is a special instrument and is a symbol of much the Lord does in a spiritual way.*

1. Some state that the "rod" is emblematic of the Word of God.

2. Some state that it is the instrument of power and/or authority. Moses used his rod to demonstrate power. The shepherd used his to discipline and protect.

3. Some describe it as an instrument for examination and counting. Ezekiel 20:37 speaks of passing under the rod. This was for personal attention.

B. *The staff was also a special instrument and it, too, is a symbol of much the Lord does in a spiritual way.*

1. The staff is considered symbolic of the Holy Spirit. The key idea is drawing. The shepherd uses the staff to reach out and draw his sheep to himself; and as he draws them, he protects, examines, and shows affection. This is what the Holy Spirit does.

2. The staff is a word for guidance. The shepherd uses it to guide his sheep through hazardous places. The Holy Spirit works in this way also.

Conclusion. To you who need comfort, look to your heavenly Father for it.

— *DRG*

* * *

SUGGESTED PREACHING PROGRAM
FOR THE MONTH OF SEPTEMBER

Sunday Mornings

"Growing Quality Christians" is the suggested theme for a series of messages relating to God's gift of the Holy Spirit to individual believers and to the church. To our own spiritual poverty, we neglect to recognize and to respond positively to this precious gift from God.

Sunday Evenings

Using the Book of Exodus as the scriptural source,. we have a series of messages centered around the theme, "How God Works With His People."

Wednesday Evenings

Continue the devotional messages based upon Psalm 23, using the theme, "With the Lord As My Shepherd, I Shall Not Suffer the Lack of Anything That I Need."

* * *

SUNDAY MORNING, SEPTEMBER 2

TITLE: **Understanding the Holy Spirit**

Text: **"And I will pray the Father, and he shall give you another Comforter, that he may abide with you for ever; even the Spirit of truth; whom the world cannot receive, because it seeth him not, neither knoweth him: but ye know him; for he dwelleth with you, and shall be in you" (John 14:16–17).**

Scripture Reading: **John 14:15–18, 26**

Hymns: **"Come, Thou Almighty King," Anonymous**
"Spirit of God, Our Comforter," Hendricks
"Teach Me Thy Way, O Lord," Ramsey

Offertory Prayer:

Holy, heavenly Father, we thank You for this day set apart for worship. We thank You for the opportunity of coming together with God's people that we might pray together and join together in praising You in song and worship. We come now, bringing tithes and offerings to express our love and our desire that others might come to know Your love through Jesus Christ our Lord. Amen.

Introduction. There are many "religious dropouts" in our churches today. They become such because they have never established a pattern of spiritual growth. Thus they are nothing more than "statistics," spiritual and ecclesiastical casualties. One of two things usually happens to these people: either they become lost in the great, faceless multitude upon whom the church has no influence and for whom it has no appeal, or else they fall victim to the persuasive enthusiasm of some religious cult.

Often the fault lies at the feet of the church, which was so concerned about the *salvation* of these persons, but lacked spiritual care and nurturing, which left them floundering in the cradle as though they, helpless babes, could take care of themselves! ~~Today and the next four Sunday mornings we shall lay a foundation for "growing quality Christians."~~ ~~To do this, we shall explore the person and ministry of the Holy Spirit.~~ For it is the power of the Spirit which motivates the Christian; it is the wisdom of the Spirit which sets afire the believer's desire to know more about God, about His Holy Word, and about the role he is to play in God's eternal purpose and plan. And it is the abiding presence of the Spirit which provides the constant assurance that one is a child of God, beloved of his heavenly Father, and kept eternally in the ~~inviolable~~ *sacred* circle of His love.

I. The Holy Spirit as He is presented to us upon the pages of the Old Testament.

A. *The Holy Spirit in Creation.* "In the beginning God created the heaven and the earth. And the earth was without form, and void; and darkness was upon the face of the deep. And the Spirit of God moved upon the face of the waters" (Gen. 1:1–2). In this first reference to the Holy Spirit in the Bible we find the key to understanding all of His works and ministry among men. The picture of earth Moses describes here is one of complete, total helplessness. But wait! Something is happening! God, in the person of His Spirit, saw potential and promise in that whirling, spinning mass of chaos and confusion. He saw not only what it *was,* but *what it could become.* The Spirit of God *moved.* Something started to happen because of the Holy Spirit. It describes the hen who broods over her nest. From her body there is transmitted life-giving warmth. Thus, in the midst of death, life began to stir.

B. *After the Creation, the Holy Spirit did not retire.* All through the pages of the Old Testament we read of events and happenings in which the Holy Spirit "came upon" men and women to continue the carrying out of God's plan and purpose. Through His Spirit, God dealt with man as a mother deals with a tiny baby. Just as a mother makes "love sounds" to her tiny infant, sounds of reassurance, so God began making "love sounds" to sinful man.

C. *Then man was brought into God's school, with the Holy Spirit as the schoolmaster, to the threshold of the New Testament era.* It almost staggers the mind to think about how much more the people of Malachi's day knew about God than Abraham knew. For whereas Abraham was nearly two thousand years away from the birth of Christ, the people of Malachi's day were scarcely four hundred years away.

II. The Holy Spirit in the Gospels, and on the Day of Pentecost.

A. *With the coming of Christ, we see a revelation of the Spirit of God that was never found in the Old Testament.* In Christ, where there was no trace of sin or human hindrance, the Holy Spirit was able to work in mighty power and freedom. Jesus possessed the Spirit of God "without measure." The total fullness of the deity of God dwelt in the body of Jesus.

B. *Just before His death, Jesus promised the disciples that He would "send another Comforter" who would abide with them forever.* He told them that this "Comforter" had been *with* them, but soon He would be *in* them. Of course, we know that this came to pass on the Day of Pentecost. When the Holy Spirit came to indwell believers, it was a permanent arrangement. He did not come in as an "overnight guest" or a "weekend visitor." He came to abide as the possessor, the owner of God's property.

C. *Three major things happened on the Day of Pentecost in relation to the Holy Spirit.* First, He became the "resident presence of God" in the world until the end of the age. He took up His abode in the bodies of believers, whom Paul called "temples of the Holy Spirit." The second thing that happened on the Day of Pentecost was the beginning of the formation of a new body or organism, the church, which the Lord Jesus had promised. It is the Holy Spirit who adds to this body as individuals receive Christ as Savior. Third, the Holy Spirit empowered believers to witness, to share the reality of their faith in God with others with boldness and assurance.

III. The Holy Spirit's ministry in the Epistles, and to our day.

A. *The Holy Spirit has a ministry to the unbeliever.* There is no way an unbeliever could know that he is lost and in need of a Savior apart from the Holy Spirit who opens his eyes to that fact.

B. *The Holy Spirit has a ministry to the believer.* He reveals God's will to him for his life; He makes the Scriptures "come alive" and speak to his heart. He works through the believer's conscience to reveal truth to him and to help him make right decisions. The Holy Spirit is the constant Companion, Supporter, and Guide of the Christian.

C. *What does all of this say to us?* It says that God, the Holy Spirit, is the Divine Mover. He is the agent in the Godhead which moves a holy, all-powerful God toward sinful man. And simultaneously, it is the Holy Spirit who moves sinful man toward God.

Then, it is the Holy Spirit who brings about the new birth. Just as He moved over the angry, chaotic waters of this shapeless, spinning world of dead matter and brought forth life, so He does in the life of the sinner, who is "dead in trespasses and sins." But He does not stop there. He continues to work in and through those whom He brings to repentance and redemption. He refines; He teaches; He encourages; He tenderly fashions, as a potter works deftly with the lump of clay on his wheel. Never for one second does He leave us alone!

Conclusion. Clearly it has been the design and strategy of Satan from the beginning to distort in every way he can the truth about the Holy Spirit, as that truth is revealed in Holy Scripture. The result has been that the teaching concerning the Holy Spirit has been subjected to everything from bizarre emotionalism to cold intellectualism. Yet, in between those two ridiculous and unscriptural extremes, there is a beautiful and vital and essential teaching concerning the Holy Spirit. Throughout the Bible He is revealed to us. Let us not neglect His vital ministry. — *DLJ*

* * *

SUNDAY EVENING, SEPTEMBER 2

TITLE: **How God Confronts Us**

Text: **"And when the Lord saw that he turned aside to see, God called unto him out of the midst of the bush, and said, Moses, Moses. And he said, Here** am I. And he said, Draw not nigh hither: put off thy shoes from off thy feet, for the place whereon thou standest is holy ground. Moreover he said, I am the God of thy father, the God of Abraham, the God of Isaac, and the God of Jacob. And Moses hid his face; for he was afraid to look upon God" (Exod. 3:4–6).

SCRIPTURE READING: Exodus 3:1–22

Introduction. A certain man went to Europe several years ago. He was excited because he had always wanted to visit the Christian shrines in England and on the continent. He went to Aldergate where John Wesley's "heart was strangely warmed," to Whittenberg and to Rome where Martin Luther's incisive turnings took place. But as he saw these places that have become shrines for many Protestant Christians, he was disappointed. He had expected to be inspired and awed, but these were just plain buildings and towns.

As he thought about his disappointment, he realized that these had been just ordinary places when the action had taken place which later made them important. In each case the thing that made these churches and cities shrines was that each was a simple setting in which a man had made a decision concerning God's will for himself—a time when someone turned with his whole life, faced God, and chose Him over "things." The events which followed were so significant that people now travel for miles just to see the site where the decision was made.

Often we look for a special place or a dramatic circumstance in which we can find God's will or do God's will. But when it actually comes to giving our lives to God, committing ourselves to Him, accepting His will for our lives, and determining to try to live the Christian life, any location will do. Anyplace where we make commitment of life to Christ can be for us a burning bush of decision.

Were we to go once again into the area of Horeb and by some means find the bush where God spoke to Moses, I am sure it would look just like any other desert bush. That particular bush had significance simply because there God spoke, there a man responded, and there a commitment was made.

For Moses it was at the burning bush. There he met God. There he had a life-changing experience. There he accepted God's commission to lead the Hebrew people out of slavery and to the Promised Land.

But for you to be confronted with God and to have an experience with God, you do not have to search out that same bush—any bush will do. Whatever it is that causes you to open your heart to God, can be for you an experience similar to Moses' experience at the burning bush. This is how God confronts us.

I. When God confronts us, we need an awareness of God.

A. *An awareness of God will allow us to see Him in any situation.* Anyone else coming along may not have seen or heard God in the burning bush. But Moses did. J. S. Whale observed that if most of us saw a bush on fire and not consumed, we would not take off our shoes in reverence, but would whip out a camera to take a snapshot of it.

Christians often talk about God's speaking to them in a situation, leading them to an action, showing Himself to them in an occurrence. This can be said when the events are interpreted through the eyes of faith. Someone looking on may call it merely coincidence, an accident, or the natural working out of events. But looking at it through eyes of faith, the Christian can call it the working of God's Holy Spirit.

B. *An awareness of God will allow faith to come alive in any situation*. With an awareness of God, faith can come alive in any situation—in loneliness, frustration, fear, anxiety, or a broken relationship. Any of the outward circumstances in which we find ourselves when we commit our lives to Him is the situation in which faith can come alive.

When faith comes alive, anyplace can become a Christian shrine. Any simple place such as a house, a kitchen sink, an office chair, or a car can be transformed into a shrine for you. The question being asked today is not the traditional religious question "What must I do to be saved?" but the contemporary question "How can I find peace, wholeness, satisfaction, and fulfillment?" As the answer to this question is found in faith in Jesus Christ, anyplace that faith comes alive becomes a holy place.

II. When God confronts us, we need an openness to God.

A. *An openness to God will allow us to recognize Him when He makes Himself known to us*. Moses asked a question of God's identity (v. 13). Notice how God identified Himself to Moses (vv. 13–14).

    1. It showed continuity: "God of your fathers."
    2. It showed self-existence: "I am."
    3. It showed divine purpose: "I AM THAT I AM."

Moses was able to recognize the God of redemption and deliverance in that burning bush.

B. *An openness to God will allow us to receive Him when He makes Himself known to us*. Moses not only asked a question of God's identity, he also asked a question of self-identity. "Who am I?" he asked in Exodus 3:11. Who was he, indeed? Was he a child of Israel? Of Egypt? A fugitive? An adopted grandson of the Pharaoh? A priest's son-in-law? A shepherd of Midian? Who was he? He was God's.

From a prison cell Dietrich Bonhoeffer asked:

> Who am I? . . .
> Am I one person today and to-morrow another?
> Am I both at once? a hypocrite before others,
> and before myself a contemptible woebegone weakling?
> Or is something within me still like a beaten army
> fleeing in disorder from victory already achieved?
> Who am I? They mock me, these lonely questions of mine.
> Whoever I am, Thou knowest, O God, I am thine!*

III. When God confronts us, we need an obedience to God.

A. *The course of obedience*. Have you ever thought how this whole experience would have turned out if Moses had refused to obey God and had refused to accept God's commission for him? We would never have heard of the burning bush. And we probably would never have heard of Moses. God would have turned to someone else and some other way to deliver His people.

But Moses was obedient. And history turned on his obedience to this encounter with God and his understanding of that experience.

B. *The characterization of obedience*. Obedience is absolutely necessary in our relationship to God.

---

*The Cost of Discipleship (New York: Macmillan, 1963), pp. 19–20.

Paul characterized Jesus Christ as being obedient—even to death on the cross (Phil. 2:8).

Paul testified to King Agrippa that he was obedient to the vision he had of Christ on the Damascus Road (Acts 26:19).

St. Augustine was obedient to the voice he heard in the garden saying, "Take and read." He read the Book of Romans and found Christ. And the church found a preacher and theologian.

C. *The courage for obedience.* But where do we get the courage to be obedient? It comes from the presence of God. God promised Moses, "I will be with thee . . ." (Exod. 3:12).

Can we be assured of the outcome when we start on the path of obedience? No, not really. We can only see the outcome when it is all over. That is what obedience and faith mean. We can know that God's presence is with us, that God accepts us, and that God will lead us. But we cannot know all that is involved until we begin the walk with God. The "sign" was given that the children of Israel would worship God on that same mountain. But many things transpired before they did so.

Conclusion. God may not confront us through such a dramatic experience as a burning bush. But God confronts each one of us. In obedience and faith we respond to Him.   — *JEC*

* * *

WEDNESDAY EVENING, SEPTEMBER 5

TITLE: The Provision of God

TEXT: **"Thou preparest a table before me in the presence of mine enemies: thou anointest my head with oil" (Ps. 23:5a, b).**

SCRIPTURE READING: **Psalm 23:1–6**

Introduction. This verse seems to mark a sudden change in approach. In the opinion of some, the change is from the shepherd-and-sheep relationship, as has been discussed thus far, to a banquet concept. However, others believe this verse continues in the same vein of thought as the previous verses.

I. An examination of the two concepts.

A. *The concept of a table being prepared conveys the idea of a banquet.*

1. The Lord God is pictured as a Host entertaining His guest at His own banquet table.

2. The guest is welcomed in the presence of his enemies, who are made powerless in God's presence.

3. The table is symbolic of the heavenly home. God's children have passed through places of trouble, sorrow, hunger, anxiety, and pain and are now at home, never to suffer again.

4. The anointing mentioned in verse 5 is often used for joyful and happy occasions.

a. The predominant use of anointing is to mark separation or distinction.

b. Each Christian needs to apply this concept to his own life. Christians are anointed with the Holy Spirit, as the Lord's special people, and thus are assured of spiritual health and welfare.

B. *The concept of a table being prepared continues the idea of a shepherd-sheep relationship.*

1. The table is a place for feeding the sheep. It was probably a plateau sort of place that was level and high. It was a place for rest and safety.

2. This place of feeding indicates several significant factors.

a. It takes planning and preparation. The shepherd would arrive at the designated place on schedule, and there the animals would find minerals, salt, and food.

b. It is a place free of poisonous weeds.

c. It is a place where the shepherd can see all about.

d. It is a place for clean water.

II. Either concept illustrates the provisions of God for His people.

A. *He is a loving, caring God who provides for His people both in this world and the world to come.*

B. *He is a God who can be trusted to supply all needs, whatever they may be.*

C. *He has wholesome plans for those who follow him.*

Conclusion. God separates His people from others and provides bountifully for them. Turn to the heavenly Father for your needs.   *— DRG*

* * *

SUNDAY MORNING, SEPTEMBER 9

TITLE: Recognizing the Holy Spirit

TEXT: "But the fruit of the Spirit is love, joy, peace, longsuffering, gentleness, goodness, faith, meekness, temperance: against such there is no law" (Gal. 5:22–23).

SCRIPTURE READING: Galatians 5:22–23

HYMNS: "All Hail the Power of Jesus' Name," Perronet
"Grace Greater Than Our Sin," Johnston
"O Spirit of the Living God," Tweedy

OFFERTORY PRAYER:

Heavenly Father, thank You for drawing us to this place of prayer and worship that we might experience Your presence through Your family. Thank You for the manner in which You dwell within the church as well as within the individual heart of each believer. Help us to let Your Spirit of grace cause us to be generous in the giving of our gifts into Your service. In Jesus' name we pray. Amen.

Introduction. One of the barriers that exists between Christians and non-Christians is that of terminology or language. There is a sense in which Christians tend to create their own manner of speaking, their own "religious vocabulary," which often sounds strange, if not a bit Pharisaical, to the unbeliever. It fosters a kind of pious exclusivism, a sort of fraternal society in which those who belong seem to enjoy a higher status of importance than those on the outside.

The result of all of these wrong concepts of "spirituality" in the life of a Christian is that the unbeliever—who is judging Christianity in general by what he sees in the lives of Christians whom he knows—and the new Christian—who is just beginning his pilgrimage with God—are both tragically disillusioned. Therefore, recognizing the Holy Spirit in His various manifestations in a believer's life is important for two reasons: from the standpoint of the believer in whom the Spirit dwells and from the perspective of those who, for whatever reason, observe us from the outside.

Today we shall outline several manifestations of the Holy Spirit in the life of a believer that are presented clearly for us in the Scriptures, and which produce a clear and true recognition of the Holy Spirit in the Christian's life.

I. The Holy Spirit produces Christian character.

A. *What* is *Christian character?* The apostle Paul has told us clearly in Galatians 5:22–23. Here we have compressed into these nine words or virtues not only a portrait of the life of Christ lived while He was on earth, but also a description of the kind of life God would have the Christian live here and now. The question is, How do we go about bringing to pass these qualities of character in our lives?

B. *Some have put on the habit of a monk and have entered a monastery, taking vows of poverty.* They have become ascetics and have tried to acquire this kind of character by various self-denial techniques. Others have tried to bring about these graces through a whirl of feverish activity. They have driven themselves to the point of exhaustion doing "good deeds" and performing good works. There is nothing evil about this *in itself.* The problem comes when we inevitably start to keep a record of our good works, expecting to be rewarded for them. Thus, instead of producing the qualities of character Paul has described for us, they start to produce in us the ugliness of pride, of projecting ourselves as "super-saints" before the world.

C. *But then, if we do not* work at *bringing to pass these nine graces or qualities of character in our lives, how do they happen?* The secret lies in the fact that Paul calls them the *fruit* of the Spirit. Fruit grows because of an inner compulsion. They develop as the believer is willing to say, "Father, I surrender to Your Holy Spirit working within me. I will not interfere with His work in my life. As You help me, I will be as clay in the Potter's hands. Produce this Christian character *in* me, not *by* me."

II. The Holy Spirit produces Christian service.

A. *Genuine Christian service is a direct result of the Holy Spirit's working in and through the believer.* Jesus told the multitudes one day that "he that believeth on me . . . out of [him] shall flow rivers of living water" (John 7:38). John editorializes and explains that Jesus was speaking of the Holy Spirit, who would come to indwell believers. Now, *we* could never produce "living waters," and certainly not "rivers." At best, we can be nothing more than the channels, or instruments, for this divine outflow. Paul said that "we are his workmanship, created in Christ Jesus unto good works, which God hath before ordained that we should walk in them" (Eph. 2:10). God has already planned a very special service for each of us to perform.

B. *Christian service is never merely a duty or chore, when one has yielded to the Holy Spirit and is letting Him direct and point out the path of service to follow.* It would be a delightful experience for any church if every member was so yielded to the Holy Spirit that he was involved in that particular area of Christian service *God* planned for him to be involved in! In that case, not only would he be doing exactly what God wanted him to do, but he would be doing it in the power and with the strength of the Holy Spirit.

III. The Holy Spirit produces understanding; it is the Holy Spirit who teaches us.

A. *Jesus said to His disciples before His crucifixion.* "I have yet many things to say unto you, but ye cannot bear them now. Howbeit when he, the Spirit of truth, is come, he will guide you into all truth" (John 16:12–13a). In other words, Jesus was saying that He was going to send the Holy Spirit, one of whose vital functions would be to teach us, to lead us beyond the range of mere human knowledge in regard to spiritual things.

B. *When does this ministry of the Holy Spirit begin in a believer's life? The moment he is born again.* All of us have known new Christians who seemingly have grown by leaps and bounds in the faith. We have marveled at their development, at the wisdom and understanding they seem to have achieved so soon. That is no mystery! It is simply the Holy Spirit doing His work in that believer's life, because that believer has yielded himself to Him. There should never become a time in any Christian's life when he is *unteachable*.

IV. The Holy Spirit produces identity—that is, He makes it possible for us to know who we are.

A. *Paul said, "The Spirit itself beareth witness with our spirit, that we are the children of God"* (Rom. 8:16). The Christian who is consciously aware of the Holy Spirit indwelling him never doubts his salvation; for one of the Spirit's blessed ministries is to whisper to us constantly that we are God's children!

It is one thing to accept with our minds the fact that the Bible declares that if we have repented of our sins and received the Lord Jesus as Savior, we are forever and eternally His. But it is quite another thing to feel the reality of that truth surging with power in our hearts.

B. *Do you know who you are—not just with your mind, but with your heart?* That is the difference between a dutiful Christian life and one that is filled to overflowing with unbounding joy.

Conclusion. *How* is the Holy Spirit recognized in a Christian's life, both by the Christian himself and by the world around him? The Holy Spirit produces our Christian character, which is manifested in these nine virtues Paul called "the fruit of the Spirit." He also produces *Christian service,* leading us to perform the "good works" *He* has planned for us. He *teaches* us the meaning and the application of the great truths of the Bible, and *He* makes it possible for us to *know who we are* constantly and continually—the people of God, the sheep of His pasture, the beloved of the heavenly Father. — *DLJ*

* * *

SUNDAY EVENING, SEPTEMBER 9

TITLE: How God Delivers Us

Text: "And the Lord went before them by day in a pillar of a cloud, to lead them the way; and by night in a pillar of fire, to give them light; to go by day and night: He took not away the pillar of the cloud by day, nor the pillar of fire by night, from before the people" (Exod. 13:21–22).

Scripture Reading: Exodus 12:29–32, 50; 13:1–2, 17–22

Introduction. James Dallas Egburt, III, was a seventeen-year-old computer genius who disappeared for twenty-eight days in 1979. A college sophomore, he seemed to be playing a real-life version of a complicated fantasy game popular at his university called "Dungeons and Dragons." Utilizing an underground sewer system, he was either hiding or being hidden and moved in a real-life, dangerous version of the game. After so many days, it no longer became a game. After twenty-eight days he was discovered in an undisclosed location. He was delivered.

The story had a tragic ending several months later when he died from a self-inflicted gunshot wound. Obviously, this boy needed deliverance.

There was a time when the Hebrews needed deliverance. They were enslaved in Egypt.

When one reflects on the deliverance of the Hebrews from Egypt, it almost looks as though the Pharaoh was playing a game. Clearly it was a contest between him and God.

Faced with the demand of God through Moses to "let my people go," Pharaoh reacted. A series of plagues occurred. At times it looked as though Pharaoh would relent and release the Hebrews. But then he would harden his heart, stiffen his neck, and not only keep them in slavery but increase their burden. Finally, the tenth plague—the death of the firstborn—was too much. Pharaoh let the Hebrews go.

The Exodus is to the Old Testament what the Cross is to the New Testament. It is the one central feature around which the activity and the revelation of God gather. God had acted decisively to deliver His people!

The Exodus itself was an amazing thing. Estimates of the number of people involved range upward to 2.5 million! Rather than take the easier route along the coast by probably the oldest highway in the world, the Hebrews went through the wilderness to the Promised Land. There were reasons for this. A negative reason was that the highway had Egyptian fortifications and patrols. A positive reason was that they needed the time to organize themselves and to comprehend what had happened.

God showed His presence with them by visible signs: a cloud by day and a pillar of fire by night.

God delivers. How do we know? God delivered the Hebrews from bondage to freedom, from oppression to life. And God delivers us today. How does He do this?

I. In considering how God delivers us, we remember that it is God Himself who delivers us.

A. *We are incapable of delivering ourselves.* It is quite obvious that God is the One who delivered. The people were incapable of delivering themselves.

They were slaves. From their behavior later on, it became clear that they were disorganized and distraught people. They complained. They lapsed into idolatry. They refused to follow by faith into the Promised Land.

Like them, in our distraught and disorganized state, we cannot deliver ourselves from our sins or our problems.

B. *God alone has the power to deliver us.* The plagues against the Egyptians were designed to show the superior power of God. The Pharaoh himself was considered a god. More than once God indicated to Moses that through these events they would know that He was God.

C. *Never forget that God delivers us.* In teaching the little children about the Passover, parents were to remind them that it was God who had delivered them.

Nor must we forget that God is the One who delivers us from all of our sin and troubles. In Romans 8:37 the apostle Paul concluded a list of frightening circumstances with the words, "Nay, in all these things we are more than conquerors through him that loved us." That phrase could be translated "super-conquerors."

II. In considering how God delivers us, we think of the things from which He delivers us.

A. *God delivers us from unrelieved oppression.* The oppression by the Egyptians against the Hebrews was unrelieved: day after day, hour after hour they were aware of it.

People today suffer from some of the same things.

1. World problems. When we think of world problems, we think of lack of freedom, of political oppression, of military dictatorships, of hungry people, of threats of war. The world is full of unrelieved hurt.

2. Personal problems. These problems can consist of continual presence of pain, sexual harassment on a job, mental pressure and harassment at work, a difficult marriage, an invalid or sick child, an aged and infirm parent. Often one calls out, "Is there any relief from the constant pressure?"

B. *God delivers us from unexplained burdens.* The average Hebrew slave on the construction site probably could not have explained why he was a slave or why his burden got worse. The unexplained burdens get us down. Is there any answer to the problem of evil and suffering?

C. *God delivers us from unrepentant sin.* What was the relationship of these people to God? It could not have been good. The demands of God were presented to them. God can deliver from the burden of sin.

In our problems and pain we turn to God. In John Killenger's book *Bread for the Wilderness, Wine for the Journey,* he told the story of a young man who had considerable mental agony due to a serious problem with his infant daughter. One of her hip joints was not growing properly, and an operation was planned.

In his personal journal he wrote that it would be easy to see the Lord's Prayer as being greatly out of touch with what really mattered to him. In fact, he penned a paraphrase of the Lord's Prayer with words that began,

> Our Father, who art in heaven,
> why aren't you down here on earth,
> doing something about my present difficulty?

But he did not pray that prayer. Instead, he tried to give thanks for his daughter and for the joy she had brought into their home. Then he reviewed the world around him as he tried to listen to the voice of the Holy Spirit to see what he could be thankful for. Again, he turned to the Lord's Prayer and this prayer began with these words,

> Our Father, in spite of the present difficulty,
> you are still in heaven and the world is still ordered.
> May my response hallow your name.
> The coming of your kingdom is more important than my own
>   difficulty—so may I not hinder its coming by my worry.

The surgery was to come a few days after the young father had come to that viewpoint. But when the doctors x-rayed the day before the surgery, the joint had begun to grow properly. Apparently she was going to be fine (pp. 52–54).

The cloud by day and the pillar of fire by night assure us that God is always with us.

III. In considering how God delivers us, we are aware of how God does deliver us.

A. *God delivers by the power of His grace.* The last plague against the Egyptians was the death of the firstborn. In many ancient religions the firstborn child was considered to belong to the diety. Some of the Hebrews' neighbors at this time even practiced the sacrifice of their firstborn child to their god.

It was by God's grace that the death angel passed over the Hebrews. God delivers by grace.

B. *Grace is obtained at God's directives.* We do not determine the ways of grace. Grace always comes on God's terms.

When the angel of death passed over the homes of the Hebrews, it was because God directed the slaying of the lamb and the blood mark on the doorpost as the means of deliverance.

In the wilderness when God delivered the people from the poisonous snakes, He directed the brass snake on the pole as the means of deliverance.

When Naaman was healed of his leprosy, the bathing had to be in the River Jordan, the place and the means of God's choosing and direction for his deliverance.

When Jesus died on the cross, this was the means of God's choice for the forgiveness of our sins.

The fact that God's grace comes on God's terms or not at all should not be so hard for us to understand; it happens all of the time. When one takes out a credit card at a department store, he agrees to the terms of the credit card at the store's terms. When one makes a loan at a bank the terms of the note and the time of its repayment are at the bank's direction.

Conclusion. God does deliver us. He delivered the Hebrew people from slavery and that became the center point of their faith in Him. He delivers us from our sin and our troubles through the death of His Son Jesus Christ upon the cross. And that becomes the center point of our faith.   *— JEC*

* * *

WEDNESDAY EVENING, SEPTEMBER 12

TITLE: **The Provision of God**

Text: **"My cup runneth over" (Ps. 23:5c).**

Scripture Reading: **Psalm 23:1–6**

Introduction. The provision of God becomes more meaningful to the readers of the Twenty-third Psalm when the true significance of "the cup" is applied, rather than an exegesis of the words themselves.

I. First, consider the biblical use of the term *cup*.

A. *Originally, it applied to the portioning out of something.* This could apply to a portion of land—one's inheritance. The Promised Land is one example; a portion of grain is another.

B. *It is more frequently used to apply to what is sorrowful.*
1. It is used in regard to the suffering of Christ (Matt. 26:39).
2. It is used for calamities attending the confession of Christ's name (20:23).

C. *It is used in reference to the Holy Supper* (1 Cor. 10:21).

D. *It is used in reference to the covenant.* The cup is the covenant of blood. It is a pledge and a seal and means the imparting of the blessings of the covenant.

E. *It is also used to refer to the blessings and joys of the children of God and the full provisions of their wants.*

II. This passage in the Twenty-third Psalm refers to the full provision of wants.

A. *The allotment or portion idea takes on a spiritual significance.* This idea is brought out in the song "Fill My Cup, Lord."

B. *The whole phrase "my cup runneth over" is a metaphor indicating a state of bliss.*
1. This is communion with God. This communion is richer by the day.
2. This is an expression of the way in which the Lord provides joys, luxuries, and the extras of life as well as the necessities.
3. This is an expression of completeness.

III. This message in the Twenty-third Psalm is a picture of contented people as children of God.

A. *Some look at this as the shepherd-sheep relationship.*
1. Here the sheep eat and drink out of the Shepherd's cup and lay in His bosom.
2. Plentiful provision is made for body and soul.

B. *Some reflections on these truths are helpful for God's children.*
1. This kind of provision is for God's children when they are committed to Him.
2. This kind of provision applies to both time and eternity, to both earth and heaven.

Conclusion. A reflection on this provision leads one to count his blessings and rejoice in them.   — DRG

* * *

SUNDAY MORNING, SEPTEMBER 16

TITLE: Cooperating With the Holy Spirit

TEXT: **"And when he is come, he will reprove the world of sin, and of righteousness, and of judgment: of sin, because they believe not on me; of righteousness, because I go to my Father, and ye see me no more; of judgment, because the prince of this world is judged"** (John 16:8–11).

SCRIPTURE READING: **John 16:8–11**

HYMNS: **"All Creatures of Our God and King," Francis of Assisi**
"I Need Thee Every Hour," Hawks
"Breathe On Me," Hatch

OFFERTORY PRAYER:

Gracious and generous Father, we thank You today for every good and perfect gift. We thank You for the gift of Your Son, that through His poverty we might become rich in our relationship with You and in the resources that You make available for fruitful living. We come bringing the fruits of our labors to place them upon the altar in dedication to the advancement of Your kingdom. Bless these gifts, we pray. In Jesus' name. Amen.

Introduction. One of the subtle insinuations about God which Satan has whispered in the ear of man from the beginning of time is *not* that God does not exist, but that He is so great, so majestic, so powerful, and thus so removed from lowly man that there is no way He can be personally and individually concerned and involved with human beings. Satan is not challenged or bothered when man believes that there is "a great God somewhere" who created everything and set life in motion with all of these natural laws which govern us.

What is the satanic motive behind all of this? It is to slowly but surely convince man that God *is not* personally involved and concerned with man; that man *is* the master of his fate and the captain of his soul; and that, ultimately, man *will* be able to manipulate and control his destiny, based on his own standard of what is right and wrong.

Satan knows that when man *cooperates* with the Holy Spirit, there is established between him and God a relationship which transcends all other human relationships and experiences man may have. And we are talking about a permanent relationship that man can have with God. As we continue our theme of "Growing Quality Christians," we shall examine what happens when a person *cooperates* with the Holy Spirit and His varied ministries in the world.

I. The ministry of the Holy Spirit to unbelievers.

A. *It is the startling revelation of Holy Scripture that God, in the person of the Holy Spirit, in a magnificent act of condescension, has determined to approach human beings as individuals.* Why does He do it? To reveal to man His love and mercy and His desire to save man from his sins.

B. *Jesus said three things about the Holy Spirit's ministry to the unbeliever:*

1. He convinces the unbeliever of sin. Note carefully the singular word for *sin*. There is only one sin in the life of the unbeliever that concerns God—the sin of unbelief. And what does it mean to believe "on" the Lord Jesus? It means not only to agree intellectually with the Scripture that Jesus lived, died, and rose again; it means to accept the "cure" He provided for man's sin in His death on the cross for oneself.

2. The Holy Spirit reveals to the unbeliever what true righteousness is. It is natural for man to believe that he can make himself good by doing good deeds, by being lawful, by being kind to his neighbor, and so forth. But as commendable as these acts are, they are not good enough for God. God wants to give His *own* righteousness to man—the righteousness of His Son, Jesus Christ.

3. The Holy Spirit declares to the unbeliever the truth about judgment. Note that Jesus said, "The prince of this world is judged" (v. 11). He meant that the forces of evil, personified in Satan, have been defeated because of Christ's death on the cross. It is not necessary for the unbeliever to "beg" God to forgive him, but rather to *accept* the fact that God has already done it in accepting the death of His Son on the cross as full payment for man's sin debt. Every claim that Satan may have had on unbelieving man because of his sin has been dissolved.

II. The ministry of the Holy Spirit to believers.

A. *When one responds to the threefold ministry of the Holy Spirit that we have just discussed, the experience of salvation takes place.* Up to this point the Holy Spirit has been on the outside; but upon the response of the sinner, the Holy Spirit presides at a birth experience. The most miraculous transformation in the universe takes place as one is born into the divine family of God. A new nature is implanted within the believer. Because the believer has "cooperated" with the Holy Spirit in His initial ministry of convicting of sin and bringing to pass the new birth, three other ministries take place simultaneously upon one's conversion.

1. The Holy Spirit baptizes. "For by one Spirit we are all baptized into one body, . . . and have been all made to drink into one Spirit" (1 Cor. 12:13). What *is* the "baptism of the Holy Spirit"? It is not a second work of grace, but the act whereby, at the moment of one's conversion, the Holy Spirit places the believer into the body of Christ. There is no other part of the salvation experience that is so far-reaching in its effect. It is by the baptism of the Holy Spirit that a believer is fused into the family of God at the moment of his conversion.

2. The Holy Spirit seals. Paul said, "And grieve not the holy Spirit of God, whereby ye are sealed unto the day of redemption" (Eph. 4:30). This is another way in which God protects His property. Not only does He "fuse" us into His family immediately upon our salvation, but He also "seals" us with His Holy Spirit. That is, His presence within us is the divine mark of ownership. It is the "heavenly brand" stamped indelibly upon every Christian. And this seal is to hold inviolably until "the day of redemption."

3. The Holy Spirit fills. Again Paul said, "Be not drunk with wine, . . . but be filled with the Spirit" (5:18). This filling is not a one-time experience, but rather it is continual. Literally, the word of Paul is "be ye kept being filled" with the Spirit. It should be a daily experience for the believer.

Conclusion. Are you "cooperating with the Holy Spirit" in your life? If you have not believed with your whole heart that Jesus is God's Son and your Savior, the Holy Spirit is on the "outside" waiting for your cooperation. If you *have* believed, then He wants you to be aware of the joys and privileges which are yours.   *— DLJ*

* * *

SUNDAY EVENING, SEPTEMBER 16

TITLE: How God Provides for Us

TEXT: "**And Moses said, This shall be, when the LORD shall give you in the evening flesh to eat, and in the morning bread to be full; for that the LORD heareth your murmurings which ye murmur against him: and what are we? your murmurings are not against us, but against the LORD**" (Exod. 16:8).

SCRIPTURE READING: Exodus 16:1–9

Introduction. On Robert Schuller's television program "The Hour of Power" there was once a testimony about God's power to help a man do the impossible. A pastor with mechanical arms and hands was standing with Schuller. Several years before, this pastor had resigned from a large church in order to work with retarded children. He dreamed of building a ranch in Arizona to serve as a home where these children could grow and develop. Selling everything he owned, he bought land in Arizona and attempted to erect his first building. While working one day, he received an electric shock which caused him to lose both hands and arms.

At first he battled with discouragement and despair. However, he refused to give up. With mechanical arms and hands he continued his work. Various state newspapers featured articles on his life. Soon thousands of donations were made to his project. He had originally hoped to have his home on a sound operating basis within ten to fifteen years. However, hundreds of thousands of dollars were given, and within a short period of time the retarded children's home was in full operation. How miraculously God provides for those who serve Him!

From the Exodus experience of the children of Israel from Egypt we can learn several things about the nature and character of God. God cares: He heard their cries and groanings in oppression. God delivers: He delivered them from Egypt and across the Red Sea. God provides: He provided care for them in the wilderness.

Focus on how God provides for His own. It took three months to get from Egypt to Mount Sinai. During this time in which they made their way across the wilderness, they experienced the care and provision of God in many ways—both during the day-to-day journey and during the crisis time God provided. God provided for the children of Israel as He provides for us today.

I. God provides in the constant processes of life.

A. *God provides for us in the common processes of life.*

Remember the pillar of fire by night and the cloud by day (Exod. 13:22)? God's presence was with the children of Israel day and night in the constant processes of life. God was with them all of the time.

B. *How God provides for us in the constant processes of life:*
　　1. God is with us. God promised Moses, in calling him to the task of leading his people, "I will be with thee" (3:12). God never relented on that promise—or any other.
　　2. God believes in us. Even at those times when we hardly believe in ourselves, God believes in us. The story of "Wrong Way Riegels"—the University of California football player who recovered a Georgia Tech fumble in the 1929 Rose Bowl game and ran the wrong way for a touchdown—is well known. The sequel is not so well known. That fateful play occurred in the first half of the football game. The University of California coach was very quiet during the half-time intermission. Roy Riegels sat in a corner with a blanket on his shoulders and his face in his hands crying. When the time came to begin the second half, the coach announced that the players who played the first half would start the second half. They all got up and filed out except Riegels. The coach asked him if he had not heard what he said. Riegels replied that he could not go out there and play again; he had ruined himself; he had ruined the coach; he had ruined the University of California. The coach then told him that the game was only half over, that he should get up and go out there to play ball. The second half Roy Riegels played inspired football.
　　3. God provides for us daily. God's everyday provision and care for us we call providence. The providence of God cares for us daily.

II. God provides in the common problems of life.

A. *An assertion: God provides in the common problems of life.*
　　Consider the logistics of moving a crowd of people who could have numbered 2.5 million people. What would be the greatest problem? It was probably that of providing food and water for them. This God did.
　　On two occasions God gave water. The first time at Marah God made bitter water drinkable, sweet (15:22). The second time at Rephidim Moses struck the rock and brought forth water (17:7).
　　God fed them with the manna and the quails. Though these are natural occurrences, we consider them miracles because of prediction, timing, and source. From the events of providing the water and the food we learn that God provides in the common problems of life.

B. *An explanation: How God provides in the common problems of life.*
　　1. God can turn the bitter to sweet. Robert L. Lee is the executive director of the Louisiana Baptist Convention and has been for many years. He had a brother who was diagnosed with cancer at the age of seventeen. The family prayed unceasingly for the boy. The sarcoma exposed on his neck was removed surgically. The tumor that had appeared on his thigh was treated with radium. Incredibly, that was the end of the dreaded disease. He became a successful high school principal. A bitter experience was turned sweet by the grace of God.
　　2. God gives to us what we cannot get in any other way. Food in the wilderness was provided by the grace of God—there would have been no other way to have obtained food. It could not have been bought. It had to come from God.
　　3. God gives us these things as we need them. Notice in the instructions concerning the gathering of the manna that it could not be kept and stored. It had to be gathered every day and used that day. The manna, in Gerald

Kennedy's words, was "fresh every morning." Dietrich Bonhoeffer once remarked that he believed that God gives us courage for each situation. But He does not give it to us in advance, lest we fail to live in faith and dependence upon Him.

III. God provides in the critical pressures of life.

A. *God provides in the critical internal pressures of life.*

Within the ranks of the children of Israel, there was a critical pressure due to their murmuring against Moses and Aaron. As they traveled, they murmured and complained. In answer to those complaints God provided food and water as they needed it.

B. *God provides in the critical external pressures of life.*

Israel also faced critical pressures from the outside. There were problems they had not caused, and they did not know how to deal with them. During the course of their journey to Mount Sinai, the Israelites were attacked by the Amalekites. The Amalekites were kinfolk. Their origins went back to the patriarchal era. Amalek was a grandson of Esau. The tribe was nomadic and ranged over the Sinai Peninsula. The attack was unprovoked.

Israel fought the Amalekites. As long as Moses' hands were lifted, they won; when his hands fell, they lost. In his flaging strength, Moses had to have his hands held aloft by Aaron and Hur.

In those critical pressures of life God provided for them as He does for us. He holds our hands aloft and gives us strength.

Ben Fisher was the executive secretary of the Education Commission of the Southern Baptist Convention. When he discovered a malignancy, he retired from his position. He had been raised in the mountains of North Carolina, and he told his wife that he wanted to go back to the old country church.

The site of the old church is now behind a power impoundment for the water of one of the rivers in that state. The Fishers drove their car as far as they could go, then they walked across a footbridge. Finally they rode in a wagon to get to the little church.

Ben Fisher slipped off by himself and went to the little churchyard cemetery nearby. He read the names, dates, and inscriptions on the tombstones. He remembered and relived some of the experiences God had given him. He thanked God for the Sunday school teacher who had led him to Christ whose name was on one of the tombstones.

Then as he was ready to go, his attention was attracted to a small marker that must have marked the grave of a child. As he stooped down and brushed away the moss, he read the words, "The Shepherd will return for His lambs someday and the valley will bloom again."

Then Fisher said, "God's timing is unpredictable. But it is absolutely dependable. He will return for His lambs and the valleys are going to bloom again. That is a part of God's prescription for your predicament."

Conclusion. God does provide. And He does it in unique and unusual ways as well as in common and expected ways. Give your life in faith to that God who provides in love.
                                                              — JEC

* * *

WEDNESDAY EVENING, SEPTEMBER 19

TITLE: That Which Follows

TEXT: "Surely goodness and mercy shall follow me all the days of my life" (Ps. 23:6a).

SCRIPTURE READING: Psalm 23:1–6

Introduction. In the last verse of Psalm 23 it seems that one passes to pure anticipation. Memory meets hope. There the psalmist's trust refuses to yield to fear and rises higher and higher in a happy faith. In this verse, he speaks of that which follows the believer.

I. First, take notice of the meaning of the words *goodness* and *mercy*.

A. *One thought is that these two words go together as do the words* rod *and* staff *in verse 4.*

B. *For the discussion in this message, we shall look at them separately.*
 1. Goodness.
  a. Goodness is that which is graceful to the senses. It looks fair to the eye. It is a pleasant sound to the ear. It is a sweet scent to the smell. It is pleasing to the taste. It is pleasant to the touch.
  b. The purpose of goodness, according to the text, is to be well adapted, useful, and profitable.
  c. The measure is abundant.
  d. The moral of it is upright.
 2. Mercy.
  a. Mercy means kindness as shown in mutual favor. It is not getting what one deserves.
  b. It is the essential quality of God and is associated with forgiveness (Exod. 34:6–7), forbearance (Ps. 145:8), and His covenant of justice, faithfulness, and truth.
  c. This mercy goes forth to all (149:9). It shows itself in pitying help (Exod. 3:7). It is everlasting and associated with grace.

C. Goodness *and* mercy *together indicate that God is abundant in lovingkindness.* This leads to repentance (Rom. 2:4).

II. Second, make an application of these meanings to each life.

A. *No evil can slip in from the rear.* No foe is able to pursue, but rather God's bright angel is there to protect.

B. *Such protection supplies spiritual courage both for the present and for eternity.*

C. *Goodness and mercy are the Master's expert hands.*
 1. This is the supreme portrait of the Great Shepherd.
 2. This is the essence of all that has gone before.

D. *This outflow is to flow from one to another.* It follows one as a legacy to others who are followers of God.

Conclusion. The Christian should have a deep desire to leave behind blessings and benedictions to others. This is his legacy—goodness and mercy. — *DRG*

* * *

SUNDAY MORNING, SEPTEMBER 23

TITLE: Yielding to the Holy Spirit

TEXT: "Quench not the Spirit" (1 Thess. 5:19).

SCRIPTURE READING: 1 Thessalonians 5:19; Romans 6:13

HYMNS: "Great Is Thy Faithfulness," Chisholm
"Abide With Me," Lyte
"Never Alone," Anonymous

OFFERTORY PRAYER:

Holy Father, today we would praise You for all of Your gifts to us through Jesus Christ and through the continuing ministry of Your Holy Spirit. Thank You for Your blessings to us through the church. Thank You for Your blessings to us through spiritual leaders. Thank You for Your blessings through Christian friends. We come now bringing tithes and offerings to express our love for You and our desire to worship You in truth. In Jesus' name. Amen.

Introduction. When someone says to you, "I wish for you God's very best," what does he mean? Most probably, the sentiment behind that good wish is our friend's desire that we experience happiness and freedom from all the troubles which come in life, or that we be blessed with an abundance of material things. From the human standpoint there is nothing particularly wrong with that.

On the other hand, when we think about "God's very best," we must go considerably beyond these fair-weather concepts of what makes life worth living. "God's very best" for those who belong to Him involves what is happening to them right now *as it relates to preparing them for eternity,* not just for the next twenty-five or thirty years.

So the keyword that will open the door to understanding God's very best for us is the word *yield.* And the dictionary states that *yield* means "to give up, to surrender, to give place to." What, then, *is* "God's very best" for us? It is simply the discovery of the divine plan and purpose God has outlined for our lives, beginning in the here and now and continuing throughout eternity. We do not arrive at this magnificent discovery as a result of the efforts of human ingenuity. Rather, God unfolds His will and purpose for our lives *as we yield ourselves to His Holy Spirit within us.*

I. God's proposition.

Let us listen carefully to the *proposition* God makes to us through the words of the apostle Paul, "I beseech you therefore, brethren, by the mercies of God, that ye present your bodies a living sacrifice, holy, acceptable unto God, which is your reasonable service. And be not conformed to this world: but be ye transformed by the renewing of your mind, that ye may prove what is that good, and acceptable, and perfect, will of God" (Rom. 12:1–2).

A. *What is involved in this "proposition" God makes to us?* "I beseech you," Paul said. It is not a command, but a pleading for the believer to live that kind of life which will mark him as a child of God. This is not something we do to be saved, but because we *are* saved. Yielding is not an act of the intellect exclusively; it is an expression of the soul, the essence of a person's being.

B. *Paul indicates that there are two areas which should be affected by this "yielding."*

1. First he calls for a dedication of the *whole body* as a living sacrifice to God. This is a dedication, not a "consecration." *God* "consecrates"; man "dedicates." The fact that Paul singled out the body suggests that man is a total being; he is not compartmentalized into "spiritual" and "physical" insofar as his dedication to God is concerned. Thus, when we dedicate ourselves wholly to God, the Lord Jesus will be seen in everything we do.

2. Paul also tells us how this dedication of our bodies is maintained: "Be ye transformed by the renewing of your mind" (v. 2). This happens as Christ moves in and "thinks through us." Charles Sheldon's classic, *In His Steps,* tells of a congregation of people who determined not to do anything until they asked themselves, seriously, "What would Jesus do?" This, then, is what is involved in the "proposition" God has made to us in regard to yielding ourselves to His Spirit within us.

II. God's pattern.

There is a *pattern* God has provided through His Son, Jesus Christ.

A. *In no uncertain terms, God sets down for us the "game rules."* One of the many evidences of perfection in the life of Jesus was His complete dedication or yieldedness to the will of His Heavenly Father. Jesus' human body was the vehicle by which He carried out His Father's will while He was on earth. Likewise, the believer should think of his body as the "vehicle" God has provided through which he carries out the will and the wishes of *his* heavenly Father. Certainly we are not perfect as Jesus was; therefore the issue with us is not our dogged determination to do something ourselves; rather it is being willing to let God do it through us, by yielding to His Spirit within us.

B. *Because Jesus was dedicated to His Father's will, three things happened in His life.*

1. He was willing to *go* where His Father chose. We sing, "I'll go where You want me to go, dear Lord." Jesus did; would *we,* really?

2. Christ was willing to *be* whatever His Father chose for Him to be. He laid aside the glory He had with the Father in heaven in order to come to earth; He was willing to be rejected, humiliated, spat upon, and crucified. That was the Father's will for *Him.* We sing: "I'll be what You want me to be, dear Lord" Jesus did; would *we,* really?

3. Jesus was willing to *do* whatever His Father chose for Him to do. He became obedient unto death, even the death of the cross. We sing: "I'll do what You want me to do, dear Lord." Jesus did; would *we,* really?

C. *We must remember, lest we become discouraged with our own imperfection: "For it is God which worketh in you both to will and to do of his good pleasure"* (Phil. 2:13). In other words, God tells us what He wants us to do; then by His Spirit within us—as we yield to that Spirit—*He does it!* He energizes us, motivates us, and enables us to do His will.

III. God's purpose.

There is a *purpose* behind it all.

A. *Why are we to yield to the Holy Spirit within us?* What will bring it to pass in our lives? It is to understand more fully, every day that we live, the will of God for our lives.

B. *How are we to yield to the Holy Spirit?*
    1. First, God will lead us, by His Spirit, *if we are willing to do what He chooses for us to do.* Someone has said, "God will speak loud enough for a willing soul to hear." It is one thing to conceive some great, vague, far-distant will that God may have for our lives; but it is quite another thing to say, "Lord, what would you have me do *today,* in the midst of this humdrum, routine, often monotonous grind in which I live?"
    2. God's leading will always be *in accordance with the Scriptures.* It is never true with God that "the end justifies the means." There is no such thing as "sacrificing a minor principle" in order to accomplish an ultimate goal.
    3. This divine leadership is provided *by the Holy Spirit who indwells the Christian.* When we yield, or dedicate ourselves to God, then increasingly we come to have "the mind of Christ." We start to think like God thinks. And thus, He is able not only to convince us of what is wrong, but also to give us a clear understanding of what is right for us.

Conclusion. Sometimes we get the idea that to "sacrifice" means to experience pain—and therefore the Christian who has "sacrificed" in order to yield himself to God's will must be a sad-faced, morbid-type person. How ridiculous! Sacrifice simply means *doing another's will.* There may be some pain along the way, to be sure; but the prevailing atmosphere will be that of joy, and the blessing of God in one's life will be that of peace. Truly, "Thou wilt keep him in perfect peace, whose mind is stayed on thee, because he trusteth in thee" (Isa. 26:3). — *DLJ*

* * *

SUNDAY EVENING, SEPTEMBER 23

TITLE: How God Teaches Us

Text: **"And when the voice of the trumpet sounded long, and waxed louder and louder, Moses spake, and God answered him by a voice. And the Lord came down upon mount Sinai, on the top of the mount: and the Lord called Moses up to the top of the mount; and Moses went up" (Exod. 19:19–20).**

Scripture Reading: **Exodus 19:16–20; 20:1–17**

Introduction. Charles Dickens' novel *Great Expectations* is the story of Philip Pirrip, a village boy who was brought up by his difficult sister and her husband, a gentle, humorous, kindly blacksmith named Joe Gargery.
    "Pip" is introduced to the house of Miss Havisham, a lady half-crazed by the desertion of her lover on her bridal night. She had brought up a girl named Estella in a spirit of revenge. Estella was taught to use her beauty as a means of torturing men. Pip falls in love with Estella and aspires to become a gentleman.
    Money and the expectation of more wealth come to him from a mysterious source. Pip thinks it has come from Miss Havisham. He goes to London and abandons the humble Joe Gargery of whom he has become ashamed.
    Then misfortunes come upon him. His benefactor turns out to be Abel Magwitch, an escaped convict for whom Pip has rendered a service when he was a boy. His great expectations fade away, and he becomes penniless. Estella had married an enemy of his who had treated her cruelly.

Taught by adversity, Pip returns to Joe Gargery and honest labor. He is finally reunited with Estella, who has also learned her lesson.

The title of this book, *Great Expectations,* has always been intriguing to me, for God, too, had great expectations for His people.

When He brought the children of Israel to Mount Sinai after three months in the wilderness after the Exodus from Egypt, He gave them the law. The law outlined the expectations of God for His people; they were to live in covenant relationship with God.

Whenever you begin to examine the law as a Christian, there are certain things that have to be considered. One matter is that the law was designed to show the Hebrew people how to live in the community. Remember: they had not been self-governing people; they had been slaves. They had to have some way to guide and regulate their relationships together.

The law also was designed to show them how to live in covenant. The law was based on a covenant relationship with God. He would be their God; they would be His people. This is how the people of God were to live.

What do they mean to us today? Some matters obviously had to do with cultural matters and contemporary problems. They can be spotted and understood as such. We no longer live in a nomadic society in a prescientific setting in a desert area. But underlying it all are some principles upon which these relationships are based. The law encapsulated in the Ten Commandments. These still hold.

God has great expectations for us as His people. He teaches us what He expects of us and how we are to live with Him and with one another. Notice how He does this.

I. God teaches us with a covenant.

A. *A covenant is a promise made with God.* All of the law is based on the covenant made between God and His people. It is expressed succinctly in Exodus 19:4–6.

We can perhaps better understand the term *covenant* as an agreement, a contract, or a promise. In the Old Testament world two kinds of covenants were practiced. One was an agreement or covenant that was made between equals. The other was an agreement or covenant made between two parties of unequal strength. Obviously the covenant made between God and the people was between two parties of unequal strength. God, the stronger party, had initiated the covenant and had dictated its terms.

Briefly and simply, the covenant between God and the people of Israel was that He would be their God, and they would be His people.

The whole matter of the law is not just a collection of good ideas. This is how people who have covenanted with God, or promised their lives to Him, should live.

B. *God keeps His promise.* It boils down to the fact that God keeps His Word. He will do what He has promised to do.

As God keeps His Word and fulfills his promises to us, we should be just as faithful and obedient to Him.

II. God teaches us with commandments.

A. *The commandments are from God.* When Moses went up the mountain to meet God, he returned with two tablets of stone, the Ten Commandments.

These ten words, as the Hebrews call them, are on two tables, and they describe two relationships: the relationship between a person and God, and the relationship between two persons. They tell us how God wants us to act both toward Himself and toward one another.

B. *The commandments are principles.* They are not stated as rules or as "do's and don'ts" for every situation of life. They are principles which help us to know how to relate to God and to persons by the attitudes and the actions developed.

The Ten Commandments are negative in statement, which means they are liberating, for they allow everything that is not forbidden. A certain self-limitation and discipline is gained from them. They are apodictic in form; they are simply stated without provisions for implementation.

C. *The commandments are inclusive.* They include relationships between the individual and God, as well as with other pesons. Notice how inclusive they are.

1. How God is known. God is known as one God. There is no other God besides Him.

2. How God is worshiped. God is worshiped in spirit and in truth. He is not worshiped in material or physical representations of Himself.

3. How God is confessed. Belief in God is confessed with sincerity, not emptily nor in vain.

4. How God is remembered. One day in seven is uniquely dedicated to God. In that way He is remembered and worshiped regularly.

5. How parents are treated. Parents should have respect and reverence. There is a continuity to life. No generation begins life anew or all on its own. The fifth commandment is a transitional commandment between the two tables of the law.

6. How human life is regarded. The sanctity of human life is expressed and kept.

7. How human personality is respected. This shows respect for human personality. No person is to be treated as an "it" or an object. The sanctity of human personality as well as human life is shown. Also, the solidarity of family life is to be maintained.

8. How personal possessions are considered. Things that belong to other persons are inviolate. They are to be used to help others; they are not to be confiscated by others.

9. How the spoken word is valued. Persons should live in trust with one another, always speaking truth.

10. How attitudes are formed. No one should be covetous or envious of others. Those attitudes lead to overt actions which break the commandments of God.

III. God teaches us through commitment.

A. *Commitment is the basis for covenant.* The people responded to Moses' announcement that they were to enter into covenant with the God who delivered them and to receive the law from Him with these words, "All that the LORD hath spoken we will do" (Exod. 19:8). They ratified the covenant with God (chap. 24). Later they had a covenant renewal ceremony (chap. 34).

B. *We commit ourselves to God.* We begin with commiting ourselves to the God who has covenanted with us. We know Him through Jesus Christ His Son: "God was in Christ, reconciling the world unto himself" (2 Cor. 5:19).

C. *We commit ourselves to living by His principles.* We commit ourselves to keeping His commandments, to living up to His great expectations for us. We commit ourselves to witness and work in the world so that being a Christian makes a difference in that world.

Conclusion. God has great expectations for us. He leads us to commitment to Himself so He might teach us how to live. Let us learn that lesson well. — *JEC*

* * *

WEDNESDAY EVENING, SEPTEMBER 26

TITLE: The Eternal Place of Abode

TEXT: "I will dwell in the house of the LORD for ever" (Ps. 23:6b).

SCRIPTURE READING: Psalm 23:1–6

Introduction. This sentence brings to a conclusion one of the greatest pieces of literature of all times. It is also the climax to this great psalm.

I. Dwelling in the presence of God is a present reality.

A. *One whose faith is fixed on God has continued communion with Him.* The Christian's life is hid in Him. His presence is wherever one goes and whatever one does.

B. *There are two other passages of Scripture that support this idea.*
1. Deuteronomy 33:25 says, "As thy days, so shall thy strength be."
2. Philippians 4:19 says, "My God shall supply all your need according to his riches in glory by Christ Jesus."

II. Dwelling in God's presence refers to the heavenly home.

A. *The hope presented in this verse rises above even that presented in verse 5 of Psalm 23, "Thou preparest a table before me."*
1. In verse 5, the singer sees himself as a guest at God's table, which is spread before him.
2. In verse 6, the singer is a dweller in the presence of God. He is not a guest but a member of the household.

B. *This verse shows that God will bring those whom He has fed, guided, and protected in journeying and conflict to an unchanging mansion in His home beyond the stars.*

C. *This brings some thoughts to the forefront that conclude the psalm.*
1. It is dwelling in the house of the Lord that enables one to realize the beauty of the Lord, as well as His unselfish love and forgiving spirit.
2. It is by dwelling in the house of the Lord that the Christian is able to throw off his imperfections and live there in perfection.
3. It is by dwelling in the house of the Lord that the dweller is able to enjoy the fullness of joy and the glorious fellowship that knows no pain.
4. It is by dwelling in the house of the Lord that makes for perfect intercourse with God, which includes perfect worship, communion, obedience, and guidance.

Conclusion. "One thing have I desired of the LORD, that will I seek after; that I may dwell in the house of the LORD all the days of my life, to behold the beauty of the LORD, and to inquire in his temple" (27:4).   — *DRG*

* * *

SUNDAY MORNING, SEPTEMBER 30

TITLE: Walking in the Spirit

TEXT: "This I say then, Walk in the Spirit, and ye shall not fulfill the lust of the flesh" (Gal. 5:16).

SCRIPTURE READING: Galatians 5:16–18

HYMNS: "Holy, Holy, Holy," Heber
"Have Faith in God," McKinney
"Holy Ghost, With Light Divine," Reed

OFFERTORY PRAYER:
Gracious Father, for Your kindness to us, we thank You and praise You. We come this morning bringing tithes and offerings as symbols of our desire to be totally available for Your glory and for the good of other people. Bless these gifts in proclaiming the message of Your love to this community and to the ends of the earth. In Jesus' name we pray. Amen.

Introduction. We come this morning to the last in our series of five studies under the theme "Growing Quality Christians." We have dealt exclusively with the ministry of the Holy Spirit in the believer's life, for it is only by means of *His* work within a believer that any kind of genuine spiritual quality can be produced. We shall conclude our study this morning on a positive note. Our theme is *continuity:* How does a Christian live his faith on a day-by-day basis so that this "quality Christianity" is maintained within one's life? We do so by "walking in the Spirit." In the New Testament, the expression "walking" did not always have reference to a physical, ambulatory activity. More often it described the daily, consistent, continuing conduct of a believer.

"Walking in the Spirit" means that we must come to the point of relying completely upon the ability and power of the One who indwells us. When we do this, the quality, or the distinguishing characteristic of a Christian, begins to be seen in us. Now *why* is this a daily necessity for the Christian?

I. Daily living in the presence of the Holy Spirit within is a necessity because of the difference between living God's way and living the world's way.

A. *The rules for living the Christian life are set down for us in portions of the Gospels, in the Book of Acts, and in the Epistles.* These are the "heavenly standards" God has set forth for Christians to live by. He never intended for the "world" to try to live by them. In fact, these principles are not lived *by* us but *through* us, as we yield to the Holy Spirit within us.

B. *What are some of these "heavenly requirements" which go to make up "quality Christianity"?* Jesus said, "A new commandment I give to you, That ye love one another; as I have loved you, that ye also love one another" (John 13:34). The Old Testament law required that one love his neighbor "as he loved himself." That is the essence of the Golden Rule. The world can adopt that standard after a fashion. It makes for harmonious living on the earth-level. But Jesus said infinitely more than that. *He* said, "Love one another *not* as you love yourselves, *but as I have loved you!"* To love as Christ has loved us is a level of love the natural man knows nothing about. It makes it possible to love an unlovable and undesirable person, one who has maligned or mistreated us.

C. *Another "heavenly requirement" which will result in quality Christianity is expressed in Paul's word to the Ephesians: "Giving thanks always for all things unto God and the Father in the name of our Lord Jesus Christ"* (Eph. 5:20). On the surface, that sounds simple enough. But it means being able to thank God for *everything* that comes into one's life—the baffling circumstances, the painful things, the heart-breaking hours—with the full awareness that God knows everything that is happening to His children, and that He is ultimately going to "turn every thorn into a rosebud"!

D. *Again, to the Thessalonians, Paul issued, in stacatto fashion, a whole list of exhortations, including these two: "Rejoice evermore. Pray without ceasing"* (1 Thess. 5:16–17). Be filled with inner joy even when circumstances on the outside are discouraging. Maintain an open line of communication with God so that prayer is a normal attitude in your life—not a crisis experience only.

II. Daily living in the presence of the Holy Spirit within is a necessity because of the enemy the Christian faces.

A. *The Bible clearly states that Satan is the archenemy of God and of God's people.* There is no controversy between Satan and unsaved people. They are already a part of his world-system. Furthermore, Satan is one of the foremost promoters of "religion." He encourages those refined, cultured religions which promote human excellence, which deify man, and which teach that man can eventually become as God because of his own goodness and through his own efforts.

B. *James told us, in his epistle, to "resist the devil, and he will flee from you"* (4:7b). But there is only one way that we can resist the devil and his temptations, and that is by submitting, yielding to the Holy Spirit within us. Though Satan is inferior to God, he is *superior* to man, and he cannot be conquered by man alone. The Christian's conflict with Satan is as fierce and unceasing as Satan can make it. Before him, we in ourselves are as nothing. But God has anticipated our helplessness before Satan, and He has provided the resources with which we can overcome him. Listen: "Greater is he that is in you, than he that is in the world" (1 John 4:4). Who is "he that is in us"? The indwelling Holy Spirit! Thus, if we would overcome the most vicious enemy of our souls, we must "walk in the Spirit"—we must live our lives daily in the conscious presence of His power.

III. The presence of the Holy Spirit within us is a necessity because of the old nature of Adam which is still a part of us.

A. *The Bible teaches that when one receives Christ as Savior, he is redeemed, that is, he is "brought back" from the kingdom of Satan.* This is an eternal and completed transaction. It is sealed in heaven, never to be repeated or undone. But we are talking about the soul, the spirit of man. On the other hand, these bodies, or our physical lives, are not yet redeemed. Our bodies will not be redeemed until Jesus comes. But in that moment, we must live in these unredeemed bodies, which are subject to sin, to disobedience toward God.

B. *Therefore, our "redeemed souls" are constantly in conflict with our "unredeemed bodies."* Satan cannot touch our souls, so he aims his attacks at our physical lives. Why? Because, as the Bible teaches, these bodies are the "temples of the Holy Spirit" who indwells us. And how do we overcome this "Adam nature" which is part of us? We daily renew our dedication to the Spirit of God within us. We "walk daily" in His power and strength. And as we do this, "we die daily" (1 Cor. 15:31). That is, the old nature which is as yet unredeemed is given a "death blow" every day. No one ever reaches the plateau of spiritual achievement where he is no longer tempted by this old flesh in which we live. Our physical nature is Satan's battleground.

Conclusion. So how can we sum up, in a sentence, all that we have tried to say during these past five weeks? Simply like this, "I live; yet not I, but Christ liveth in me: and the life I now live in the flesh I live by the faith of the Son of God, who loved me, and gave himself for me" (Gal. 2:20). Quality Christianity "happens" as the Christian surrenders, in glorious acquiescence, to the Holy Spirit within him.　　　　　　　　　　　　　　　　　　　　　　　*— DLJ*

* * *

SUNDAY EVENING, SEPTEMBER 30

TITLE: How God Reaches Us

TEXT: **"And there I will meet with the children of Israel, and the tabernacle shall be sanctified by my glory. . . . And they shall know that I am the LORD their God, that brought them forth out of the land of Egypt, that I may dwell among them: I am the LORD their God" (Exod. 29:43, 46).**

SCRIPTURE READING: **Exodus 25:1–9; 29:43–46**

Introduction. Several years ago the London *Daily Mirror* carried a story about an elite community in Massachusetts. The reporter wrote about wealthy neighbors who met for fellowship on Sunday mornings at the town dump. These cultured people carted their week's trash in their Chryslers and Thunderbirds to the dump, then stayed on to gossip and occasionally pick out of the debris some item to carry home. The writer reported that at one dumping party they brought their martinis and plates of hors d'oeuvres for a Sunday-morning get-together. Instead of fellowship with one another at the Lord's house on the Lord's Day, these people had fellowship with one another at the town dump—in the midst of the rubbish, broken chairs, discarded mattresses, old crates and boxes, and refuse.

We get what we go after. If fellowship with other people is all we want, the town dump may be as good as anyplace to go. If fellowship with Almighty God is what we want, then the church of the Lord Jesus Christ is the place to go.

A recurring human problem is how and where we are to worship God. This was one of the problems faced by Moses and the children of Israel. They stayed at Mount Sinai for nearly a year. Then they began their journey to Canaan and the Promised Land. A bleak desert separated Mount Sinai from Canaan. They were destined to wander in that desert for forty years before they crossed the Jordan River into the Promised Land. They would never have survived the years of wilderness wandering had not God accompanied them and watched over them. The symbol of His presence in their midst was the tabernacle.

Actually a tent within a tent, the tabernacle was built according to the specific instructions of God. Moses spent forty days and nights on Mount Sinai receiving the instructions for building the tabernacle. God showed him the form of the tabernacle with all its furnishings.

We often face two extremes when we come to the tabernacle: one is to avoid it, the other is to allegorize it and thus distort its meaning. We should steer clear of both these extremes. The tabernacling presence of God with the people of Israel was a central and important fact of their existence. It was how God reached them.

A great deal of the Book of Exodus is given over to instructions for worship, specifically the tabernacle, which was a portable sanctuary. God reaches us as we worship Him. The tabernacle and worship through it show how God reaches us in worship.

I. God reaches us in the symbols of God.

A. *The tabernacle was a symbol of the presence of God with the Israelites.* This was the glory of God (shekinah) that was always with them. God is always present with us.

1. God tabernacled with the children of Israel in the wilderness. The tabernacle always reminded the people that God was with them. Martin Buber once described Israel's God as a great deity of the road. They never went anywhere without the presence of God.

2. God tabernacled with us more completely in Jesus Christ. John 1:14 reminds us, "And the Word was made flesh, and dwelt among us, (and we beheld his glory, the glory as of the only begotten of the Father,) full of grace and truth." The word that is translated *dwelt* really means "tabernacled." In Christ, God pitched His tent among us. The tabernacling presence of God is known through Jesus Christ.

3. God promised His eternal presence with us. Listen to the promise of God as expressed by John in the Book of the Revelation, "And I heard a great voice out of heaven saying, Behold, the tabernacle of God is with men, and he will dwell with them, and they shall be his people, and God himself shall be with them, and be their God" (21:3).

B. *Symbols continue to remind us of the presence of God with us.* Symbols have always been a part of worship. The most common symbol in Christian worship is the cross, which always reminds us of the cost of our salvation. Places of worship are constructed in ways that use symbolism to remind us of God's presence in worship. Many church buildings are built in the form of a cross. The placing of the pulpit in the center of the platform, the focus of attention, emphasizes the importance of the proclamation of the Word of God. The spire points our thoughts heavenward.

II. God reaches us through service to God.

The tabernacle was built according to God's specifications, but it was built by God's people. Worship is not simply being reminded of the presence of God; it also must issue in service to God. In the construction of the tabernacle we see something of how we can serve God.

A. *Sacrifice.* We can serve God by sacrificing what we have to God and to His use. The children of Israel took an offering of the things needed to build the tabernacle. The people gave of what they had. In fact, they brought so much, they finally had to stop the giving.

"And Moses gave commandment, and they caused it to be proclaimed throughout the camp, saying, Let neither man nor woman make any more work for the offering of the sanctuary. So the people were restrained from bringing. For the stuff they had was sufficient for all the work to make it, and too much" (Exod. 36:6–7).

B. *Skill.* Skilled workmen were enlisted from among the people. They were enlisted to do the work on the tabernacle. Observe: "And Moses called Bezaleel and Aholiab, and every wise hearted man, in whose heart the LORD had put wisdom, even every one whose heart stirred him up to come unto the work to do it" (36:2).

Their ministry was what they were skilled in doing. The Lord never calls us to do what we cannot do for Him. But He does call us to use the skills we have in service to Him.

III: God reaches us through salvation from God.

A. *Salvation is the result of worship.* The end result of worship is that we might know the salvation of God. Worship is to bring us into communion and fellowship with God.

B. *Salvation must come on God's terms.* We often wonder why the Book of Exodus goes into such detail about the construction of the tabernacle and the performance of worship. The reason is that the worship of God that results in salvation must be done on His terms, not on ours. Some people feel that all of the other religions of the world are the expressions of humankind's attempt to reach God. God tells us how He reaches us. He reaches us in the worship of God.

Salvation is the gift of God's grace. In Exodus the Lord kept reminding the people that deliverance came to them from God's hand. And that the God whom they now worshiped according to those specifications was the very same God who had delivered them from the hands of the Egyptians. Just as in the Exodus experience God specified how the people would be delivered in the Passover—by the blood of the lamb on the doorpost—so does God specify how persons might be saved now—by the blood of the Lamb of God shed on the cross.

The promise of salvation from God is expressed in Exodus 33:14, "And he said, My presence shall go with thee, and I will give thee rest." In the *Broadman Bible Commentary* Roy Honeycutt observed that this promise to Moses is that God will lead persons to that rest in which the hope of unhindered communion and wholeness will become a reality. That is salvation.

C. *Salvation is the transformation of life.* Goodness is not enough. What we need is the salvation that God gives to us through the transformation of life.

Some years ago the *New York Times Book Review* reviewed a book on the life of Mahatma Gandhi. It detailed his accomplishments in the achievement of independence for India through nonviolent revolution. But it also indicated that many of the things that Gandhi had advocated hindered the progress of India. They needed industrialization, but Gandhi emphazied cottage crafts. They needed population control, but Gandhi advocated large families. They needed to end the caste system, but at the death of Gandhi there were more untouchables whose lives were miserable than there were when he began his movement. The final statement of the review indicated that the major lesson to be learned from the brilliant life of Mahatma Gandhi was that goodness was not enough.

That is the Christian message. Goodness is not enough. What is needed is transformation, a new birth, salvation through Jesus Christ. Whenever God reaches us in worship, we are once more made aware that goodness is not enough, that the transformation of life through salvation is needed, and that comes through faith in Jesus Christ.

Conclusion. God reaches us in worship. There in the presence of God we can receive salvation from God and enter into service to God. In worship God reaches us and our lives are made new.   *— JEC*

* * *

SUGGESTED PREACHING PROGRAM
FOR THE MONTH OF OCTOBER

Sunday Mornings

On every Lord's Day the plan of salvation should be explained. We should be busy at the task of sharing the good news of salvation along the way every day. It is suggested that during the month of October a special emphasis be placed upon evangelistic preaching. The suggested theme is "The Urgency of Deciding for Christ Now."

Sunday Evenings

These messages are evangelistic in objective. The theme is "Christ Can Bring About Great Change for Good in Your Life If You Will Let Him."

Wednesday Evenings

A series of devotional messages based on the great messianic types and figures of the Old Testament is suggested. The theme is "Foregleams of Christ in the Old Testament."

* * *

WEDNESDAY EVENING, OCTOBER 3

TITLE: Christ and Adam's Rib

TEXT: "And the LORD God caused a deep sleep to fall upon Adam, and he slept: and he took one of his ribs, and closed up the flesh instead thereof; and the rib, which the LORD God had taken from man, made he a woman, and brought her unto the man" (Gen. 2:21-22). "For this cause shall a man leave his father and mother, and shall be joined unto his wife, and they two shall be one flesh" (Eph. 5:31).

SCRIPTURE READING: Genesis 2:21-24; Ephesians 5:30-32

Introduction. There are many reasons why the Bible is a miracle book; but perhaps the most remarkable reason is that its focal point, its central figure, is the Lord Jesus Christ. From Genesis, which commences at the beginning of time as we know it, to Revelation, which brings to a consummation all things relating to man and this universe, Jesus is there—either in full focus or standing in the shadows of prophetic symbolism.

Every major event recorded in the Bible has some connection with God's revelation concerning Christ, either directly or indirectly. In the resurrected Savior's conversation with the two on the Road to Emmaus, he said, "O fools, and slow of heart to believe all that the prophets have spoken: ought not Christ to have suffered these things, and to enter into his glory? And beginning at Moses and all the prophets, he expounded unto them in all the scriptures the things concerning himself" (Luke 24:25-27).

For thirteen Wednesday evenings, we shall take a grand tour down the hallways of the Old Testament. The purpose of this study shall be twofold: first, to point to Jesus as the Savior, and second, to stimulate in believers the habit of searching for Jesus every time any portion of God's Word is read.

Our study begins with the sixth day of creation—the day on which God made man—and we stand amazed at the marvelous foregleam of Christ we find there.

I. Adam as a picture of the Lord Jesus.

A. *It is common, in a study of the Old Testament patriarchs, to point out how a number of them are types of the Lord Jesus Christ.* Abel, Isaac, Jacob, Joseph, David, and many others demonstrated human likenesses to the perfect life Jesus lived on earth. But seldom do we think of Adam as being a type of Christ. Yet in 1 Corinthians 15, Paul refers to Christ as "the second man" and the "last Adam."

In Ephesians 5, Paul teaches that Christ is the Savior and Redeemer of the church, His chosen bride. In speaking about the relationship between husband and wife, Paul says, "For this cause shall a man leave his father and mother, and shall be joined unto his wife, and they two shall be one flesh" (Eph. 5:31). There Paul quotes directly from Genesis 2:24. Then Paul concludes his analogy by stating, "This is a great mystery: but I speak concerning Christ and the church" (v. 32).

B. *What is this "great mystery" Paul refers to?* It must be that Jesus Christ, the spotless, sinless Son of God, should be willing to leave His Father's house in heaven and come into the world to save a fallen, sinful, unfaithful "wife," even by dying on the cross for her! *This* is the mystery, and Paul says plainly, "I speak concerning Christ and the church." Adam, therefore, becomes a type of Christ in his relationship to His beloved bride, the church. When Eve partook of the forbidden fruit, she broke God's commandment and became a fallen sinner under the sentence of spiritual death. Adam had lost his bride; communion between them had been broken. They were no longer one.

But Adam loved Eve above all things. Eve needed a Redeemer, and this Redeemer must be of *her seed*. But how could Eve bring forth a seed without a husband? Adam could not be the father of her seed as long as he was separated from her by her sin. How then could this gulf be bridged between the two of them? Eve could not be raised to Adam's level of innocence without a Redeemer, and that Redeemer must be the seed of woman, and the only man who could become the father of that seed was Adam. Thus Adam lowered himself to *her* level, assumed her guilt, became partaker of her sin and condemnation, and then became the father of her seed. Adam deliberately, willingly, and with full knowledge of the consequences took the fruit and "did eat."

C. *Adam had now made Eve's sin his own responsibility and made himself subject to death by becoming partaker of the curse.* Paul commented on this: "For Adam was first formed, then Eve. And Adam was not deceived, but the woman being deceived was in the transgression. Notwithstanding she shall be saved in childbearing, if they continue in faith and charity and holiness with sobriety [earnestness]" (1 Tim. 2:13–15).

Adam was not deceived; he knew what he was doing. Adam partook of Eve's sin and thus made it possible for her to bear children. Jesus could not have been born save "through the seed of woman," according to God's plan. In Romans 5:14, Paul said, "Nevertheless death reigned from Adam to Moses, even over them that had not sinned after the similitude of Adam's transgression, who is the figure of him that was to come." Paul was obviously comparing Adam with Christ. *We* sin because we are sinners by nature. *Adam* became a sinner because he deliberately chose to share in the sin of Eve. In this, according to Paul, he was the "figure" (or type) of Christ. Of course, the "type" can never do justice to the "antitype." Adam was a sinner; Jesus was not. In no way are we exalting Adam or exonerating him from his sin. Yet Jesus *became sin* (though not a sinner!) for us, that we might be saved.

II. The significance of Adam's rib.

While Adam slept, God created from his wounded side a wife, who was part of himself; and Adam paid for her by the shedding of his blood. Adam said, "This is now bone of my bones, and flesh of my flesh." And Paul said, "For we are members of his [Jesus'] body, of his flesh, and of his bones" (Eph. 5:30). The Lord Jesus left His Father's house to gain His bride at the price of His blood. Jesus, the last Adam, like the first one, must be put to sleep (i.e., death) to purchase His bride, the church. Jesus' side, too, was opened while He was on the cross, and from that wounded side redemption flowed.

In the creation of Eve, Adam shed his literal blood. God opened his side, and this implies a wound and bloodshedding. Here then, at the very dawn of creation, even before man had sinned, we have an implied reference to a "new creature" taken from the side of a man and becoming a part of him, even of his flesh and bones. The church, which is Christ's body, was also purchased by the Lord Jesus. His side, too, was opened and the cleansing water and His justifying blood flowed forth.

Conclusion. Through Adam's disobedience and sin, God has provided for us a picture, a shadow, of what the perfect, *sinless* Christ Jesus did in "becoming sin" for us. And today, every time a person receives Christ as his Savior, the Holy Spirit is continuing His work on that "rib"; and one day He will present the completed bride, the church, to the Bridegroom, the "second Adam," the Lord Jesus Christ.   —DLJ

* * *

SUNDAY MORNING, OCTOBER 7

TITLE: **Death Is Defeated**

TEXT: **"And as it is appointed unto men once to die, but after this the judgment: So Christ was once offered to bear the sins of many; and unto them that look for him shall he appear the second time without sin unto salvation" (Heb. 9:27–28).**

SCRIPTURE READING: Hebrews 9:27–28

HYMNS: "Low in the Grave He Lay," Lowry
          "On Jordan's Stormy Banks," McIntosh
          "Amazing Grace," Newton

OFFERTORY PRAYER:

O eternal God, You have made everlasting life with You a possibility through Jesus Christ. By placing our faith in Him death is no longer a tragedy. It is but a transition into a higher and better existence. As we think of the multitudes who have never discovered the hope of eternal life, we become more aware of our opportunity to give without reservation. Your gift was so generous to us; help us also to be generous as we give to You. In Jesus Christ's name we pray. Amen.

Introduction. *They Shoot Horses, Don't They?* is the title of a book written in 1935 and made into a film in 1970. It is the story of two desperate young people who are carried relentlessly toward their fate. That fate is death.

This story leaves a person a little bit sympathetic and very sick. But it does do one thing. It brings one face to face with hardship and death. In days gone by everyone talked about death. But now no one wants to talk about death. Hebrews 9:27-28 talks candidly of death.

I. Death is a reality.

Some time ago a famous evangelist made the comment that "Death is as much a part of life as living itself."

Hebrews 9:27 says it is appointed unto men once to die. No one can live forever. Even the patriarchs of the Bible who lived hundreds of years came to the time they had to take leave of life. How close is death? It is as close as one malignant cell, one heartbeat, one breath, one blood clot, one bad decision on a motorcycle. Death is a reality.

II. Death is inescapable.

One of Aesop's fables tells of a wealthy man who sends his servant down to the marketplace in Baghdad. After a brief time the servant returned as white as a sheet. "Well," said the master, "what is wrong with you?" The servant replied, "Oh, sir, I was down in the marketplace. I felt something strange behind me. I turned and I saw Death. She beckoned for me to come to her. Master, master, let me have your swiftest horse that I might ride to Samaria and escape Death." The master gave him permission. The servant rode as fast as he could to escape the icy fingers of death. Later in the day the master himself went down to the marketplace. There he too saw Death. "Death," said he, "why did you frighten my servant by beckoning him to come to you?" Death replied, "Sir, my gesture was not one of beckoning, rather it was one of surprise. I was surprised to see your servant in Baghdad, for I have an appointment with him tonight in Samaria."

In the Book of Amos we are told of a man who was taking a walk. He turned a corner and faced a ferocious lion. Realizing that his life was in danger, he climbed a tree. The lion sniffed around the trunk and went on his way. The man came down and started walking again. He topped a hill and came face to face with a mother bear and her cubs. She began to chase him. He realized his life was in danger once again. He ran as quickly as possible to his home and slammed the door of his house in the face of the bear. He was safe! In order to rest himself, he leaned his hand against the wall. Out of the cranny of the wall a viper struck his hand. He was dead within the moment. The Book of Hebrews says that death is inescapable. It is appointed by God and ordained that all men die. This includes businessmen, housewives, professional football players, young people, and children.

III. Death has spiritual dimensions.

Hebrews 9:27 says, "It is appointed unto men once to die, but after this the judgment.'' The decisions you make in life determine your destiny. The Bible tells us that there are three types of death. All are caused by rebellion and sin. Each type of death represents a kind of separation.

A. *Physical death.* Genesis 1–3 tells how God created Adam and Eve. He put them in the Garden of Eden. He gave them liberty to eat of all the fruit of the trees except one. That one tree was placed in the midst of the garden to test character and develop conscience in the lives of the first man and woman. Then Satan came along and said to Eve, ''The Lord has said that you can't eat from any of the trees in the garden.''

She replied, ''No, that is wrong. We can eat from any of the trees in the garden except one. The day that we eat we shall die.''

''No,'' said Satan, ''you'll not die, for God knows that the day you eat, you shall become like Him with the ability to discern between right and wrong. Look at the fruit. It is good to eat. It will make you wise. It will give you wisdom. It is beautiful. Take and eat.''

Eve ate. Adam ate. They didn't die on that day, but they were separated from the garden in which grew the Tree of Life. In time, they did die. Romans 5:12 says, ''When Adam sinned, sin entered the entire human race. His sin spread death throughout all the world, so everything began to grow old and die, for all sinned'' (LB).

B. *Spiritual death.* Ephesians 2:1 says, ''You . . . who were dead in trespasses and sin.'' The moment a person sins he is immediately separated from God. One is alienated from Him. You who sin are alive, and He is alive; but for all practical purposes you are dead to each other. That is spiritual death.

C. *Eternal death.* He who is spiritually dead and dies physically without Christ will be condemned to the eternal death. Revelation 21:8 says, ''But the fearful, and unbelieving, and the abominable, and murderers, and whoremongers, and sorcerers, and idolators, and all liars, shall have their part in the lake which burneth with fire and brimstone: which is the second death.'' The second death of this verse refers to an eternal separation from God. The worst thing about hell is that separation. All of this leads to the question, ''When you get where you're going, where will you be?''

IV. Death is defeated by Christ.

In the same way that the cure for smallpox is a cowpox germ and the cure for a poisonous snake bite is snake venom, man's cure for death was the death of Jesus Christ on the cross. *Christ's resurrection* proved that He was the victor over death and that there is a life beyond.

Conclusion. Some time ago a Christian was talking to a Mohammedan. In his witness he said, ''We believe that God revealed Himself through the book that is called the Bible.''

The Mohammedan replied,''We believe that God has revealed Himself through the book that is called the Koran.''

The Christian said, ''We believe that God has revealed Himself climactically through Jesus Christ.''

The Mohammedan said, ''We believe, too, that God revealed Himself through a man. His name is Mohammed.''

The Christian said, ''We believe that Jesus Christ died on the cross for our sins.''

The Mohammedan said, "We believe that Mohammed died for the benefit of his followers."

The Christian said, "We believe that Jesus Christ rose from the grave on the third day."

The Mohammedan bowed his head for a moment and thought seriously. Then he raised his eyes and said, "We do not know what happened to our religious leader after his death."

Jesus Christ is the only founder of a world religion who died and was raised from the grave.

This resurrected Christ gives victory in the midst of struggle. He gives hope in the world of darkness. He gives real meaning to life. He takes the sting out of death. He gives confidence in the face of death.

All ought to trust Christ and experience the results of His promises.   — *GW*

* * *

SUNDAY EVENING, OCTOBER 7

TITLE: What Must I Do to Be Saved?

TEXT: "And after he brought them out, he said, 'Sirs, what must I do to be saved?' And they said, 'Believe in the Lord Jesus, and you shall be saved, you and your household' " (Acts 16:30–31 NASB).

SCRIPTURE READING: Acts 16:19–34

Introduction. There are many important questions in life, but this question is the most important of all: "What must I do to be saved?"

It is life's most important question because it is about salvation, man's greatest need and God's greatest gift.

It is a personal question, "What must *I* do to be saved?" Each one stands individually before God and answers for his own relationship to Him.

It is an urgent question, one that emphasizes "must." It is life's most fundamental necessity. We cannot ignore it without personal and eternal damage to ourselves.

Let me tell you simply how to be saved.

I. If you are to be saved, you must know that you need to be.

The jailer saw his need and asked the question. He knew something was wrong in his life and was honest enough to acknowledge it.

However, it is hard to be honest with ourselves about our spiritual need. Three Scripture verses indicate why: (1) Satan blinds our eyes from Christ (2 Cor. 4:4); (2) sin deceives us (Heb. 3:13); and (3) our own hearts deceive us (Jer. 17:9).

The truth is, we have many needs—physical, mental, material, and social—but our greatest need is spiritual. The Bible says that everyone is a sinner (Isa. 53:6; John 3:18; Rom. 3:23). It also says that everyone is spiritually lost (Luke 15; 19:10), and that everyone who is without Christ is spiritually and eternally lost (Matt. 13:41–42; Rom. 6:23; Rev. 21:8). The need to be saved is deep and urgent and personal!

II. If you are to be saved, you must know that you can be.

There is hope or the jailer would not have asked for it. That hope is real! The answer to the question says you can be saved, "Believe in the Lord Jesus, and you shall be saved." The Bible says two strong things.

A. *God wants to save you.* This is what John 3:16 means. God loved the world and God gave His Son. God did something for you that you cannot do for yourself. Ephesians 2:8 says that it is by grace that we are saved and not of ourselves. God must do something, and He did it because He wanted to.

B. *God provided salvation through Jesus Christ.* Jesus Christ is God's provision (1 Tim. 1:15). Jesus Christ is our sacrifice for sins (John 14:6; Acts 4:12; 1 Cor. 15:3). Jesus Christ is God's gift of salvation (Rom. 6:23). Jesus Christ is the living Savior and Lord (Heb. 7:25). What hope there is for you in Him!

III. If you are to be saved, you must respond to Jesus Christ in your life.
Acts 16:31 says, "Believe on the Lord Jesus. . . ."

A. *You must want to be saved.* Salvation is impossible without that desire. God will not force you, nor can any man do so. You must want Him for yourself. C. H. Spurgeon once said, "Wanting to be saved is nine-tenths of salvation."

B. *You must receive Jesus Christ through repentance and faith.* Acts 20:21 says, "Solemnly testifying to both Jews and Greeks of repentance toward God and faith in our Lord Jesus Christ" (NASB).

Repentance is a change of mind, an expression of desire, and an act of the will. It is knowing we have sinned, we sorrow for it, and we turn from it. We turn from sin to God!

Faith is trusting Christ alone for salvation. It involves belief, acceptance, and surrender. Faith acknowledges the truth of Christ; it accepts the facts of His life, death, and resurrection; and it commits, trusts, and surrenders to Him. It is "receiving" Him, as John 1:12 says. It is "opening the door" of our hearts to Him, as Revelation 3:20 says. Right then and there Jesus Christ comes into your heart.

IV. Then, because you are saved, you confess Christ before men.
Romans 10:9–10 says that you believe in your heart and confess with your mouth. Matthew 10:32–33 says we either confess or deny Christ before men.

This is what the jailer did. He believed! He surrendered to Christ and openly confessed this new relationship with Him.

Conclusion. Now is the moment for you to ask your personal question and receive Christ's answer. The result will be eternal salvation and spiritual joy. Purpose this moment to say to Christ, "I open the door of my heart and receive You as my Lord and Savior."   *— TSB*

* * *

WEDNESDAY EVENING, OCTOBER 10

TITLE: The Protevangelium—The First Gospel Message

TEXT: **"And I will put enmity between thee and the woman, and between thy seed and her seed; it shall bruise thy head, and thou shalt bruise his heel" (Gen. 3:15). "Do not think that I will accuse you to the Father: there** is one that accuseth you, even Moses, in whom ye trust. For had ye believed Moses, ye would have believed me: for he wrote of me. But if ye believe not his writings, how shall ye believe my words?" (John 5:45–47).

SCRIPTURE READING: **Genesis 3:15; John 5:45–47; 1 Peter 1:8–11**

Introduction. Genesis 3:15 stands at the head of a long line of thrilling statements in the Bible which gave mankind assurance that God would send a Redeemer to salvage lost human beings from their eternally hopeless state. We call Genesis 3:15 the "Protevangelium" because it is the first promise of a coming Redeemer in the Scriptures. The New Testament passage we have chosen as part of our text (John 5:45–47) is evidence that Jesus took special pains to emphasize His firm belief in the truth of the Pentateuch—that it was historically accurate and divinely authentic. On the particular day Jesus spoke these words, the Jews were criticizing Him for healing the lame man at the Pool of Bethesda on the Sabbath. Again and again, throughout His teaching and preaching, Jesus quoted from the books of Moses.

Thus, this evening we shall examine this remarkable foregleam of our Savior's coming to be mankind's Redeemer.

I. What was its cause?
What was the occasion which prompted it?

A. *The first two chapters of Genesis contain the brilliant account of the creation of the world, climaxing, like the mighty crescendo of an orchestra, with the creation of man.* But into that scene of pristine beauty and total innocence came the Serpent, Satan. And the third chapter of Genesis brings the first darkness into this picture. In a moment Satan wiped away man's innocence. Adam and Eve sinned; they disobeyed God; they openly, blatantly, willfully defied the command of the almighty God.

B. *When Adam and Eve realized what they had done, they tried to hide themselves from God.* But they could not, for in the cool of the evening they heard God's steps in the garden. God called, "Adam, where art thou?" In his answer, Adam said four things to God.

1. "I heard thy voice." God could have abandoned Adam and Eve. He could have said, "I will start over. I will make another creature who will obey Me, and who will appreciate all of this beauty and perfection I have created." But because God's nature is love—a kind of love we cannot understand as human beings—He immediately reached out to that sinning pair. So Adam "heard the voice of God" in the garden, and the voice was a plea of searching love.

2. Then Adam said, "I was afraid." This was the first by-product of sin. He was seized with a new emotion he had never experienced before—fear. Ever since that day fear and anxiety have plagued people. Many of our illnesses, both physical and mental, are the result of fear and anxiety.

3. The third thing Adam said was, "Because I was naked." Why was he afraid? Because he knew that his sin was open before God. He could not cover his sin and hide himself from God. He was humiliated before God.

4. The fourth thing Adam said was, "I hid myself." That is man's natural reaction when he sins. He wants to run, to get away from the light of truth. Jesus said, "Men love darkness rather than light, because their deeds are evil."

II. The content of this fantastic foregleam of Christ in Genesis 3:15.

A. *In his first epistle, the apostle Peter tells his readers that the prophets of old, including Moses, had been inspired of God to speak and to write both of the sufferings of Christ and of the glory or vindication of Christ which would follow* (1 Peter 1:8–11). What was Christ's "suffering"? It was His rejection by mankind. And what was His "glory"? It began with His resurrection and ascension back to the Father; and it shall end with His eternal glory, as He shall reign as "King of kings and Lord of lords." Therefore, Genesis 3:15—the words of God spoken initially to Satan—contains two statements: one concerning the suffering of Christ and the other describing His ultimate victory.

B. *About this verse as a whole, we note two things.*

1. It was spoken to Satan, although it was clearly in the hearing of Adam and Eve. This means, consequently, that the great drama of redemption has repercussions *beyond* the human race. The cross of Christ meant not only salvation for sinful man, but also the defeat of the devil and the deliverance of *natural* creation from Satan's deadly grip and blighting power.

2. The second thing we see about this statement God made is that it was a promise of redemption made *immediately upon the fall of man.* There is nothing that could illustrate the love, goodness, and grace of God better than this.

C. *Then God said to Satan, "I will put enmity between thee and the woman."* The woman represents redeemed humanity, or more specifically, the church. This means there will be a continual warfare between Satan, the archenemy, and the people of God.

III. The conclusion of this marvelous foregleam of the coming Christ.

"It [the seed of the woman] shall bruise thy head, and thou shalt bruise his heel" (Gen. 3:15b).

A. *The seed, of course, is Christ.* And the word *bruise* in the Hebrew means literally "to desire to swallow up." The idea seems to be that of bitter pursuit and hatred. And from the time of Christ's birth, that is what happened. Satan dogged our Lord's steps and determined to destroy Him if he could. But he couldn't; and Jesus summed it all up in the Garden of Gethsemane when He said to the arresting soldiers, "No man taketh my life from me: I lay it down of myself."

B. *Thus, in the dawning of time, God told Satan conclusively that he would be destroyed, and He told him who would do it!* On the cross Satan bruised the "heel" of Christ by causing Him to suffer physical death. But this suffering was not final. Christ rose victorious, never to suffer or die again. God will bruise Satan under *our* feet. For He said to us, "Resist the devil, and he will flee from you" (James 4:7). And He also said, "Greater is he that is in you, than he that is in the world." In Christ, Christians are invincible before Satan.

Conclusion. So what do we have? In this remarkable conversation between God and Satan, God revealed one of the most glorious of all the Old Testament foregleams or promises of the coming Savior. And all of this He did because He is love—and His love permitted Him to prepare a way for us to return to Him and to be received into His family. That is "the way of salvation." It is open to all who will receive it.   — *DLJ*

* * *

SUNDAY MORNING, OCTOBER 14

TITLE: Fake Forms of Conversion

TEXT: "And now, behold, I go bound in the spirit unto Jerusalem, not knowing the things that shall befall me there" (Acts 20:22).

SCRIPTURE READING: Acts 20:21–22

HYMNS: "Jesus Saves," Kirkpatrick
"Jesus Paid It All." Grape
"The Great Physician," Stockton

OFFERTORY PRAYER:

O Holy Father, Your Son stated that we would know the truth and the truth would set us free. This morning we pray for freedom from hypocrisy, superstition, our culture, and our selfishness. So work in our hearts that we may give generously to Your cause that others might be set at liberty. In the name of Christ. Amen.

Introduction. The bizarre incident began Sunday afternoon with phone calls to the First Baptist Church of Dallas. The callers, identifying themselves as executives of a television network and the Dallas News, suggested that Leonard Bernstein, Jr., was on his way to the services at the church. They said he had been given grant money and was looking around for ideas for the New York Philharmonic Orchestra. That evening the visitor, escorted to a front-row-center seat, got up halfway through the service saying that he was so impressed with the choir that he was returning to the hotel for a check to present to the church.

He was introduced to the congregation by the church's pastor. With tears in his eyes the man praised the performance and presented a $20,000 check to the pastor. He said it was to take the church's 410-voice choir to New York to perform with the New York Philharmonic Orchestra. It was an emotional moment for the choir and the members attending the evening worship service.

As often happens with magic moments, this one was short lived. The church's business manager began to investigate. He learned through the conductor's office that a man using that name had been arrested in other cities for giving the impression he was the conductor's son, running up bills, and then leaving. The Leonard Bernstein, Jr., who so graciously presented a $20,000 check to the church, was nothing but a fake.

There are many fake items in the world. There are fake diamonds, fake money, and fake love. There are also fake conversions. Someone has suggested that one of the greatest fields of evangelism is within the church itself. There are many whose names are on the church rolls, but whose names have never been inscribed on the Lamb's Book of Life.

I. Three types of fake conversions.

A. *Intellectual conversion.* This occurs when a person changes one set of ideas for another. Take an atheist, for instance. He does not believe in the existence of God or a future life. Then he comes across the rational proofs of the existence of God. He looks at the beauty of nature and the complexity of the inner man. He says to himself, "Maybe I have been wrong. Perhaps there is a God. I think I'll change my mind. I now believe in the existence of a supreme Creator."

Just because the atheist decides to change his idea concerning the existence of God does not mean that he has become a Christian. The only way a person can honestly be converted is to have an experience with the Creator by faith in Christ. By so doing he becomes a child of God.

Examine your own experience. Do you think you are a Christian simply because you believe in the existence of God?

B. *Emotional conversion.* Culbert G. Rutenbur tells of a young woman who attended a revival meeting. She heard a sad song sung during the invitation and began to cry. The pastor saw her and said, "Honey, do you believe that Jesus Christ was the Savior and that He died on the cross for your sins?"

She replied, "Yes." She had been reared in a Christian home and had been taught by rote memory to believe. The minister put his hand on her shoulder, prayed for her, and presented her to the church. She was baptized. Her parents gave her a Bible and a prayer book. Everyone was excited about her conversion. For the next twenty-five years she was miserable. She was miserable because she had had an emotional experience, but had never had a genuine conversion experience (*The Reconciling Gospel* [Philadelphia: Judson Press, 1960], pp. 160–62).

One can have all sorts of experiences with God and not receive spiritual salvation.

1. One can have an experience with God in which God saves him physically but not spiritually. In many a foxhole-conversion God has saved a soldier from physical death, but not from spiritual death.

2. A person can have an aesthetic experience with God. Have you ever been on a mountaintop and experienced a beautiful sunset in the west? You have the feeling that God is hovering upon you like a bell. You know that God is there, and you stand in awe at His presence. A person can have that kind of experience with God and still not be converted.

3. A person can have an experience with God in which he shouts, cries, and praises the Lord. That does not mean that he has had a conversion experience.

Ask yourself the question: Is my conversion experience genuine or was it just an emotional experience?

C. *Moral conversion.* This occurs when a person exchanges one set of ideals for another. Have you ever known someone who lived a sorry life? Perhaps he drank, ran around, gambled, beat his children, and cheated on his wife. One morning that person got up and said, "What a mess I am. I am going to change." He does change. He stops drinking, cursing, gambling, cheating, and cleans up his language. He brings his family to church and joins. But just because he joins the church and changes his lifestyle doesn't mean that he has had a genuine conversion experience. Reformation without commitment to Christ is not conversion.

A person can be converted to all kinds of people who challenge him to live right. A person can be converted to a pastor. As long as the pastor fills the pulpit, that person is faithful to the church. When the pastor is called somewhere else, the person drops out and is never seen again.

To be converted to anyone but Christ is not a genuine conversion.

II. True conversion.

What constitutes a true conversion? In Acts 20 Paul recites his experience in Ephesus. He tells how he went from house to house sharing the full truth with the

Ephesians, both in public and in the privacy of their homes. He said, "I have had one message for Jews and Gentiles alike—the necessity of turning from sin to God through faith in our Lord Jesus Christ." (Acts 20:22 LB). These are the ingredients for true conversion.

A. *Repentance toward God.* To be genuinely converted a person must repent. Repentance is the migration of the mind from self to Christ. It is reorientation. It is to stop thinking your own thoughts and start thinking God's thoughts. It is to stop trying to save yourself in your own way and allow God to save you His way.

B. *Faith in Jesus Christ.* Paul said that true conversion means repentance toward God and faith in the Lord Jesus Christ.

1. A faith that saves is a faith in Christ and in Christ alone. Faith in Allah, Buddha, or Krishna will not save. Acts 4:12 says, "Neither is there salvation in any other: for there is none other name under heaven given among men, whereby we must be saved." Jesus said, "I am the way, the truth, and the life: no man cometh unto the Father, but by me" (John 14:6). So the faith that saves is faith in Christ and Christ alone.

2. A faith that saves is a faith that costs. There are many people who want to put business, family, amusement, girl friend, boyfriend, school, or sports first and then tack Christ on the very end of their list of priorities. This will not work. It must be Jesus Christ first, business second; Christ first, family second; Christ first, amusement second; Christ first, boyfriend or girl friend second; Christ first, school second; and Christ first, sports second. Christ must be first in our lives.

3. A faith that saves is a faith that identifies. When a woman marries, she identifies herself completely with her husband. She identifies herself with him to such an extent that she drops off her name and takes up his name. She identifies herself with his past, present, and future. She identifies herself with him for better or worse, richer or poorer, in sickness or in health, until death bid them part.

Whenever a person becomes a Christian he identifies himself with Jesus Christ. He identifies himself with His name. He becomes a Christ-ian, or Christian. He identifies himself with Christ's past, present, and future. He identifies himself with Christ for better or worse, in sickness or in health, in riches or in poverty, but it is not an until-death-bid-you-part identification. Once you identify yourself with Christ by faith, you become His and He becomes yours forever and ever.

Conclusion. A legend tells of a pastor who died and went to heaven. He stood before the judgment bar of God. God said to him, "Pastor, give me an account of your sheep." The pastor bowed his head and didn't say anything. A moment later God said, "Pastor, I asked you to tell me about your sheep."

Once again the pastor didn't say anything.

At last God insisted, "Pastor, you must give Me an account of your sheep."

To which the pastor replied, "Dear God, they were not sheep. They were wolves dressed in sheep's clothing."

The saddest words spoken may well be found in Matthew 7:21 when Jesus said, "I never knew you: depart from me." Examine your life. Have you been genuinely converted, or was your conversion a fake?   — *GW*

* * *

SUNDAY EVENING, OCTOBER 14

TITLE: Life's Greatest Experience

TEXT: "And Jesus said to him, 'Today salvation has come to this house. . . . For the Son of man came to seek and to save the lost' " (Luke 19:9–10 RSV).

SCRIPTURE READING: Luke 19:1–10

Introduction. Miracles are still happening today! A young Australian student en route to the West Coast arrived at the Honolulu Airport at four o'clock one afternoon. He bought a newspaper, read about a Billy Graham Crusade, left the plane, hitchhiked to the International Center, went to the meeting, and gave his life to Christ. His counselor took him to the airport; and at nine o'clock that evening, he was on another plane, bound for college in Chicago—and rejoicing!

In the Bible Zacchaeus had his moment of miracle. Jesus stepped beneath the tree, looked up at Zacchaeus and called for him to come down. Something happened to Zacchaeus that day! Jesus said with finality, "This day is salvation come to this house"! Life's greatest experience became his. He was lost, but then was found. Christ truly saved him, and he gave evidence of new life within him in his relationship toward others.

This story can impress you with four simple lessons about life's greatest experience, salvation.

I. The need for salvation.

Zacchaeus had all life could offer materially, but he was lost spiritually. A person may lose health, home, friends, or business, but the greatest loss of all is the loss of one's soul. Zacchaeus almost lost himself forever, but didn't.

The Bible says that a person is lost spiritually when he does not have Christ in his heart. God made us for Himself for fellowship. Man sinned against God and has, therefore, separated us from God, so that man is a sinner and lost from God. This is Jesus' term for man's spiritual condition—*lost*.

A person doesn't wait until he is an adult before he is lost. Each person is lost now—without Christ! Children are lost without Christ. So many people are truly lost today! Without life, lacking peace, needing forgiveness, without direction or certainty for life, existing, but not living.

II. The hope for salvation.

A. *Hope for salvation is in Jesus Christ.* "For the Son of man is come to seek and to save that which was lost" (v. 10).

Salvation is not of ourselves, it is in Christ! John 3:17 says that He came not to condemn but to save. Acts 4:12 says that "there is no other name under heaven given among men by which we must be saved" (RSV).

Salvation is not in what we do; it is God's gift. Romans 6:23 says, "The gift of God is eternal life through Jesus Christ our Lord." Ephesians 2:8 says that salvation is not by our character, but by God's grace to us. And that grace is in Christ!

B. *Hope for salvation is available for any person.* Salvation is possible no matter who the person is, for the Bible says, *"Whosoever* believes in Him."

Zacchaeus was a tax collector and was considered a social and spiritual outcast. He was hated by the people because he was fraudulent, dishonest, and hard-hearted. Was there any hope for him? Jesus said about Zacchaeus that "today salvation has come to this house"! What does Jesus say about you?

III. The attitude for salvation.
The attitude for salvation basically involves two things.

A. *Desire.* There is the desire to be saved that grows out of spiritual need. There is a hunger for help, fellowship, cleansing, and peace.

The desire is the work of the Holy Spirit convicting and drawing you to Christ.

B. *Decision.* Salvation comes to the willing heart. There are two sides, God's and ours. He is active; we are passive. He gives; we receive. Our part is to respond to Christ by opening our lives to Him in repentance, trust, and confession. We must decide!

IV. The opportunity for salvation.
Jesus said "today" is salvation come—that very day, not later. It was sometime during Zacchaeus' conversation.

For Zacchaeus, it was his only opportunity for salvation. It was Jesus' last time to pass through Jericho on the way to the cross.

We never know when time will run out, but it is certain to do so sooner or later. The opportunity will not always be ours to have. We may not be in the right frame of mind or we may not be listening for God's voice.

Conclusion. Now is your opportunity to experience life's greatest miracle! The Holy Spirit speaks to your heart. He prompts you and calls you to decision. Will you listen to His voice and receive Christ into your heart now?   *— TSB*

* * *

WEDNESDAY EVENING, OCTOBER 17

TITLE: Christ and the Animal Sacrifices

TEXT: "Unto Adam also and to his wife did the LORD God make coats of skins, and clothed them" (Gen. 3:21).

SCRIPTURE READING: Genesis 3:21; 1 Peter 1:18–19

Introduction. As we began our study of these foregleams of Christ in the Old Testament, we discovered a picture of Christ in the very first verse of the Bible: "In the beginning God created" (Gen. 1:1). In the New Testament we read that "all things were made by him [Christ], and without him was not anything made that was made" (John 1:3).

Then the shadow became even a bit more detailed when we saw the creation of Eve from Adam's wounded side, and we discovered another picture of the Lord Jesus. The light increased as we saw Adam as a type of Christ in his love for his bride, which was so great that he was willing to die in sin that she would be able to produce seed, from which would eventually come the Savior, the Lord Jesus.

Last Wednesday night we studied the first prophecy of the coming Redeemer in Genesis 3:15. Tonight, we move six verses forward—to Genesis 3:21—and we see an unmistakable picture of how our Redeemer would accomplish His wonderful salvation. Someone has described this as the first clear gospel sermon ever preached, and it was preached in the form of an object lesson for Adam and Eve by God Himself.

I. The situation.

A. *Adam and Eve had sinned.* They had openly and willfully disobeyed God's commandment, which had expressly forbidden them to eat of the fruit of the tree of the knowledge of good and evil. When they sinned, a number of disastrous things happened. They were seized with a new emotion—fear. They experienced shame and humiliation, which they had never known before. They had the urge to run and hide, which was another new experience for them. Sin had so distorted their thinking that instead of running *to* God for help, they ran *from* Him and frantically began trying to *do* something in order to make themselves presentable before God once more.

Before Adam and Eve sinned they were clothed with innocence. But when they sinned, their innocence was stripped away. "And the eyes of them both were opened, and they knew that they were naked; and they sewed fig leaves together, and made themselves aprons" (v. 7).

B. *Their act of making fig-leaf coverings for themselves is a picture of the general procedure of the sinner who is conscious of his spiritual nakedness or guilt before God.* The "spiritual aprons" the sinner makes come with various descriptions. Sometimes they are in the form of religious observances. The ancients threw their children in the Ganges River to appease their god. The Muslims make their pilgrimage to Mecca to worship at that shrine. And there are those who will "do good deeds" in order to quiet their guilty consciences before God.

When Adam and Eve came face to face with God, they saw the total inadequacy of the coverings they had made. So it is when the sinner is truly faced with his sins. He knows, in that humiliating moment, that all of his efforts to hide and cover his sins have been totally futile. Thus we have the *situation* in which Adam and Eve were found. They were trapped, cornered. There was nothing they could have done to alleviate that terrible situation. There was no place to hide and no place to go.

II. The sacrifice.

We move now to the glorious intervention of the Lord God in order that this situation might be saved from its hopelessness.

A. *While Adam and Eve were hiding, having realized, upon hearing the voice of God calling them, that their fig-leaf aprons were insufficient, God had embarked on a new approach, a new potential means of relating Himself to Adam and Eve.* While Adam and Eve were hiding from God, He was seeking for them. What a thrilling demonstration of God's grace! That is what Paul meant when he said, "Where sin abounded, grace did much more abound" (Rom. 5:20).

The beautiful thing about this was that God sought them *not* to accuse them (their guilty consciences had already done that), nor to condemn them (again, they were already condemned by their guilt), but *to make a way for them to come back to Him.*

B. *So what did God do?* He took an animal, shed its innocent blood, and from its skin made coverings for the guilty pair. When God did this, He laid down an eternal principle from which man cannot escape. In this first animal sacrifice—which is a type of the Lord Jesus' death on the cross—God laid down three inviolable rules for an acceptable sacrifice or atonement for sin.

1. It was all done by God. The animal was God's gift; it was not provided by Adam. So was the Lord Jesus God's gift to sinful man (John 3:16).

2. The atonement must be by the death of an innocent substitute. The animal, or animals, that God killed in order to provide the skins to cover Adam and Eve's nakedness had no part in their sin. Thus Jesus, "who knew no sin," became sin for us (2 Cor. 5:21).

3. This atonement must be by the shedding of blood. While the blood is not specifically mentioned in the account here, it is certainly implied, for there would have been no way for God to have procured the skins from the animals without shedding their blood.

III. The significance of this sacrifice.

A. *From this event—when God killed the animal and made coverings for Adam and Eve—we can trace the doctrine of atonement by blood for our sins throughout the Bible.* Where these conditions are met, God accepts the provision; but where any part of this is missing, God must reject it. But then, as the noon-day sun rises higher in the sky, the shadows disappear, and the One to whom all of this pointed appears on the scene. In the fullness of time God sent His Son, and He was proclaimed by John the Baptist as "the Lamb of God which taketh away the sin of the world."

B. *Jesus met every one of the requirements of that first clear picture of Him in Genesis 3:21.*

1. Jesus was God's free gift—"For God so loved the world, that he *gave* his only begotten Son" (John 3:16). The fig-leaf apron Adam made himself, the product of his own labor, was not sufficient.

2. Christ *died* as a substitute for sinners. "For if, when we were enemies, we were reconciled to God by the *death* of his Son, much more, being reconciled, we shall be saved by his life" (Rom. 5:10).

3. Redemption through Christ must be by the shedding of His blood. In the New Testament portion of our text we read, "Forasmuch as ye know that ye were not redeemed with corruptible things, . . . but with the precious blood of Christ, as of a lamb without blemish and without spot (1 Peter 1:18–19).

Conclusion. So what do we have here? All of this was foreshadowed and promised in the first acceptable sacrifice—an animal sacrifice—recorded in the dawn of human history. God has made provision for man's sins, and it is all His doing. We cannot do anything except receive, by faith, this incomparable gift of God's Son.

Indeed, God has etched upon every page of the Bible the person of our Lord Jesus Christ. If we open this Book, we shall see Him. Truly man is "without excuse" if he passes by and refuses the grace and love of God.   —*DLJ*

* * *

SUNDAY MORNING, OCTOBER 21

TITLE: Is There a God?

Text: **"In the beginning God created the heaven and the earth" (Gen. 1:1).**

Scripture Reading: Genesis 1:1

HYMNS: "To God Be the Glory," Doane
"Holy, Holy, Holy," Dykes
"O Worship the King," Haydn

OFFERTORY PRAYER:

Our Father, we thank You that You are the great Sovereign of the universe. You are all-powerful, all-wise, and everywhere present. We stand in awe before You. Today we are grateful that You are a personal God who has revealed Yourself through Jesus Christ. Through His death and resurrection You have made it possible for us as finite beings to come boldly into Your presence.

Thank You that You have included us in the redemptive process. May our offerings be used to share the truth of Christ with others in our own surroundings and throughout the world. In Christ's name. Amen.

Introduction. The Bible begins with one of the most dynamic and controversial statements ever made: "In the beginning God." If this statement is untrue, Christians might as well burn their Bibles and withdraw membership from churches. Some might say, "I'll believe in God if you can prove He exists." Is there anyone who can measure out five yards of love? Can you fill a cup with justice? Yet who will deny the existence of love and justice?

You may not be able to see, taste, touch, or hear God, but once you meet Him by faith in Christ, you will see the results of that experience.

There are many reasons for believing in God.

I. Design in nature.

In Psalm 8 the psalmist exclaimed, "When I consider thy heavens, the work of thy fingers, the moon and the stars, which thou hast ordained" (v. 3). Romans 1:20 reads, "Since earliest times men have seen the earth and sky and all God made, and have known of his existence and great eternal power" (LB).

If I found a watch on a beach and noted that it gave the second of the moment, the moment of the hour, the hour of the day, the day of the week, I would know that behind this watch there had to be a watchmaker.

If someone handed me a copy of the Gettysburg Address and I read it, I would have to believe that it was the product of a mind such as Abraham Lincoln rather than the product of a monkey in a print shop.

When I look at our earth, I note that it is just the right size. If it were any smaller, the atmosphere would be impossible for human survival, such as mercury in the moon's atmosphere. If it were any larger, the atmosphere would contain free hydrogen such as Jupiter and Saturn. The earth is also exactly the right distance from the sun. If it were any closer, it would be burned to a crisp. If it were any farther away from the sun, it would freeze as if it were in a giant deep freeze. The tilt of the earth is just right to ensure the seasons of summer, winter, spring, and fall. The moon is just right for the earth as it controls the ocean tides. The ocean is just right as it serves as a giant thermostat for the earth. When I note all of these things, I have to say that behind this earth and universe there must be a God.

II. Purpose.

Purpose calls for the existence of God. Listen to the atheists of the present and past. Jean-Paul Sartre has suggested that man is a tragic joke in the context of a total comic absurdity. Clarence Darrow said that the outstanding fact that cannot be dodged by thoughtful men is the futility of it all. H. L. Mencken stated that life is not worth the living. What could be more logical than suicide and more preposterous than remaining alive? B. F. Skinner says that man is born by chance; he dies by design. This is the beginning and ending of man. In contrast to this, the existence of God stands for intelligence behind the universe, purpose running through the universe, and a logical outcome for the earth's destiny. Purpose calls for the existence of God.

III. Unusable energy.

Unusable energy calls for God's existence. Although America and the world have been faced with an energy crisis, experts agree that there are billions of gallons of oil under the ground. Add to that the existence of coal, uranium, and oil shale, and the earth seems to have enough energy for hundreds of years. But what happens then?

The first law of thermodynamics states that energy is never destroyed though it changes in form from usable energy to unusable energy. The second law of thermodynamics states that this loss of energy is irreversible. Nature moves in only one direction. The sun is slowly but surely burning out. The stars are dying embers. Everywhere in the cosmos heat is turning to cold. Matter is dissolving into radiation. Energy is being dissipated into empty space. The universe is moving toward a maximum entrophy or ultimate heat death where all energy will be unusable. The world will be like a cold tomb.

If the world is moving toward an end, it must have had a beginning. If the universe is running down like a clock, the clock must have been wound up at a point in time. Nature cannot explain its own existence; therefore, God is the winder of the clock. He is the first cause of the universe. Genesis 1:1 simply states, "In the beginning God created the heavens and the earth."

IV. Observation.

Observation calls for the existence of God. Examine the civilization of men. From ancient times until now all peoples who have not been brainwashed have had a seed thought of God. Egyptians, Babylonians, Assyrians, Indians—all have believed in some type of god. From whence did this idea come? Is it the result of wishful thinking? Did man create a universal father image and turn around and worship the figment of his own imagination? Is it a matter of whistling in the dark? No. God placed the idea of Himself in the minds of men. Romans 1:19 reads, "For the truth about God is known to them instinctively; God has put this knowledge in their hearts" (LB).

V. Mercy.

Mercy calls for the existence of God. Romans 5:5 says, "The love of God is shed abroad in our hearts by the Holy Ghost which is given unto us." Christians, because of the love of God within their hearts, have established educational institutions to educate the minds of men. Because of this love they have established hospitals for the healing of the body, homes for unwed mothers, orphanages for children of negligent parents or children without parents at all, and homes for senior citizens. Ask yourself these questions: Have I ever visited a hospital over which there was this sign: Atheistic Memorial Hospital? Have I ever heard anyone who was a member of the Atheistic Alcoholics Anonymous? Mercy calls for the existence of God.

VI. Revelation.

Revelation reveals the existence of God. One hundred years ago Herbert Spencer popularized agnosticism. He observed that a bird could never fly out of space. He concluded by analogy that it was impossible for the finite to break through to the infinite. He was correct in his observations, but he was incorrect in his conclusion. He overlooked two things. He overlooked that the time would come when astronauts would break out of the atmosphere and fly to all parts of the universe. He also missed the possibility that while the finite could not break through to the infinite, the infinite could break through to the finite. Galatians 4:4 says, "But when the fulness of the time was come, God sent forth his Son, made of woman, made under the law." Hebrews 1:1–2 says, "Long ago God spoke in many different ways to our fathers through the prophets . . . telling them little by little about his plans. But now in these days he has spoken to us through his Son to whom he has given everything, and through whom he made the world and everything there is" (LB).

There is a comic strip entitled "B.C.," which is about cavemen, flowers, dinosaurs, ants, and anteaters. On one occasion the comic strip showed one ant saying to another, "Wouldn't it be a miracle if we could be transformed into human beings?" It would be a miracle if an ant could become a human being; but a greater miracle happened two thousand years ago when Jesus Christ, the very Son of God, came to the earth in the form of a man. He came to the earth to tell us that God is. He came to the earth to tell us what God is like.

If by faith in Christ you meet God, God will reward you with victory over troubles. Note that the Bible does not promise that if a person accepts Christ as his personal Savior, He will give him a bed of roses, easy sailing, or a life uninhibited by sickness. No, He said that He would give him victory in the midst of the normal struggles of life.

He who comes to God by faith in Christ will be rewarded by a peace when the rest of the world is at war. He will receive a companionship so that when all others have forsaken him, God will stand by his side. He who comes to God by faith in Christ will receive confidence in a confused world and power over sin.

Conclusion. Some time ago two men, father and son, were proponents of atheism. Their lives were devoted to projecting the doctrine that there was no God. At last the father lay on his deathbed and said, "Son, what if we have been wrong all of this time? What if there is a God?"

The son replied, 'Oh, dad, don't say that. Hold on. Hold on."

The father gasped, "That's just the point, son. There's nothing to hold onto."

Faith in Christ brings hope and confidence for the future. Would you come to God today by faith in Christ? — *GW*

* * *

SUNDAY EVENING, OCTOBER 21

TITLE: Four Aspects of Christlikeness

TEXT: "You are the salt of the earth. . . . You are the light of the world. . . . Let your light so shine before men . . ." (Matt. 5:13–14, 16 RSV).

SCRIPTURE READING: Matthew 5:13–16

Introduction. A Christian young man went to work one summer in a lumber camp. Some of his friends told him that the rough lumbermen would make life miserable for him because of his Christian faith. Bravely he went and spent the summer. When he came home, his friends asked him if the men had laughed at him for being a Christian. He said, "No, they didn't laugh at me because of my being a Christian. They never found out!"

This is not the way Jesus wants us to live. In fact, there are two descriptions of the Christian life that make it impossible for others not to know that we are Christians. Jesus said that we are the salt and light of the world. There are four aspects of Christlikeness in those two metaphors.

I. Personality of Christlikeness.

Jesus was speaking to His disciples, to people. He was not speaking to intellectual, philosophical, or even religious people. He was talking to everyday folks whom He had called, changed, and challenged to Christlikeness. Christlikeness resides in persons who know Jesus and who are becoming like Him.

As Christians, then, we are described by two powerful metaphors, salt and light. Salt was a scarce and valuable commodity in Jesus' day. It was an irreplaceable item, desperately needed. Salt is so powerful that a little goes a long way. As Christians, we are "salt."

The fact that Christians are light is related in other Scriptures. In John 8:12, Jesus states, "I am the light of the world." He is the source of spiritual light; He alone gives us light. He is the Light in us! Ephesians 5:8 says, "For ye were sometimes darkness, but now are ye light in the Lord: walk as children of light." And Philippians 2:15 says, ". . . ye shine as lights in the world."

So there is something powerful at work in us—divine life, light, salt, and the light of Christ. We have a strategic place in life, on the earth, in the world.

II. Purpose of Christlikeness.

Salt and light possess some unique functions.

A. *Salt.*

1. Salt purifies. Salt is glistening white and is said to be the purest of all things. Christians, as the salt of the earth, are to be examples of purity, creating pure and wholesome conditions wherever we go. "Blessed are the pure in heart . . ." (Matt. 5:8).

2. Salt preserves. It prevents corruption and decay. It is put on meat to prevent spoiling. There are forces at work in the world today that only the salt of Christ's life and attitudes in us can counteract. Our lives are like divine salt when contact with another life saves it from moral and spiritual corruption.

3. Salt seasons. Food without salt is insipid. Salt adds taste and flavor. We are to so live the Christian life that other people will see that life without Christ is stale and meaningless, but life with Him is full of spiritual flavor, the joy of living, and the abundant life.

B. *Light.*

1. Light dispels darkness. When Robert Louis Stevenson was about six years old, he stood at a window watching the lamplighter work. It fascinated him to see the street lamps lighted one by one. His nurse asked him what he was doing. He answered, "I am watching a man making holes in the darkness." This is what Christ came to do! And this is what we do as we let the light of Christ shine through us.

2. Light illumines life. It lights the way and gives direction. One who is in Christ walks in light and not darkness (John 8:12). When we walk by the Word of God, we walk by the light of God's truth and we "give the light" (2 Cor. 4:6). Our purpose is to turn on the light of the Lord for others and to show them Christ.

III. Peril to Christlikeness.

The peril to Christlikeness is twofold. It is possible for salt to lose its savor, its saltness. And it is possible to hide a light, to prevent it from fulfilling its purpose.

The point is that we as Christians can lose our flavor, our influence upon others. And it is possible for us to hide our spiritual illumination and, therefore, our usefulness.

How is this done? It happens when we allow some sin in our lives or some attitude to control us. We do this by violating the Beatitudes and being unwilling for Christ to develop us. Or we may do this by compromising Christ, thus manifesting little distinctiveness to the world about us. These are awful dangers! The responsibility for Christlikeness is serious.

IV. Penetration of Christlikeness.

The "blessed life" (Matt. 5:3–12) is to be a "blessing." Where do we begin?

A. *We begin with ourselves.* We apply Jesus' teachings to our own lives first. Is He changing your habits? Do you, for example, have any driving habits that are not Christlike? Do you observe the laws of the "stop sign" and the "speed limit"? What are your shopping habits? Do you push ahead of other shoppers and are you demanding of the clerk? How are your work habits? Do you work in a grumbling spirit? Are you excited about making your boss or your company successful? Begin with yourself.

B. *We continue at home.* Does your light give light "to all that are in the house"? Do you practice Christlikeness with your parents, your brothers and sisters, your spouse?

C. *We penetrate then to the outside world.* As verse 16 says, "Let your light so shine before men," throughout the community and the world.

Conclusion. What happens when Christlikeness characterizes your life? Verse 16 answers this by saying that men see your good works and glorify your Father who is in heaven. This is worth it all!   *— TSB*

* * *

WEDNESDAY EVENING, OCTOBER 24

TITLE: **Christ and Noah's Ark**

TEXT: **"And God said unto Noah, The end of all flesh is come before me; for the earth is filled with violence through them; and, behold, I will destroy them with the earth. Make thee an ark of gopher wood" (Gen. 6:13–14).**

SCRIPTURE READING: **Genesis 6:13–15; Hebrews 11:7**

Introduction. There are few Bible stories which lodge more securely in our memories than the story of Noah and the ark. But our concern in this study is to see if there indeed can be a picture of our Lord Jesus in Noah's ark. And we shall discover that Noah's ark provides for us one of the clearest foregleams of Christ in all of the Old Testament. The writer of Hebrews declared: "By faith Noah, being warned of God of things not seen as yet, moved with fear, prepared an ark to the saving of his house; by the which he condemned the world, and became heir of the righteousness which is by faith" (11:7).

Noah was saved because he had faith in the Word of God concerning the construction of an ark in which he and his family would escape destruction. We are saved in the same way—by faith in God's Word concerning His Son, who is *our* Savior, from the coming judgment of God which is going to be poured out in the world. Therefore it is obvious that the ark of Noah is a shadow, a type, of the coming Savior, the Lord Jesus Christ.

I. The plan of God.

A. *"And God said unto Noah."* We do not know how God communicated with Noah. But that is not important; Noah received the message clearly and plainly. God told Noah that "the end of all flesh is come before me." In other words, all sin, evil, sorrow, trouble, and suffering was about to come to a final end. Violence and corruption were rampant. God said, "I will destroy them with the earth." When Jesus preached and taught concerning the coming judgment of God upon the earth, He used the Flood in Noah's day as a picture of that last, great event (see Matt. 24:37–39).

B. *So the countdown in Noah's day was begun.* But note: There is always mercy mixed with judgment. There were a few righteous people on the earth. In fact, there were *eight people:* Noah and his wife and his three sons and their wives.

Then God proceeded to give Noah explicit and detailed instructions for building the ark. It was not to be constructed by Noah's plans. So we see that the idea of an ark for the preservation of Noah and his family originated in the mind and heart of God. It wasn't the brainchild of Noah. It was not the invention of man. In fact, there is no hint that Noah even anticipated a flood.

C. *Just as the ark was planned by God alone, down to the last detail, so the Lord Jesus Christ, the antitype of the ark, was foreordained by God to make provision for those who would be saved by receiving Him.* Peter wrote, "Who verily was foreordained before the foundation of the world, but was manifest in these last times for you" (1 Peter 1:20)—and, of course, he was speaking of Christ.

II. The purpose of God.

A. *In our last study we saw how God made provision for the covering of the nakedness of Adam and Eve by killing the animals and making coats from their skins.* It was God's idea and God's provision all the way through. The point is that man must have no part in the plan of salvation.

Incidentally, modern shipbuilders tell us that these dimensions God gave Noah for the building of the ark are the most ideal measurements to insure the safest and most seaworthy craft. The ark was built on dry land, miles from the nearest water. Noah had no model to work from, and yet the ark had the ideal dimensions for a ship accepted by shipbuilders even today!

B. *The beautiful thing to note is that Noah believed what God said about the ark.* Never did he appear to doubt God's Word or the feasibility of His instructions. He believed God and accepted God's instructions by faith. Likewise, Jesus, a type of the ark, must be accepted by faith. Peter wrote, "Whom [Christ] having not seen, ye love; in whom, though now ye see him not, yet believing, ye rejoice with joy unspeakable and full of glory" (1 Peter 1:8).

Just as Noah had nothing else to base his faith on than the Word of God, so we today must receive Jesus Christ only on the authority of the Word of God.

C. *But not only was the purpose of God to provide* a *way of salvation for sinful man, but to provide* the only way *whereby man must be saved.* There was *only one door* in the ark. Today such an arrangement would not be permitted. A ship of this size would have to have several exits, and be equipped with life rafts and life preservers for its passengers. But none of these things is mentioned, for they were completely unnecessary. As we shall see, God provided for the complete safety of the occupants of the ark, for God was with them. "God was in Christ reconciling the world to himself."

III. The provision of God for the salvation of helpless and hopeless man.

A. *Note that, with all of the careful details and dimensions God gave to Noah concerning the building of the ark, there are no dimensions for the size of the door.* We do not know how high it was or how wide. And this was for a reason in its symbolism: *all can gain entrance.* The invitation God extended sinful man is universal. It is for "whosoever will" come. The door is wide enough and tall enough to admit any who will believe and receive Christ as Savior.

Jesus said, "I am the door"; and by that He meant that He was the only entrance to the kingdom of God. He was not *a* door, but *the* door. There are not *many* ways to heaven; there is only one way. "Sincerity" is not the key that opens heaven's door, but rather *obedience* to the stipulations laid down by Holy Scripture.

B. *Then the Scriptures declare also that it is not the Father's will "that any should perish, but that all should come to repentance"* (2 Peter 3:9). Again the door is swung wide to receive all who will come. But there came that moment when God shut the door of the ark. That meant that His extended invitation through Noah's preaching was over. Mercy and grace were finished. Likewise there will come that time when God's grace will be through as far as inviting sinful man to come to the Savior is concerned. Then "the door will be shut."

Conclusion. In that fantastic sea-going vessel Noah built, in which he followed explicitly the plans and blueprints God set forth for him, we have a marvelous foregleam of the Lord Jesus. There is room in Him for all who will come and believe. The door is open now to receive all who will respond. And, as in the ark of Noah, there is safety in Christ from the storms of eternity which would forever separate man from God, for those who are in Christ. — *DLJ*

* * *

SUNDAY MORNING, OCTOBER 28

TITLE: Put Aside Your Excuses

TEXT: "Then said he unto him, A certain man made a great supper, and bade many" (Luke 14:16).

SCRIPTURE READING: Luke 14:16–24

HYMNS: "I Am Coming to the Cross," Fischer
"I Am Resolved," Fillmore
"Pass Me Not, O Gentle Savior," Doane

OFFERTORY PRAYER:

Dear God, we thank You that You are consistent in Your love toward us. Your love is sweet, and it never fails. Because of Your love You have offered Your Son as a vicarious sacrifice. He became poor that we may become rich. In this offering we have an opportunity to offer to You a portion of our possessions that Your deep love may be shared with others. Work in our hearts to lead us away from excuses that would hinder our fulfillment of this opportunity. In Christ's name. Amen.

Introduction. This parable in Luke 14 highlights excuse-making. Three or four self-evident truths come to the surface.

The three who sent their regrets had probably told themselves these excuses so many times that they finally deemed them to be valid reasons. A person can tell himself a lie so often that at last he will accept it as the truth; however, a lie is always a lie, and an excuse is always an excuse.

The invitation from God is spiritual. Excuses are usually based on the material. There is nothing wrong with buying land, working, or getting married. It is wrong when any person places these things above the invitation of God.

Their excuses were foolish in the light of so gracious an invitiation. Yet they are no more foolish than the excuses given in our day. Think of those excuses.

I. Excuse number one: "I am too busy."

In Luke 14 the three men who made their excuses were preoccupied. They were busy with land, oxen, and marriage. Which is most important in the long run: land, John Deere tractors, and women—or eternal salvation? Put it this way. Suppose you owned two businesses. One was worth one thousand dollars and the other was worth one million dollars. It would not be reasonable for you to give all your time to the one-thousand-dollar business and none of your time to the million-dollar business. When you compare heaven and the world, this world is the one-thousand-dollar business and heaven is the million-dollar business. It is not right for you to spend all your time with the world and be too busy to give any time to heaven. Beware, lest you sell your life for cut glass when God is offering you rare jewels.

II. Excuse number two: "I don't understand enough."

The master who gave this banquet did not expect those who were invited to know everything about it. He did not expect them to understand all about the food that was being served or about the entertainment. He did expect them to come to the banquet.

Pascal, the French philosopher and mathematician, pointed out that the supreme function of reason is to show man that some things are beyond reason. With all our knowledge there are some things that the most brilliant person cannot understand. God does not expect any person to understand all the mysteries of His kingdom. He does expect us to come to Jesus Christ and confess Him as Savior.

If one understands enough to realize that sin has separated him from God and that God sent Christ to bridge the sin gap, he understands enough to be saved.

III. Excuse number three: "The great number of denominations is confusing."

As long as people are people, there will be differences of opinion. As long as there are differences of opinion, there will be differences of denomination. The Bible does not forbid different denominations. It does forbid rejection of Jesus Christ. God is not so concerned about what denomination you join as He is about whether or not you join yourself to Jesus Christ.

John 3:36 says, "He that believeth on the Son hath everlasting life: and he that believeth not the Son shall not see life; but the wrath of God abideth on him."

IV. Excuse number four: "People at church don't suit me."

A. *Some claim that church members are unfriendly and cliquish.* It may be said, in all honesty, that when a person becomes a Christian and relates himself to some local church, the people may not run up to him, shake his hand, pat him on the back, or greet him with a holy kiss. However, one should not be so concerned about being accepted by Christians. What he should be concerned about is being accepted by Christ.

B. *Some make the excuse that people go to church only to parade their new clothes.* When a Christian gets a new suit, certainly he wears it to church. He also wears it to town, to work, and to other places. The clothes we wear will not justify us before God. The master who sent out the invitations for the banquet put no stipulations on what kind of clothes were to be worn. Neither does God care whether we come to Him in a tuxedo or a torn shirt. It is not the clothes we wear that count. It is who is on the inside.

C. *Some argue that there are hypocrites in the church.* There also are hypocrites in other areas of life. Some bankers are hypocrites. Does that mean that when you need money you will not go to the bank to get a loan? Of course not.

Some in the medical profession are hypocrites. We call them quack doctors. Does that mean that you will not take your children to a physician when they get sick? Of course not.

The fact that there are Christians who are hypocrites does not mean that you should refuse to come to Jesus Christ and accept Him as your personal Savior.

V. Excuse number five: "I am a pretty good person. God will probably accept me as I am."

It depends on what one means by "good." Some people feel they are good because they have a low concept of sin. If you consider wearing lipstick a sin, then all you have to do to live above sin is to leave off the lipstick. If you think it is a sin to wear jewelry, then all you have to do to live above sin is to not wear jewelry. Many think they are good because they have a low view of sin.

It is not by works that a person is made acceptable to God. It is by faith in Jesus Christ. You should turn from your sins and come to Him through Jesus Christ.

VI. Excuse number six: "I am too wicked."

Thank God for your conviction concerning the power, penalty, and effect of sin. You should have the same kind of conviction about the power of God to forgive your sin. First John 1:9 speaks to Christians saying, ''If we confess our sins, he is faithful and just to forgive us our sins, and to cleanse us from all unrighteousness.''

When the lost person confesses his sins, God is ready to forgive him, too.

VII. Excuse number seven: "I am too timid."

Some people are more bashful and timid than others. The timid person needs to heed the warning of Revelation 21:8. Note that the timid person, as indicated by the word *fearful,* is placed alongside people guilty of horrible sins. A person should not allow his timidity to keep him from accepting Christ as his personal Savior.

VII. Excuse number eight: "I am not ready."

It is apparent that those who refused the invitation of the master to the banquet took that invitation too lightly. However, the master considered it very important. Luke 14:24 indicates that those who rejected the invitation would never have another opportunity to come to that banquet.

To say no to Jesus is a dangerous thing.

A. *It is dangerous because of the impending wrath of God that hangs over the lost.*

B. *There is a danger of the drifting and hardened heart.* Each time a person says no to Christ, it becomes easier to say no the next time. Hebrews 3:7–8 says ''. . . the Holy Ghost saith, To day if ye will hear his voice, harden not your hearts. . . .''

C. *To say no to Jesus is dangerous because of accidents and death.* How far away is death? Death is just one breath away, one heartbeat away, one malignant cell away, one car accident away.

Proverbs 27:1 says, ''Boast not thyself of to morrow; for thou knowest not what a day may bring forth.''

Conclusion. Now is the time of salvation. — *GW*

* * *

SUNDAY EVENING, OCTOBER 28

TITLE: Allowing Christ to Change Us

Text: ''And when Jesus came to the place, he looked up and said to him, ''Zacchaeus, make haste and come down; for I must stay at your house today' '' (Luke 19:5 RSV).

Scripture Reading: Luke 19:1–10

Introduction. A favorite children's game is hide-and-seek. The person who is "it" closes his eyes, counts to one hundred while his friends seek hiding places, and then tries to find all those who have hidden. In the Bible it's no game. The great God, who always knows where we are and what we are up to, is forever seeking His hiding children. The gospel tells all about God's love and God's search for us. The work of the church is to carry the message about the love of Christ to all those who have found some dark place in which to hide.

The hide-and-seek drama is familiar and is as real as life. Adam and Eve, feeling guilty and afraid, hid from God in the Garden of Eden (Gen. 3:8). All of us since that time have been playing the same game. The sermon today is about one of these, a hated little man named Zacchaeus.

Jesus found Zacchaeus in Jericho during his last visit to that town. Zacchaeus was one of the last men on record whom Jesus called to Himself during His earthly ministry. Of greater importance, he is one of the best examples we have of God's power to change wicked men.

I. Zacchaeus knew he needed to be changed.

Though wealthy and living in a human paradise, Zacchaeus was miserable. He lacked inner peace, dignity, and self-respect. He was rated with cutthroats, robbers, informers, and traitors. As a chief tax collector he had become rich by collecting customs on the famous balsam of Jericho and on the costly imports from Damascus and Arabia. The tough collectors working under him kept money pouring into his account and gave the townspeople of Jericho more reason to hate the little man who had made a deal with Rome.

Money cannot buy one moment of happiness or peace for the person who has sold out to evil. Zacchaeus may have taken the job as a way to get rich quick, without giving a thought to how this business would affect others; but now his conscience jabs at him day and night. He needs relief. He needs somebody willing to listen to him. He needs a friend.

II. He decided to take a look at Jesus.

Why? Was it conscience and maddening guilt, emptiness, loneliness, curiosity? Or was it an inspiration from above? Surely he had heard numerous reports about the ministry of Jesus. He may have heard that Jesus had attended a party for tax collectors. Or he may have heard about Jesus' kindness to sinful women, to lepers, and to little children.

Zacchaeus was determined to see Jesus. He apparently had hoped to melt into the crowd where he would go unnoticed by Jesus, but he was short and the hostile crowd was in no mood to do a favor to a hated tax collector. What could he do? He decided to act like a little boy again. He ran ahead of the crowd, found a sycamore tree by the side of the road, and perched himself in the tree where he could get a good look at Jesus.

He had taken one right step. Jesus was the One he needed to see. But just seeing Jesus is never enough. Zacchaeus' future depended on his next step.

III. He accepted change readily and joyfully.

"When Jesus came to the place, he looked up and said to him, 'Zacchaeus, make haste and come down; for I must stay at your house today.' So he made haste and came down, and received him joyfully" (vv. 5–6 RSV). What a day! The hidden traitor had been found and challenged. But Jesus hadn't denounced him nor yelled at him.

Zacchaeus was on the spot. Everybody was looking at him, and the crowd was waiting to see how Jesus would handle Zacchaeus. What Jesus did was to invite Himself to Zacchaeus' home. We don't have much of the conversation that followed, but we know how the story unfolded. Zacchaeus neither argued nor excused himself. He apparently saw that moment as one charged with the tingle of destiny. Face to face with the life-changing Christ, he would not worry about the vengeful onlookers. He was ready to be changed, even if it meant being exposed in the presence of enemies. With joy he received Jesus, without hesitation and without bargaining.

IV. He gave evidence he had really been changed.

His profession showed he had a new heart. "Zacchaeus stood and said to the Lord, 'Behold, Lord, the half of my goods I give to the poor; and if I have defrauded any one of anything, I restore it fourfold' " (v. 8 RSV). He faced his situation frankly and made a radical break with his past. He had found the life-giving Christ, and in Christ Zacchaeus saw himself and his money in a new light. His money could feed the poor and provide some restitution for his evil past. He no longer found security in money. The accepting, forgiving Christ had forgiven him. He was a new man.

Zacchaeus' confession both challenges and condemns many modern Christians. How much have we been changed? Have we allowed Christ to change our attitudes, our habits, our lifestyles, our reasons for living, our character?

V. Zacchaeus received the only necessary assurance of change.

The hostile crowd murmured, saying, "He has gone in to be the guest of a man who is a sinner" (v. 7 RSV). With one stroke they condemned both Jesus and Zacchaeus, showing their prejudice, their hatred, and their spiritual blindness. Zacchaeus could have anticipated their accusing response.

But Zacchaeus heard the word every guilty sinner needs to hear. "Jesus said to him, 'Today salvation has come to this house, since he also is a son of Abraham' " (v. 9 RSV).

Conclusion. The story of Zacchaeus is the message of Jesus in miniature. He came to seek and to save the lost. He would die for the lost. He offered hope for all the lost who would receive Him.

Zacchaeus shames us. He was a bad man who found joy and peace when he turned everything over to Christ. We are often unwilling to risk even a little embarrassment in order to let Christ change us.

Zacchaeus also offers us hope. We're no worse than he was. We, like him, can see Jesus as the difference between life and death, the difference between hope and despair, the difference between joy and misery. We can throw caution to the wind and courageously confess Christ as our living, loving Lord. We can let Christ change us completely, and can lay everything we are and have before Him.

Jesus is now looking up into the sycamore tree in which we are hiding. Let's follow the example of Zacchaeus without another moment's delay.

— KF

* * *

WEDNESDAY EVENING, OCTOBER 31

TITLE: **Christt and Isaac, the Son of Promise**

TEXT: **"Now the LORD had said unto Abram, Get thee out of thy country, and from thy kindred, and from thy father's house, unto a land that I will shew thee: And I will make of thee a great nation, and I will bless thee, and make thy name great; and thou shalt be a blessing" (Gen. 12:1–2).**

SCRIPTURE READING: **Genesis 12:1–2; 18:10–12; 21:1–3; 22:1–3**

Introduction. The first eleven chapters of Genesis cover the record of the Creation, the fall of man, the coming of the Flood, and the building of the Tower of Babel; and they give brief histories of a large number of individuals.

However, soon after the Flood, man again forgot God and began to worship idols. Yet before the knowledge of the true God should disappear, God stepped in and called a man named Abram. In God's sovereign grace He separated Abram from his idols in Ur of the Chaldees. God came seeking Abram, just as He comes today seeking sinners. Man does not seek God; God seeks man.

This relationship with Abram was to be a new beginning on the earth, which would find its full expression in the coming of Jesus to provide salvation for sinful man. God's promise to Abram was that his offspring, his children, would bless the entire world. So the key to the fulfilling of this promise God made to Abram lay in the birth of his heir, his son. And it is in this event that we find our "foregleam" of the Lord Jesus Christ.

I. The promise God made to Abram (Gen. 12:1–2).

A. *As always, the initiative came from God, who moved at this point in His sovereign power to continue the unveiling of His plan of redemption for sinful man.* The call of God to Abram came without Abram's having taken a single step toward God. He was, as Paul would describe him, "dead in trespasses and sin." But God broke into his life. And so it is with every person who becomes a believer. No one can move toward God until God first calls him. In various and sundry ways, God "breaks into" our lives and calls us to Himself.

B. *God told Abram to leave three things.*

1. His *country.* For Abram this meant the literal, physical, geographical breaking of ties. He was to begin a journey, become a pilgrim. He was to break with his old life—socially, politically, idealogically.

2. He was to leave his *kindred.* Even though Abram took Terah, his father, and Lot, his nephew, against God's will, he was told to leave his family behind. This means, for the Christian, that there are times when family interest, when it is opposed to the plan and purpose of God, must be by-passed. There are times when a person must go against his worldly wishes and the desires of his family in order to follow God.

3. Abram was to leave *his father's house.* This was the break that was too great for Abram's strength. Therefore, it was not until his father died, two years later, that Abram was able to enjoy the fullness of God's blessings in his life. Many Christians today are not enjoying the fullness of God's blessings in their lives because they have not fully relinquished those things which are contrary to God's will for them.

C. *We must see also, however, that God's call to Abram was not entirely negative.* There was a positive side, and this was by far the most important part of his call. Abram would be led by God "to a land that I will show you." He had a plan, a purpose, for something better. The separation was a means to an end. When God insists that we renounce certain things, certain patterns of life, it is because He has something better in store for us.

Then God made a promise to Abram: "And I will make of thee a great nation." That meant one thing: Abram would have a child or children—and through that child, and his children, and his children's children, a great and mighty nation would arise through which God would carry out His plan and purpose for the salvation of sinful man.

II. The preparation.

A. *Years passed, and Abraham and his wife, Sarah, had no children.* To their dismay, they discovered that Sarah was barren. In their impatience they made a tragic mistake: they decided to "help God out." With Sarah's permission, Abram had a son, Ishmael, by his wife's servant. That was not God's plan. So one day, when Abram was one hundred years old and Sarah was ninety, God moved again to fulfill His promise (see Gen. 18).

B. *Sarah, like the Virgin Mary, was totally baffled and confused at this news.* The angel said to Mary, "For with God nothing shall be impossible" (Luke 1:37). This is identical in meaning with God's words when He announced the miraculous birth of Isaac: "Is any thing too hard for the LORD?" (Gen. 18:14). So, thus far, we can see emerging the striking details of the birth of Isaac, which parallel those events surrounding the promise and preparation for the coming of Jesus.

III. The presentation (Gen. 21:1–3).

A. *We need to understand that, whereas the births of Isaac and John the Baptist were not as great as the birth of Jesus, their births were wonderful miracles nonetheless.* They were the result of a supernatural act of God.

Abram had such great faith in God that he *believed* this miraculous thing—that he and Sarah could have a son in their old age—was possible. Paul described Abram's faith in Romans 4:20–22. Abram believed what God said about the promise of a son because God said it, and for no other reason. And Sarah, though at first she laughed in unbelief, later believed (see Heb. 11:11).

B. *Isaac then, as a type of Christ, is a shadow and a type of the Virgin Birth of our Savior.* To be saved, one must accept by faith the record which God has given us concerning His Son. "Whosoever believeth that Jesus is the Christ is born of God" (1 John 5:1).

IV. The prophecy in the story of Isaac, which points to the Lord Jesus (Gen. 22:1–2).

A. *This event is a sermon in itself.* It is one of the most sacred moments in Old Testament history. The parallels and similarities between Jesus and Isaac at this point are remarkable. Isaac was Abram's "only begotten son." Like Isaac, Jesus was "the only begotten of the Father" in heaven. All of Abram's love was centered upon Isaac. Jesus, too, was the well-beloved of the Father.

B. *The land of Moriah, where Abram took Isaac, was the region in Pales-*

tine where the city of Jerusalem was built. In this region was Mount Calvary. See, also, how that the entire transaction was between father and son. No other person was to have a part in it. Someone has said that when the final moment came with Jesus on the cross, God "closed the door, snuffed out the lights of heaven, drew a black curtain across the windows of the sky, hung a black crepe on heaven's door, until the final, agonizing cry was heard, 'My God, my God, why hast thou forsaken me?' "

Conclusion. Thus we have in the story of Isaac, the son promised to Abram and Sarah, a beautiful Old Testament foregleam of the Lord Jesus. His birth was miraculous, and the plan for his sacrifice on Mt. Moriah was a beautiful picture of our Lord's death on the cross.   *— DLJ*

* * *

SUGGESTED PREACHING PROGRAM
FOR THE MONTH OF NOVEMBER

Sunday Mornings

Man is basically an acquisitive creature. He is selfish because of his insecurity away from God. One of the great changes that Christ desires to make is to change man from being "a getter" into being "a giver." The suggested theme is "Understanding and Developing the Grace of Giving."

Sunday Evenings

The suggested theme is "Sharing the Good News of Salvation." Those who are experiencing the salvation of Christ have a story to tell.

Wednesday Evenings

Continue with the theme "Foregleams of Christ in the Old Testament."

* * *

SUNDAY MORNING, NOVEMBER 4

TITLE: **The Grace of Giving and the Glory of Christ**

TEXT: **"As for Titus, he is my partner and fellow worker in your service; and as for our brethren, they are messengers of the churches, the glory of Christ" (2 Cor. 8:23 RSV).**

SCRIPTURE READING: **2 Corinthians 8:7–9, 16–23**

HYMNS: **"All Creatures of Our God and King," Williams**
"Saved, Saved!" Scholfield
"Grace Greater Than Our Sin," Towner

OFFERTORY PRAYER:

Father in heaven, help us to recognize that You are always the Giver of every good and perfect gift. Thank You for giving to us the great salvation that we have through Jesus Christ. Thank You for the gift of Your Holy Spirit as an indwelling presence. Thank You for the opportunities to cooperate with You in ministering to a needy world. We come today bringing tithes and offerings that they might be used to help those who are seeking to proclaim the message of Your love to the ends of the earth. In Christ's name. Amen.

Introduction. Paul writes to the church at Corinth in order that he might encourage them to follow through on the plans that they made the previous year to provide a generous relief offering for the poor saints who were in Jerusalem. Paul writes of his practice of encouraging gentile converts to Christianity to be generous in benevolent gifts to Jewish Christians in his Epistle to the Galatians (2:9–10). He had given more specific instructions to the church at Corinth regarding this offering in his first epistle (cf. 16:1–4).

The apostle Paul was eager that Jewish Christians recognize the genuineness of the conversion experience of those who came to know Jesus Christ out of idolatry and paganism. Jewish Christians were sincere and conscientious in doubting whether these people could be genuine followers of Jesus Christ unless they also followed all of the traditions, customs, and rituals associated with Judaism. Because generosity was such a remarkable trait, Paul saw that this would be a means by which Gentile Christians could convince Jewish Christians of the genuineness of their relationship to Jesus Christ.

Second Corinthians chapters 8 and 9 are concerned with the response of the followers of Christ in Corinth to this opportunity for ministering through a generous offering.

In this passage of Scripture, the apostle imparts to us the truth that generous and joyous giving is a grace that is to be developed by the followers of Christ (8:7).

Generosity is not instinctual. Generosity does not come easily to humanity, which has believed from the dawn of human history that one must arrange for his own well-being. It has been the strategy of Satan to imply that God is not good and that He is trying to deprive and restrict us rather than enrich and help us. The apostle is urging upon these immature believers that they accept the philosophy of Jesus and come to believe that it is more blessed to give than to receive. He encourages them by the example of Jesus Christ, who demonstrated the grace of God by giving Himself so completely on behalf of all of us (v. 9). Because of God's grace, Jesus Christ became poor that we through His poverty might become rich. Paul encourages us to have that same kind of an attitude and engage in that same kind of activity.

As Paul describes the process by which this offering is to be carried from Asia Minor to the church in Jerusalem, he goes into great detail to describe how people who have been appointed by the congregation in Corinth will accompany him and others as this generous offering is taken to Jerusalem. Then he makes a shocking statement as he comes to the end of the words of our text. He describes the arrival of these messengers with the offering as ". . . the glory of Christ" (v. 23). What does that mean? What was he trying to communicate to these givers? What was he trying to communicate to us today as we give generously in the name of Christ to meet the needs of others?

The word *glory* is used in many different ways throughout Scripture. It is used as an adjective and as a verb. And in this particular passage it is used as a noun to describe those who come with a generous gift to relieve the pain of those who are experiencing great poverty and who are in great need. He describes them as being "the glory of Christ."

When used as a noun the word *glory* describes "a visible manifestation of the invisible God" throughout the Old Testament.

I. The Lord appeared by day "in a pillar of cloud . . . and by night in a pillar of fire to give them light, that they might travel by day and by night" (Exod. 13:21).

This pillar of cloud by day and the pillar of fire by night were visible symbols of the presence of the invisible God that was leading the Israelites out of the bondage of Egypt and into the liberty of the Land of Promise.

The following chapters describe this visible presence of the invisible God in such a way that the people were both comforted and frightened by this manifestation of the invisible God.

II. "The glory of the LORD settled on Mt. Sinai" (Exod. 24:16).

At this particular juncture in the journey of the children of Israel, the glory of the Lord settled on Mt. Sinai. The glory of the Lord concealed the presence of the Lord, while at the same time revealed His presence to the people. When the glory of God moved, they moved. When the glory of God remained in one place, they remained there.

III. "The glory of the LORD filled the tabernacle" (Exod. 40:34).
The tabernacle had been built as a visible symbol of the dwelling place of the Most High God. It contained the sacred furniture that was to be used in the sacrificial system. In the Holy of Holies, the invisible God was to dwell, and He was to be reverenced.

When they completely finished the construction of the tabernacle, "the glory of the LORD filled the tabernacle."

The word *glory* is the word used to describe the visible manifestation of the invisible God.

IV. "The glory of the LORD filled the house of the LORD" (1 Kings 8:11).
When Solomon had completely finished the construction of the magnificent temple on Mt. Moriah, they conducted a dedication service. God honored their gifts and their worship by filling the temple with the visible manifestation of His invisible presence, and this is described as "the glory of the Lord."

V. "The whole earth is full of his glory" (Isa. 6:3 RSV).
In the year that King Uzziah died, Isaiah, a young man, went into the temple where he had a life-changing experience with the eternal God. With the thoughts of an empty throne filling his mind and heart, the eye of his soul was opened, and he was given a vision of God on a throne. He heard the angelic beings speaking of this holy God and that "the whole earth is full of his glory." What he saw was the glory of the Lord. He saw the visible presence of the invisible God, described as the glory of the Lord.

VI. Ezekiel saw the glory of the Lord (Ezek. 1:28).
Ezekiel's inaugural vision by which he became a prophet of God contains a verbal description of the indescribable God who came to him in a far country to anoint him and to commission him to be His spokesman to the exiles. Ezekiel describes this experience as, "Such was the experience of the likeness of the glory of the LORD" (v. 28).

Conclusion. Peter, James, and John saw the glory of the Lord on the Mount of Transfiguration when He was transfigured before them (Matt. 17:2–8).

The apostles saw the glory of the Lord when a cloud took Him out of their sight following His resurrection (Acts 1:9). This was no mere atmospheric condition. This was the shekinah glory that had both revealed and concealed the presence of God throughout the Old Testament ages.

The thrilling, exciting truth that Paul communicates in His epistle to the Corinthians is that these messengers who come bringing generous gifts to the poor out of hearts that are filled with the presence of Christ are in reality "the glory of Christ" in the world today.

That givers are "the glory of Christ"—the visible presence of the invisible God—could excite and challenge and warm our hearts as we seek to give ourselves in service to Him today.

Let us go out and give truly genuine, caring love and be "the glory of

Christ'' in the world today. Let us go out and give affirmation to those about us and be "the glory of Christ'' in the world today. Let us go out and give kindness to others that we might be "the glory of Christ'' in the world today.

Truly it is more blessed to give than to receive. There is more happiness to the person who lives to give than there is for the person who lives to get. When we give generously and gladly, we become "the glory of Christ'' in the world today. We become the visible presence of the invisible Christ. May God help each of us to rise to this opportunity. — *TTC*

* * *

SUNDAY EVENING, NOVEMBER 4

TITLE: **A Testimony of Redemption**

TEXT: **"Let the redeemed of the LORD say so, whom he has redeemed from the hand of the adversary" (Ps. 107:2 NASB).**

SCRIPTURE READING: **Psalm 107:1–32**

Introduction. The phone rang loudly in the silent room. I thought, "Who would be calling at eleven o'clock Wednesday night?" It was a person I had known several years before. She said, "You'll never guess what happened to me tonight. The most wonderful thing in the world! I replied, "You got married." And she said, "No, something far more wonderful than even that! I was saved! I truly repented of my sins and trusted Christ, and I know that He saved me. It's wonderful! I just had to tell somebody."

After I rejoiced in that wonderful news and had hung up the phone, I thought about her last statement, "I just had to tell somebody." That's the way it is when we are saved. We want to share the news.

However, the writer of this psalm is not writing in the glow of a recent experience of redemption. He is reflecting upon a lifetime of blessings which have come through God's redemption.

The psalm is carefully construed like a hymn with four verses and a refrain which is sung with each verse. It is an inspiring testimony of what the Lord has done in our redemption.

I. The Lord has satisfied the longing soul (vv. 1–9).

A. *The plight of the unredeemed* (vv. 4–5).

1. "They wandered in the wilderness." Life without God is without direction. Life without direction makes the journey one of wandering and getting nowhere.

2. "They found no city to dwell in." The soul without God cannot find a peaceful dwelling place, no matter how many places he or she may look.

3. They were "hungry and thirsty." After one has searched for life and peace and found only wilderness and frustration, he hungers and thirsts for life and peace.

4. "Their soul fainted in them." Their longing souls were ready to give up.

B. *The redemption of the Lord when they cry out to Him* (vv. 6–9 NASB).

1. "Then they cried out to the Lord in their trouble" (v. 6a). When

sinful, selfish living leads where it always does—to trouble and heartache—then some will wisely cry out to the Lord.

2. "He delivered them out of their distresses" (v. 6b). The Lord is the Great Deliverer! By the sacrifice of Jesus Christ, the Lord can offer deliverance from the guilt of sin.

3. "He led them forth by the right way" (v. 7). Having received the Lord's redemption, the people never return to their wanderings again. The same Lord who saves them also leads them in the right way. There is a certainty in the way they travel and the destination toward which they progress. For He leads them so "that they might go to a city of habitation," a place of belonging, of security and peace.

4. "He satisfies the longing soul" (v 9a). The longing souls are fully satisfied, filled with goodness, because the Lord performs this miracle in them.

This first verse of the hymn of redemption leads to the refrain. "Oh that men would praise the LORD for his goodness, and for his wonderful works to the children of men!" (v. 8).

II. The Lord has broken the chains of sin (vv. 10–16).

A. *The slavery of sin described* (vv. 10, 12).

1. "They sit in darkness" (v. 10a). Those who live in sin go into darkness, not into the light.

2. They are "in the shadow of death" (v. 10b). Death hangs ominously before the lost sinner, for "the wages of sin is death" (Rom. 6:23).

3. They are "bound in affliction and iron" (Ps. 107:10c). Not only do the sinful experience afflictions, but they are helpless to overcome or escape them. Sin enslaves just as if one were bound with iron.

4. "They fell down, and there was none to help" (v. 12b). Their slavery in sin, their helplessness in their chains, overcomes them and they fall. There, ruined by sin and helpless to overcome it, "there was none to help."

B. *The cause for such terrible slavery is seen* (v. 11).

1. "Because they rebelled against the words of God." God's words make imperative demands upon all, but these refused to obey, and turned away from the words of God.

2. They "spurned the counsel of the Most High" (v. 11b NASB). God called upon them to repent, but they rejected His call. God does this through the preaching of His Word and through the concerned counsel of Christians. It is clear that the cause of terrible slavery is sin against God.

C. *The Lord gives complete salvation, breaks the chains of sin, when they call upon Him* (vv. 13–14, 16).

1. "He saved them out of their distresses" (v. 13b). When they cried desperately for God to help them, He saved them completely. He will hear your cry today.

2. "He brought them out of darkness and the shadow of death" (v. 14a). He provides complete deliverance—no more darkness and no more fear of death.

3. He "brake their bands in sunder" (v. 14b); and verse 16, "He hath broken the gates of brass, and cut the bars of iron in sunder." He broke away the handcuffs and leg irons, and then destroyed the cell and the jail with it. That's complete deliverance.

The refrain is, "Oh that men would praise the Lord for his goodness . . ." (v. 15).

III. The Lord has healed their backslidings (vv. 17–22).

A. *The picture of backsliding.*

1. Backsliding is the mark of fools. "Fools because of their transgression . . . are afflicted" (v. 17).

2. Backsliding is caused by starving the soul of spiritual food. "Their soul abhorreth all manner of meat" (v. 18).

3. Backsliding produces distress and troubles.

B. *The way out of backsliding.* "Then they cry unto the LORD in their trouble" (v. 19).

C. *God heals the backslider.* "He sent his word and healed them" (v. 20). The same Word they neglected, and so starved their souls, is then sent to heal them. So the refrain is, "Oh that men would praise the Lord. . . ."

IV. The Lord calms the storms of life (vv. 23–31).

A. *The storms of life vividly described:* "The stormy wind . . . the waves . . . They mount up . . . They go down again . . . their soul is melted . . . and are at their wit's end." The storms of life can overwhelm us.

B. *God's answer to those who cry out of the storm.*

1. They cried to the Lord in desperation and total dependence. So must we.

2. "He brings them out . . . he makes the storm a calm. . . . Then are they glad" (NASB).

3. "He brings them into their desired haven" (NASB). After the storms of life, the Lord takes us to the wonderful haven of rest.

Conclusion. All of this complete redemption comes from the merciful God. This gives us, the redeemed, a great testimony of our great God. So the writer concludes: "Oh that men would praise the LORD. . . . Let them exalt him also in the congregation of the people" (vv. 31–32). So we ought to gladly give testimony of God's saving grace in Christ, and exalt His name in the assembled church.   *— JFE*

* * *

WEDNESDAY EVENING, NOVEMBER 7

TITLE: Christ and Isaac's Bride

TEXT: **"But thou shalt go unto my country, and to my kindred, and take a wife unto my son Isaac"** (Gen. 24:4).

SCRIPTURE READING: **Genesis 24:1–4**

Introduction. Last week we saw a beautiful foregleam of Christ in the life of Isaac—in the promise of his birth, in his being offered as a sacrifice on Mt. Moriah, and by his being rescued from death. Now, in the remainder of Genesis 22, Isaac is not mentioned again until he goes out into the field to meet Rebekah, his bride. His name is not mentioned once in the rest of chapter 22, or in all of chapter 23. There is a symbolism here, perhaps. After Jesus was crucified on Calvary, He disappeared for three days. (Later, after forty days, He ascended back to his Father in heaven.) The entire story of the securing of the bride for Isaac sparkles with foregleams of Christ and *His* bride, the church.

I. The role of the servant.

A. *When Isaac was forty years old, Abram called his servant Eliezer, which means "God's helper or guide," to go into a far country and bring back a bride for his son.* When the servant of Abraham, Eliezer, who represents the Holy Spirit, met Rebekah, he showed her all of the wealth and riches of Isaac, and told her the purpose for which he had come.

Note the hard proposition which the servant put to the prospective bride for Isaac. First, she was asked to believe a man she had never met before. Second, she was requested to go to a land from which she was never to return. She was to totally abandon her old lifestyle and begin anew in a new land. Third, she was asked to marry a man whom she as yet had not seen.

B. *As we have noted, Eliezer represents the Holy Spirit and His mission in the world.* Just as Eliezer went into the "far country" to seek out a bride for Isaac, so the Holy Spirit has come into the "far country" of the world to gather together the bride of Christ, the church.

No one could come to Christ, become a part of His church, His bride, unless the Holy Spirit introduced Him. For one must first feel conviction of his sins and a desire to receive Christ. God came calling and looking for Adam and Eve. Likewise the Holy Spirit came into the world for the primary purpose of seeking out a bride for Christ. Every time a person is born again, a part of the Holy Spirit's mission is being fulfilled.

II. The reaction of the bride.

A. *This was a monumental test of faith for Rebekah.* Yet she believed the word of the servant whom Abraham had sent; and upon the evidence of the jewels which he presented as a token of the reality of the transaction, she was willing to set out with him to this strange land. We have no record of how much "convincing" the servant had to do in order to win Rebekah. The story tells us that Rebekah prepared herself and went with this man, Eliezer, into a strange country with which she was totally unfamiliar. She hardly knew the direction they were traveling, but she simply trusted her leader. She believed that he knew the way.

B. *One day she lifted up her eyes and saw a man walking toward her.* She had never seen him before, but she must have recognized him because of the faultless description Eliezer had given her.

The prophetic symbolism is clear. God the Father also had an only Son. After He had offered Him up to die on the cross, He too sent His servant, the Holy Spirit, into the far country of this wicked world to call out a bride, the church, for His Son, the Lord Jesus. The same questions that were put to Rebekah are put to sinners today: first, believe someone you have never met before—the Holy Spirit who whispers in your heart and tells you that you are a sinner in need of a Savior. Second, go with Him, allow Him to lead you into the land of the redeemed, from which you will never return. And third, you will be joined to One whom you have never seen before. You must accept by faith the Lord Jesus, your "Bridegroom," though you have never seen Him.

III. The rest of the journey.

A. *As Christians, we may not know the next step we are to take, but we trust our Lord, and we permit Him to lead.* Rebekah did not know the way to the land of her beloved bridegroom, Isaac, but she trusted Eliezer, the servant, to lead her there. Sometimes our days are dreary and hard; but when the journey seems long, the Holy Spirit tells us more about the One whom we shall one day meet face to face. And we take courage and press on.

Then the Holy Spirit will take some of those precious jewels from the Book of our blessed Master, and with the glittering promises of its truth, He encourages us along the way. The Holy Spirit talks to us *not* of Himself, but only of Him whom we are going to meet. This is what John means when he said, "When he, the Spirit of truth, is come, he will guide you into all truth: for he shall not speak of himself; but whatsoever he shall hear, that shall he speak: and he will shew you things to come. He shall glorify me: for he shall receive of mine, and shall shew it unto you" (John 16:13–14).

B. *One of these days, as the shadows of this life start to fall, we will lift up our eyes and there–suddenly in the heavens–we shall see Him, just as Rebekah saw Isaac approaching in the field.* And the Spirit within us will say "That's He!" And we shall rise to meet Him in the air, going into the open arms of Him whom, though we have not seen Him, we have learned to love.

Conclusion. In this beautiful story of Abraham's search for a bride for Isaac, we have the incomparable picture of the Holy Spirit's search for those who will receive Jesus as Savior, and become a part of His bride, the church. The invitation is extended, and it is a universal one.   —*DLJ*

* * *

SUNDAY MORNING, NOVEMBER 11

TITLE: Generous Sowing Means a Generous Harvest

Text: "The point is this: he who sows sparingly will also reap sparingly, and he who sows bountifully will also reap bountifully" (2 Cor. 9:6 rsv).

Scripture Reading: 2 Corinthians 9:6–12

Hymns: "To God Be the Glory," Crosby
            "I Stand Amazed in the Presence," Gabriel
            "I Gave My Life for Thee," Havergal

Offertory Prayer:
Father God, we want to thank You for the privilege of worship today. Thank You for letting us come to Your house. Thank You for letting us be associated with these people as we come together to worship You and to praise Your holy and good name. We come now bringing love gifts to express our gratitude for Your generosity. Bless these gifts to the end that others shall come to know Your love and Your mercy. Through Jesus Christ our Lord we pray. Amen.

Introduction. In 2 Corinthians, chapters 8 and 9, the apostle Paul is writing to the disciples of our Lord in the city of Corinth regarding a generous benevolent offering which they have made plans to provide for the poor saints in Jerusalem. He has commended them for their generosity and their eagerness to be a part of providing relief for those who were in genuine need.

The apostle was particularly interested in this being a generous and worthy offering because it would not only relieve the conditions of distress in Jerusalem, but it would also serve as a bridge to unite Jewish believers with those who were converts from paganism and idolatry to the Christian faith. Paul knew that if a generous offering came from Gentile converts, that this would be very helpful at the point of breaking down the cultural and religious barriers that separated Gentile believers from Jewish believers (cf. Acts 6:1; Gal. 2:9–10).

In these two chapters Paul deals with the subject of the proper motivations for generous giving, and he also discusses the principles of proper giving to God and for the needs of others.

This section of the epistle contains a plea for generosity. It also contains a plea for enthusiasm in the giving of the offering. It contains a plea for a great faith in God, and it also contains a word of encouragement concerning their entering into a real partnership with God and with others in relieving the needs of those in great need.

Paul encourages them to be generous by reminding them of one of the basic laws in agriculture. The gardener or the farmer will reap in direct proportion to his using a proper amount of seed for the planting of a garden plot or a field. He emphasizes the fact that it is foolish to be stingy with the seed in sowing time. He who would be stingy with the seed during the sowing time is in reality robbing himself of the potential harvest in the future. The apostle applies this to the practice of giving for the glory of God and for the good of others. This principle works in every area of life.

I. We reap in the measure that we have given ourselves to Bible study (Josh. 1:8).

Many people are not even acquainted with biblical characters, much less the great events of biblical history. They have no knowledge of the provisions of God's great salvation, which is offered through the ministry of Jesus Christ and through the abiding presence of the Holy Spirit. Their lives are greatly impoverished because they have never given themselves to the study of God's Holy Word.

If we neglect to feed ourselves on the truth of God's Word, we cannot possibly grow up in the salvation which God has provided (1 Peter 2:1–3).

The psalmist describes the happy and successful man as one who delights in and meditates upon the great truths of God's Word (Ps. 1:1–3).

We reap in biblical knowledge according to the measure in which we have given ourselves to Bible study.

II. We reap in the measure that we have given ourselves in prayer (Matt. 6:6).

Jesus specifically and dogmatically declared that there are spiritual rewards that come to those who develop the habit of going apart into the private place for communion with the Father God. These rewards and blessings are too numerous to list, but many people miss these rewards because they never give themselves to prayer. James writes in his epistle, "You do not have, because you do not ask" (4:2 RSV). This does not mean that we can get anything we ask for. It does mean that God has many things for those of us who wait upon our asking.

He who neglects to give himself much to prayer misses the blessings that would come from prayer. We reap according to the measure in which we have sown.

III. We reap in the measure that we give voice to our Christian testimony (Ps. 126:6).

One of the greatest sins that we are guilty of is the sin of being silent about the goodness of God and about the grace of God revealed in and through Jesus Christ.

It appears that some of us are either ashamed of our relationship with Jesus Christ or we are afraid to speak concerning His presence in our lives.

The Holy Spirit of God can take our personal testimony and use it to impart the gift of faith to the nonbelievers about us. When we neglect to "plant the seed" of our personal testimonies concerning what God has done in our own lives, we are depriving others of the blessing that they could receive. At the same time, we are robbing ourselves of the joy of the harvest time that God wants us to experience.

IV. We reap in the measure that we give of our material resources in the service of God and for the good of others (2 Cor. 9:8).

The apostle Paul did not believe that God was a beggar or that God's treasury was in danger of going bankrupt. He did not believe that God became richer because of the gifts of His people. Instead, he encouraged these people in Corinth to become generous givers because God is a generous Giver. The apostle declares, "God loves a cheerful giver" (9:7 RSV). God does not love the generous giver because the gifts enrich the heavenly treasury; God loves the cheerful giver because that giver is becoming Godlike. When we give out of a heart of love and meet the needs of others, God sees in us those character traits that remind Him of His own nature and character. To be generous is to be godly. To be stingy is to be ungodly.

Paul declares in verse 8 of this chapter that God responds to the generosity of His children by blessing them in the manner in which they have given of themselves into His service and for the good of others. God blesses not just by addition, but by multiplication. Paul declares that God will bless the generous person with divine generosity, and that his needs will be met.

The word which is translated "cheerful" is the Greek word *hilarion*. This is the word from which we get our word *hilarious*. One cannot be a hilarious giver if he has a great feeling of insecurity. He who finds his security only in the possession of material things can never be a hilarious giver, because he can never accumulate enough to be totally secure. Paul is encouraging the people to find their security in God, and then, out of the resources that He blesses them with, to be a hilarious helper of others.

Conclusion. It is never wise to be stingy with the seed at the time of planting. The gardener or the farmer will actually be very generous with his seed because he recognizes that if the seed is not planted, there can be no harvest. This law works in the realm of the spirit exactly as it does in the realm of nature. We can become hilarious givers of ourselves and of our substance if we can somehow muster the faith to trust God to give us an abundant harvest.   — *TTC*

* * *

SUNDAY EVENING, NOVEMBER 11

TITLE: **The Salvation of a Scarlet Woman**

TEXT: **"Jesus answered and said unto her, Whosoever drinketh of this water shall thirst again: But whosoever drinketh of the water that I shall give him shall never thirst; but the water that I shall give him shall be in him a well of water springing up into everlasting life"** (John 4:13–14).

SCRIPTURE READING: **John 4:4–30, 39–42**

Introduction. There was a village which needed salvation. It was of great concern to Jesus. The people were a despised group—Samaritans, half-breed Jews. They were rejected by society, both Jewish and Gentile. But they were not rejected by Jesus! They needed Him, so "he *must* needs go through Samaria" (John 4:4). Most Jews traveled around that region, but Jesus felt compelled to go there.

How to reach a village for salvation? One way would be to save a sinner who would witness to the rest. This is the method Jesus chose. Though this was a casual contact, it was not an accident. This woman, so frustrated in seeking true love and immoral in conduct, came to the community well at high noon. No doubt she was lonely and empty. Certainly she did not dream that a miracle was about to happen—and to her! Take the steps with her.

I. Curiosity aroused (4:4–14).

A. *Why?* Why would this Jew travel through Samaria? Why would he talk to her? For a rabbi to talk to a woman in public was a violation of custom. And to talk to a sinful Samaritan woman was totally taboo. But Jesus broke the racial and social barriers because all people are equally important to Him, and He wants to save all.

B. *What?* What was this living water? He certainly spoke truly when He said that water from the community well would satisfy thirst only temporarily. But His water would stop thirst forever. Living water? What was that?

C. *Who?* Who is this man? "Art thou greater than our father Jacob?" Her curiosity was really aroused.

Are you curious about Jesus? Does the offer He makes of eternal life intrigue you? Does the transformed life of your friend who trusted Christ make you wonder if Jesus could do that in your life, too?

II. Craving awakened (4:15).

"Sir, give me this water." Her soul desired something that satisfied.

A. *She could have understood His meaning.* She seemed to have some understanding of the Scriptures, and the term "living water" could have had real meaning to her. Isaiah, Jeremiah, Ezekiel, the Psalms, and Zechariah all used it to refer to salvation and messianic blessings. Her words "That I thirst not, neither come hither to draw" may have been words of jesting sarcasm to cover her deep craving for salvation.

B. *Her craving for life was unexpected.* The people of the village expected nothing good of her. No one dreamed that she would have a hunger for cleansing and salvation.

III. Conviction felt (4:16–24).

A. *Her sinfulness was revealed.* When craving for forgiveness awakens, then sinfulness must be revealed. For no salvation comes until we deal with our sins and confess our guilt and need. When the reluctance to repent comes, then conviction can convulse one's soul. Jesus knew this woman needed to face herself as a sinner, so He said, "Go, call thy husband, and come hither." He then informed her that He knew she had been married five times and now lived with a man without marriage.

B. *Her escape from admittance of sin was blocked.* She tried to change the subject to religion rather than her sins. She wanted to discuss *where* people should worship, but Jesus talked about *how* people worship. "God is a Spirit: and they that worship him must worship him in spirit and in truth" (v. 24).

IV. Conversion experienced (4:25–26).

A. *"Christ: when he is come. . . ."* As the woman heard Jesus tell her that the way to God did not depend upon place or race, but upon the heart, she thought about the promised Savior, the Christ.

B. *Jesus revealed Himself as the Messiah, the Christ.* "I that speak unto thee am he." Jesus is the One who shows us the Father. He *is* the way. The woman's reaction now must be to more than a Jewish man or even a prophet. She was in the very presence of the promised Savior.

C. *She forgot her thirst and even her waterpot.* Her inner thirst had to be satisfied.

V. Confession expressed (4:28–29).

This woman was unashamed to talk about the One who had revealed all her sins. She challenged the townspeople with the question, "Is not this the Christ?"

Her confession was powerful in effect. The men of the city came out to see and hear Jesus for themselves. As a result, many believed in Him. "Many more believed because of his own word; and said unto the woman, Now we believe, not because of thy saying: for we have heard him ourselves, and know that this is indeed the Christ, the Saviour of the world" (vv. 41–42).

Conclusion. Every person, whether he recognizes it or not, is thirsty for the living water, salvation from sin. Everyone desires the fountain of eternal life. It is available in Jesus Christ. If there is curiosity enough to listen to Christ, craving enough to want the abundant life, conviction enough to recognize and confess sin and guilt, faith enough to experience salvation, then it will be natural to express confession of Christ as Savior and Lord. The salvation of the scarlet woman sets the pattern for the conversion of all who need to be saved. — *JFE*

* * *

WEDNESDAY EVENING, NOVEMBER 14

TITLE: Christ and Joseph

Text: **"And God sent me before you to preserve you a posterity in the earth, and to save your lives by a great deliverance. So now it was not you that sent me hither, but God: and he hath made me a father to Pharaoh, and** lord of all his house, and a ruler throughout all the land of Egypt" (Gen. 45:7-8).

SCRIPTURE READING: **Genesis 45:1-15**

Introduction. Four men stand out in the last thirty-nine chapters of Genesis, who, in a sense, are symbolical of four successive steps in God's program of redemption. Abraham is the great example of divine, sovereign election by grace. Abraham was not searching for God at all; God came looking for Abraham. Likewise to this very day no unbeliever takes the initiative and searches for God. Then Isaac is the example of selective calling. He was the child of promise, born miraculously to Abraham and Sarah in their old age. He represented the Lord Jesus Christ as the sacrifice for sin. Then came Jacob, the twin brother of Esau, who represented the miracle of salvation by grace alone. There was nothing commendable in Jacob which would have qualified him for his place of distinction in God's plan. Yet God saw through the imperfections and weaknesses in Jacob's life, and saw one whom He could use to carry along the development of His plan of redemption.

Finally came Joseph, who is the great picture of *glorification*. Joseph was vindicated and exalted by God, after having suffered at the hands of his family *and* his enemies. Thus, beginning with divine election and ending with glorification, God revealed in type His plan which Paul undoubtedly had in mind when he wrote in Romans 8:30: "Whom he did predestinate, them he also called: and whom he called, them he also justified: and whom he justified, them he also glorified."

In many ways, Joseph is the most complete and satisfying type of the Lord Jesus in Genesis. Between chapters 37 and 50 of Genesis there are over one hundred incidents and details in the history of Joseph's life which point to the Lord Jesus. Tonight we shall lift out of the story of Joseph the three most obvious facts which point unmistakably to the Lord Jesus.

I. Joseph was beloved of his father (Gen. 37:1-4).

A. *Two of the most thrilling moments in the earthly life of Jesus must have been His baptism and His transfiguration on the mountain with Moses and Elijah, in the presence of Peter, James, and John.* On those two occasions, God thundered from heaven His love and approval for His Son.

Likewise, Joseph was loved by Jacob because "he was the son of his old age." Jacob had other sons, but they were not close to their father. There is a contrast here. Jesus was the *only* "begotten son of God the Father"; God did not have other offspring.

B. *To further prove that Joseph shared the favored position with his father, Jacob gave him "a coat of many colors."* In Old Testament times, this was the dress of the heir, the one who was to receive the inheritance of his father. In the same way, Paul tells us that Christ has been appointed by God as "heir of all things" (Heb. 1:2). And the wonderful thing about this is that we who are His *share* in this inheritance! We are "heirs of God, and joint-heirs with Christ" (Rom. 8:17).

Thus in the beginning of the record of Joseph's life we see this significant fact that he was beloved of his father in a special and unique way. And we hear Jesus say to His own disciples, "I and my Father are one. . . . He that hath seen me, hath seen the Father" (John 10:30; 14:9).

II. Joseph was hated by his brethren.

A. *Joseph's brothers had been a disappointment to their father.* Obviously there was lacking a relationship of trust between them and Jacob, for Jacob felt it necessary to send Joseph out into the fields to "check on" his brothers, to see if they were tending the flocks as they should. And sure enough, they were not. They had refused to accept their father's will and follow his instructions.

Thus, when they saw Joseph *obeying* his father and seeking to please him in all things, they hated him bitterly. The Scripture states that they "could not speak peaceably to him." Here is an example of the lost person who cannot love God within himself. We know, also, that this was the attitude of the kinsmen of Jesus toward Him—His own half-brothers who grew up with Him in Nazareth, as well as His fellow Jews.

B. *Then, Joseph caused his brothers to hate him all the more when he came forward with the strange dreams that he had.* These were prophetic dreams, dreams God had given to him for the purpose of warning his brothers. In the dreams Joseph saw his brothers as "sheaves of wheat" in the field, bowing down to him. In a second dream, Joseph saw the sun and moon and the eleven stars making obeisance, giving honor, to him. By the time Joseph related the second dream to his brothers, their anger toward him was at the boiling point (37:8).

In all of this, we can see a graphic picture of the enemies of Jesus. They hated Him, too, for what He claimed to be. John tells us: "Therefore the Jews sought the more to kill him, because he . . . said also that God was his Father, making himself equal with God" (John 5:18).

III. Joseph became the savior of his people.

A. *The story of Joseph's life after he was sold by his brothers to the Ishmaelite slave traders reads almost like a mystery novel.* But through it all we see a parallel in the life of Jesus. He, too, was tried and convicted on false charges. He was "numbered with the transgressors" and treated as a common criminal, as was Joseph.

Then, to shorten a rather lengthy story, Joseph interpreted Pharaoh's dream and ultimately was exalted to a high position in Egypt. During this time a great famine in Canaan forced his father Jacob to send his sons (Joseph's brothers) to Egypt to purchase grain. They had no idea that their brother Joseph, whom they hated and had sold into slavery, was still alive, much less the "number-two ruler" in Egypt!

B. *The dealings which resulted between Joseph and his brothers were at once agonizing and beautiful.* All that Joseph did was not out of revenge and vengeance; there was a purpose and plan in it all. For conviction came upon these brothers while they were in jail. They remembered how they had dealt with their brother Joseph. Finally Joseph wrung from them a confession of their guilt and sin. The result was that Joseph "fell upon his brother Benjamin's neck, and wept; and Benjamin wept upon his neck. Moreover he kissed all his brethren, and wept upon them: and after that his brethren talked with him" (Gen. 45:14–15).

Conclusion. What a beautiful picture indeed do we have of the Lord Jesus Christ as foreshadowed and prefigured in the life of Joseph! He was "beloved of his father," a special son, with a special mission to perform. He was "hated by his brethren"; He "came unto his own, but his own received him not." He was, most gloriously, "the savior of his people." He loved his brothers in spite of their sin against him. So too the Lord Jesus loved His enemies and even died for them. — *DLJ*

* * *

SUNDAY MORNING, NOVEMBER 18

TITLE: It Is a Good Thing to Give Thanks

TEXT: "It is good to give thanks to the LORD, to sing praises to thy name, O Most High" (Ps. 92:1 RSV).

SCRIPTURE READING: Psalm 92:1–4; Ephesians 5:18–20

HYMNS: "Praise to the Lord, the Almighty," Neander
"Come, Ye Thankful People, Come," Elvey
"Now Thank We All Our God," Cruger

OFFERTORY PRAYER:
Father God, we join our hearts with the heart of the psalmist in praising You for Your love and faithfulness. We come today indicating our love for You by bringing tithes and offerings. Faithfully we would be generous and supportive of Your work in the world, not only with our treasures, but with our time and talents and testimony. Through Jesus Christ our Lord we pray. Amen.

Introduction. The psalmist experienced the joy of being thankful and became verbal in his giving of thanks to the Lord. He declares, "It is good to give thanks to the LORD." The psalmist was talking to himself. We too need to recognize the wisdom of talking to ourselves about this matter of giving thanks to God.

The psalmist is talking to the church as well as to himself. It would be good for us as a church to give thanks to our God in the presence of His people. In Paul's Epistle to the Ephesians, he urges them to speak to each other in psalms and hymns and spiritual songs, giving thanks to God. He declares that this is the will of God for us in Christ Jesus (5:17–20).

The psalmist talks about the subjects for which he could be thankful. He expresses thanks for the lovingkindness of God. He believes in the steadfast, enduring love of God, and for this he offers thanks. He was also grateful for the faithfulness of God. He discovered God to be reliable, trustworthy, and dependable. Not only does he speak about the subjects for which we should be thankful, but he also reveals the seasons in which we should be thankful. He speaks of giving voice to thanksgiving both in the morning and at night.

I. It is a good thing to give thanks to God.

James recognized that every good and perfect gift finds its source in the generosity of God (1:17).

A. *It is a good thing for you personally to give thanks to God.* Paul wrote to the saints at Thessalonica and said, "Give thanks in all circumstances; for this is the will of God in Christ Jesus for you" (1 Thess. 5:18 RSV).

1. Offering thanks will disperse your depression.
2. Offering thanks to God will increase your joy in life.

3. Offering thanks to God will encourage your faith and hope for the future.

4. Offering thanks will make a great contribution toward your having a positive mental attitude.

5. Giving thanks will encourage you to be generous toward God and toward others.

B. *Giving thanks is a good thing for those about you.*

1. Your offering of thanks to God will encourage others to have faith in God.

2. Your thanksgiving will encourage an attitude of gratitude within those about you.

C. *The offering of thanks brings joy to the Father God.* Every earthly parent is caused to rejoice when a child comes and says, "Daddy, thank you. I love you." We are not bringing God down by making the assumption that our thanksgiving brings joy to His loving heart.

II. It is a good thing for you to give thanks to others.

A. *It is a "good thing" to give thanks to your parents.* Shakespeare puts into the mouth of one of his characters, "How sharper than a serpent's tooth it is to have an ungrateful child." You can bring joy to the heart of an aged parent by thanking him for what he has done for you and for what he has meant to you.

B. *It is a "good thing" to give thanks to your mate.* Let us thank God for and offer thanks to our mate, for the quality of marriage is nourished by an attitude of gratitude. A husband or wife can never say "thank you" too much to the one who is sharing his or her life.

C. *It is a "good thing" to give thanks to your children.*

1. Most parents are hypercritical of their children rather than being complimentary. This can be a serious defect in parenting.

2. We need to affirm and applaud that which is good in the conduct and choices of our children.

3. We need to applaud our children for choosing the good and avoiding the bad.

How long has it been since you sincerely offered thanks to your children for what they mean to you and for what they have done for you?

D. *It is a "good thing" to give thanks to your friends.* Rich indeed is the man who has lots of friends. Rich indeed is the man who has one genuine friend. All of us would have more friends if we nourished the relationships that we have with others with expressions of thanksgiving.

E. *It is a "good thing" to give thanks to those who serve you in a significant manner.*

1. Have you offered thanks to the teachers of your children?

2. How long has it been since you offered thanks to the sheriff or the police force in your community for helping promote the safety of the community or to the fireman who would come to your rescue should your house become enflamed?

3. How long has it been since you have expressed thanks to the hospital where people wait to minister to your family should an emergency arrive?

4. How long has it been since you have thanked the garbage collector who comes to pick up the garbage at your house?

5. How long has it been since you offered real thanks to a salesperson who helped you make a proper purchase?

6. How long has it been since you have offered thanks to your neighbors?

Conclusion. It is a good thing to give thanks to God. It is also a good thing to give thanks to others.

The best way to give thanks to God is to give Him your heart. Give Him your confidence. Give to Him the gratitude and the trust of your heart. Let your life be a life of thanksliving and you will experience far more joy in life and you will be a far greater blessing to others than if you neglect to develop the habit of being a thankful person.   — *TTC*

* * *

SUNDAY EVENING, NOVEMBER 18

TITLE: Reconciliation

TEXT: "If any man be in Christ, he is a new creature" (2 Cor. 5:17).

SCRIPTURE READING: 2 Corinthians 5:17–21

Introduction. Four pastors were discussing how much churches today need revival. One spoke of how many members did not have any joy in their salvation. Another spoke about so many who were spasmodic in attendance and who did not witness to the lost. Then one of the men said, "I think the real need of most of my congregation is a true understanding of what it means to be reconciled to God." That deals with the heart of the problem. Reconciliation is the very heart of the New Testament. It is imperative that we come to a new appreciation of what we have in Jesus Christ.

I. The meaning of reconciliation.

The word *reconciliation* is used often in older English, primarily referring to former enemies becoming friends. In the New Testament it is nearly always used of a changed relationship between a person and God. For example, "Being now justified by his blood, we shall be saved from wrath through him. For if, when we were enemies, we were reconciled to God by the death of his Son, much more, being reconciled, we shall be saved by his life" (Rom. 5:9–10). The unsaved person lives a lifestyle in opposition to God and is destined to suffer the wrath of God. But God so loved us that he gave His Son to experience our punishment and death and to make a way for us to have peace with God, which is salvation through faith in Christ.

An illustration of this is seen in the Old Testament story of Hosea and Gomer. They were married, but she was unfaithful to him. She left him and went into a life of sensual, sinful pleasure. She represents all people who are unfaithful to God. The marriage relationship was broken, and this brought tragic results to Gomer. So sin causes us to be lost from God. But it also broke the heart of Hosea. He represents our loving God. Then when sin had run its course, Hosea, who still loved his wife in spite of her unworthiness, paid the price for her redemption. The relationship was restored. She could no longer continue the old life. She was to be exclusively devoted to the one who loved her and redeemed her. So we have been bought with the high price of the blood of Christ; we belong to Him, and so are reconciled to Him.

II. The agent of reconciliation.

"God . . . hath reconciled us to himself by Jesus Christ" (2 Cor. 5:17).

A. *The agent of reconciliation is Jesus Christ.* He is the One promised by the prophets, who fulfilled the words they wrote. Having been born of the Virgin Mary, He lived the perfect life. He went willingly to the cross to bear our sins (1 Peter 2:24). He rose from the dead and is alive forever. "This man, after he had offered one sacrifice for sins for ever, sat down on the right hand of God. . . . For by one offering he hath perfected for ever them that are sanctified" (Heb. 10:12, 14).

B. *The Agent was made sin for us.* "For he hath made him to be sin for us, who knew no sin; that we might be made the righteousness of God in him" (2 Cor. 5:21). When Jesus died, He took our sins and made them His own.

C. *This was all the work of God.* "God was in Christ, reconciling the world unto himself, not imputing their trespasses unto them" (v. 19). The very heart and person of God were in the sacrifice of Christ. God is truly the God of love and sacrifice!

III. The totality of reconciliation.

A. *In Christ the reconciled person is a new creature.* Literally, he is a new creation—completely new!

B. *The old has passed away.* The old life, the sins, the guilt, the deadness, the rebellious heart are all gone. The perfect sacrifice of Christ guarantees this.

C. *"All things are become new"* (v. 17). When all of the old has been removed, the heart is not left empty. In Christ everything in life, in fact, life itself is all new. There is new life, a new presence, as one is now indwelt by the Holy Spirit. New peace, new power, a new family, new love, new purpose, and a new destiny. All things are new in Christ!

D. *See the wonderful wholeness of the new life.* "And all things are of God" (v. 18). This includes the whole plan of life—the spiritual, the physical, the mental, and social and family life. This also includes the whole span of life—"*are* of God." This present tense indicates that the new life is still new every today that comes. It is God-centered. All are "of God." So the focus of life changes from self to God.

IV. The secret of reconciliation.

A. *The secret is to be "in Christ."* This happens by faith. When you put your faith and trust in Christ, you and Christ enter into a complete, unchangeable relationship.

B. *There is a terrible possibility.* It is *if* any man is in Christ. *If.* This indicates that there is the possibility that a person might miss Christ. This would be the most awful tragedy imaginable.

C. *Consider the open invitation:* "any man." The way to reconciliation is open to any person. It is a "whosoever" gospel. God, who is no respecter of persons, wants all people to be saved and says, "Whosoever will, let him take the water of life freely" (Rev. 22:17).

V. The ministry of reconciliation.

A. *God has given us this ministry.* "And hath committed unto us the word of reconciliation" (2 Cor. 5:19). So the main work of each Christian and each church is to call people to reconciliation through faith in Jesus Christ. This should have top priority.

B. *This ministry gives us a noble status.* "Now then we are ambassadors for Christ" (v. 20). We are Christ's official representatives with His message, His power, and His authority to give that message.

C. *This ministry involves us in urgent evangelism.* "As though God were making his appeal through us. We implore you on Christ's behalf: Be reconciled to God" (v. 20 NIV). We implore, we beg, we exhort people to be reconciled to God. This describes the urgent appeal which comes from caring hearts committed to obeying Christ.

Conclusion. So we have a great salvation by which we are completely reconciled to God. This gives us life that is completely new and completely God-centered. It also involves us in evangelizing others for our Lord. We should be grateful for our new life, and we should be totally committed to reaching others for salvation. — *JFE*

* * *

WEDNESDAY EVENING, NOVEMBER 21

TITLE: "Build Me a Sanctuary!"

TEXT: **"And let them make me a sanctuary; that I may dwell among them" (Exod. 25:8).**

SCRIPTURE READING: **Exodus 25:1–9**

Introduction. In our study of "Foregleams of Christ in the Old Testament," we come to one of the most fascinating of all the Old Testament types and symbols—the tabernacle, or tent of worship, which God instructed Moses to build in the wilderness between Egypt and the Promised Land. There are many remarkable things about the tabernacle. To begin with, it was the very first place of worship ever built in honor of the Lord Jehovah. And it is most significant that God gave Moses detailed and specific instructions for its building. It was not an edifice born out of Moses' imagination and ingenuity.

In this study session, we shall concentrate on an overview of this unusual place of worship. In subsequent studies, we shall study it, part by part, from the standpoint of its furnishings, its design, and its place of importance among the people of God.

I. The Designer.

A. *After God had delivered Israel from their four hundred years of Egyptian slavery, Moses had led them down to the southern tip of the Sinai peninsula.* He had moved, and the people had followed him, as the cloud of God's glory had moved in the sky above them. Finally they came to majestic, awesome, craggy Mt. Sinai. While they were camped at the base of the mountain, God had given Moses the Law, and along with it instructions for the building of the tabernacle.

The purpose of the tabernacle was to allow God to dwell among His people in order to meet their needs (Exod. 25:8–9). Here we see God's compassion for His people. They knew so little about Him. They had no sacred Scriptures. God longed to identify Himself with His people and to dwell among them. God wants fellowship with those who place their faith in Him.

B. *And note that it was* God *who wanted to dwell with the people.* Never had they asked this of God. God sought them! Over and over we have seen that fact in our study of the Old Testament. It has always been God who has first come seeking man.

But because of the sinfulness of the people, God could not dwell in their midst in just any way. So He prescribed the way that this could be done. Throughout the Scriptures, we can note the progress God made in the way He revealed Himself to man. First, He walked in the Garden of Eden in the cool of the day and revealed Himself to Adam and Eve. Second, He revealed Himself to Moses in the burning bush. Third, when the Israelites had been delivered from Egypt, God revealed Himself to them in a pillar of cloud by day and fire by night. Fourth, after Moses had completed the tabernacle as God had instructed him, God appeared over it in the same cloud. "The cloud of the LORD was upon the tabernacle by day, and fire was on it by night, in the sight of all the house of Israel, throughout all their journeys" (40:38). And fifth, God later revealed Himself in the temple built by Solomon, after the design of the tabernacle.

Sixth, during the New Testament era, God dwelt among His people in the person of the Lord Jesus Christ. Jesus was the radiance of God's glory among us—the express image of the Father in heaven. Then, after Jesus ascended to the Father, He sent the Holy Spirit to indwell every believer.

II. The design of this strange building.

A. *As we have noted, God was careful to lay out for Moses the exact design for the tabernacle.* Moses was not given "free reign" to experiment with some design of his own.

The tabernacle building itself was forty-five feet long and about fifteen feet wide. The back end of it and the two sides were constructed of boards, and the entrance had a curtain of fine linen in blue, purple, and scarlet. The building itself stood in a courtyard surrounded by a fence made of curtains of fine, white, pure linen about 8½ feet high, enclosing an area 175 feet long and 87½ feet wide. Within the enclosure, or courtyard, there were two pieces of furniture. First, at the one entrance to the courtyard there was the "brazen altar," an altar made of brass, upon which the sacrifice of a spotless lamb was burning continually.

Next, between this altar and the tabernacle itself there was a laver, a washing basin, at which the priest washed his hands and feet before entering the Holy Place of the tabernacle.

B. *As one entered the tabernacle building, he found that there were two rooms—a larger one and a smaller one.* The larger room was called "the Holy Place," and there were three pieces of furniture in that room. As one entered, at the right there was the "table of shewbread." Then straight ahead, placed in front of the curtain dividing the Holy Place from the smaller room, there was a golden "altar of burnt incense." On the left side of the room was the golden, seven-branched candelabra, the flames of which were kept burning continually.

Next came the smaller room, called "the Holy of Holies," the most sacred and awesome part of the tabernacle and its complex. There was one piece of furniture inside that room, called "the ark of the covenant." This chestlike object contained the two tables of stone upon which the Ten Commandments were inscribed, a pot of manna, and Aaron's rod, which represented the God-ordained priesthood among the people. And incidentally, no one could enter this room except the high priest, and he could do so only once a year—on the Day of Atonement, when he brought the sacrificial blood in to make atonement for his sins and the sins of the people.

III. Those for whom it was designed.

A. *To do this, we must leave the Old Testament briefly and go to the New Testament.* The order of approach to God on the part of sinful man, as outlined in the tabernacle, is shown beautifully in the Gospel of John. John the Baptist introduced Jesus as "the Lamb of God, which taketh away the sin of the world" (1:29). This points to the sacrifice which burned on the brazen altar in the courtyard. That, representing the sacrificial death of Christ on the cross, is the first step in one's reconciliation with God. The laver for washing represents the continual cleansing of the Word of God, as it is read, studied, and digested. The table of shewbread speaks of Jesus as "the Bread of Life," and the golden candelabra points to Him as "the Light of the World." The golden altar of burnt incense represents the prayer of the priest ascending to God on behalf of the people. Jesus' prayer in John 17 was for us. This altar also represents the privilege *we* have, as "priests of God," to pray before heaven's throne of grace.

B. *Finally, inside the veil separating the Holy Place from the Holy of Holies, there is the mercy seat—the throne of God, the presence of God, where we are told to "come boldly" and place before Him our needs, our petitions, the yearnings and pleadings of our hearts.*

Conclusion. So here we have the overview of the tabernacle and its teaching to us. Next week we shall walk slowly and deliberately through the courtyard of this complex and through the building, and we shall look at the details of its structure. Thus we shall see even *more* of our Lord Jesus Christ symbolized here. In all of it, we can determine God's purpose in providing salvation for sinful man.

— DLJ

* * *

SUNDAY MORNING, NOVEMBER 25

TITLE: **God Makes Things New**

TEXT: **"A new heart also will I give you, and a new spirit will I put within you"** (Ezek. 36:26).

SCRIPTURE READING: **Ezekiel 36:22–31**

HYMNS: **"His Way With Thee," Nusbaum**
"Have Thine Own Way, Lord," Pollard
"Whiter Than Snow," Nicholson

OFFERTORY PRAYER:
Our Father, help us never to take for granted the blessings that we have but always to remember they come from You, and that we shall never truly

show our gratitude for them until we also learn that it is "more blessed to give than to receive." Bless us in this offering. We pray in Jesus' name. Amen.

Introduction. The prophets of the Old Testament were God's spokesmen to their generation. They came with an authentic message that was relevant to the situation in which they found themselves. The prophets were not primarily predictors. They were primarily authentic, inspired spokesmen for God to their generation. Often their messages have a double application. There was both a present fulfillment and a future fulfillment.

Isaiah was not alone at being a messianic prophet. Ezekiel, the prophet among the exiles, had a message for his day; but there were also truths in his prophecies of great messianic significance. As we enter the Advent season of the year, in which we rejoice in the coming of the Christ, we can enrich our spiritual lives as we look at the messianic predictions coming to us through the prophet Ezekiel.

The Book of Ezekiel is one of the most logically organized books among the canonical prophets. The first twenty-four chapters warn that the city of Jerusalem will be destroyed, and the people there will join the captives in Babylon. Chapters 25 through 32 are foreign prophecies, directed against the nations surrounding Judah and warning them of their fate. In chapters 33 through 39, Ezekiel gives messages of hope for Israel's future. The first few chapters of this section deal with the responsibility of the prophet as a watchman and the hearers as individuals, and contain an oracle concerning God's concern for his flock. Chapters 35 and 36 deal with the destruction of Edom and the restoration of Israel. It is in the latter chapter that our text appears.

God promised to deliver and bless His people bountifully. He had made a covenant with Abraham that his descendants would be a blessing to the world. The messianic promise had not yet been fulfilled, and God was determined that nothing would prevent it.

I. Motivation—for the sake of the Lord's name.

Although the Old Testament makes it abundantly clear that God is compassionate and merciful toward all people, a fundamental fact that accompanies many of His declarations is that God wishes to vindicate His own name. Why is He concerned about this? The answer goes back to the call of Abraham. Rather than destroy the world again by flood, God decided to start a new people and allow them to be missionaries to the rest of the world. In those days, every nation and culture had a god of its own. Some, such as the Egyptians, had a multitude of deities whom they worshiped. God chose Abraham, first of all, in order to let the rest of the world know there is only one God and that He personifies holiness as well as redeeming love.

When the city of Jerusalem was destroyed and the temple fell in 586 B.C., skeptics considered this proof that Israel's God was weak and unable to protect His people. Restoring the nation then would be an act which proved that the monotheistic God lives and has unlimited power.

A person's name was always important because it stood for his entire character. These proper nouns had meanings, given to people either at birth or at some significant time in their lives, to stand for a trait that the namer saw or hoped would develop in the person. Since Israel's God possessed a name that meant "I am that I am," signifying external existence, God wished to make it clear He had all power and could redeem His people at any time He chose. This fact prevented others from casting doubts upon the ability of the true God. God loved His name and wanted others to respect it because it stood not only for unlimited existence but suggested the covenant that God had made to Abraham to protect His own people and accomplish the work He had given to them.

II. A new relationship.

Since sin always separates from God, forgiveness is necessary in order to bring either a nation or an individual back to God. As Ezekiel, under the inspiration of God, surveyed the scene, he saw that Israel's greatest need was the restoration of a relationship which had been broken by the nation's rebellion against God. As he delivered God's message concerning the future, the first thing he felt needed to be done was for the sin to be removed that severed the relationship between Israel and God.

Likewise, sin destroys the relationship of an individual with God. In Adam, we all die; but in the death of Jesus Christ, God dealt with sin, and the resurrection vindicated all that Jesus did on the cross. When one receives Jesus as Savior, the sin debt is dealt with "once and for all." Guilt is removed and a person has a new standing before God, forgiven of his sin through the atoning work of Christ on the cross.

A new relationship is thus established that cannot be destroyed. Fellowship may vary as a believer is obedient or disobedient. Growth may take place more at certain times in one's life than at other times. The person, however, who has been genuinely saved by receiving Christ as Savior enjoys a relationship that is new and cannot be taken away by anything or anyone.

III. A new heart.

The Hebrew word translated "heart" has more than the idea of feeling. In fact, emotion is only a small part of its meaning. To the Hebrews, feeling was associated with the kidneys or the intestines. The heart, to the Jewish mind, was the seat of intelligence, understanding, and action. A person did not "feel with his heart," rather, he "thought with his heart" and, therefore, acted as a result of volitional choices.

God promised His people a new heart. No longer would their understanding be dead and lifeless. Rather, God would impress into the heart an understanding that would produce a living knowledge, resulting in voluntary obedience.

IV. A new spirit.

When the restoration came to the nation, God would deal with His people on a different basis. A new living principle or motivation would be placed in their lives. His very breath would permeate their attitudes. No longer would they live for self and their own glory, but their great delight would be to be a part of God's purpose in the world.

Although material prosperity was promised, this was not to be the priority. Underlying the promises of physical abundance, the prophets always, whether explicitly stated in every instance or not, held out the spiritual aspect of God's work as the most important.

So much depends upon one's attitude! The spirit of a local fellowship is, in many ways, the most important thing about it. So with a nation! God looked forward, and promised through His prophet, to the time when He would make everything new about the nation.

Conclusion. What God did for Israel He wishes to do for every individual. As Israel had rebelled against God's will, so all of us have sinned and "come short of the glory of God" (Rom. 3:23). Everyone needs the forgiving grace and mercy of God.

In addition to forgiveness, the lost person needs something else and God stands ready to give it. A change within must accompany the forgiveness of sin. In justification, man secures a new standing before God. In regeneration, however, he becomes a new person and all things become new to him. His manner of life will be different and his entire approach to everything will stand transformed because God has made him a new person in Jesus Christ.   *— FMW*

* * *

SUNDAY EVENING, NOVEMBER 25

TITLE: Faith Worth Passing On

TEXT: **"When I call to remembrance the unfeigned faith that is in thee, which dwelt first in thy grandmother Lois, and thy mother Eunice; and I am persuaded that in thee also" (2 Tim. 1:5).**

SCRIPTURE READING: **2 Timothy 1:1–2:2**

Introduction. That afternoon during the revival the pastor and the evangelist were visiting prospects. As they drove up to a lovely brick home, the pastor said, "In this home the mother is a Christian, but is not an active church member. The father is not a Christian and never attends church. Their seventeen-year-old son is not a Christian but does attend our services." As they arrived, the son was coming out the front door to get in his car. He explained that his parents were away, and that he had to hurry to make an appointment. As they invited him to the services, he said, "You know, preacher, I sure wish mother were faithful to the church. I think if she really meant business with her faith, it wouldn't be very long until dad and I both would go all the way with God." There was only one person in that home with faith, and hers was not worth passing on.

This is true of many people in our churches today. They have professed faith in Christ and joined the church. Perhaps for a brief time they were faithful. Then they became indifferent and negected the Lord and His church. This is a great detriment to evangelism. It blocks the road to salvation for countless persons.

Thank God it was not that way with Paul. He went to Lystra and preached the gospel. God opened the heart of a lady named Lois, and she believed and was saved. She had the kind of faith that was contagious, and soon her daughter Eunice believed. She passed on the faith to her son, Timothy. He became a co-laborer with Paul in the work of world evangelization. Later, when Paul wrote to him, he described this "faith worth passing on."

I. Faith worth passing on originates in a personal experience with Christ.

Paul had been saved. Then Lois was saved. In this chain of evangelism, each link is a fresh experience of salvation in Christ. That is always the starting place.

II. Faith worth passing on has a faithfulness about it.

A. *Note the quality of it.* "Unfeigned faith" means with no pretense. It is totally sincere with no hypocrisy. So our Christian faith must be completely sincere. We must be the same on weekdays as we are on Sunday.

B. *Note the permanence of it.* "Faith . . . which *dwelt* first in thy grandmother. . . ." Phillips translates it, "Faith which found a home in the heart of Lois first." That's the idea. It was faith that was permanent, living in a home. This is descriptive of daily, sincere commitment to Jesus Christ.

III. Faith worth passing on has a fruitfulness about it.

A. *The fruit of faith's contagiousness.* When several cases of chicken pox are reported in an elementary school, no promotion campaign is needed to spread chicken pox. It spreads because there is exposure and it is contagious. It is the same way with faith in Christ that is transparently loyal and constant.

B. *The fruit of faith's practical service.* Jesus went about doing good, and the common people thronged to Him. So when Christians take every opportunity to "do good to all," others catch their faith.

C. *The fruit of faith's direct witness for Christ.* Saving faith is a faith to share with others. We are all witnesses. We must witness face-to-face with persons.

IV. Faith worth passing on has a fearlessness about it.

To be dominated by fear is a paralyzing experience. Many people endure this awful lifestyle month after month. But that kind of fear is not from God. "God hath not given us the spirit of fear" (v. 7). Faith is trust without reservations. God's love overcomes fear, for "there is no fear in love; but perfect love casteth out fear" (1 John 4:18). Young Timothy was pastor in a large city where persecution was a real possibility. But he could serve without fear!

V. Faith worth passing on has a forcefulness about it (2 Tim. 1:7).

A. *It is the forcefulness of power.* This is the word from which we get the English word *dynamite* and which refers to the innate power of Almighty God. That divine power our Lord has made available to us, His children!

B. *It is the forcefulness of love.* God's kind of love is not only powerful, but it is the guiding force for the power He gives us. It is unlimited power, limited in its use only by love.

C. *It is the forcefulness of a sound mind.* It is the forcefulness of unlimited power, limited in its use by love, and guided in its service by the kind of sound mind that only God can give.

Conclusion. This is the faith that is certainly worth passing on, and must be passed on—and on—and on. But even this kind of faith must be renewed regularly. "Wherefore I put thee in remembrance that thou stir up the gift of God, which is in thee . . ." (v. 6).

Will you examine your faith? Will you ask the Lord to "stir it up" again until it blazes afresh in power, love, and a sound mind to reach out to all about you who do not yet know our Lord?   — *JFE*

* * *

WEDNESDAY EVENING, NOVEMBER 28

TITLE: One Way—the Curtains of the Tabernacle

TEXT: **"And there I will meet with thee, and I will commune with thee from above the mercy seat, from between the two cherubims which are upon the ark of the testimony, of all things which I will give thee in commandment unto the children of Israel" (Exod. 25:22).**

SCRIPTURE READING: Exodus 26:1–14

Introduction. Last week we presented a bird's-eye view of the tabernacle, or the tent of worship, which God instructed Moses to build. We listened as God told Moses *why* he was to build this unusual tent with all of its furnishings. We saw the thrilling symbolism of each piece of furniture as it spoke prophetically of the coming Savior, the Lord Jesus Christ. Tonight we shall focus on the curtains of the tabernacle.

I. The fence enclosing the courtyard (Exod. 27:9).

A. *The amazing thing we discover about this fence is that it was not constructed of boards or slats; but between the pillars or posts there was fine-twined, white linen!* But then, before we consider the curtained fence itself, we might ask: Why was this outer court necessary, since God actually dwelt inside the building, in the Holy of Holies? With all other things considered, it would appear that the outer court says that God demands *separation* from the world. There had to be a place where the priest could become "separate" before coming into the presence of God. God's presence cannot be contaminated with sin.

This does not mean that God expects His people to withdraw from the world, from the standpoint of living lives cut off from any contact with the world. We are "in" the world, just as the tabernacle was in the midst of the people. But there should be that about us which makes us obviously different from the world—not in an obnoxious way, however. Rather there should be a refreshing difference about the Christian's life which the unbeliever cannot find in his own life or in the world.

Certainly this was so with Jesus. No life ever lived on earth was more "separate," more different than His. Yet He was constantly mingling with the people, rubbing shoulders with them, giving Himself to them.

B. *The panels of this fence were made of white linen—this pure color represents righteousness.* Concerning the church, the Scripture declares: "And to her was granted that she should be arrayed in fine linen, clean and white: for the fine linen is the righteousness of the saints" (Rev. 19:8). Thus, the indication is that the courtyard was encircled with the righteousness which God demands. We cannot provide this for ourselves; God provides it for us. Before we can come into His presence in prayer, we must be surrounded by and enveloped in the righteousness of His Son.

C. *The posts which supported these linen panels were high enough that no one could climb over them.* No person could scale this "fence of righteousness" on his own; he had to enter by the gate God had provided. Man still would rather enter God's presence by his own method, by way of his own good works.

As we walk around that white linen fence, too tall to climb over, we feel a sense of hopelessness. First, the brilliant whiteness of it blinds us; we cannot look at it. We are cut off! God is inside, and He is perfect and sinless. We are outside, and in spite of our finest efforts, we are still far short of *God's* quality of goodness. Any way you look at it, it seems to be an impossible situation.

II. As we circle the courtyard, we come to the east end and there we find one gate, and only one (Exod. 27:16).

A. *There was no other entrance to this courtyard, just as there is no other way to God the Father except through Jesus Christ* (John 10:7–9). Thus the one gate points to the Lord Jesus Christ, who is the only way of salvation. Throughout the New Testament we find abundant evidence and references to the fact that Jesus Christ is man's only hope for salvation.

B. *Then, there were four colors in the curtains of this gate—blue, purple, scarlet, and white.* All through the tabernacle we shall find these colors. They, too, represent the Lord Jesus, by symbolizing several characteristics of His being.

1. Blue is the color of heaven; it speaks of Christ's heavenly character. He was *with God* before He came to earth.

2. Purple, which is a mixture of scarlet and blue, was the color most frequently associated with royalty. So this color pointed to Jesus as Christ the King. As a mixture of blue and scarlet, the purple color also pointed to Christ as the One who combined the heavenly nature He had with the sacrifice for sin—the shedding of His blood.

3. Scarlet is the color of blood. This color in the curtains of the gate looked forward to Jesus, who would come and give His life and shed His blood on the cross for our sins.

4. Finally, white symbolizes purity and perfection. Thus it spoke of Christ's perfect character. Even when Jesus was born into this world and entered a body of human flesh, still He "was in all points tempted like as we are, yet without sin" (Heb. 4:15). Never at any time while Jesus was on earth was there anything about Him which even hinted at the imperfect, sinful nature of our humanity.

C. *These colors on the gate, representing the character of our Lord Jesus Christ, are seen throughout the tabernacle.* They were on the door leading into the Holy Place and woven into the great veil that separated the Holy Place from the Holy of Holies. Always they represent Christ who is the only means of access to God. There is no other way.

This is the amazing, inconceivable glory of our God. He is perfect, holy, sinless. He is the essence of everything that man is not. And to make the distance between man and God infinitely farther apart, man chose to turn away from God and to choose sin. Why didn't God write man off, annihilate him, obliterate him from the face of the earth?

This is the mystery of God's love which we will never understand in this life. Even in the eternity of heaven we shall only be amazed at it and glorify God for it throughout endless eons.

Conclusion. Thus, the gate is there. The entrance is provided. The invitation from God is given. It is for whosoever will come. It is for everyone who will repent of his sins and receive this all-sufficient Christ.   *— DLJ*

* * *

Sunday Morning

With the beginning of the Advent season, it is suggested that a good theme would be "Listening to the Angels' Proclamation." The messages find their primary source in the Nativity account in Luke 2.

Sunday Evenings

During the Christmas season many people experience exhaustion and frustration. "Christ and Our Deepest Needs" is the suggested theme for these messages.

Wednesday Evenings

We conclude the series of messianic studies using the theme "Foregleams of Christ in the Old Testament."

* * *

SUNDAY MORNING, DECEMBER 2

TITLE: Recognizing and Responding to the Messiah

Text: "Lord, now lettest thou thy servant depart in peace, according to thy word; for mine eyes have seen thy salvation which thou hast prepared in the presence of all peoples, a light for revelation to the Gentiles, and for glory to thy people Israel" (Luke 2:29–32 rsv).

Scripture Reading: Luke 2:22–35

Hymns: "Angels We Have Heard on High," Old French Carol
"The First Noel," Old English Carol
"O Come, All Ye Faithful," Wade

Offertory Prayer:

Father God, help us to respond fully to the messianic Savior whom You have sent to live within us. Help us to let Your love flow through us during this season of the year when we remind ourselves of Your great gift to us through the Lord who was born in Bethlehem. Bless our gifts to the telling of the Good News. Amen.

Introduction. The saints of ancient Israel longed for the coming of their Messiah. There were many different ideas concerning Him and expectations for Him. Some of these expectations were exaggerations and literalistic interpretations of poetic descriptions of the expected Messiah.

Some of the prophecies concerning Him have what the scholars call a double significance. There was a fulfillment of the prophecy in the time in which it was spoken by the prophet, but there was a secondary fulfillment of the prophecy with the coming of the Christ.

In our Scripture we read of the recognition and response of the aged man Simeon to the Christ child. He was given a special insight into who Jesus was and the significance of His birth. Perhaps the primary purpose of this was for the benefit of Mary and Joseph who needed divine reinforcement at this particular time in their spiritual pilgrimage as they faced the responsibility of caring for and rearing to maturity the Christ child.

Simeon recognized Him and rejoiced over the fact that God's Messiah had been born.

Have you recognized and responded appropriately and positively to the Messiah? Do you have some false expectations of Him? Have you missed the Messiah? Have you failed to recognize and respond to Him?

The ministry of the Messiah was to be variegated and many-faceted. Some looked for one thing and others looked for another. Some were expecting Him to be a military leader who would overcome the tyranny of the Roman army of occupation. Others expected the Messiah to produce great prosperity. It is significant to look at some of the Old Testament expectations and the New Testament fulfillments.

I. The Messiah was to be a prophet of God (Deut. 18:15–19).

The Messiah was to be an authentic spokesman of God to His people as Moses was God's authentic spokesman to His time.

A prophet was not primarily a predictor of the future. The prophet came with a word from God to the people. Someone has described the prophets as being "forth-tellers" more than "fore-tellers." We have come to think of the prophet as a predictor primarily on the basis of the messianic prophecies of the Old Testament.

Jesus was the true messianic Prophet in that He is God's last Word to man. He is God's supreme Word to man (Heb. 1:1–2).

We need to not only hear God's Prophet, but we also need to heed Him.

II. The Messiah was to be God's Priest (1 Sam. 2:35).

A. *A priest was one who ministered in the presence of God on behalf of the people that he might bring about the removal of the guilt and condemnation for sin.*

B. *The priest had access into the sacred presence of God.* In the Old Testament priests offered sacrifices for their own sins first, and then they offered sacrifice for the sins of the people.

The writer of Hebrews describes Jesus as being the Great High Priest of God who has entered into the holy presence of God Himself, not with the blood of sacrificial animals, but with the sacrifice of His own blood in order to obtain eternal redemption for us (9:11–12).

The contemporaries of our Lord did not even begin to understand this aspect of His life and ministry until after His death and the coming of the Holy Spirit on the Day of Pentecost.

It is in Jesus Christ as the High Priest that God comes to us; and it is through Jesus Christ as the Sacrifice that we have access into the presence of the Holy God.

III. The Messiah was to be a suffering servant.

A. *The ministry of the Messiah as a suffering servant on behalf of a guilty race was unrecognized and unappreciated by His contemporaries.* They could not believe that the Messiah described in Isaiah 53 was one and the same with the Son of David who was to be King.

Isaiah 53, which tells of the wounded Savior whose stripes heal us and upon whom our sins were placed, was understood only after Jesus opened both the Scriptures and the minds of His disciples to understand those Scriptures following His victorious resurrection from the dead (Luke 24:44–47).

IV. The Messiah was to be the King of God's kingdom (Isa. 9:6–7).

The Old Testament has many references to the expected Messiah who would be the King and who would rule on David's throne. It was only normal and human that believers during those days would long for a king who could come and deliver them from the tyranny of all of their enemies. This came to focus during the lifetime of Jesus in terms of deliverance from the tyranny of Rome.

On one occasion the people began to talk in terms of forming a conspiracy to force Jesus to assume kingship (John 6:15). They wanted a political Messiah who would assert nationalistic claims to the throne of David and reestablish the sovereignty of the nation of Israel among the nations of the world. Jesus repeatedly repudiated this kind of kingship.

Jesus came that he might be King in the hearts of men and that He might establish the rule of God as a present reality in the hearts of men.

Conclusion. How have you recognized the Messiah who was born to be King of the Jews? Have you responded to Him in a positive way?

Herod treated Christ as a usurper, a rival, a disturber. He wanted to eliminate Him. Some today seek to eliminate Jesus by simply ignoring Him.

Nicodemus recognized and responded to Jesus as the Teacher sent from God (John 3:2). There were others who recognized and responded to Jesus as a prophet who spoke for God (Matt. 16:14). John the Baptist proclaimed Him as being the Lamb of God who came to take away the sin of the world (John 1:29). The wise men recognized Him and responded to Him as the King of the Jews (Matt. 2:10–12). Following His resurrection, Thomas recognized Him and declared Him to be "My Lord and my God" (John 20:28). Each of us needs to do likewise. Do so today for your good and for the glory of God.   — *TTC*

* * *

SUNDAY EVENING, DECEMBER 2

TITLE: Spiritual Burn-out

Text: **"And let us not be weary in well doing: for in due season we shall reap, if we faint not" (Gal. 6:9).**

Scripture Reading: **Galatians 6:7–9**

Introduction. I am a keen observer and a careful listener when I travel by airplane. I am fascinated with take-offs and landings. I also like to watch the airline personnel. One activity of pilots caught my attention when I first traveled by airplane. They would often walk around their aircraft and make close examinations. My curiosity could not be contained, so I asked one pilot, "Why do you inspect the airplane?" He said, "We check for metal fatigue. This is caused sometimes by the stress of flying and most of the time by longevity of service."

Paul wrote to some churches in Galatia which evidently experienced the stress of continuous work for the Lord. Some false teachers known as Judaizers had confused the believers. The church leaders became fatigued over fighting the heresy and proclaiming the truth of the gospel. Paul encouraged these leaders not to burn out. The word for "weary" describes the idea of fainting or losing heart. In modern terminology this would be called "burn-out."

Burn-out seems to be a prevalent problem in today's churches. Jerry Edelwick in his book *Burn Out* described this condition as "a progressive loss of idealism, energy, and purpose experienced by people in helping professions." Without a doubt there are some tired Christians today. To examine this condition let us get some insights about spiritual burn-out.

I. There are some recognizable cases of spiritual burn-out.

A. *Look first in the Bible for some recognizable cases of spiritual burn-out.* Perhaps the first case of burn-out was Noah. After the Flood, he was exhausted.

Moses was another case of burn-out. He was weary with the wilderness wanderings and the rebellious people. He demonstrated his weariness by striking the rock instead of speaking to it.

Elijah is another case of spiritual weariness. After his high moment of victory over the priests of Baal on Mt. Carmel, he sat under a juniper tree with a good case of burn-out.

The Galatian Christians were weary. They had fought the Judaizers so long and with such intensity that they became weary.

B. *Look around you, and you will see recognizable cases of spiritual burn-out.* Burn-out prevails in many professional people, especially among those in the business of helping people.

Burn-out prevails among those involved in church work. Brooks Faulkner in his book *Burnout in Ministry* points to the growing problem of spiritual burn-out among those who serve in various areas of church life.

C. *Look within yourself, and maybe you can see some symptoms of burn-out.* Being exhausted, irritable, frustrated, helpless, discouraged, critical of others and of self, wanting to change jobs, feeling dull, lacking enthusiasm, and being spiritually dull represent some symptoms of spiritual burn-out.

II. There are some noticeable characteristics of spiritual burn-out.

A. *Burn-out is characterized by a noticeable lack of activity.* The Galatians were tempted to quit. They were tired; they wanted to take a rest. Paul encouraged them, "And let us not be weary in well doing" (6:9a).

B. *Burn-out is also characterized by a noticeable lack of enthusiasm.* Being identified so fully with a matter tends to cause a lack of enthusiasm. Maybe the believers were so identified with the threats of the Judaizers that they were losing their enthusiasm.

C. *Burn-out is further characterized by the noticeable presence of frustration.* Close examination of the Galatian believers might have disclosed a great sense of frustration. The Judaizers frustrated their efforts in the Lord's work. Those believers became weary in doing good work.

D. *Burn-out is also characterized by a noticeable presence of stagnation.* Often believers can go through religious routines. Even the Lord's work can become weary.

III. There are various causes of spiritual burn-out.

A. *Burn-out may be caused by overextending ourselves.* The Christians in Galatia worked long and hard on the problems raised by the Judaizers. Doing good things will not mean endless rest. Christian workers are neither supermen nor wonder women. Exhaustion comes to believers.

B. *Burn-out may be caused by the failure to express ourselves.* Maybe the Galatian Christians did not express themselves as Paul did toward the Judaizers. "I would they were even cut off which trouble you" (5:12).

C. *Burn-out is often caused by the act of condemning ourselves.* The Judaizers practiced the fine art of making the believers feel guilty. They said, "You are not doing enough." Condemnation from others and from within ourselves can lead to burn-out.

IV. There are some therapeutic cures for spiritual burn-out.

A. *Listen to the encouragement of God's precious Word.* Paul had a word from the Lord: "Let us not be weary in well doing" (6:9). God has an appropriate word for our situations, and in each case we should listen to His Word.

B. *Look at the great task God has for you.* Whenever one looks at new challenges of God's mission, the present activity seems mundane compared to God's greater work.

C. *Lean on God's power and strength.* Paul gave a great promise: "For in due season we shall reap, if we faint not" (v. 9b). Leaning on God's strength will bring renewal. "But they that wait upon the LORD shall renew their strength; they shall mount up with wings as eagles; they shall run, and not be weary; and they shall walk, and not faint" (Isa. 40:31).

Conclusion. Take time to examine your work for the Lord. Ask yourself, "Do I have the symptoms of spiritual burn-out?" If so, take advantage of the cures for spiritual weariness. God will help you. — *HTB*

* * *

WEDNESDAY EVENING, DECEMBER 5

TITLE: The Brazen Altar and Laver—First Steps Toward God

TEXT: "And thou shalt make an altar of shittim wood, five cubits long, and five cubits broad; the altar shall be foursquare: and the height thereof shall be three cubits. . . . Thou shalt also make a laver of brass, and his foot also of brass, to wash withal: and thou shalt put it between the tabernacle of the congregation and the altar, and thou shalt put water therein" (Exod. 27:1; 30:18).

SCRIPTURE READING: Exodus 27:1–8; 30:17–21

Introduction. Last week in our study we stood before the awesome, white-curtained fence which surrounded the courtyard in which that unusual tent of worship stood. We saw that the pure, white linen which comprised the fence represented the righteousness of God. And we also saw that it was this perfection and holiness that kept sinful man away from God.

As we circled the courtyard, we discovered that there was only one gate. And with great relief and joy, we saw that the curtains of this gate—blue, purple, scarlet, and white—represented the redeeming characteristics of our Lord Jesus Christ. We saw that He is the one Door into the presence of God. As we receive Him, His righteousness becomes *our* righteousness, and we are able to stand in the presence of God and be accepted by Him.

Tonight we shall walk through that gate, on our way toward the presence of God, represented by the fire burning on the mercy seat in the Holy of Holies, inside the tabernacle.

I. The brazen altar.

The first object we encounter as we enter the courtyard is the brazen altar, the place of sacrifice. The brazen altar foreshadowed the cross on which Christ shed His blood for the sins of the world. (Exod. 27:1–2).

A. *This impressive altar was seven and a half feet square, standing four and a half feet high.* On the hot coals of that altar lay the sacrificial lamb, which had been slain and was being offered as a burnt offering to God for the sins of the people. The lamb being sacrificed represents the Lord Jesus Christ, who shed His blood and gave His life that our sins might be forgiven.

We can see that the altar represents *sacrifice.* After the flood waters had receded in Noah's day, the first thing Noah did when he and his family stepped out of the ark onto dry land was to *build an altar.* In Genesis 12 we read that Abraham built an altar even before he pitched his tent. These men were careful to put God first in their lives. Thus the first and most important lesson we learn as we approach this altar is that something must be done there which we cannot do for ourselves. There must be offered in our stead a sacrifice—there must be shed innocent blood.

B. *Let's look a bit more closely at this altar itself.* It was made of wood and covered with brass. Brass, in the Old Testament, was considered the most fire-resistant of all metals. In fact, the brass of the Old Testament probably was closer to our copper than it was to the brass that we know today. Brass represents the fierceness of God's wrath against sin.

The altar was foursquare, saying to us that the gospel message is for the whole world—north, south, east, and west, for all people everywhere. This is what Jesus meant when He said, "Go ye into all the world, and preach the gospel" (Mark 16:15).

Wood speaks of the humanity of our Lord Jesus; He was God manifest in the flesh. Brass is that which is capable of enduring fire. While He hung on the cross, our Lord endured the awful fire of God's wrath on the sins of the world, which had been placed upon Him.

C. *The altar stood flat upon the desert sand in the courtyard.* It was not upon some high, exalted place. There were no steps to climb, leading up to it. It was right on the ground, level with sinful man. This was not true with pagan altars where sacrifices were made to pagan gods. They were always in high places, with steep, ascending steps, making it difficult for man to reach them.

Thus the brazen altar could be approached with no effort. There were no steps up to the altar—no "stepping stones" to Christ, no "good works" required in order to be saved. One comes to God just as he is. God meets man at the point of his need, and there provides total and complete salvation.

II. The laver.

Having identified with the spotless lamb being offered as a sacrifice upon the altar, we proceed to the only other piece of furniture in the courtyard that stands between us and the tabernacle. It is the laver, or the washing basin (Exod. 30:18–21).

A. *Where did Moses get the brass for making the laver?* Exodus 38:8 states that he made it "of the lookingglasses of the women." Mirrors of that time were made of polished brass. We shall refer to this fact and its significance later in the study.

The laver is the "second step" in our progress toward God's presence. It is a type of the Word of God. Paul teaches us that the Word of God is like water. As we read and study it, we are "washed" and cleansed. The Word of God has a purifying and cleansing effect upon us.

The Word of God is compared with a mirror. James tells us that as we look into these Scriptures, we "behold ourselves as a man looking in a mirror." God's Word shows us what we are. It reveals the progress we are making, or are *not* making. So we see our need of daily washing in the Word of God. Every day we commit sins, either of omission or of commission. We must daily seek God's forgiveness for these sins.

B. *In the New Testament there is a remarkable comparison.* John 13 contains the account of the Last Supper, the Feast of the Passover. After the Passover meal was finished, Jesus arose, took a towel and a basin of water, and began to wash the disciples' feet. What was He doing? He was fulfilling the type of the laver! The feet represent the daily walk, during which we come in contact with the dirt and dust of the earth. Likewise, as Christians we encounter daily defilement because of sins and temptations yielded to.

It is between the brazen altar and the laver, which represents daily consecration, that many believers stop growing spiritually. They do not read and study God's Word.

Conclusion. Peter objected to Christ washing his feet, suggesting that he needed washing all over. Jesus said to him, "If I wash thee not, thou hast no part with me" (John 13:8). He was talking about fellowship and growth. Perhaps *you* have not gone past the altar, the Cross. You have problems with temptation and sin in your life. Your thoughts wander into areas where they should not be. You need to advance to the laver, the place of washing. You need to look in the "mirror" of the word of God and receive daily cleansing as you read and study its message. — *DLJ*

* * *

SUNDAY MORNING, DECEMBER 9

TITLE: Good News of Great Joy to All the People

Text: "Be not afraid; for behold, I bring you good news of a great joy which will come to all the people" (Luke 2:10 rsv).

Scripture Reading: Luke 2:8–14

Hymns: "God, Our Father, We Adore Thee," Frazer
　　　　"Jesus Loves Me," Warner
　　　　"Whosoever Will," Bliss

OFFERTORY PRAYER:

Thank You, Father God, for the blessed good news that a Savior has been provided. Thank You for the light that He has brought upon the dark places of life. Thank You for the love that He has brought into our hearts. Thank You for the hope that we have through Him. Today we would join with all of those who give of their time, talents, and resources for the advancement of Your kingdom in the world. In Jesus' name we pray. Amen.

Introduction. Many people think of Christianity as being some good advice for those who want to do good. There is a great deal of difference between good advice and good news. The gospel is Good News.

Benjamin Franklin is famous for giving much good advice. The angels, the shepherds, and the apostles are famous because they communicated the good news of what God did and wants to do through Jesus Christ.

Jesus Christ came into the world to communicate good news from God to all people.

I. Good news for other people.

From time to time we read and hear about good news that has come to others.

The angels announced some good news that had the potential of producing great joy for all the people. Up until this point Jewish people thought that their God belonged in a special way to them alone. They did not recognize that their God was also concerned about the Gentiles, the pagans, and the outcasts.

II. The Good News of Jesus is for all the people.

Luke's gospel is the gospel for the underdog, the outcast, and the underprivileged.

A. *In Nazareth Jesus preached the Good News to the people.* He announced, "He hath anointed me to preach good news to the poor" (Luke 4:18).

B. *To the sick Jesus came with health* (4:40).

C. *To the demon possessed He came as the liberator from demonic powers* (4:41).

D. *To the leper who was unclean and untouchable and consequently very depressed, Jesus brought cleansing, health, and wholeness* (5:13).

E. *To the paralytic Jesus forgave his sins and then enabled him to walk* (5:25).

F. *To Levi, the hated tax collector, Jesus extended a gracious invitation that lifted him from obscurity to significance and prominence when Jesus said, "Follow me"* (5:27).

G. *To the woman of the city who was a great sinner, Jesus granted the gift of forgiveness and cleansing* (7:48).

H. *To the demoniac who was possessed by a legion of demons, our Lord brought liberation and the restoration of a right inward attitude.* He brought peace to him and then commissioned him to return to his home, there to give testimony concerning what God had done for him (8:39).

III. The nature of the good news which Jesus brought.

A. *Jesus brought good news regarding cleansing of the heart and soul from sin.* Deep in the heart of man there is a feeling of being unclean, unworthy, and unprepared to enter into the presence of a holy God. Jesus came that we might be clean and acceptable to a holy God. God sent Him and made it possible for us to experience righteousness and grace through Him (2 Cor. 5:21; 8:9).

B. *Jesus brought good news regarding acceptance into the family of God.* Some children are cursed into this world by having parents who are something other than they ought to be.

Some children are fortunate in the heritage which they receive through birth and belonging to a good family.

Some children are millionaires on the day of their birth because of rich parents.

On the day of our spiritual birth, we become the sons and daughters of the eternal God. We are accepted into the family of God. This gives to us the privilege of belonging to God.

C. *Jesus brings good news regarding spiritual resources for living.* Through faith in Christ we receive the gift of a new nature.

Through faith in Christ we receive the gift of the indwelling presence of the Holy Spirit.

Through faith in Christ we receive the gift of the spiritual power that we need for coping with life.

Through faith in Christ we receive the good news of an eternal home at the end of this life.

Conclusion. The gospel is Good News for all the people. Through this Good News we receive the offer of forgiveness, the offer of life, and the offer of acceptance into the family of God. We receive the assurance of help and friendship with God.

Let each of us listen to the Good News.

Let each of us believe this Good News for ourselves.

Let each of us respond affirmatively to the Good News.

Let all of us rejoice today in the privilege of responding to this Good News through Jesus Christ.   — *TTC*

* * *

SUNDAY EVENING, DECEMBER 9

TITLE: In Celebration of Solitude

Text: "And the word of the Lord came unto him, saying, Get thee hence, and turn thee eastward, and hide thyself by the brook Cherith, that is before Jordan" (1 Kings 17:2-3).

Scripture Reading: 1 Kings 17:1-7; 18:1-6

Introduction. Richard Foster has written a significant book entitled *Celebration of Discipline: the Path to Spiritual Growth.* He has written: "In contemporary society our Adversary majors in three things: noise, hurry, and crowds. If he can keep us engaged in 'muchness' and 'manyness' he will rest satisfied" (p. 13).

One of the greatest needs of believers in our world is to plan times of solitude.

Elijah lived in a busy time. The kingdom in which Elijah lived was a divided one. It had split in approximately 931 B.C. A new kingdom was in the process of being established. Elijah, a prophet of the northern kingdom, was busy in the affairs of the new kingdom. In the midst of his busy time God spoke, "Go hide yourself." Without a doubt Elijah thought God's word about solitude was an unusual one. Nonetheless, Elijah did as the Lord commanded and practiced solitude for a time.

Believers are involved in "muchness" and "manyness." Yet God is speaking. If we would listen to Him, we would hear Him say, "Go hide yourself." Let us ask, What will solitude do for us? There are some benefits of solitude.

I. Solitude will strengthen our relationship with God.

A. *Authentic Christianity is a relationship with God.* Elijah could have been caught up more with religious activity than with a personal relationship with the Lord. He could have been caught up with the routine of meetings and other activities and lost sight of his need for a fresh relationship with the Lord.

True religion consists of a personal relationship between God and man. This means there are times of mutual talking and listening. There are times of sharing life together.

B. *Relationships are strengthened in times of mutual togetherness.* Elijah could not have enhanced his relationship with God by mere religious routines. He had to spend quality time with God.

Solitude affords an excellent opportunity to be with God. John Killenger in his book *Prayer: the Act of Being With God* wrote of prayer as a time of just being alone with God.

What else will solitude do for us?

II. Solitude will develop our trust in the Lord.

A. *Humanism can take over the management of our lives.* Elijah was a gifted, courageous, and articulate person. God needed to teach him that intelligence and strength are not enough.

In our scientific and technological age, one can easily come to the idea that strength and smartness will suffice for living. Times of solitude teach us to trust in the Lord.

B. *Trusting in the Lord will develop the idea of transcendence in us.* Elijah was in awe of God when he received from the Lord food from the ravens and water from the brook. He learned that Someone from beyond provided.

What else will solitude do for us?

III. Solitude will help put life in focus.

A. *Life is constantly getting out of focus.* The life of Elijah was one of both agonies and ecstasies. At one moment he could be on a spiritual high, and the next moment he could be at a spiritual low. Circumstances change, thus life is this way.

B. *Getting alone with God will put life in focus again.* Elijah in his time of solitude was able to put the circumstances of the times in focus.

Being alone with the Lord helps one to put life in focus. It is to put God in the center, and the rest of life may be viewed in reference to God.

What else can solitude do for us?

IV. Solitude will give direction for ministry.

A. *The Lord wants a balance in ministry.* Having a balance will mean times of solitude followed by times of service. God never intended for Elijah to stay in the wilderness. He wanted Elijah to stay for a while and then "go show himself to Ahab."

Ministry is like a pendulum swinging back and forth. It is a time of solitude and then a time of service. It is never just hiding. It is never just serving. It involves both solitude and service.

B. *Solitude leads to service.* The order of priority is solitude and then service. God told Elijah first to "hide himself," and then He told him to "go show himself."

Solitude should lead to a ministry to the world. Being alone with God is not intended to get us away from the world but to prepare us for the world.

Conclusion. Today's world is a noisy one. It is also a busy world. Don't let the noises of the world deafen God's instruction, "Go hide yourself." Also, don't be too busy to practice times of solitude with the Lord.   — *HTB*

* * *

WEDNESDAY EVENING, DECEMBER 12

TITLE: **The Table of Shewbread and the Golden Lampstand—the Body of Christ and the Light of the World**

TEXT: **"Thou shalt also make a table of shittim wood: two cubits shall be the length thereof, and a cubit the breadth thereof, and a cubit and a half the height thereof. . . . And thou shalt make a candlestick of pure gold" (Exod. 25:23, 31).**

SCRIPTURE READING: **Exodus 25:23–40**

Introduction. Tonight, as we step inside the tabernacle itself, we enter the Holy Place, or "the place of fellowship." On the north wall of the room is the table of shewbread. Upon it were placed twelve freshly baked loaves of bread each week. On the south wall of the Holy Place stands the golden lampstand, also known as "the candlestick," one of the most beautiful and elaborate pieces of furniture in the tabernacle.

Although each piece of furniture was distinct in itself, each also related to the other. We cannot grasp the full significance of one without understanding the others. As we shall see tonight, the table of shewbread speaks of Christ, the Living Word upon whom we are to feed to receive spiritual nourishment. The golden lampstand cast light on the table of shewbread. Thus, as we study the Word of God, the Holy Spirit "sheds light" on it and enables us to understand it.

Every believer is privileged to enter the Holy Place and have fellowship with God by feeding on His Word at the table of shewbread, which is illumined by the Holy Spirit in the candelabra. Or we might say it this way: Our *relation-*

ship with God is established in the outer court at the altar of sacrifice and at the laver of cleansing. Our *fellowship* is established and maintained by the study of the Word, by the illuminating work of the Holy Spirit.

I. The construction of the table of shewbread (Exod. 25:23–24).

A. *The wood of the table represented the humanity of Jesus, whereas the gold with which it was overlaid spoke of His deity.* Though He was man, He was also God. On the table Moses was instructed to place loaves of bread, a symbol of Christ's body. The bread was made from the fine flour which resulted from a grinding process. Jesus experienced extreme suffering (symbolized by the grinding of the grain), and yet He retained His sinless purity.

The bread was to be unleavened. Leaven, or yeast, is used in the Bible as a symbol of sin. The unleavened bread was a symbol of the sinless Christ.

B. *The bread was the result of a process of death and suffering, for the wheat had been harvested, ground to powder, and baked in a hot oven.* So Christ went through the experience of Gethsemane and the burning heat of Calvary.

II. The table's provision for the people.

A. *The table and its contents symbolized God's provision for the people during their wilderness journey.* It symbolized the "spiritual food" God made available for them. Because of its symbolism, it points to Jesus Christ. Jesus *was* the Word of God in human flesh. As we learn of Him, we gain spiritual sustenance for strength, and we grow and develop as Christians.

B. *But what of the bread itself?* Very practically, the bread was intended to be food for the priests as they ministered daily in the Holy Place before the Lord. Jesus said, "I am the bread of life: he that cometh to me shall never hunger; and he that believeth on me shall never thirst" (John 6:35). Jesus is telling us that He, in the person of His Word, is the sustaining food of the Christian.

III. The construction of the lampstand (Exod. 25:31–32).

A. *This lampstand, which was to be made of a talent of pure gold (which weighed over ninety pounds!), was not to be cast in a mold.* That is, it was not to look like anything else that had been made. It was to be hammered out so that the entire lampstand was formed from the one piece of gold. Unlike our tapers, the candles on this stand did not consume themselves as they burned. Rather each branch supported a small golden pot which was kept filled with oil, in which a burning wick floated.

B. *What did the golden lampstand do for the Holy Place?* It provided the only source of Light. Jesus said to His disciples that they were to be "the light of the world." It was important that the wicks which floated in the seven golden pots be kept trimmed so that the light would not grow dim. Therefore, as believers come daily to the light of the Word, Christ draws us close to Himself. He cleanses us and takes away the things that are not of the Spirit, so that our light may shine more brightly.

Conclusion. Thus we thank God for the beautiful and meaningful symbolism in the table of shewbread and the golden lampstand. We can say that Jesus is the "Bread of Life" and "the Light of the World."   *— DLJ*

* * *

SUNDAY MORNING, DECEMBER 16

TITLE: The Joys of Christmas

TEXT: "Be not afraid; for behold, I bring you good news of a great joy . . ." (Luke 2:10 RSV).

SCRIPTURE READING: Luke 2:8–15

HYMNS: "Jesus Shall Reign Where'er the Sun," Watts
        "Angels, From the Realms of Glory," Montgomery
        "Glory to His Name," Hoffman

OFFERTORY PRAYER:

Father God, You are the Giver of every good and perfect gift. You have given to us the indescribable gift of Your Son Jesus Christ to us and for us. Today we come bringing ourselves and our substance in the form of tithes and offerings. Bless these gifts to the honor and to the glory of Your name and to the advancement of Your cause on earth. Amen.

Introduction: For many Christmas is a sad time rather than a glad time. Psychiatrists are busier following Christmas and New Year's than at any other time of the year. It is said that the psychiatric rooms at our hospitals are more likely to be filled to capacity at that time of the year than at any other period. Perhaps this is due to the fact that many people are reminded of how empty and meaningless life without God has become for them.

Jesus came into the world to bring joy. He came to communicate love. He came to make peace possible.

A part of the joy of Christmas is the joy of receiving. Many people have never learned how to graciously and humbly receive from others. There are many who cannot believe that God is the great Giver. Perhaps this is due to a low sense of self-esteem and a feeling of great unworthiness. Some are unable to accept a gift from others without trying to repay them in some form or another. There is no way that one can truly experience the richest joy of Christmas unless he develops the fine art of learning how to be a grateful receiver.

Another of the great joys of Christmas is the joy of giving. God so loved that He gave. God loves the cheerful giver. God is generous, gracious, even extravagant in His gifts.

To experience gracious, undeserved giving is a shocking experience to those who have built their lives upon the development of their acquisitive instinct. Many never enter into the joy of Christmas because they have become like Scrooge. They live only to get.

The angels sang about the possibility of a great joy that could come to those who would properly recognize and respond to what God was doing in the gift of the Christ child.

I. The joy of Christmas is the joy of knowing that God is for us (Rom. 8:31–39).

Living in a "performance-oriented society," in which success is judged on the basis of performance and in which rewards are bestowed in recognition of achievement, some find it difficult to believe that God is a gracious and loving Giver.

A sense of guilt often brings an attitude of self-condemnation, and we find ourselves unable to believe that the great God who gave the Ten Commandments and who spoke through Christ the words of the Sermon on the Mount is really for us.

The whole message of Christmas is intended to declare that God always has been for us and always will be for us if we will but trust Him and let the Christ have the place that by right belongs to Him in our lives.

II. The joy of Christmas is the joy of belonging to the family of God.

Christmas is usually a family-oriented affair. For some this can be a painful experience, while to many it is indeed a joyous and pleasant experience.

At Christmastime many are deprived of the joys of family relationships because of deaths that have taken place or because great distances separate them from the members of their families. At such a time we need to recognize and respond to the joys of being a member of the family of God. We enter this family through the spiritual birth (John 1:12). We can stand in amazement before the joy of knowing that now we are the children of God (1 John 3:1–2).

At Christmastime let us rejoice more in the family of God than we do in earthly family relationships.

III. The joy of Christmas is the joy of experiencing liberation from fear
(Luke 2:10).

It was normal and proper for the shepherds to respond to the presence of the shekinah glory of God with a holy awe and a reverential fear. The angels spoke words to dispel that fear. Christmas can bring the joy of letting us know that we need not live our lives under the tyranny of fear.

A. *We need not be afraid of the past.* Through Jesus Christ we receive forgiveness for all of our sins (1 John 1:9).

B. *Because of the promise of His abiding presence, we need have no fear in the present* (Matt. 28:20). Our living Lord has promised to be with us day by day as the Light of the World. When we follow Him we do not stumble in the darkness (John 8:12).

C. *We need have no fear of the future because our Lord has promised to prepare a place for those who love Him* (John 14:1–3).

We can live our lives with fullness of joy if we will recognize Jesus as the great Liberator and Deliverer from fear.

IV. The joy of Christmas is the joy that comes to those who become givers.

A. *We cannot give away what we do not have.* Many fret and are unhappy because of their inability to give some things that they would like to give.

B. *What do we have that we can give at Christmastime?*
    1. We can give the gift of our faith to those who have not yet come to know Jesus Christ as Savior. We can share the testimony of what He has come to mean to us and encourage others to put their confidence in Him.
    2. We can give the gift of helpfulness to those about us who carry heavy burdens.
    3. We can give the gift of encouragement to those who are depressed.
    4. We can give the gift of friendship to those with whom we are associated.

5. We can give the gift of forgiveness to those who have mistreated us.

6. We can give the gift of acceptance and affirmation to those who are uncertain and insecure.

7. We can give the gift of kindness to those who are suffering physically, emotionally, or spiritually.

8. We can give the gift of gratitude to those who have been kind to us and to those who have ministered to others.

Conclusion. To truly experience the joy of Christmas, we must recognize and respond to Him who was born to be our Savior and King. He is the great joy-bringer. He wants to use us in helping other people to find joy, which is deeper and richer and finer than happiness. Happiness is the result of something that happens. Joy is an inward condition of the heart that comes about as we recognize the greatness, the graciousness, and the goodness of God. May yours be the joy of Christmas during this season of the year. —*TTC*

* * *

SUNDAY EVENING, DECEMBER 16

TITLE: **Strength Out of Weakness**

Text: **"And he said unto me, My grace is sufficient for thee: for my strength is made perfect in weakness. Most gladly therefore will I rather glory in my infirmities, that the power of Christ may rest on me" (2 Cor. 12:9).**

Scripture Reading: **2 Corinthians 12:1–7**

Introduction. Often the world considers trouble to be a terrible intruder into life. For many people the problems of life are viewed as nothing more than minus factors. According to many people the weaknesses make a person weak.

The Christian perspective of trouble changes that pessimistic perspective. Paul experienced a thorn in the flesh, and this weakness made him strong. He learned how to be strong in the broken places. His weaknesses did not destroy him. With God's help he gained strength out of his weaknesses.

Life breaks all of us. There seem to be two alternatives to this problem. On one hand the problems can keep us down. Yet, on the other hand, the problems can make us strong. Let us learn from one who was broken and made strong how we may benefit from the weaknesses of life.

I. The weaknesses of life drive us to deepen our faith in God.

A. *The apostle Paul had a great faith in the Lord.* His faith was not just an assent to religious beliefs. His faith was a personal relationship with the Lord Jesus Christ. His favorite expression to describe this relationship was "in Christ." "For I know whom I have believed, and am persuaded that he is able to keep that which I have committed unto him against that day" (2 Tim. 1:12).

B. *Only a genuine faith in God is adequate during the weaknesses of life.* Faith is no casual nod to God. It is allowing God to join our lives. The presence of the Lord helps during the times of weaknesses.

II. The weaknesses of life keep us aware of life's greater concerns.

A. *Paul had other concerns in his mind more than the agonies caused by the thorn.* Paul had two overwhelming purposes in his life. First, he wanted every person in his world to accept Jesus Christ as Savior. Second, he wanted every believer to be Christlike in thoughts and actions. Paul refused to let the thorn detour him in his purposes.

B. *Being consumed with the larger purposes of life overshadows the weaknesses.* A person's lack of mission forces him to focus on selfish discomfort. To be possessed by a great mission will mean that selfish discomforts will become secondary.

III. The weaknesses of life motivate us to become a part of a support group.

A. *Paul had a support group during times of weaknesses with churches.* Soon after his dramatic conversion believers in Damascus welcomed him. Ananias called him "Brother Saul" (Acts 9:17). Barnabas also "took him" (v. 27). Churches across Asia Minor, in Macedonia, Achaia, and Italy helped him.

B. *To help us with our weaknesses God provides a supportive group of people known as the church.* God's people are bound together in an intimate fellowship. They receive one another, love one another, minister to one another, forgive one another, pray for one another, and make many other supportive gestures.

IV. The weaknesses of life afford opportunities to be wounded healers.

A. *Paul was able to help others because of his thorn in the flesh.* He was able to empathize with a greater intensity. He knew what it was to suffer. As he found strength from God during his weaknesses, he told others who were hurting where to find help.

B. *People who have been hurt and have been helped prove to be good helpers.* Henri Nouwen in his book *The Wounded Healer* advocates that only the wounded can be authentic healers.

V. The weaknesses of life force us to look for a greater hope.

A. *Paul looked beyond the weaknesses to a greater time.* The thorn did not cause Paul to have a pessimistic view of life. Instead, in the midst of his weaknesses he loved life. Part of his great love for life was his optimistic view of the future. He believed that God would ultimately remove the thorn. "This mortal nature must put on immortality" (1 Cor. 15:53b RSV).

B. *There is a greater hope for believers.* The weaknesses of life may last for a lifetime, but they will not last throughout eternity. The believer will get a body which is immune from physical or emotional disorders.

Conclusion. The weaknesses of life do not have to make us weaker. By God's help we may gain strength during times of weaknesses.   — *HTB*

* * *

WEDNESDAY EVENING, DECEMBER 19

TITLE: The Golden Altar—the Place of Prayer

TEXT: "And thou shalt make an altar to burn incense upon: of shittim wood shalt thou make it. . . . And thou shalt put it before the veil that is by the ark of the testimony, before the mercy seat that is over the testimony, where I will meet with thee" (Exod. 30:1, 6).

SCRIPTURE READING: Exodus 30:1–10

Introduction. As we continue our tour through the tabernacle Moses built in the wilderness, we shall stand before the last of three pieces of furniture in the Holy Place, the larger of the two rooms comprising this unique and magnificent "tent of worship." As we examine the furniture that was in the Holy Place, it is important to remember that we are discussing the place of *fellowship.* This is the most important element in the believer's life—fellowship with God Himself. God is not so much concerned with what we *do* as He is with what we *are,* for the *doing* comes from the *being.* And it is only from our fellowship with God that we *become* what we ought to be.

So now we come to the golden altar of burnt incense. It stood before the veil, which hung between the Holy Place and the Holy of Holies.

I. The construction and position of the altar.

A. *Note carefully the position of this altar in the Holy Place.* It was located as close to the Holy of Holies—that sacred, smaller room where the presence of God dwelt—as it could possibly be. Thus, the nearest one could be to the presence of God, without being inside that awesome Holy of Holies, was to be at the altar of prayer. This says to us that we are never as close to God as when we are at prayer.

B. *Because of the importance of prayer in a believer's life, Satan does all in his power to interrupt this privilege.* A prayerless Christian is a virtual stranger to God. Any relationship loses its vitality without communication. Thus, the altar of burnt incense, placed closest to the place of God's presence, was a continual reminder to the people that God wanted to communicate with His people through prayer.

II. The offering upon it.

A. *God told Moses that an offering of incense was to be on the coals of fire of the altar continually.* This was a type of Christ who, now in the Father's presence in heaven, makes continual intercessory prayer for us (Heb. 9:24). John said, "My little children, these things write I unto you, that ye sin not. And if any man sin, we have an advocate with the Father, Jesus Christ the righteous" (1 John 2:1). John was saying that when we as Christians sin, we are not to panic; we have a representative standing by in heaven. He is seated at the right hand of the Father. He knows us and loves us and is ready to plead our case before the Father.

B. *Outside the tabernacle, in the courtyard, there was the brazen altar we discussed earlier.* On this altar made of wood and brass, a spotless lamb was sacrificed. It represented the cross of Calvary, where Christ, the Lamb of God, gave His life for our sins. So this "brazen altar" was the first stop one must make on his way to God. *Salvation* —redemption and reconciliation—took place at the brazen altar outside; that was for the sinner, lost and undone, without hope in the world. *Intercession* —continual prayer—takes place at the "golden altar" and it is Christ praying for all of us who have received Him as Savior. And the Christ we see there is not the dying Savior on the cross, but the risen Lord, who is seated at the right hand of the Father in heaven, making intercession for us.

To summarize, then, we can say that Christ saves us from much more than just condemnation of sin—He saves us from everything that contaminates us in our daily lives.

III. The golden altar as it relates to our prayer life.

A. *The altar had a continual fire, and incense was burning upon it; but there also were regular times of the day when it was specifically attended.* We are to pray continually, yet there are to be times for special prayer. Paul admonished us, in his first Thessalonian epistle, to "pray without ceasing."

B. *Even though we cannot intercede for others as Jesus does, we are personally responsible to pray for others.* When the people of Israel asked Samuel to pray for them, he replied: "God forbid that I should sin against the LORD in ceasing to pray for you" (1 Sam. 12:23).

The most important thing we can do, as believers, is to engage in intercessory prayer for others. This is a part of true worship, and it is more precious to God than much of the "activity" in which we are sometimes engaged.

Conclusion. Therefore, the golden altar of burnt incense is important in our understanding both of the ministry of Jesus for us *now* —as our Intercessor seated at the right hand of the Father in heaven—and the ministry He expects *us* to have for others. Are you a "stranger" at the altar of prayer?   —*DLJ*

* * *

SUNDAY MORNING, DECEMBER 23

TITLE: **The Glowing Light of the Lord's Presence**

TEXT: **". . . and the glory of the Lord shone around them, and they were filled with fear" (Luke 2:9 RSV).**

SCRIPTURE READING: **Luke 2:8–14; Matthew 5:14–16**

HYMNS: **"Hark! the Herald Angels Sing," Mendelssohn**
    "Good Christian Men, Rejoice," German Carol
    "O Come, All Ye Faithful," Wade

OFFERTORY PRAYER:
    Father in heaven, we are reminded at this time of the year of the greatness of Your gift to us in the Christ child, who became our Savior and Lord. Today we would bow before Him in awe and reverence. We would worship Him as the wise men did. We come bringing gifts to indicate our love and our concern that the rest of the world will come to know about the good news of His birth, His life, His death, His resurrection, and His living presence today. Bless these gifts to that end. In Jesus' name we pray. Amen.

Introduction. On the night of our Lord's birth, the shekinah glory of the Lord appeared, and the shepherds were made aware of the presence of the eternal God in a unique and unprecedented manner. If they were familiar with the Old Testament Scriptures, they would have recognized that this light that shone around them was a visible symbol of the presence of the invisible God. We see them in the tradition of the men of faith throughout the Old Testament who responded to this manifestation of the presence of God with fear and awe.

I. The radiant light of the Lord's presence.

Throughout the Old Testament our God is often pictured as the light which brings life and illumination for the path of life, enabling one to walk without falling.

God manifested Himself to the Israelites as a radiant light: "And the LORD went before them by day in a pillar of cloud to lead them along the way, and by night in a pillar of fire to give them light, that they might travel by day and by night" (Exod. 13:21 RSV). To be able to travel by night without stumbling was an unprecedented experience for human beings. This was made possible by the glory of the Lord which shone about them as a radiant light.

The children of Israel made their way through the wilderness by means of this radiant light of the Lord's presence: "The pillar of cloud by day and the pillar of fire by night did not depart from before the people" (13:22 RSV).

The glory of the Lord filled the tabernacle when it was dedicated (40:34).

II. Jesus Christ was the radiant light of the Lord's presence in the world (John 1:4–8).

A. *This radiant light of the Lord's glory was present at the birth of the Christ* (Luke 2:9).

B. *The radiant light of the Lord's presence was manifested in the Transfiguration experience* (Matt. 17:1–8; Mark 9:2–13; Luke 9:28–36). In this experience the deity of Jesus Christ shone through the veil of the flesh of His humanity.

C. *The radiant light of the Lord's presence accompanied the angels who announced the resurrection of the Christ.*

D. *There was this manifestation of the radiant light of the Lord's presence when the gift of the Spirit was bestowed at Pentecost.* "And there appeared to them tongues as of fire, distributed and resting on each one of them" (Acts 2:3 RSV).

E. *The glory of the Lord as a radiant light served to bring about the conversion of Saul of Tarsus on the road to Damascus.* "Now as he journeyed he approached Damascus, and suddenly a light from heaven flashed about him. and he fell to the ground and heard a voice saying to him . . ." (Acts 9:3–4 RSV). There can be no doubt that the memory of the glory of the Lord shining on the face of Stephen as he experienced execution by stoning was used as one of the goads to bring about conviction in the heart of this persecutor who was to become the great apostle Paul.

Satan has created darkness in the world and in the heart in order to prevent this radiant light of the Lord's presence from shining into the hearts and faces of the unsaved (2 Cor. 4:4).

III. Believers are to be the glowing light of the Lord's presence in the world today.

The Living Bible translates, or interprets, the words of Jesus in the Sermon on the Mount as follows, "You are the world's light—a city on a hill, glowing in the night for all to see. Don't hide your light! Let it shine for all; let your good deeds glow for all to see, so that they will praise your heavenly Father" (Matt. 5:14–16). There is something very exciting about the implications of this translation of the Scriptures in which the followers of Christ are described as "a city on a hill, glowing in the night for all to see." This implies that as followers of Christ we are to do something more than to merely reflect light. We are to let the living Christ, who dwells within us in Spirit, shine forth through our humanity so that an unbelieving world finds the pathway to God illuminated and made clear.

A. *Paul speaks of the messengers who bring the benevolent gifts of Gentile converts to Jewish believers in Jerusalem as being, "the glory of Christ"* (2 Cor. 8:23 RSV). If the glory of God is the visible symbol of the invisible God, then it follows that those who are generous in benevolent giving become "visible symbols of the invisible Christ."

B. *By means of good works that are helpful to others, we become the glowing light of the Lord's presence in the world that attracts men to our God:* "Don't hide your light! Let it shine for all; let your good deeds glow for all to see, so that they will praise your heavenly Father" (Matt. 5:15–16 LB). These good works are designed to glorify or to "advertise" God. Jesus specifically declares that we must not do our good works in order to glorify ourselves (6:1–4). If this translation is correct, and I believe it is, we have the privilege of being living, mobile symbols in the world today of the presence of our God similar to the manner in which the cloud by day and the pillar of fire by night symbolized the presence of the living God.

C. *If we render works and ministries of mercy to "the least of these" in the name and on behalf of Christ, then in a very real sense, we become the "glowing light of the Lord's presence" to them.*

D. *When we practice genuine caring love for others, we give proof of our relationship to Christ and in a sense become His representatives in the world today* (John 13:35).

Conclusion. We may be surprised to discover that in the world today, we can be angels of the Lord announcing, not only the birth, but the life, death, resurrection, and living presence of Jesus Christ. It is possible for us to be the radiant light of the Lord's presence by which others can come to know God today.

There are angels singing of His birth today. If you have not let Him come into your life, then listen to these songs and learn from them. Let Jesus Christ come into your heart and home.

There are shepherds in the world today still telling the Good News. There are wise men and women who have already given Him their hearts and treasures; and instead of becoming poor, they have become enriched beyond words by trusting Him and giving themselves to Him.

You would be wise to give yourself to this Christ.   — *TTC*

* * *

SUNDAY EVENING, DECEMBER 23

TITLE: When Jesus Gets Angry

TEXT: "And they come to Jerusalem: and Jesus went into the temple, and began to cast out them that sold and bought in the temple, and overthrew the tables of the moneychangers, and the seats of them that sold doves" (Mark 11:15).

SCRIPTURE READING: Mark 11:15-19

Introduction. Numerous questions have always come to my mind about Jesus Christ. Some of the questions are serious, while others may be mere curiosity. For example, How did Jesus sound? Was His voice high or low? What did Jesus look like? Was He short or tall? What was the disposition of Jesus? Did He have the full range of human emotions?

Let us look at an incident in the life and ministry of Jesus. This will give an insight into His disposition. All four of the gospel writers record the incident of Jesus cleansing the temple. The Master went to Jerusalem and to the temple. When He came to the outer court, the Court of the Gentiles, He observed something He did not like. People were involved in the buying and selling of animals as well as the exchange of Roman currency into Jewish currency. This aroused the anger of Jesus. He was concerned about reality in religion, and the abuse of religion aroused His anger.

Jesus still visits religious gatherings. Often He becomes angry. We would profit from a close examination of the incident in Jesus' ministry, for it would tell us when Jesus becomes angry today.

I. Jesus gets angry when routine takes the place of a relationship.

A. *The Jews visited the temple and transacted religious business without the sense of God's presence.* There was no absence of religious activity. The people attended the temple services, participated in the religious rituals, paid their tithes, and even offered sacrifices. Yet there was no sense of the presence of the Lord.

B. *Religious activities are opportunities for personal encounters with the Lord.* Going to church services on the Lord's Day affords an excellent opportunity to meet the Lord and to share life together. It is not just a time for religious routine. It is a time for a person to encounter the living Lord. "For where two or three are gathered together in my name, there am I in the midst of them" (Matt. 18:20).

This is one occasion that prompts the anger of Jesus, but there is another.

II. Jesus gets angry when convenience takes the place of discipline.

A. *The Jews sought to reduce the limits of their commitment to God.* At one time the sacrificial system had a significant meaning. It was a time of making a personal sacrifice to God.

The sacrificial system had been perverted. Instead of thinking about how much they could give, most of the people thought of how little they could give. A marketplace was established in the Court of the Gentiles so that people could conveniently buy an animal and make a sacrifice.

B. *An authentic relationship with the Lord has a demand with it.* Jesus calls people to follow Him. Accepting His invitations is no half-hearted commitment. Following Christ has preeminence over any other commitment.

Without a doubt Jesus becomes angry over the lack of discipline, but we can detect another time when He becomes angry.

III. Jesus gets angry when self-seeking takes the place of self-giving.

A. *The Jews had progressed to the point where they wanted to profit from their religion.* No foreign money could be used to pay the temple tax. Consequently, money changers erected places in the Court of the Gentiles to change foreign currency into Jewish currency. Of course an interest was charged. In other words many people participated in religious activities for a profit.

B. *Believers serve God because He is God and not for what they can profit.* Often one mistakes a commitment to Christ to mean prosperity or fame. No, one does not serve God for what he or she can get from it. Christ wants self-giving, not self-getting.

Jesus gets angry over self-getting, but there is also another time Jesus gets angry.

IV. Jesus gets angry when exclusion takes the place of inclusion.

A. *The Jews were selected to be a mission to the nations.* Careful study of Hebrew history will disclose that God intended the Jews to reach "all the families of the earth." Even in their places of worship, God told them to provide a place for the outsiders. In both the tabernacle and the temple, there was a Court of the Gentiles. It was a place where outsiders could come and learn of God.

When Jesus visited the temple, He saw that the moneychangers and merchants had excluded the Gentiles. This exclusion made Jesus angry.

B. *Relationship with God leads to an inclusion of others.* There can be no healthy church which excludes people from interest in the kingdom. Jesus becomes angry when exclusion is practiced.

Conclusion. Jesus is alive today. He visits our religious gatherings. Is He satisfied? Or is He angry? I encourage you to examine your religious rituals and see if they are pleasing to the Lord. — *HTB*

* * *

WEDNESDAY EVENING, DECEMBER 26

TITLE: The Ark of the Covenant—the Presence of God

Text: "And there I will meet with thee, and I will commune with thee from above the mercy seat, from between the two cherubim which are upon the ark of the testimony, of all things which I will give thee in commandment unto the children of Israel" (Exod. 25:22).

Scripture Reading: Exodus 25:10–22

Introduction. In this final study in our series, "Foregleams of Christ in the Old Testament," we shall step with reverence and holy awe behind the veil or curtain separating the Holy Place from the Holy of Holies in the tabernacle—that small room built with the perfect dimensions of a cube. According to the directions and specifications God gave to Moses, this room was a fifteen-foot cube. It was God's dwelling place among His people. In Old Testament days it was the holiest place on earth. Why was this small room so sacred and mysterious? Because in it rested one piece of furniture, called "the ark of the covenant." The lid of this chestlike piece of furniture was called "the mercy seat," and upon it burned continually a fire called "the shekinah glory of God." It represented the presence of the Almighty God among His people. In the final verse of our text passage we read God's words to Moses in regard to this ark: "And there I will meet with thee, and I will commune with thee from above the mercy seat" (Exod. 25:22).

I. The ark and its contents.

A. *Like the table of shewbread and the golden altar of burnt incense, the ark of the covenant was made of wood overlaid with gold.* But the ark of the covenant differs from the other pieces of furniture in the Holy Place. They all pointed to some aspect of Christ's *work*. The ark of the covenant spoke of His *person*. It did not reveal what He had done, but who He is. We can never appreciate or properly evaluate the ministry of the Lord Jesus until we come to understand who and what He is.

B. *The ark was a chest, in which were kept certain cherished articles.* There were the two tables of stone upon which were written the Ten Commandments; the golden pot containing a sample of the manna, which fell in the wilderness to feed the people; and Aaron's priestly rod or staff, which had budded, representing the continuing perpetual priesthood of his family. The ark was made of acacia (shittim) wood, the common wood of the desert where they were encamped—not from the cedars of Lebanon or the oak or gopherwood of Palestine. Likewise, God did not send us His Son in the form of an archangel, but rather in human flesh, to be as a man upon the earth.

C. *At both ends of the lid of the ark, called the "mercy seat," there was a cherub, an angellike being, sculpted of gold.*These two cherubim faced each other with their wings outstretched, covering the mercy seat. They were sculpted so that they were looking forward and down, their gaze focusing on the middle of the mercy seat. It was here that the blood was applied when the high priest entered on the Day of Atonement to offer the annual sacrifice for the sins of the people. Thus, as the cherubims' attention was constantly focused upon the shed blood of those sacrificial animals in Old Testament times, how much more should *our* attention be centered upon the cross, where Christ's blood was shed for our sins.

D. *Then, there was a visible manifestation of God's presence on the ark, in the form of a brilliant light or glow, called the shekinah glory of God.* It hovered over the mercy seat in the space between the two cherubim. Sometimes it was called a "fire."

The pot of manna in the ark reminded the Israelites how God sustained their physical lives in the wilderness. It was a fitting symbol of Jesus Christ, who sustains *our* lives spiritually. The other item in the ark was the Law—the tables of stone. The first set of tables of stone which Moses broke because the people were worshiping the golden calf represents man's continual breaking of the law of God. The second set represents Christ, who did *not* break the law when He came to earth to live among men. They represent God's perfect standards for man's life, which only Jesus could meet. Thus all *we* can do is cast ourselves upon *His* mercy; and when we do, He *has* mercy on us and saves us from our sins.

II. The lid of the ark, called the mercy seat.

A. *The mercy seat of pure gold represented God's throne in the midst of a sinful people.* Since it was placed on the top of the ark, it revealed the fact that God could *cover* the ark, containing the Law revealing His standards for man, and show mercy. Although God had to remain just and righteous without lowering His standards, He could extend mercy through the sprinkling of blood on the mercy seat. The shedding of blood made it possible for God to "be just, and the justifier of him which believeth in Jesus" (Rom. 3:26).

B. *As we noted earlier, a blood sacrifice had to be offered on the mercy seat once every year in order to atone for the sins of the people.* There was no chair in the tabernacle, because the work of the priest was never finished. From the time of the giving of the law on Mt. Sinai to the time Christ died on the cross, the priest had to come again and again with sacrifices for the people. But in Hebrews we read concerning the Lord Jesus: "Every priest standeth daily ministering and offering oftentimes the same sacrifices, which can never take away sins: but this man [Jesus Christ], after he had offered one sacrifice for sins for ever, sat down on the right hand of God" (Heb. 10:11–12).

C. *Now let's consider some of the special blessings of the mercy seat.* It was the place where God told Moses He would communicate with him. It covered the ark and thus overshadowed the law, which was represented by the tables of stone. It tells us Jesus lived and kept the law perfectly, and then offered Himself as the sacrifice for our sins committed in breaking that law. Then, another special blessing of the mercy seat was that it was the place where God met the sinner through a representative. Today Christ is our High Priest, for He has made the way into the Holy of Holies available to all who come by means of His shed blood.

Conclusion. When Jesus died on the cross, the veil which separated man from God's presence in the Holy of Holies was rent in two. We no longer have to stand outside and wait while an earthly priest enters the presence of God and pleads our case. We can come boldly and with assurance to this mercy seat in prayer. We come *not* because we are "good," but because of what Jesus Christ has done for us. — *DLJ*

* * *

SUNDAY MORNING, DECEMBER 30

TITLE: Teach Us to Number Our Days

TEXT: **"So teach us to number our days that we may get a heart of wisdom" (Ps. 90:12 RSV).**

SCRIPTURE READING: **James 4:13–15**

HYMNS: **"Majestic Sweetness Sits Enthroned," Stennett**
   "Jesus Shall Reign Where'er the Sun," Watts
   "Forward Through the Ages," Hosmer

OFFERTORY PRAYER:

Holy Father, as we come to this Lord's Day we look back through the year with great gratitude in our hearts for all of the blessings that You have so abundantly bestowed upon us. Help us to see all of these blessings as a part of Your providential plan to prepare us for ministry and helpfulness in the future. Thank You for Your blessings of the past. Thank You for Your promises for the present and the future. Accept these gifts and use them for the advancement of Your kingdom. We pray in Jesus' name. Amen.

Introduction. We come to the end of a year with joyful thoughts combined with solemn thoughts. We recognize that we are one year closer to the end of our earthly pilgrimage. We need to be reminded of the brevity of time and of the importance of being at our best at all times. It is true as the wise thinker said, "We live in deeds, not years; in thoughts, not breaths; in feelings, not in figures on a dial." Life is meant to be something much more than "a tale told by an idiot, full of sound and fury, signifying nothing." Time is given to us to be used in God's service.

Time is precious. Time is short. Time is passing. Time is uncertain. Time is irrevocable when gone. Time is that for which we are accountable.

Fuller said, "He lives long that lives well, and time misspent is not lived but lost." Each moment, as it passes, is the meeting point of two eternities.

As we come to the end of the year we need to recognize a number of things:

1. The brevity of time;
2. The swiftness of life;
3. The certainty of death;
4. The importance of ultimate values;
5. The years are slipping away.

I. The child of God may live with a noble disregard for time if death is no barrier, but only a door opening into the Father's home.

A. *"And this is eternal life, that they know thee the only true God, and Jesus Christ whom thou hast sent"* (John 17:3 RSV).

B. *"Beloved, we are God's children now; it does not yet appear what we shall be, but we know that when he appears we shall be like him, for we shall see him as he is.* And everyone who thus hopes in him purifies himself as he is pure" (1 John 3:2–3 RSV).

C. *The apostle Paul communicated words of faith, hope, and assurance as he wrote to the saints in Corinth: "So we are always of good courage; we know that while we are at home in the body we are away from the Lord, for we walk by faith, not by sight.* We are of good courage, and we would rather be away from the body and at home with the Lord" (2 Cor. 5:6–8 RSV). God did not make us to be earthlings alone. He made us for eternity, and He has given to us the Holy Spirit as an indwelling presence and as the guarantee that He shall rescue believers from death so they can live with Him for eternity (v. 5).

II. The nonbeliever should accept God's offer in Christ with great joy now.

A. *We need to gently and lovingly and appropriately remind our dear friends who are nonbelievers that the number of their days of opportunity are decreasing.*

B. *With the help of the Holy Spirit we need to help our unsaved friends recognize that their days of opportunity for serving God after being saved are declining with the passing of every day.*

Behold now is the acceptable time. Behold now is the day in which God offers the gift of forgiveness and the granting of mercy.

III. We should live every day as if it were our last day.

What would you do if this were the last day of your life? A farmer who knew God and who had lived a faithful life said in response to that question, "I would go plow." If we would live each day of our lives as if it were the last, there are a number of things that we should do.

A. *Begin the day with a prayer of thanks to God for His blessings upon you.* Name them one by one.

B. *Accept the day as an opportunity to help.*
1. Help God do His work in the world today.
2. Help yourself to be a better person and do a better job.
3. Help your family members to achieve their goals.
4. Help others in the sphere of your influence to achieve worthwhile goals.
5. Help others along the way through the day as you have time and opportunity.

Respond to everyone with love—a persistent, unbreakable spirit of good will that relates to others in terms of their highest possible good.

C. *Plan the day with top values out front.*
1. Draw up a list of the things that need to be done.
2. Number them in the order of their importance.
3. Concentrate on the most important item first.
4. Do one thing at a time.

D. *Schedule the day and allow for some interruptions.* Recognize that while some interruptions are time-killers, other interruptions are divine appointments.

Conclusion. The psalmist prayed that God would help him to number his days that he might secure wisdom and face life with the highest possible intelligence and the deepest possible insight.

Do not postpone living. Make those important decisions that need to be made. Procrastination can cause you to

1. Kill time
2. Lose time
3. Waste time

Today is the only day you have.

Decide today for Jesus Christ if you have not let Him become your Savior up to this point.

Decide today to build a Christian home with your partner.

Decide today to ask for and to grant forgiveness.

Decide today to find a usefulness beyond the value of the marketplace.

Decide today to find a means of extending life's usefulness.   — *TTC*

* * *

SUNDAY EVENING, DECEMBER 30

TITLE: "Have a Good Day"

TEXT: **"Take therefore no thought for the morrow: for the morrow shall take thought for the things of itself. Sufficient unto the day is the evil thereof" (Matt. 6:34).**

SCRIPTURE READING: **Matthew 6:25–34**

Introduction. Several months ago I made a business trip from New Orleans to Atlanta. As the day started an interesting chain of events happened. The person who parked my car said, "Have a good day." Then the person who checked my airline ticket said, "Have a nice day." As I left the airplane, the flight attendant said, "Have a nice day." After I paid for my lunch, the cashier said, "Have a nice day."

The courteous expression "Have a good day" became obvious. It was a good expression. The more I thought about it, the more I recognized that while several people told me to have a good day, no one had told me *how* to have a good day. Let us stop and think for a moment about how to have a good day.

Our lives are lived in various time segments—years, months, weeks, days. Each day is divided into hours, minutes, and seconds. Learning to manage our time is one of the prominent priorities of life. Our Lord wants us to fill each day with meaning. Let us notice now how to have a good day.

I. Begin each day with God.

A. *Good beginnings are important.* This fact is evident in many areas of life. Students need to get a good beginning in school. Preachers need to have effective beginnings for their sermons. Television programs need to have good leads. In numerous areas of life good beginnings are essential.

Beginning each day with God will align the day with the prominent priority. The Lord will be considered first, and the rest of the day will be considered in the light of His will.

B. *Beginning the day with God may have varied exercises.* Several exercises will be beneficial in beginning the day with God, for example, Bible reading, prayer, and contemplative thinking. Other exercises could be practiced as well.

C. *Beginning each day with God will have positive benefits.* Our relationship with the Lord will be strengthened. Life with its ideas and happenings could be placed in proper perspective. One can get direction for the living of the day. If a person begins the day like this, he is on the way to having a good day.

II. Maintain healthy interpersonal relationships.

A. *Relationships with people are inevitable occurrences of the day.* There is no way we can get away from contact with people. Much of our lives involves contact and interaction with people.

At times we may want to get away from people. This desire represents a legitimate occasional need, but it is a permanent impossibility.

B. *Relationships may be enhanced.* Believers have the possibility of having good interpersonal relationships. There are several reasons Christians may have healthy interpersonal relationships. First, believers are to respect each individual as a person of importance. Second, believers are to listen carefully to other human beings. Third, Christians are to seek the highest good of other people. This gesture is what is meant by loving one another.

C. *Reconcile ruptured relationships.* Closely akin to enhancing relationships is repairing relationships. Our day may be enhanced by settling our grudges by eliminating our revenge. "Therefore if thou bring thy gift to the altar, and there rememberest that thy brother hath aught against thee; leave there thy gift before the altar, and go thy way; first be reconciled to thy brother, and then come and offer thy gift" (Matt. 5:23–24).

III. Watch your conversation.

A. *Talking comprises a large part of our day.* Have you ever thought about how many words are said in the course of a single day? We cannot live through a day without speaking words. Talking is a large part of our daily activity.

B. *Words have the power of influence.* Words directed to us have the power either to bless us or to curse us. Someone may speak an encouraging word to us, and it will enhance our day. Or someone may speak a derogatory word to us, and it will ruin our day. Words directed to us have amazing power to affect our day. Likewise, the words we speak have the capacity of affecting a person either for good or bad.

C. *Our conversation needs to be controlled.* To have a good day we need to filter words from others. At times we need to listen carefully to the critical words others as well as to their complimentary words to us. Let us also guard our conversation to others. The appropriate words spoken to others are about how God will help. Only God can control our conversation.

IV. Fill your mind with good thoughts.

A. *Thoughts are inevitable occurrences during the course of the day.* Ideas come to our minds from unexplainable origins. Human beings cannot prevent thoughts from coming to mind.

B. *Thoughts have the possibility of lodging in our lives.* To entertain good thoughts will lead to good actions. To entertain bad thoughts will lead to immoral actions. "For as he thinketh in his heart, so is he" (Prov. 23:7).

C. *Thoughts can be controlled.* The apostle Paul helped us with our thoughts: "Finally, brethren, whatsoever things are true, whatsoever things are honest, whatsoever things are just, whatsoever things are pure, whatsoever things are lovely, whatsoever things are of good report; if there be any virtue, and if there be any priase, think on these things" (Phil. 4:8).

V. Engage in meaningful activities.

A. *Working for our livelihood is a part of most days.* "Six days shalt thou labour, and do all thy work" (Exod. 20:9). There is a commendable quality to those who fill their days with good work. To have a good day would mean that you enjoy your work and strive to do your best with it.

B. *To have a good day one day of each week needs to be devoted to worship.* "But the seventh day is the sabbath of the LORD thy God: in it thou shalt not do any work, thou, nor thy son, nor thy daughter, thy manservant, nor thy maidservant, nor thy cattle, nor thy stranger that is within thy gates'' (v. 10). One day of each week should be given to worship. It will enhance the other days.

C. *A meaningful day will be filled with significant activities.* In addition to giving your best to your work there are some other meaningful activities, such as, visiting for your church, helping some person in need, and others.

Conclusion. You can have a good day. The best day is when you open your life to Jesus Christ. Subsequent days will be more meaningful. Each day can be enhanced by beginning with God, by maintaining healthy relationships, guarding our conversation, thinking good thoughts, and engaging in meaningful activities. Now, have a good day! — *HTB*

* * *

COMMUNION SERVICES

TITLE: **Making the Lord's Supper Memorable**
TEXT: **"Do this in remembrance of me" (1 Cor. 11:24 RSV).**
SCRIPTURE READING: **1 Corinthians 11:23–25**

Introduction. On Communion tables all over the world you will find inscribed in many languages the simple phrase "In remembrance of me." It's a verse from the Bible, and it's probably the one verse that is in plain view of millions of Christians every time they come to worship the Lord. Many of us grew up seeing those words.

Those words were first used with reference to the Lord's Supper by Jesus Himself. The apostle Paul recorded them in First Corinthians, chapter 11. He quoted Jesus as saying of the broken bread and the cup of the covenant, "Do this in remembrance of me." Those words remind us of two basic facts: that Jesus wants us to remember Him, and that we are prone to forget.

The Lord's Supper makes clear to us that Jesus wanted His followers to remember that His magnificent ministry on earth was completed on a cross, where He suffered and died for the sins of the world. He wants us to remember the cross as the ultimate demonstration of His love for undeserving, self-centered sinners. And He wants us to remember that following Him means being identified with Him. It means taking up a cross—suffering as He suffered, forgiving as He forgave, loving as He loved, and dying as He died.

In our meditation today we shall be thinking about making the Lord's Supper memorable. That should not suggest that we make the Lord's Supper take on the character of a World's Fair attraction or cast it in high drama suitable for a Broadway production. We do need to make every effort, however, to make sure the celebration of the Supper is not routine ritual.

I. Through preparation.

A. *The Lord's Supper can be made memorable through recall.* Our minds travel back to that night when Jesus was betrayed. We remember the setting of the Supper and the meaning He gave it. We cannot view the Supper as a casual observance when we are meditating on that night.

Then, too, it helps us to recall former meaningful experiences of worship around the Lord's Table. Many of God's faithful children have felt closer to Him when they celebrated with joy the Lord's Supper than at any other time in worship.

B. *The Lord's Supper can be made memorable through anticipation.* Having had numerous uplifting experiences of Communion with the Lord while observing the Supper, we look forward to the next time we shall break the bread and take the cup together.

C. *The Lord's Supper can be made memorable through our involvement with Christ in the world.* When we walk with Him and take some of the licks He took, we find it easy to identify with Him, especially on the night when He instituted the Supper.

II. Through participation.

A. *For a memorable observance of the Supper we need to come to the house of worship in the right spirit.* We need to be still and remember that the God before whom we bow is our Creator, our Redeemer, our sovereign Lord. We want to approach Him in a spirit of reverence and humility. We have been counting our blessings and want to thank Him in the most expressive way possible. We want to open our whole lives to God.

B. *For a memorable observance of the Supper we need to feel the warmth, strength, purpose, and vibrancy of our brothers and sisters in the body of Christ.* The apostle Paul had some harsh words for a fellowship that ignored the poorer members. "When you meet together," said he, "it is not the Lord's supper that you eat. For in eating, each one goes ahead with his own meal, and one is hungry and another is drunk." Pointedly he inquired, "Do you despise the church of God and humiliate those who have nothing?" (1 Cor. 11:20–22). God's people should love each other, rejoice and sorrow with each other, and pray that each other will sense God's nearness.

C. *For a memorable observance of the Supper we need to examine ourselves and confess our sins to God.* Though standing before God's full-length mirror causes us to be aware of every flaw, we should without hesitation try to see ourselves as God sees us. For a moment, this vision of ourselves will be painful and humiliating. That's the way God wants it. He wants us to be uncomfortable in seeing our selfishness, our rebellion against Him, and our resistance to His will. When we see ourselves as He sees us, we want to get on our knees, confess all our sins, and ask Him to forgive us.

D. *For a memorable observance of the Supper we should partake of the elements in faith and meaningful remembrance.* While we believe the bread and the grape juice received in faith remain bread and grape juice, we also believe that partaking of them in the spirit Jesus demonstrated will heighten our awareness of God's presence and of His call to us to bear our crosses with honor. Gathered around the Lord's Table, we remember we are celebrating the Lord's Supper, conscious of the Lord's presence, the Lord's power, and the Lord's purpose. From the Table, we look back to the cross on which Jesus died and we look forward to His coming in glory. When we compress all that meaning in a worship setting, we need to be prepared for a jolt from heaven.

Conclusion. Communion should be memorable. It is sacrilege to let it become a monotonous, routine ceremony. Thorough preparation and meaningful participation will enable us to sense God's presence at the Lord's Table and to be charged with God's power and purpose as we serve Him in the world. — *KF*

* * *

TITLE: What Is Communion to Us?

TEXT: **"The cup of blessing which we bless, is it not a participation in the blood of Christ? The bread which we break, is it not a participation in the body of Christ?" (1 Cor. 10:16 RSV).**

SCRIPTURE READING: **1 Corinthians 10:16–17; 11:20–26**

Introduction. What's Communion to us? Considering the way we observe

Communion, we might come up with several answers: It's everything in worship; it's nothing; it's something we have to do; it's a meaningful act of worship.

One Catholic priest reported that a noisy, drunk man once came for Communion. The priest passed him. "Give me my Jesus," the man demanded, creating an embarrassing scene for everyone present. He wanted to take Communion, but he felt no need to prepare himself for an uplifting experience of worship.

Now take a look at a general in the army. On his last Sunday before leading his troops in battle, he took part in six Communion services. He spent his whole day traveling to and sharing in these services. Did he feel that Communion would give him added protection in battle?

Communion ought to be a central act of worship, but there is no magic to it. It won't make a bad man good, a weak man strong, or a dense man clear-headed.

I. The meaning of the Supper.

A. *It is known as a memorial.* "For as often as you eat this bread and drink the cup, you proclaim the Lord's death until he comes" (1 Cor. 11:26). At the Table we look back.

B. *It is communion with Christ.* "The cup of blessing which we bless, is it not a participation in the blood of Christ? The bread which we break, is it not a participation in the body of Christ?" (10:16). At the Table we sense God's presence in a special way. Standing for Christ's body and blood, the bread and the juice call us to worship a Christ who died for us and who was raised from the dead. As we commune with Him, we know we are not alone, that we need never give in to fear or despair.

C. *It is the Lord's Supper.* The apostle Paul chided the Corinthian Christians for their selfishness. "When you meet together, it is not the Lord's supper that you eat. For in eating, each one goes ahead with his own meal, and one is hungry and another is drunk" (11:20–21).

Communion is not the church's supper. It is all about the Lord. We break the bread and drink from the cup to remember the Lord and to sense His presence with us.

D. *It is sometimes referred to as a Eucharist, meaning thanksgiving.* Thanksgiving is a vital part of our celebration of the Lord's Supper. Following the example of Jesus, we thank the Lord for the bread and the fruit of the vine.

E. *It is a form of prophecy.* In Communion, wrote Paul, "you proclaim the Lord's death until he comes" (11:26). The great victory over sin has been won. Christ died for our sins and was raised in triumph. But God has more for us. Jesus will return. Until He does return, we shall praise Him around His Table.

F. *It is called a sacrament by some.* Many Christians, fearing possible magical associations, avoid the use of that word. But *sacrament* is a good word. It means a pledge or vow of loyalty. We may not choose to call Communion a sacrament, but we cannot avoid pledging our lives to Christ.

II. The quality of our celebration.

Knowing the profound meaning of Communion, we still may not experience a meaningful celebration around the Lord's Table. To a large extent the quality of our celebration depends on us.

A. *It depends on our feelings at the time of the celebration.* Kidney stones and unvented anger can prevent us from having a soul-stirring worship experience in a Communion service. Many hurtful things can bring our spirits down and cause us to center our minds on ourselves. When we're depressed and hurt, we need to open our lives again to God—confessing our sins, asking for His help, thanking Him for His mercy, and offering ourselves totally to Him.

B. *It sometimes depends on what is going on around us.* There are few worship services without distractions. Horseplay and rude whispering may cause us to forget why we came to God's house. On the other hand, our spirits may be lifted to glorious adoration by inspiring music or an effective presentation of God's Good News. Obviously, we should be so determined to worship the Lord that we let nothing get between us and Him.

C. *It sometimes depends on what Christ means to us.* If we take for granted His loving sacrifice on the cross and the salvation we have received as a gift of His grace, Communion will be dull to us. If Christ means more to us than anything or anybody else, we shall be in awe of Him as we take the bread and the cup. We shall be overwhelmed with gratitude and expectation.

D. *It also depends on what we now are doing for Christ and hoping to do for Him.* Those who take their lumps for Christ in the world realize how much they need Him and how much worship can do to renew their spirits. Communion is sweet to these people, for they find strength in His presence and solace in their sorrow.

Conclusion. What's Communion to us? It is not everything, but it is a significant worship experience for those who recognize the centrality of the cross in the plan of God. Let us approach the Lord's Table with prepared hearts, knowing we now need and always will need the presence and the power of the Lord.   — *KF*

* * *

TITLE: Proclaiming the Lord's Death

TEXT: "For as often as you eat this bread and drink the cup, you proclaim the Lord's death until he comes" (1 Cor. 11:26).

SCRIPTURE READING: 1 Corinthians 11:23–26 - 34

Introduction. The Lord's Supper is a proclamation of the Lord's death. It is never just a "whatchamacallit" we do from time to time. There is no magic in it. There is faith behind it, and because of that faith there can be miracles involved in the meaningful celebration of the Supper.

Every celebration of the Lord's Supper is a proclamation of Jesus' death on the cross for us. It is the central message of the Christian faith. We may seek to discover innovative approaches for celebrating the Supper, but we are only trying to find ways to make the death of Christ more real to us and to point up the significance of the Lord's death.

I. Proclaiming the historical details of the Lord's death.

A. *The time and place.* Historical details are important in the Bible. God works in history. His revelations are given to people struggling with their trials and troubles in the world.

Jesus was crucified after a brief ministry of about three years. The place was outside the city walls of Jerusalem.

B. *The manner in which Jesus died.* Jesus was interrogated without respect or mercy. He was lied about and falsely charged. He was denied by Simon Peter, leader of the apostles. Judas, treasurer of the group, betrayed Him. He was jeered and mocked, spat upon, scourged with whips that cut His back to shreds, crowned with a crown of thorns, and crucified between two thieves. Death by crucifixion was an especially cruel form of capital punishment. It usually involved a long period of physical torture and public shame of the worst kind.

C. Jesus had faced the torture and shame of the cross in the Garden of Gethsemane. There He prayed, "Abba, Father, all things are possible to thee; remove this cup from me; yet not what I will, but what thou wilt" (Mark 14:36 RSV). On the cross He suffered valiantly and victoriously, praying for those who had crucified Him and commending His spirit to the Father.

Recalling the details of Jesus' crucifixion and the abuse that preceded it should bring tears to us all. Indescribable brutality was matched by unbreakable love.

II. Proclaiming the religious significance of the Lord's death.

A. *Jesus' death on the cross demonstrated the depth of God's love for us.* Paul's witness was, "But God shows his love for us in that while we were yet sinners Christ died for us" (Rom. 5:8 RSV). John wrote, "By this we know love, that he laid down his life for us" (1 John 3:16 RSV).

B. *Jesus' death on the cross made salvation available to us.* The cross was the culmination of God's plan for our salvation. "He destined us in love to be his sons through Jesus Christ," wrote Paul (Eph. 1:5 RSV). "In him we have redemption through his blood, the forgiveness of our trespasses, according to the riches of his grace which he lavished upon us" (vv. 7–8 RSV). The writer of the Book of Hebrews noted the significance of Jesus' death by saying, "He entered once for all into the Holy Place, taking not the blood of goats and calves but his own blood, thus securing an eternal redemption" (Heb. 9:12 RSV).

C. *Jesus' death on the cross pictured the way of life God had in mind for us.* "If any man would come after me," declared Jesus, "let him deny himself and take up his cross and follow me" (Mark 8:34 RSV). It is clear that Jesus wants His followers to accept cross-bearing as a way of life. People who would honor Jesus with their lives must be willing to suffer as He suffered and die as He died.

The early church got Jesus' point. Part of the apostle Paul's testimony was, "I have been crucified with Christ" (Gal. 2:20). Paul drew the same kind of anger and venomous opposition from his adversaries that Jesus received. He, too, was hated, misunderstood, misrepresented, and physically abused.

Another faithful Christian called on Jesus' followers to pay the ultimate cost in representing Him. "So Jesus also suffered outside the gate in order to sanctify the people through his own blood. Therefore let us go forth to him outside the camp, and bear the abuse he endured" (Heb. 13:12–13 RSV).

Conclusion. As we again proclaim the Lord's death we remind ourselves that the cross was at the center of God's plan for our salvation and was the culmination of that plan.

The cross reveals to us God's baffling wisdom and limitless power. Though He allowed despicable sinners to expose Jesus to shame and kill Him by crucifixion, God demonstrated His sovereign power and His redemptive plan by raising Jesus from the dead. He wants us to believe that he can bring good to us out of the worst things we ever shall have to pass through.

As we proclaim Jesus' death, we recognize that he was crucified for us; we confess our awful sin of unbelief; we thank Him for His sacrifice; and we commit ourselves to live the rest of our days for Him, trying with all our hearts to become like Him.　　　　　　　　　　　　　　　　　　　　　　　　　　　— *KF*

* * *

FUNERAL MESSAGES

TITLE: **Facing the Death of a Loved One**

TEXT: **"But we would not have you ignorant, brethren, concerning those who are asleep, that you may not grieve as others do who have no hope"** (1 Thess. 4:13 RSV).

SCRIPTURE READING: **1 Thessalonians 4:13–18**

Introduction. We feel intense pain this hour. We've lost someone we love, and life can never be the same for us again. Death cuts us to the bone—frustrating our schedules, upsetting our plans, reminding us of our weakness, closing doors we wanted to stay open, and piercing us with a pain that won't go away. This is a day for grieving, and the months ahead of us will be an extended time for grieving.

Grief can be healthy or sick, good or bad. It all depends on the faith and the outlook of the grief-stricken. The apostle Paul was concerned that his friends in Christ not grieve the way hopeless unbelievers do. That is our concern today. Let us begin the grief process with faith in God's character and power, and let us resolve to strengthen our faith in God as we live with our pain and work through our grief one day at a time.

How shall we face the death of this one who has touched our lives for good and made God seem more real to us? First, we shall try to see death through the eyes of God. And then we shall try to respond to our loss by looking back, by looking inside ourselves, by looking around us, and by looking up to God.

I. Seeing death through the eyes of God.

A. *As an end.* Death is the end of all the good things we have enjoyed with and cherished in this loved one who has just died. So much of our lives have been tied to and built around this loved one. While we're not ready to loosen those ties, we know that the loving fellowship, the intimate conversations, and the shared pleasures we had are now finished. Our lives can still be moved by his compelling example, but we no longer can see his face or hear his voice. His active service to God and to us is all over.

Jesus must have had this reality in mind when He said, "We must work the works of him who sent me, while it is day; night comes, when no one can work" (John 9:4 RSV).

While we sorrow to see death as the end of a good life on earth, we rejoice to see death as the end of all the bad things that brought sadness to our loved one. God revealed to John that tears, death, mourning, crying, and pain were all part of the things that will have passed away when we are in the immediate presence of God in our heavenly home (Rev. 21:3–4). For this man we love there will be no more loneliness, no more doubts, no more disappointments, no more misunderstanding, no more physical limitations, no more injustices, no more bitterness, no more weaknesses or failures.

B. *As a continuation.* Death has been described as a horizon that marks the limit of our sight. That's a good way to see it. The ship sailing beyond the horizon is still nestled in the sea; and though we can see it no longer, it is still progressing toward its ultimate destination. This dear child of God has moved beyond the horizon.

Death cannot rob him of the warm communion he has been maintaining with God through the years. The apostle Paul declared that Jesus Christ "died for us so that whether we wake or sleep we might live with him" (1 Thess. 5:10 rsv). In Christ life goes on. The relationship is sustained.

C. *As a beginning.* Death ushers us into the nearer presence of God and enables us to enjoy perfect fellowship and to share the glories of heaven with believers who have completed their lives on earth. "For we know that if the earthly tent we live in is destroyed, we have a building from God, a house not made with hands, eternal in the heavens" (2 Cor. 5:1 rsv).

At death life's puzzles will be answered for the children of God. We shall have our eyes opened to see our problems in God's perspective.

II. Responding to our loss with the help of God.

A. *By looking back.* Looking back on the life of this man of God brings sorrow to us now, for it reminds us of the magnitude of our loss. We remember his heritage, his faith, his character, his contributions, his influence, and the convictions he lived by. It hurts us to have to speak of him in the past tense. We grieve because we are unable to thank him for all the reminders of his love which are everywhere about us.

Still we must look back. We need to thank God for this good man. We need to learn to reproduce his sterling qualities. We need to deal realistically with our grief. And all of these require us to look back with appreciation and to marvel at what God has done for us through him.

B. *By looking inside.* We need to make a microscopic study of who we are, what we are, where we're coming from, how we feel, and what our dreams are.

When we try to look inside ourselves, we recognize our finitude. We know we are weak and that we, too, shall die. We feel forced to examine our faith: Do we know enough? Do we trust God enough? Can we face the future unafraid? And we must deal honestly with our feelings. After we have admitted our feelings, we need to decide whether we should vent them, learn to live with them, or change them.

C. *By looking around.* The apostle Paul wrote, "If one member suffers, all suffer together" (1 Cor. 12:26). We're in the boat together, and we sink or float together. We hope you'll never be ashamed or embarrassed or uneasy about leaning on any of us when you need support. Later you'll be able to help those who are going through your present crisis (see 2 Cor. 1:3–4).

D. *By looking up.* God is our ultimate source of help. We recognize His goodness, His greatness, and His love. We trust Him to hear us, to accept us just as we are, to put up with us when we get down in the dumps, to be with us at all times, to guide us where we should go, to see us through this long tunnel of sorrow, to encourage us, and to give us all we need to make us whole again.

Conclusion. We face this day without the comprehensive understanding we want, without the clarity of vision we'd like to have, without the buoyant spirit we yearn for. That simply means we face our great loss as weak, finite human beings. But we take heart in the promises of God. We believe that the great God who created us now holds us in His hands, and that one day He will unite us with this loved one and with all the rest of God's children.

"May the God of hope fill you with all joy and peace in believing, so that by the power of the Holy Spirit you may abound in hope" (Rom. 15:13 RSV). — *KF*

* * *

TITLE: **God's Consolations for Our Cares**

TEXT: **"When the cares of my heart are many, thy consolations cheer my soul" (Ps. 94:19 RSV).**

SCRIPTURE READING: **2 Corinthians 1:3-5**

Introduction. Out text is like a treasure rescued from the fire. The psalmist, a man of tested and proven faith, was perplexed by his suffering and hard times; but he was absolutely sure that the Lord was on his side and would see him through. His testimony gives light and encouragement to all of God's children in their times of suffering and mental anguish.

We need to hear and believe that in the worst of times the Lord can cheer our souls with His presence and with a message that is above and beyond us. The settings for our daily lives and the schedules we follow are all tied up with the choices we have made and the lifestyles we have followed, but the sorrows we have experienced are timeless. Like the ancient psalmist we recognize that "the cares of our hearts are many." Our hearts, wearied from toil and trouble, need to be cheered; and God is the only one who can do that. His consolations make all the difference in the world.

In this service we shall consider two great consolations which have cheered God's troubled people through the centuries: (1) God will take care of us now. (2) God has a great future planned for us.

I. God will take care of us now.

Certain people, overwhelmed by their sense of powerlessness in the presence of ungodly forces, have cried out: "This is a God-forsaken world." We would agree that there is a lot of evil in this world, but we know God has not forsaken it. With Christ in our hearts, we are never alone.

Emmanuel was a name given to Jesus. It means "God with us." God is with us in Jesus. We live in a God-inhabited world.

The great God who is always with us knows all about us. He knows where we live, how much money we have in the bank, what our favorite foods are, what our secret sins are, and how hard we try to be good. He knows our strengths and weaknesses, our anger and our fears, our dreams and our doubts, our burdens and our blessings. We may or may not be willing to make full disclosure of our true selves, but God knows the whole story already. He stands by us not as a neutral, but as our dearest Friend. And He walks with us not as a well-intentioned weakling, but as the all-powerful, sovereign Lord.

We must not understand, however, that His presence with us and His power in us mean that he will deaden our pain or give us a detour around trouble.

Instead, God usually blesses us by leading us through the trouble and giving us wisdom and enabling power when we face the worst there is in life.

The writer of the Book of Lamentations declared, "Gone is my glory, and my expectation from the Lord" (3:18). His soul was depressed as he thought about his afflictions and his bitter experiences. Then he took another look. "But this I call to mind, and therefore I have hope," he reflected. "The steadfast love of the Lord never ceases, his mercies never come to an end; they are new every morning; great is thy faithfulness" (3:21–23 RSV). He caught the Lord's vision and found His peace when his soul was troubled.

The apostle Paul, frustrated and depressed by what he called a thorn in the flesh, prayed earnestly that the Lord would take it from him. The Lord didn't give Paul what he asked for, but He gave him what he needed. He said to Paul, "My grace is sufficient for you, for my power is made perfect in weakness" (2 Cor. 12:9).

That is the way God works. He doesn't keep us away from heartache and trouble, but He stands by us and takes care of us.

II. God has a great future planned for us.

God is eternal. He holds tomorrow in His hands. He has planned for us a future so glorious our minds cannot now begin to comprehend it; and He in majestic power and with unbridled authority will bring His plan to fulfillment in His own time and in His own way. "To die is gain," said Paul (Phil. 1:21). He had caught a glimpse of God's plan for His people in the future.

God's plan involves quality of life. John heard a voice from the throne saying, "Behold, the dwelling of God is with men. He will dwell with them, and they shall be his people, and God himself will be with them; he will wipe away every tear from their eyes, and death shall be no more, neither shall there be mourning nor crying nor pain any more, for the former things have passed away" (Rev. 21:3–4 RSV).

God's plan involves full understanding. Daily we are plagued with unanswerable questions that jab at our spirits. Why did God let the child die? Why did God allow the plane to go down? Why does God let communism and the underworld thrive? Why? Why? Why? The questions are endless, and the absence of answers is almost unbearable. That is an earthbound problem, and for it we need a heavenly answer. The apostle Paul assured us God has an answer. "For now we see in a mirror dimly," he said, "but then face to face. Now I know in part; then I shall understand fully" (1 Cor. 13:12).

God's plan involves a new self for each of us. Paul assured us that the returning Christ "will change our lowly body to be like his glorious body" (Phil. 3:21). The witness of John was that "we know that when he appears we shall be like him, for we shall see him as he is" (1 John 3:2).

Conclusion. In this sad hour when our hearts are broken, we find comfort in knowing that God is good and that He is in control. We look to Him for the goodness, guidance, calmness, and strength we now desperately need. With faith, hope, and love we would trust ourselves completely to Him—body and soul, everything we are or ever shall be—now and forever, in sunshine and in shadow, in life and in death. And to God be the glory!   — *KF*

* * *

TITLE: Really Believing in Heaven

TEXT: "In my Father's house are many mansions: if it were not so, I would have told you. I go to prepare a place for you" (John 14:2).

SCRIPTURE READING: John 14:1–3

Introduction. God has made it clear to us that this quaking world, marred by sin and intimidated by death, is not our final home. He has something infinitely better for His children. In mercy He has prepared a place beyond this world, a place marvelous in beauty and custom-designed for people who have been transformed by a personal encounter with Jesus Christ. That place is heaven.

We long to see heaven and to be in the immediate presence of Jesus and all those who belong to Him. If we aren't careful, however, we shall give a pious nod with our heads to the idea of heaven while our hearts in despair regard heaven as well-intended fiction. We know Jesus promised He would prepare a place for us, and we want to believe everything He said; but we still have trouble really believing in heaven.

I. Why we have difficulty believing in heaven.

A. *It's not on earth.* Though we as God's children are not earthbound in perspective, we soon learn to settle comfortably into this world. Our eyes moisten as we recall the home of our childhood, the birthday parties we celebrated there, and the furnishings that turned a house into our home. As we grow older, we become more deeply involved with this world. We become attached to the things of this world and find security in bank accounts, houses, a system of government, schools, and churches. We find it hard to believe life can be good without the things and happenings that have brought us joy in this world.

B. *It's beyond death.* That for us is unexplored territory. Cemeteries remind us of our powerlessness and our lack of knowledge.

We have read in the Bible that Christ is Lord both of the dead and of the living (Rom. 14:9), but death still strikes fear into our hearts.

C. *It sounds too good to be true.* Even those with great imaginations cannot envision the glories of heaven. Who on earth can picture a place not contaminated by sin, sickness, and death? Who can dream what it will be like to see God and to become like Jesus?

II. Why we should believe in heaven.

A. *This world is not enough.* God is a God of justice, and in this world injustice can be seen everywhere. We are not supposed to be satisfied with this world where good people suffer and bad people thrive, where angel-faced children die of leukemia and underworld characters live to be ninety.

B. *Jesus promised it.* "I go to prepare a place for you," He said (John 14:2). The perfect Son of God never lies, but always keeps His word. Our dull minds will never be able to comprehend all God has in store for us in heaven, but we can wisely and safely leave that in Jesus' hands. He will take care of every detail.

The Christ who promised heaven was raised from the dead and now lives within us. His Spirit is our guarantee of full redemption in heaven (2 Cor. 1:22; 5:5; Eph. 1:13–14).

III. What really believing in heaven should do to us.

A. *It should cause us to realize that we as God's children have the only real security there is.* Real security is not in property, insurance, bank accounts, and retirement income. We are secure in God alone. Thus, those like poor Lazarus can rejoice because they know they have life that never will end.

B. *It should keep us from despairing when we think of our loved ones who have died in Christ.* They are with the Lord now. Their future with God is sure. We need not worry about them.

A three-year-old boy was perplexed and indignant when his playmate's father died suddenly. His mother assured him that his friend's daddy was with God. "Oh! Then he's still real," the troubled boy replied. Of that we can be sure. When our loved ones die, we shall see them no more in this world; but we know they are just as real as they were on earth, living in other rooms of our Father's house.

C. *It should help us avoid fear or resentment of our own coming death.* We are safe in Christ. We need not worry about coming down with cancer or having our life snatched away in a plane crash.

D. *It should prepare us to be our best and do our best on earth.* If we know that the leading character in a story is victorious in the end, we don't become disturbed when he is getting his lumps in the middle of the story. It is the same with us. Being sure of heaven should free us to live creatively, without being terrorized by temporary frustrations and hardships. With the apostle Paul we can say, "For to me to live is Christ, and to die is gain" (Phil. 1:21). With that kind of faith we should be willing to take any necessary risks without fear, seeking only to become like Christ and to honor Him with our lives.

Conclusion. Horatio Spafford, a popular nineteenth-century Chicago lawyer, was jolted to learn that his wife and daughters had been spilled into the sea due to a shipwreck, and that all his daughters had drowned. Spafford joined his wife, and on the high seas near the place of the tragedy he wrote the hymn "It Is Well With My Soul." His inner peace was built on the conviction that God held the whole world in His hands, and that heaven was real.

Really believing in heaven is a must. We remain miserable and fearful when we only half believe in heaven or when we believe in heaven only half the time. The bottom line is that we must take Jesus' promise seriously. We should really believe in heaven because we unquestionably believe in Jesus.   — *KF*

* * *

WEDDING CEREMONIES
TITLE: A Wedding Ceremony

"O magnify the LORD with me, and let us exalt his name together" (Ps. 34:3).

"Let us come into his presence with thanksgiving; let us make a joyful noise to him with songs of praise! For the LORD is a great God" (Ps. 95:2–3 RSV).

"The steadfast love of the LORD never ceases, his mercies never come to an end; they are new every morning; great is thy faithfulness" (Lam. 3:22–23 RSV).

On this happy day as _____ and _____ have come to exchange their marriage vows and to become one by the plan of God, we want to assure them of our love for them and of our prayer that the Lord will smile upon them all the days of their lives. Let us worship God as we bow together in prayer.

Invocation by the minister
God in sovereign love and by holy design has gathered us into families; and through our family relationships He has enabled us to realize life's highest ideals and to achieve life's noblest purposes. _____ and _____ feel that God has blessed them by bringing them together. They want the home they establish this day to honor God and to fulfill the high dreams of their parents. In their hearts they seek the loving approval and the encouragement of those who are most dear to them. With this realization I now ask, who gives _____ to be married to _____?

Listen to the compelling words of Jesus which conclude the Sermon on the Mount. "Every one then who hears these words of mine and does them will be like a wise man who built his house upon the rock; and the rain fell, and the floods came, and the winds blew and beat upon that house, but it did not fall, because it had been founded on the rock" (Matt. 7:24–25 RSV).

_____ and _____, my counsel to you on this important day in your life is simple and direct: Build your house upon the Rock.

Decide now that you're going to have a Christian marriage, a marriage in which Jesus has the first and the last word. You already have made a significant beginning by giving your lives to Jesus Christ and by seeking His direction in your marriage. But yesterday's commitment must be reaffirmed today and all of your tomorrows. Each day you live you will need to offer to God your dreams, your feelings, your motives, your thoughts, your words, and your deeds.

Next, I would suggest that you let the Bible and the church be important to you. As you meditate on the Bible, your minds will be saturated with eternal truth, with assurance of God's never ending love, and with hope-infusing promises. In God's house you will find inspiration, fellowship, encouragement, inner peace, and soul-bracing strength.

My third word of counsel to you is that you demonstrate the highest kind of love to each other at all times and under all circumstances. Genuine love is a commitment, an act of the will; and the highest will you can have is to want to love as Jesus loved.

One final word of counsel: Try with all that is in you to work together as a team, knowing that God has made you one, that He has yoked you together so that you can pull your maximum load together.

You can see that I'm suggesting that the two of you should love and serve God with all your hearts and should love each other fully, joyfully, and unselfishly.

Please join right hands.

Vow: (*Groom, bride*), in taking _____ to be your (*wife, husband*), do you promise you will seek to fulfill the high purposes of God in your marriage by demonstrating the purest kind of love you know in your every thought, word, and deed?

From ancient times, the ring has been worn as a symbol of loyalty and faithfulness. The wedding ring tells of your possessing for the benefit of the other and of your being possessed for your own highest good.

Ring Pledge: "I give you this ring as a sign of my faithful love for you."

Forasmuch as you, _____ and _____, have consented together in holy wedlock and have witnessed the same before God and this company of family and friends; I, therefore, pronounce that you are husband and wife, Mr. and Mrs. _____ _____, in the name of the Father, and of the Son, and of the Holy Spirit.

Let us pray: "Our Father, may Your infinite blessings be upon _____ and _____ in this moment of dedication and during all their days together. May their marriage be a thing of beauty as they live together unselfishly by Your rule of love, as they encourage each other, and as they become one in a very real way. May they through Your grace be able to meet every day's challenges with humility and dignity and honor. In all the struggles of life may they bring glory to Your holy name through their dreams and their love and their labors. Guide them in paths of righteousness, dear Father, and rule over their hearts in love, through Jesus Christ our Lord. Amen!" — *KF*

* * *

TITLE: A Wedding Ceremony

"Blessed be the name of the LORD from this time forth and for evermore! From the rising of the sun to its setting the name of the LORD is to be praised!" (Ps. 113:2–3 RSV).

Let us hear the words of Jesus. "Abide in me, and I in you. As the branch cannot bear fruit by itself, unless it abides in the vine, neither can you, unless you abide in me. I am the vine, you are the branches. He who abides in me, and I in him, he it is that bears much fruit, for apart from me you can do nothing" (John 15:4–5 RSV). Thanks be to God for the good news of the gospel. May the light of His truth penetrate the darkness of our lives, that we may understand His will and commit ourselves to do it.

Invocation by the minister, concluded with Lord's Prayer

Mr. (*father of the bride*), your daughter, _____ , has come today to be united in the holy bond of marriage with _____. Do you now affirm before God and this congregation that you give your consent, and do you promise them the continuing support of your prayers, your encouragement, and your love?

_____ and _____, as you stand together before the altar of God, you are indicating that you want the present sanction and future blessings of God to dignify your marriage and to give it character that lasts. We who have gathered here to share this happy hour with you want that for you, too. We want you to have a life that is filled with all the good things God has in store for His obedient children.

The apostle Paul gave to husbands and wives one of the most significant words of counsel in all the Bible as he charged them to "be subject to one another out of reverence for Christ" (Eph. 5:21). In those words he was placing marriage in its most sublime context—reverence for Christ; and he was affirming that the genius of a happy marriage is the mutual submission of husbands and wives.

A Christian marriage begins with reverence for Christ. We reverence Christ by acknowledging His lordship and by committing our lives to Him, allowing Him to rule over our hearts in love and to stabilize our homes with His presence. We start with Him and we stay with Him—looking to Him daily, leaning on Him daily, listening to Him daily, learning from Him daily, and living for Him daily. With hearts aglow we reverence Christ.

Then we can gladly and safely subject ourselves to each other. To our great surprise we learn that in this mutual submission we experience life's ultimate joy. In the warmest of ways we come to know the grace of unquestioning acceptance and the glory of unselfish sharing. There is no other relationship in all the world so exalted of God. I hope that you in mutual submission will begin your marriage with a deep respect for each other. I hope that each of you will be willing at all times to accept each other, to forgive, to lift, to steady, and to cheer. I hope you'll never stop growing in your love for each other and in your devotion to each other. I encourage you to keep your covenant vows renewed by continually doing the little things that remind you of the deep love you share. I wish for you joy unending as you with united purpose reverence Christ as the Lord of your lives and submit yourselves happily to each other.

I shall ask you now to join hands as you face each other to recite your sacred vows.

Vow: I, _____, take you, _____, to be my _____: to have and to hold from this day forward, for better or for worse, for richer or for poorer, in sickness and in health, to love and to cherish until death alone shall separate us.

Ring Pledge: *(Address the appropriate question to both parties with each ring.)* _____, do you present this ring to _____ as a token of your love and a pledge of your loyalty to _____?

_____, do you accept this ring and the spirit of its giver with the earnest intent of keeping your vow to _____with all sacredness?

Jesus our Lord said, "Have you not read that he who made them from the beginning made them male and female, and said, 'For this reason a man shall leave his father and mother and be joined to his wife, and the two shall become one flesh'?" (Matt. 19:4–5 RSV). You have decided to symbolize your oneness as husband and wife by lighting a unity candle. May God bless us all with a new appreciation of the oneness He planned for us from the beginning! You may now proceed.

Prayer of Dedication by the minister
Forasmuch as you, _____ and _____, have committed yourselves to be faithful to each other as husband and wife, and before God and these witnesses have exchanged your vows and your rings in token of this commitment, I now proclaim that you are husband and wife, Mr. and Mrs. _____ _____.

"The LORD bless you and keep you: The LORD make his face to shine upon you, and be gracious to you: The LORD lift up his countenance upon you, and give you peace" (Num. 6:24–26 RSV).   *— KF*

* * *

TITLE: A Wedding Ceremony

"May God be gracious to us and bless us and make his face to shine upon us" (Ps. 67:1).

We have gathered today in this house of God to unite _____ and _____ as husband and wife for the glory of God and for their special joy. We want this ceremony of public commitment to be an occasion for rejoicing and an experience of worship for us all.

_____ and _____, we commend you to God that your life together may be grounded in His love and mercy; and we commend God to you believing He is worthy of your first choice and of your total commitment. Let us pray.

Invocation by the minister
In infinite wisdom and boundless love the good Lord gathered His people into families. He commanded parents to teach His way diligently to children. His compelling word to children was, "Honor your father and your mother" (Exod. 20:12). We believe that command is the foundation of a good marriage and of a strong society. It is therefore both fitting and important that there be parental consent, extended warmly and lovingly, to those preparing to enter marriage. I now ask, who gives _____ to be married to _____?

The lesson today is from the Gospel of Matthew. Let us hear with faith and appreciation the words of Jesus our Lord. "Have you not read," said Jesus, "that he who made them from the beginning made them male and female, and said, 'For this reason a man shall leave his father and mother and be joined to his wife, and the two shall become one flesh'? So they are no longer two but one flesh. What therefore God has joined together, let not man put asunder" (Matt. 19:4–6 RSV).

Thanks be to God for instituting the home and revealing His plan for it in His Holy Word.

_____ and _____, the great God who is our loving Father has made it clear to us that He wants husbands and wives to find the best there is in life as they share their lives and become one in Him. He wants them to set their hearts on the same goals and to share a kind of life that gives meaning and satisfaction to both as long as they live.

To achieve the unique togetherness God wills in marriage, husbands and wives need to commit themselves to Christ, to be filled with His kind of love, and to demonstrate that love morning, noon, and night, summer, winter, spring, and fall.

In First Corinthians, chapter 13, the apostle Paul described the special kind of love Christ showed to us and expects from us. "Love is patient and kind," he wrote; "love is not jealous or boastful; it is not arrogant or rude. Love does not insist on its own way; it is not irritable or resentful; it does not rejoice at wrong, but rejoices in the right. Love bears all things, believes all things, hopes all things, endures all things. Love never ends" (vv. 4–7 RSV).

When you have that kind of love in your hearts, you want what is best for each other at all times, and you do all you can to bring out the best in each other. I wish for you that kind of love. I hope that as you live joyfully by the plan of God and in the power of God you will be able to appreciate fully and to share freely with each other Christ's transforming, self-giving, never-ending love.

Please join right hands as you prepare to exchange your vows of marriage.

(*Groom*), the Bible tells us that God wants a man to take a wife for himself in holiness and in honor. He commands the husband to live considerately with his wife and to love her as Christ loved the church. As you prepare to enter into this sacred covenant of marriage, I shall ask that you do so in a spirit of dedication to the high purpose of God. I shall now ask you to face _____ and pledge to her your sacred vow by repeating after me.

Vow: "I, _____, take you, _____, to be my wife. With God's help I promise to love you unselfishly, to stand by you faithfully, and to serve with you honorably as long as we both shall live."

(*Bride*), the Bible says that a wife should be reverent and chaste. It refers to her and her husband as joint heirs of the grace of life. That means that from this hour forward you and _____ will be bound together in all of life's heartaches and all of life's joys. It follows that the covenant you now make is one of the most significant ones you will ever make. I, therefore, shall ask you to make your pledge of loyalty to him with all the genuineness of your heart. Face _____ now and pledge to him your sacred vow by repeating after me. *(Same vow as above)*.

The rings you now exchange, symbols of good faith and tokens of promised loyalty, are visible reminders that someone you love is committed to you and that you consider it an honor to be identified with that person. Exchange your rings now with love and joy, and from this moment on wear them with pride and devotion to each other.

_____, I shall ask you to take this ring, place it on _____ finger and repeat after me: "With this ring I pledge to you my life and my loyalty as we become one, in the name of the Father, and of the Son, and of the Holy Spirit."

_____, take this ring, place it on _____ finger, and repeat after me: *(Same ring pledge as repeated by groom)*.

A closing prayer by the minister

_____ and _____, you are united in marriage in the name of the Father, and of the Son, and of the Holy Spirit. Now that you have fulfilled all requirements for marriage and in the presence of a loving God and these assembled friends have exchanged your vows and your rings in token of your commitment to each other, I do, therefore, with personal pleasure and with a sense of God's sanction pronounce you husband and wife, Mr. and Mrs. _____ _____.

May the good Lord, who holds the whole world in His hands, protect you from all evil and cause you to feel secure in the warmth of His love. May He enrich your lives each day as He fills you with His wisdom, His strength, His joy, and His peace. May He enable you "to live in such harmony with one another, in accord with Christ Jesus, that together you may with one voice glorify the God and Father of our Lord Jesus Christ" (Rom. 15:5–6 RSV). Go with God. He will surely go with you.

You may now seal your promises with a kiss.   — *KF*

* * *

MESSAGES FOR OLDER CHILDREN AND YOUNG PEOPLE

TITLE: Thou Art the Potter

TEXT: **"And the vessel that he made of clay was marred in the hand of the potter: so he made it again another vessel, as seemed good to the potter to make it" (Jer. 18:4).**

SCRIPTURE READING: Jeremiah 18:1–4

Introduction. Some of the lessons of living can be learned by observation. It is erroneous to think that one can only learn by attending a class or by reading a book. Educators say that people learn by observing. The first five years of life are filled with learning by observation.

Jeremiah learned a great lesson by watching a potter at work. On one occasion Jeremiah visited the potter's house, which was located on the outskirts of the city. The potter selected a lump of clay and started to mold a vessel. It became marred. Instead of throwing the clay away, the potter made it into another vessel. By this Jeremiah learned about how Jehovah worked with Israel.

In our minds we need to visit the potter's house and observe his work. We can learn a lot about the qualities of God's character.

I. We can learn about the intention of God.

A. *The potter had an intention for the piece of clay.* He did not cast it on the trash pile when it did not suit his intention. Something happened to the clay. It was not meeting the intention of the potter. Maybe some sand had gotten into the clay. Or it could have been what some would call "a stubborn piece of clay." The potter could have chosen to abandon the clay. But he did not.

B. *God's grace has been particularly noticeable throughout Israel's history.* From Israel's earliest beginnings and throughout her subsequent history rebellions against God were frequent. In each case of rebellion, God extended His grace. God could have discarded Israel and selected another nation, but He did not. The Lord extended His grace.

C. *God will not let sinners be discarded.* The Lord observes human beings becoming marred. Will He allow them to be destroyed? No, God extends His grace to make them into new persons. God allows a person to make a fresh start, a new beginning.

II. We can learn about the power of God.

A. *The potter had the capacity to take the marred vessel and to mold it into a new vessel.* Jeremiah observed a skilled potter, who took great pride in his work. The potter had the ability to take a spoiled situation and rectify it. Through this deed Jeremiah caught a glimpse of God's redemptive power.

B. *God's power may be seen throughout history.* When God called Abram out of the land of Ur of the Chaldees, God promised that He would make a great nation from this small beginning. Whenever Israel rebelled, God promised new beginnings. These promises are evidences of God's amazing power.

C. *God has the power to change any marred human life.* There is no case so severe that God cannot change the life. God has the ability to change the vilest sinner.

III. We can learn about the joy of God.

A. *The potter was delighted to see his final product.* Evidently Jeremiah observed the potter throughout his work. He saw the potter's creative ability. When the vessel was finished, Jeremiah saw the look of delight on the potter's face. There was joy over the completion of the vessel.

B. *God has been pleased to see times of renewal in Israel's history.* Nothing brought greater joy to God than when there were periods of renewal and repentance with His people.

C. *God continues to rejoice over restoration.* Jesus told three stories about recovery—a lost sheep, a lost coin, and a lost son. In each case there was joy over recovery. Nothing would please God more than for you to repent of your sins.

Conclusion. God is in the process of making human beings into what He wants them to become. The human race has become spoiled. God could choose to cast the whole race away, but He has not. He wants to make each person into a new person.

Clay is good only in the hand of the potter. It is powerless to shape its own destiny. Likewise, human beings can be actualized only in the hands of the divine Potter. Will you allow Him to shape your life?   *— HTB*

* * *

TITLE: The Foolish Person

Text: **"But God said unto him, Thou fool, this night thy soul shall be required of thee: then whose shall those things be, which thou hast provided?"** (Luke 12:20)

Scripture Reading: **Luke 12:16–21**

Introduction. People have been known to do foolish things. Once I read in a newspaper about a man who purchased a new car. Hours after he had purchased it, an irresponsible driver hit the car and damaged it considerably. The man looked at his new car, and he was heartbroken. He went to the glove compartment, got a gun, and killed himself. How foolish!

Jesus told a story about a farmer who lived life in a foolish manner. The man gave himself to farming. There was nothing wrong with his thrifty and industrious farming. The problem was that he missed the real meaning of life while pursuing a worthy vocation.

The story of Jesus is not antiquated. People today pursue good things in life, but they fail to give preeminence to the real meaning of life. To miss the real meaning of life is a foolish matter. Let us notice the times a person can act foolishly.

I. A person can be foolish when material matters take priority over spiritual matters.

A. *The foolish farmer gave attention solely to the material side of life.* The farmer's interests and energies were devoted to barns and larger barns. Of course there was nothing wrong in being an excellent farmer. But the farmer lost sight that barns and larger barns were not the main matters of life.

B. *Life and its meaning have to do with more than the material side of life.* The physical is a real part of life. No one can deny its importance. Much of the pursuits of life are spent in taking care of various physical needs.

Another vital dimension of life is the spiritual. A human being is made in the image of God and has great capacity for fulfillment in God's will. One can never be happy in life until primary attention is given to one's relationship with God or the spiritual side of life. To neglect this dimension is to be a foolish person.

II. A person can be foolish when self matters more than others.

A. *The foolish farmer devoted his life to himself.* It is no accident that the personal pronouns "I" and "my" were used eleven times in the farmer's words. He centered his life on his own selfish desires. In his mind the world existed for him. In his reasoning he thought of "his barns," and never what his barns could do to help others.

B. *Authentic living includes awareness and involvement with other people.* "Me-ism" cannot be the prevailing philosophy. The essence of sin is to want our way. The tragic result of sin is to be insensitive to others. To neglect others and to live life for self are deeds of a foolish person.

III. A person can be foolish when today means more than tomorrow.

A. *The foolish farmer looked only at the existing moment.* He said rather presumptuously to himself, "You have got a long time to live. Take it easy." He treated seriously the pleasure of the moment, but he neglected the future.

B. *To live life means that one has to be concerned both about today and tomorrow.* It is a mistake to think only of tomorrow. The wise person thinks of both. The foolish person neglects to plan for eternity.

IV. A person can be foolish when life is planned without God.

A. *The foolish farmer made plans, but he made them without God.* The farmer made plans about his work. Seeing the productivity of his crops caused him to plan for expansion of storage facilities. Without a doubt he gave consideration to planning. The problem was that he left God out of his plans.

B. *God wants and needs to be considered in our plans.* He gives life. He gives the ability to work. He wants to be considered in planning for life. To leave God out of our plans is to act foolishly.

Conclusion. All of us do foolish things. Some of these foolish gestures are inconsequential, but some can be of serious consequence. The worst fool is one who lives life without settling his or her relationship with the Lord.   — *HTB*

* * *

TITLE: Precious Treasure

TEXT: **"Again, the kingdom of heaven is like unto treasure hid in a field; the which when a man hath found, he hideth, and for the joy thereof goeth and selleth all that he hath, and buyeth that field"** (Matt. 13:44).

SCRIPTURE READING: **Matthew 13:44–46**

Introduction. Have you ever searched for something which you lost? It happened to me several years ago when I lost the stone out of a tie pin. I retraced my steps. I looked every place where I thought I had been. I rented a metal detector. Yet the stone was never found. That experience taught me the anguish of a searcher. There are many inward dynamics of one who searches for something precious and valuable.

Jesus told two stories about people who found something significant. A farmer found some treasure as he plowed in a field. He hid the treasure, and he went to buy the field so he could possess the treasure. Another man, a merchant, while shopping for gems, found a precious pearl. He wanted to own it, so he sold all his other gems that he might possess it. Both the farmer and the merchant knew something of searching and finding.

What do these stories mean to us? These stories focus upon searchers. As we examine these stories, we can get some insights about the character of God. The search of the farmer and the merchant disclose the attitude and action of God as He searches and finds the precious treasure of human beings.

I. The searcher places great value upon the treasure.

A. *The farmer placed great value on the treasure he found in the field.* There were no banks for people to deposit their money. Often they buried their treasures. Various disasters such as death, wars, and captivity caused people to forsake their treasure.

The farmer about whom Jesus told was plowing in a field. His plow struck a sharp object. He thought it was a rock; but when he checked, he discovered a box of money. He covered the box, and he went to buy the field. He knew the value of the treasure.

B. *God makes great sacrifice for the precious treasure of the human race.* When God came to earth in flesh, He was willing to leave the glory and splendor of heaven to come to earth. The Incarnation is a demonstration of God's great sacrifice.

An old car might seem to some people to be just a piece of junk. But to an antique car collector the car may be seen as a treasure. Some people may be viewed as worthless and others average. However, God looks upon every person as a precious treasure.

II. The searcher makes great sacrifice for the treasure.

A. *The farmer sacrificed to buy the field.* As soon as the farmer found the treasure in the field, he sold all that he had to possess the treasure. He knew that the treasure was worth great sacrifice.

B. *God makes great sacrifice for the precious treasure.*
of the human race. When God came to earth in flesh, He was willing to leave the glory and splendor of heaven to come to earth. The Incarnation is a demonstration of God's great sacrifice.

In addition to the Incarnation, the Atonement on the cross discloses how much God was willing to sacrifice. Jesus gave His life in order to possess the treasure.

III. The searcher makes great use of the treasure.

A. *The farmer had many great uses for the treasure.* He could have used the treasure to purchase more property or to purchase farming tools. The farmer had many uses for the treasure.

B. *God makes good uses of His possessions.* When God possesses a human being, He makes several uses of a saved person.

1. First, He utilizes a saved human being to show to the world His power to change a human being. God uses believers to show the world His character and power.

2. Second, God uses a person to accomplish His mission on earth. Believers are used by God to accomplish the Lord's purpose.

Conclusion. People are precious treasures to God. He has made the ultimate sacrifice to possess the treasure. Have you allowed the Lord to possess you? He has been searching for you. Nothing would please the Lord more than for you to open your life to Him.

— *HTB*

SENTENCE SERMONETTES

1. "God's mercies are fresh with each new day."
2. "Worry never climbed a hill."
3. "No one hates a job well done."
4. "Is your spiritual experience up to date?"
5. "The filling of the Holy Spirit is not for enjoyment but for employment."
6. "Don't trouble trouble until trouble troubles you."
7. "Courage is fear that has said its prayers."
8. "Worry is pulling tomorrow's cloud over today's sunshine."
9. "The Bible is to be trusted and not just dusted."
10. "You never completely test the power of God until you attempt the impossible."
11. "Prayer is the greatest sin-killer in the world."
12. "Christ is the centerpiece of the human race."
13. "Prejudice is being down on something that you are not up on."
14. "God stands by us in all our needs; we should stand by Him in all our deeds."
15. "Your life is a sermon, so be careful how you preach it."
16. "True greatness lies not in trying to be somebody, but in trying to help somebody."
17. "Religion should not be carried like a burden on your back, but like a song in your heart."
18. "When God measures a man, He always measures his heart, not his head."
19. "The Bread of Life never becomes stale."
20. "God sometimes snuffs out our brightest candle that we may look up to His eternal stars."
21. "The thermometer of a church is its prayer meeting."
22. "God will mend even a broken heart if we give Him all the pieces."
23. "Life is marching on. Are you in step?"
24. "Worry never robs tomorrow of its sorrow; it only saps today of its strength."
25. "Instead of being an 'if thinker,' become a 'how thinker.'"
26. "The Bible promises no loaves to the loafer."
27. "Be kind, for everyone you meet is fighting a hard battle."
28. "The more we can endure with patience and grace, the stronger we grow and the more we can face."
29. "He who sows courtesy reaps friendship, and he who plants kindness gathers love."
30. "You'll never get a busy signal on the prayer line to heaven."
31. "Delayed obedience is disobedience."
32. "No reformation can ever take the place of regeneration."
33. "The will of God will never lead you where the grace of God cannot keep you."
34. "Happiness is happiest when shared."
35. "If you have not felt the pangs of sorrow, you cannot dry the tears of those who weep."
36. "Daily prayers help dissolve your cares."
37. "In hours of discouragement God is our encouragement."
38. "God's music is in the hearts of those who accept His conductorship."
39. "As soon as you are born, you are old enough to die."

40. "Life is only one time around."
41. "A smile is a curve that can set a lot of things straight."
42. "The perfume of kindness travels even against the wind."
43. "Make every decision carefully and prayerfully."
44. "Time will not tarry."
45. "Little is much when God is in it."
46. "Children follow in the direction their parents lead, rather than in the direction their parents point."
47. "Death shows no favorites."
48. "Ten two-letter words can change your life: "If it is to be, it is up to me.""
49. "The church is not a museum for saints but a hospital for sinners."
50. "A baby is God's opinion that the world should go on."
51. "Jesus is King of the land of beginning again."
52. "Two little words that make the difference—Start Now!"   — *BCC*

* * *

TOPIC INDEX

SCRIPTURE INDEX

(Sermon texts are in bold type)